WORK COMMUNICATION

WORK COMMUNICATION
Mediated and Face-to-Face Practices

Maureen Guirdham

First published 2015 by
PALGRAVE

Palgrave in the UK is an imprint of Macmillan Publishers Limited, registered in England, company number 785998, of 4 Crinan Street, London N1 9XW.

Palgrave Macmillan in the US is a division of St Martin's Press LLC, 175 Fifth Avenue, New York, NY 10010.

Palgrave is a global imprint of the above companies and is represented throughout the world.

Palgrave® and Macmillan® are registered trademarks in the United States, the United Kingdom, Europe and other countries.

ISBN 978–1–137–35144–9

This book is printed on paper suitable for recycling and made from fully managed and sustained forest sources. Logging, pulping and manufacturing processes are expected to conform to the environmental regulations of the country of origin.

A catalogue record for this book is available from the British Library.

Typeset by Cambrian Typesetters, Camberley, Surrey, England, UK.

Printed in China

CONTENTS

list of figures and tables   viii

list of abbreviations   ix

acknowledgements   x

preface   xi

part **I**   **the revolution in work communication**

chapter **1**   **introduction**   **3**
            1.1   contemporary interpersonal work communication
                   skills   5
            1.2   the nature and importance of mediated interpersonal
                   work communication   7
            1.3   introduction to alternative ways of working   12
            1.4   skilled interpersonal communication: its importance
                   and complexity   23
            1.5   about this book   25

chapter **2**   **work communication modes**   **27**
            2.1   affordances of different work communication modes 28
            2.2   factors that influence patterns of media usage   37
            2.3   factors relating to individuals that influence mode
                   choice   42
            2.4   work-related factors influencing mode choice   47

part **II**   **core processes in work communication**

chapter **3**   **social cognition and impression formation**   **53**
            3.1   social cognition   54
            3.2   forming impressions and perceiving groups   62
            3.3   perceiving events and environments   71

chapter **4**   **contributing to communication, self-presentation and
                   impression management**   **79**
            4.1   contributing a communication   80

4.2   self-presentation   90
4.3   impression management   99

chapter **5**   **interaction**   **105**
5.1   how we interact   107
5.2   interaction skills   113

chapter **6**   **demography, culture, situation and mode as influences
on communication**   **131**
6.1   demography and culture as influences on
communication processes   132
6.2   social influence theory and interaction   142
6.3   situation and mode as influences on communication:
important theories   145

chapter **7**   **intrapersonal influences on communication**   **155**
7.1   motives, motivations and goals   156
7.2   affect: moods and emotions   161
7.3   cognitions: thoughts and beliefs   167
7.4   attitudes and values   177
7.5   intentions, abilities and competencies   184
7.6   traits, personality and the self   186

chapter **8**   **influencing, handling conflict and negotiating**   **193**
8.1   influencing   194
8.2   handling conflict   205
8.3   negotiating   211

part **III**   **the impact of the communication revolution on work and
organization**

chapter **9**   **cooperation, work relations, knowledge sharing and
coordination**   **221**
9.1   cooperation, competition and work relations   222
9.2   sharing knowledge   229
9.3   coordination   239

chapter **10**   **working in groups and teams**   **244**
10.1   groupwork   244
10.2   decision-making by groups   251
10.3   teamwork   256
10.4   effects of diversity in groups and teams   259

10.5 how communication modes affect working in groups and teams   261

10.6 virtual teams and global virtual teams   267

chapter **11**   **management and leadership**   **277**

11.1 communication management, knowledge management and governance   278

11.2 managers' interpersonal communication as managers of people   286

11.3 leadership and interpersonal communication   300

chapter **12**   **organizational structures and cultures**   **305**

12.1 organizational structures and interpersonal communication   305

12.2 interpersonal communication and organizational cultures and climates   308

12.3 communication mode and organizational structures and cultures   312

12.4 interpersonal communication in multinational enterprises   316

chapter **13**   **inter-organizational relations**   **320**

13.1 control in inter-organizational relations   320

13.2 inter-organizational knowledge sharing   326

13.3 communication mode and inter-organizational, international and intercultural relations   327

cases and exercises   331

further reading   344

references   346

glossary of terms   405

index   415

LIST OF FIGURES AND TABLES

FIGURES

1.1 What is network density?   11
2.1 Choosing a communication mode   28
2.2 Factors influencing whether email is the chosen communication mode   41
2.3 Factors influencing e-service adoption in Saudi Arabia   45
4.1 How framing was used to communicate the vision of a Total Quality Program   103
5.1 How different modes affect choice of uncertainty reduction strategies   125
5.2 Shared reality theory   127
6.1 Cultural values and choice of mode for deception   141
7.1 Self-evaluation traits and job performance   190
8.1 How having power may positively affect how people think and act   197
10.1 Factors that affect the level of an individual's social loafing in a group   247
10.2 Factors that help improve group performance   249
10.3 Factors that affect group members' feelings towards the group   258
11.1 Benefits and governance dangers from workplace instant messaging   284

TABLES

2.1 Affordances of different communication modes   36
7.1 A comparison of types of regulatory focus   158
7.2 A comparison of Western and non-Western negotiators' assumptions   169
8.1 Characteristics of different conflict handling styles   207
12.1 Four kinds of organizational culture, their foci and values   309
12.2 Relationships among three types of organizational culture, subsequent sales growth/organizational efficiency and employee satisfaction   310

LIST OF ABBREVIATIONS

BPO	business process outsourcing
CA	communication apprehension
CEO	chief executive officer
cmc	computer-mediated communication
CompA	computer apprehension
CTs	collaborative tools
DPSNs	distributed problem-solving networks
FTAs	face-threatening acts
ftf	face-to-face
ftfc	face-to-face communication
GDSS	group decision support systems
GSS	group support system
IM	instant messaging
LMX	leader-member exchange
mc	mediated communication
MNC	multinational corporation
MNE	multinational enterprise
MRT	media richness theory
PDM	participative decision-making
PIU	problematic internet use
R&D	research and development
RSC	reduced social cues theory
SIDE	social identity model of deindividuation effects
SIPT	social information processing theory
SMS	short message service (texting)
SPM	social presence model
VoIPs	voice over internet provider services
VR	virtual reality

ACKNOWLEDGEMENTS

The author wishes to thank the people who so generously gave their time to be interviewed for this book and gave their consent for extracts from the interviews to be quoted. Thanks are also due to the academics around the world who reviewed the proposal and the typescript and whose suggestions were very helpful. Finally, particular thanks are due to Abigail Williams for her invaluable contribution to the research.

PREFACE

A revolution in interpersonal communication took place at the end of the twentieth and start of the twenty-first century, as new media came into widespread use. The fact that these new media were so quickly and so widely adopted made this a global revolution; its nature made it an unprecedented revolution. Its implications are still to be fully understood as more research is undertaken.

The overall purpose of this book is to familiarize readers with interpersonal communication in the world of work and to help them to communicate effectively in that world. Unlike my earlier texts, it takes as full a note as possible of the new communication media. I take the position that it is not enough to know how to use these technologies in a purely instrumental sense; rather, it is also vital to understand how people's behaviour changes when the communication mode changes and when there are new communication media available. The changes brought about by computer-mediated communication have led to it being called 'a new communication activity';[1] significant among these changes is the fact that people now can, do, and – to be effective – should choose what communication mode to use for different purposes, taking into account their different consequences for understanding others, self-presentation and interaction.

Being a skilled interpersonal communicator has always had great value in a work context; that has not changed, though its value has become more widely appreciated. What has changed is the range of skills required to use all the available communication modes to interact effectively with the much wider range and larger number of people contacted through the new media. This book addresses these skill needs using what research has taught us about both face-to-face and mediated interpersonal work communication.

In some ways this book is premature: the research literature on mediated interpersonal communication at work is currently inchoate, even chaotic. In five years' time, it is to be hoped, findings will be more conclusive, more topics researched, better theories proposed and tested. And yet the need for a book is pressing: no-one now can either understand or be prepared for the modern world of work without a grasp of the impact of mediation on communication. Readers of this book will acquire the necessary understanding to enable them to function effectively in this context.

One issue here is that while the vast majority of research on work communication has been conducted in the context of face-to-face communication, if or until research is done which proves otherwise we have to assume that it applies to all modes of communication. Fortunately, while as this book shows there are important differences in how people behave when using mediated communication, it is emerging that much that we have learnt from face-to-face interpersonal communication research still applies.

One limitation that might be assumed, but which would be wrong, is that this book concerns only business. My contention is that most modern fields of work require a high level of interpersonal communication skills. From medicine to the law, finance to marketing, education to fashion, and, yes, plumbing to politics, people everywhere engage in work-related mediated interpersonal communication – and the skill or the lack of skill with which they communicate strongly affects both individual and organizational outcomes.

MAUREEN GUIRDHAM

Note: terms emboldened in the text are explained in the Glossary.

Part I

The Revolution in Work Communication

Part I of this book introduces interpersonal work communication, demonstrates its importance, describes alternative ways of working – that is, the different communication modes and technologies of the modern world – and explains why the subject requires study. It then turns to the important question, effectively a new one, of the choice of mode. Here it outlines the various affordances of different modes and explicates the factors that influence how people decide which mode to use, with a particular focus on work-related factors.

1 INTRODUCTION

Until the end of the nineteenth century, most people at work who needed to communicate with colleagues, customers or suppliers, clients or agents had only two choices: they could meet face-to-face (ftf) or write a letter (or its equivalent, the internal memorandum). These choices were so distinct that choosing between them was generally straightforward: who, if a meeting was practical, would choose to undertake a business negotiation by letters, each of which might take days to arrive?

By early in the twentieth century, a third alternative, the telephone, became available. Almost intermediate between the letter and the ftf meeting, the telephone was quickly adopted by businesses; bridging distance like a letter, but, like ftf, allowing and requiring the use of **paralinguistics** (voice tone, speed of speech) and immediate responses, it both substituted for and complemented the existing modes. Its limitations, however – no record of the conversation, lack of a visual channel, the need for the respondent to be within earshot of the instrument when a call was put through – meant that it did not replace the earlier modes but found its place alongside them. This remained the situation for most of the rest of the twentieth century, with only small additions to the communication arsenal becoming available – innovations such as 'fax' to transmit written messages over the telephone and then print them out, and answering machines to record voice messages.

Near the end of the twentieth century, however, technology brought in a virtual explosion of communication modes: mobile telephony and text messaging, electronic mail (email), instant messaging, video- and audio-conferencing. These changed the situation dramatically, allowing and requiring users to choose among them and to adapt their communication to the chosen mode by, for instance, using appropriate language and ways of expression.

The new communication technologies, though widely adopted in the personal sphere, made an at least equal and perhaps greater impact on working life. In a study performed before the use of communication technology became widespread Mintzberg (1973)[1] demonstrated that managers spent most of their time in communication, and much of that time then was spent face-to-face. Now, however, technological innovation offers many new communication media choices and people have been quick to make use of them.[2] In only 25 years, the new communication technologies have become indispensable aids.

As early as 1987, Culnan and Markus pointed out that this introduction of new technologies that alter communication activities in organizations has the potential to influence key aspects of organizational structure and process.[3] Furthermore, the impact of mediated communication (mc) extends beyond what happens within organizations to their contact with publics and to inter-organizational relations. Already by 1997, public bulletin boards, listservs and discussion groups provided broadcast (one-to-many) ways for organizations to reach customers and other stakeholders, while email had become an important method of task and social inter-organizational communication, information dissemination, problem-solving and project coordination. Educational activities and the creation and maintenance of personal contacts by mc fulfilled social functions for the organizations' members.[4] By the end of the first decade of the twenty-first century, mc had become all-pervasive, taken-for-granted and, sometimes, problematic.

The purpose of this book is in part to explain how communication modes affect **interpersonal communication** at work and so affect the work itself, the people who do it and the organizations in which the work is done. In addition, on most of the topics covered in this book – from interpersonal communication at work in general, mediated interpersonal communication at work, to decision-making, working in groups, managing work relations and working inter-organizationally – people also want to know how they should do it. What is the best way to do it? How can a person produce appropriate communication behaviour? How can they improve at doing it? Another purpose of this book is to try to answer these questions – in other words to show how to communicate skilfully and effectively.

> Ask someone who was working for at least ten years before the 'communication explosion' about the changes they have noticed since it happened.

The purpose of this introductory chapter is to set out the scope of the book, to motivate the reader to study the subject seriously and to explain some of the key concepts. There are five sections. Section 1.1 explains the significance of interpersonal work communication: why people interact at work; Section 1.2 explains the importance of mediated interpersonal work communication; Section 1.3 introduces alternative ways of communicating at work, especially using contemporary mediated communication such as mobile telephony, SMS (text messages), email, instant messaging (chat), social media, listservs, and audio and video-conferencing; Section 1.4 explains the complexity and importance of skill in interpersonal work communication; Section 1.5 outlines the other chapters of the book.

1.1 CONTEMPORARY INTERPERSONAL WORK COMMUNICATION SKILLS

All the elements in the title of this section are important for this book:

- We can start with 'communication', which here refers to the science and art and skills of interaction with other people. It is the discipline that provides the scholarship, research and practical applications that are at the core of this book.
- 'Interpersonal' here implies 'two-way', so broadcast communication is not a focus. Some scholars limit interpersonal communication to the communication between pairs of people (dyads), but in this book it has a wider meaning: communication within and between groups and even organizations, providing it has the capacity for being two-way, is included.
- 'Work' narrows our focus to the world of work; this becomes particularly relevant in conjunction with 'interpersonal' because interpersonal communication is sometimes considered to be confined to the sphere of family, friends and lovers.
- The word 'contemporary' means that our focus will be on interpersonal communication exercised through computers, mobile instruments, the internet or the telephone as well as ftf.
- 'Skills', of course, embrace a very wide range of competencies, from plumbing to political abilities, embroidery to software design. Interpersonal communication work skills are those communication-based abilities and competencies that allow people to work effectively together; they therefore exclude those skills required for working alone, such as using a keyboard efficiently or working out the solution to a problem in your head.

> ❝ Communication has four essential elements. The 'sender' is the person transmitting the message, the 'message' is the data that the sender is transmitting, the 'channel' is the medium used to transmit the message, and the 'receiver' is the person receiving the message. Communication exists when all four elements are in place.
>
> Other important aspects of communication include: the 'signal', the degree to which the message is received and understood; the 'noise', anything that interferes with the clarity of the signal; the 'feedback', the receiver's response to the sender's message; and the 'reply', the data sent during feedback.[5]

Communication with other people is so obviously a part of most work that it sometimes receives little attention by comparison with topics like strategy, marketing, accounting and finance or human resource management. In reality,

Do you agree with the explanation of communication given in the quotation above? Why or why not?

BOX 1.1

'In the European bank where I am working, the members of the fifteen-person team I work with are allocated to different jobs and different seats in the office on a daily basis. I don't understand why. The information about the work is sent through on a spreadsheet; a junior member of staff tells you where to sit.'

'There is a lack of communication. One process has to start at a particular time, but I wasn't told when, and missed the start the first day. Also I need two screens for my work, but kept being given a desk with only one, and I did not know whom to ask.'
(Author's interview with a bank regulatory reporting specialist who has worked on a series of temporary contracts)

---

however, none of those functions could be performed at all, let alone effectively, without a great deal of interpersonal communication. Providing information, discussing issues, clarifying influencing factors, proposing and considering solutions, choosing among alternatives and implementing decisions are all communication-based processes in most organizations. In fact, to some scholars, organizations are constituted by communication. In the words of Williams (1998), 'an organization can be viewed as a human communication system in which **networks** of human nodes are linked internally, in a variety of ways, and with the external environment'.[6]

While effective and efficient communication makes it possible for organizations to survive and grow, poor or inadequate communication, as Box 1.1 suggests, disrupts work, reduces productivity and creates confusion. It can also lead to low job satisfaction, stress, poor work relations and conflict.

There is a continuing need for information that is only available from interpersonal sources: this includes the kind of knowledge that can allow experienced sales managers to 'know' that a business's customers will object to a proposed change, or allow an experienced market researcher to 'know' that there is something wrong with a set of survey findings. As Chapter 9

To develop skill in interpersonal communication, whether mediated or ftf, you need to know the processes involved in behaviour and the factors that affect it, to become more self-aware, more aware of others, more aware of what happens when you interact with other people, and to practise, observe and get feedback.

To learn more about developing skills in interpersonal communication at work, visit www.palgrave.com/companion/Guirdham-Work-Communication... 1.1.1.

Section 2 will show, this kind of unarticulated knowledge, referred to as 'tacit' knowledge, makes a big difference to how efficient and effective an operation is and gives businesses a competitive edge. Although technology plays a part, communication is central to transmitting tacit information to other people in the organization who can or should use it.

> To learn more about changes such as globalization and their impact on work communication, visit the companion website... 1.1.2.

Adding to the importance of interpersonal communication at work in recent years have been changes in the way work is done and organized, in the scope of industries and businesses through **globalization**, as well as the expansion of the service sector and increases in workforce **diversity**. Technological change, in particular the exponential growth of communication technology and its use at work, which is a central theme of this book, has vastly increased the number and types of people with whom we typically communicate at work. It has thereby expanded our communication opportunities but also our communication challenges.

Summary

Interpersonal work communication is the process of interaction (two-way communication) at and about work. This can be between pairs of people, but it can also be within and between groups and organizations. Interpersonal communication underpins most other workplace processes: strategy, marketing, accounting and finance, for example, would rarely happen at all without it. Technological innovations combined with changes in the ways organizations operate, due to globalization and other factors, have profoundly affected the ways we interact at work, and how many and what kind of people we interact with.

1.2 THE NATURE AND IMPORTANCE OF MEDIATED INTERPERSONAL WORK COMMUNICATION

'Mediated interpersonal communication' refers to any situation where a medium is introduced into interpersonal interaction. It includes telephone conversations, letters, CB radio and electronic mail. Computer-mediated communication (cmc), which includes email, instant messaging, computer conferencing and voice mail, 'is simply the application of computing machinery to the process of communication,'[7] or 'the process by which people create, exchange, and perceive information using networked telecommunications systems that facilitate encoding, transmitting, and decoding messages'.[8] This second definition has advantages: it 'encompasses the delivery mechanisms, derived from communication theory, and the importance of the interaction of people that the technologies and processes mediate'.[9] Interpersonal cmc is more narrowly defined and involves an interactive relationship via electronic media directly among individuals or groups of individuals.[10]

This book will, in fact, include all these modes, although when it is not concerned with face-to-face communication (ftfc) it will tend to concentrate on cmc. In 2006 Spitzberg pointed out that technological convergence means that cmc includes many media not ordinarily considered to be computers, 'as more and more media involve digital technologies'.[11]

In the words of Rettie (2009), 'mediated interaction has become a feature of everyday life, used routinely to communicate and maintain contacts'.[12] Cmc has also created entirely new forms of interaction: 'discussion list archives, and the saving of interesting messages by individuals, which they may then reuse within later discussions, provide for new forms of group interaction, and suggest features unlike those seen in communities based on face-to-face interaction and the spoken word'.[13] Such a group 'through an exchange of written texts has the peculiar ability to recall and inspect its entire past'.[14] Between them, as this book will explore, mediated communication technologies have permitted and encouraged profound changes in how we spend our time at work (consider email inboxes), work locations (tele-working), how businesses operate (**offshore outsourcing**), how organizations in general function (**virtual teams**) and in forms of organization (the network economy).

At work, cmc can increase organizational performance,[15] adjust **roles** and redistribute power[16] as well as modify organizational communication.

> To see the research evidence for this, visit the companion website... 1.2.1.

There is widespread agreement that cmc is not only a new communication medium but also a new communication activity: for instance, when writing business letters people often allow for an interval since their last correspondence and so begin by a phrase that allows the receiver to identify it (as in 'With reference to your letter of 16th inst.'). By email, however, they may create continuity simply by appending responses to received messages.[17]

> To see more of the research evidence on this, visit the companion website... 1.2.2.

As Box 1.2 suggests, despite its benefits cmc has the potential for damaging productivity, work satisfaction and work relationships. The challenge, for individuals and organizations, is to use it appropriately and effectively.

> ## BOX 1.2
>
> 'In the department of a European bank where I am working now, we all get over 100 emails most days, but for about three weeks after I started there, I was getting all those but I wasn't getting all the ones I needed for my work. My name had not been put on the appropriate distribution list.
>
> About 40 of the 100 emails will have a symbol on them which means the work on them is completed; in principle you can tell which of the other 60 you need to open from the subject line, but in practice I open them all because people might have altered them and I want to check. Most of the banks I've worked in have a system of flagging up when an email is important or urgent, but this bank doesn't have one or it is almost never used.
>
> Basically, people who are sending out emails save themselves the trouble of deciding who to send them to, and so we all get the trouble of reading lots of emails irrelevant to our work.'
>
> (Author's interview with a bank regulatory reporting specialist who has worked on a series of temporary contracts)

Networks

Networks are a critical concept for understanding the impact of work-related cmc. While communication networks existed and were important before the cmc revolution, following that revolution they were ubiquitous both within and between organizations. Communication networks are:

> ❝ the patterns of contact that are created by the flow of messages among communicators through time and space. The concept of message should be understood here in its broadest sense to refer to data, information, knowledge, images, symbols and any other symbolic forms that can move from one point in a network to another or can be co-created by network members. These networks take many forms in contemporary organizations, including personal contact networks, flows of information within and between groups, strategic alliances among firms, and global network organizations, to name but a few.[18]

Relations among members of networks (who are usually referred to as 'actors') build and sustain the network. These relations, which are conceived as strong or weak 'ties', typically result from exchanges of resources. The resources may be material, informational or social-psychological. Patterns of who is tied to whom and at what strength show how resources flow within the network. Tie strength depends on the frequency, quantity and quality of transfers between actors. So, for instance, ties within a nuclear family are usually strong, because its members share many different resources and interact frequently on a range of topics. Strong ties both reflect themselves and support more flows of resources, including information; however, much of this information may be redundant rather than new because actors with strong ties possess similar information. Weak ties are more likely to provide new inputs, particularly of information, as actors who have weak ties possess resources that differ from those of other actors; weak ties can, for instance, create international trade opportunities:[19]

> **"** Many opportunities for international exchange result from ... existing weak ties with others; these 'idiosyncratic' connections with others both promote and inhibit international exchange. Tie-based opportunities lead to higher-quality and more valuable exchanges but they are constrained by geographic, psychic and linguistic distance.[20]

One of the first studies to deal with cmc networks was by Eveland and Bikson (1989).[21] They compared four groups in two conditions (cmc and ftf) for a year-long project. Their objective was to investigate network density, that is, the proportion of potential connections between people in the network that are actual connections. For example in a tiny organization consisting of five people there are ten potential connections, as Figure 1.1 shows. If all but one of these potential connections are actual connections, the network's density is high; in the unlikely but possible event that only four of these potential connections are actual connections, the network's density is low. Eveland and Bikson (1989) found that cmc networks had higher density than ftf networks, meaning that more of their potential ties were active.

Surprisingly, in view of their findings on comparative network density, Eveland and Bikson (1989) also found that email is not just a substitute for other media: on the contrary it increases the use of traditional media. They also found that participation is higher in cmc settings than ftf, and leadership roles emerge flexibly in electronic networks: in ftf networks leadership roles are more stable (held for longer by the same individual). Recognition, reciprocal acknowledgement and communication increase over time in electronic networks.[22]

Some individuals benefit from network advantages: they have a higher chance of proposing good ideas, more positive evaluations and recognition, higher compensation and faster promotions. These advantages arise when a person is connected to a variety of different 'clusters' of other people who possess different knowledge, in other words when they are a network '**broker**'. Being connected to different clusters gives an individual 'access to

What type of organization has a low density network corresponding approximately to that shown in Figure 1.1?

Figure 1.1 What is network density?

Potential connections

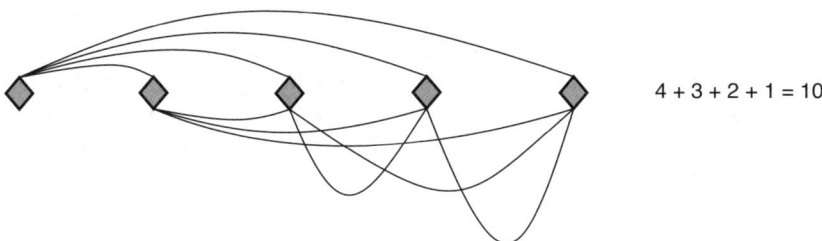

$4 + 3 + 2 + 1 = 10$

Actual connections if the network density if high

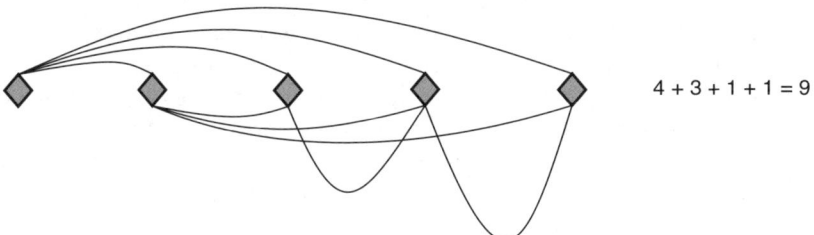

$4 + 3 + 1 + 1 = 9$

Actual connections if the network density is low

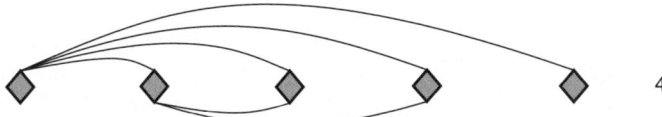

4

Based on Eveland, J.D. and Bikson, T.K. (1989) 'Evolving electronic communication networks: An empirical assessment', *Information Technology & People*, **3**(2), 103–28.

less redundant information'; being 'at a crossroads in the flow of information between groups' will make an individual 'early to learn about activities' in a number of groups, often being 'the person introducing to one group information on another'; and being connected to different clusters also makes an individual 'more likely to know when it would be rewarding to bring together separate groups', which gives the individual 'disproportionate say in whose interests are served when the contacts come together'. Building bridges between clusters 'does not guarantee achievement, [but] it enhances the risk [chance] of productive accident: of encountering a new opinion or practice not yet familiar to colleagues, enivisioning a new synthesis of existing opinion or practice, finding a course of action through conflicting interests, discovering a new source for needed resources'.[23]

Summary

Mediated interpersonal communication refers to any situation where a technological medium is introduced into interpersonal interaction. With cmc, that technological medium involves a computer. At work cmc is ubiquitous, used routinely and useful: it can connect people in ways that they were not able to connect before, and has been found to affect pre-established roles, hierarchies and forms of power, and to increase organizational performance. Cmc can profoundly change the way people work, how groups function and how organizations operate, though it presents new challenges for efficiency.

Networks are created by a flow of resources, including communication and information, both between individuals and larger entities. Network theory argues that strong ties within networks support more flows of resources, including information, while weak ties provide more new resources to the network. If people have ties with a variety of different 'clusters' of people within a network, they can enjoy some advantages: being connected to different clusters gives them access to a range of information and enables them to pick up on information and activities relatively early. Cmc networks are denser than ftf networks.

1.3 INTRODUCTION TO ALTERNATIVE WAYS OF WORKING

This section begins to analyse the similarities and differences of communicating ftf or by telephone, audio or video-conferencing, email, instant messaging, SMS, listservs and social media. As well as these widely known and used forms of cmc, there are many apps (applications) that are tailored to the uses of organizations. A sample of them is described in Box 1.3.

Face-to-face communication

When people interact in one another's physical presence they usually have multiple ways of sending and receiving messages. They have speech, that is verbal behaviour (words and their meaning) and paralinguistic behaviour, which includes voice tone, pace, loudness, pauses, silence and the alterations to each of these over the duration of the interaction. They also have a range of non-verbal behaviours (or, more colloquially, body language) including the controllable aspects of appearance, facial expression, posture, gesture, **proxemics, kinesics** and the alterations to each of these over the duration of the interaction. This multiplicity creates a great wealth of opportunities and subtleties but also complexities for interaction. Ftfc has been regarded as the 'gold standard' because it offers most channels, though it too has restrictions – principally that of the need for co-location. Moreover its high levels of complexity create difficulties which are

---

BOX 1.3

The following are types of app that are useful for small businesses:

- Voice over internet provider (VoIP) allows free or cheap calls, including international calls.
- Apps that allow presentation slides to be shown on several people's screens simultaneously in different locations, attend and schedule meetings in high-definition (HD) video around the world and arrange and host webinars.
- Customer support apps that allow seeing and engaging with all the business's customers in one place; they look at channels such as email, Facebook and Twitter and give the most important alerts in real time.
- Apps that allow keeping abreast of the business's social media accounts on the go, scheduling tweets and sharing company news; they are also useful for keeping up to date with industry influencers.
- Conferencing clients that allow users to interact in real time over the internet. Most people call these a 'video-conferencing client', but they are actually capable of much more than that, including a file transfer application for sending files, a chat client, similar to Instant Messenger, an audio and video-conferencing client, a whiteboard, which is a shared drawing space where people can collaborate in real time, and application sharing.

compounded by the usual need to respond almost immediately to an interaction partner.

Some techniques for improving work coordination depend on continuous ftf interaction for their effect. One such method is radical co-location:

> Companies are experimenting with putting teams into their own large rooms (an arrangement called radical collocation). A field study of six such teams, tracking their activity, attitudes, use of technology and productivity found that radically collocated teams showed a doubling of productivity. Schedules, too, were shortened in comparison with both the industry benchmarks and the performance of past similar projects within the firm; the teams reported high satisfaction about their process and both customers and project sponsors were similarly highly satisfied.[26]

In this example radical co-location facilitated learning as well as work coordination and allowed high visibility to some of the products of work when artefacts were pasted on the walls of the room. While acknowledging that some aspects of co-located work are poor – for example meetings where 'nothing happens' – the researchers concluded, 'seeming inconsequential interactions serve critical functions such as co-ordination and learning'.[27] However, 'face-to-face communication does not cope well with organizational constraints such as time pressure or the geographic distribution of team members'.[28]

Mediated communication

Mc includes telephone, SMS, email, instant messaging, social media, listservs and video-conferencing. In comparison with ftfc, mc provides the opportunity to work together without being co-located, but its various channels also differ both from ftfc and from each other on a range of characteristics, which may be affordances or limitations.

An **affordance** is 'the design aspect of an object which suggests how the object should be used'.[29] Not all media characteristics are affordances: for instance, a distinction is often drawn between text-based and non-text-based modes, but being text-based is not an affordance, though it does sometimes, as in the case of most email systems, provide the affordance of searchability – key-word and other searches facilitate finding records and specific information within records. Again, the number and type of channels a medium provides do not in themselves define its affordances. Norman (1988), who coined the term 'affordances' in this context, described them as follows:

> **"**the term *affordance* refers to the perceived and actual properties of the thing, primarily those fundamental properties that determine just how the thing could possibly be used. A chair affords ('is for') support and, therefore, affords sitting. A chair can also be carried. Perceived properties that may or may not actually exist [include] suggestions or clues as to how to use the properties. Affordances can be dependent on the experience, knowledge, or **culture** of the actor and can make an action difficult or easy.[30]

To learn more about the elements of ftfc, visit the companion website

Does the following finding surprise you? Why or why not?

According to Keyton et al. (2013) verbal communication in the workplace is used for multiple purposes, but the 36 most frequently used communication behaviours can be categorised as composed of four factors: information sharing, relational maintenance, expressing negative emotion and organizing.[24]

S. Jackson, CEO of Applied Semantics Inc. in Los Angeles, said, 'I can be anywhere and connect to the office but most of my job is much more individualized and face to face. You can only manage clients and employees and strategy so well when you are trying to do it remotely. I have to be able to have face-to-face meetings with my teams'.[25]

'Of all the many hirings I have done, those few that have turned out badly have all been where I did not meet the person face-to-face.'
(Author's interview with the CEO of a medium-sized knowledge business)

BOX 1.4

'I think I now use email more than phone – partly because you know they'll see the email if they want to, but also they might just be too busy or too unwilling to speak to you [on the telephone].'
(Author's interview with an executive from a media and information company)

'I don't like eternal email strings with multiple people copied in on them. They lead to people passing off responsibility, avoiding taking decisions or taking action. All that happens is that nobody does anything. They amplify our more human traits – procrastinating, passing off responsibility. I can't see that new technologies, whether computers or email, have made organizations more efficient.

I must admit, emails are useful as a workflow tool, because you've got a record. For instance, I've stopped keeping a database of contacts. I know I'll be able to find them with an email search.

They can also be useful in work-related social situations that you might find awkward. For instance calling a prospective customer – emails let you make a warm call instead of a cold one.'
(Author's interview with an executive from a media organization)

As the need for co-location for ftfc shows, communication modes also have limitations. Box 1.4 shows that users have found email to have both affordances and limitations.

Electronic mail (email) has been defined as 'the entry, storage, processing distribution and reception, from one account to one or more accounts, of digitized text by means of a central computer'.[31] Another definition views email as a computer system for the exchange of messages and other information that may include text and numerical data, computer programs, video, graphics and sound.[32]

Email affordances allow asynchronous (but not synchronous) communication, digital storage, rapid communication retrieval and notification of delivery or non-delivery, though it is 'unforgiving' about textual errors in the address. Email affordances also include the possibility of providing detailed contextual background information; it allows multi-media documents to be attached – pictures, images, audio, video and animations can be integrated into the electronic text or attached to an email. 'Hence, we see here that email affords contextual information and persistence communication which are valuable

> *Look back critically at the last five work- or study-related emails you wrote before reading this material. Are they 'readable?' How could they be improved?*

for enhancing communicators' competency.'[33] Another affordance of email is the ability to document communication. However, poor email readability can lead to considerable ambiguity of information transfer.

By comparison with ftfc, email has these characteristics:

- Constraints are fewer. There is no need to know the target receiver. The sender can select the target. There is no need for participants to be using the medium at the same time or to be in the same location. The participants can more easily store, retrieve or process the contents of the discussion.
- There is a lowered ability to communicate by physical presence, non-verbal behaviour or paralinguistic cues. (However, of course this 'lowered ability' can sometimes be an advantage.)
- The receiver decides reception and response times.
- Either party can terminate the interaction simply by not responding, instead of having to turn their back or make some other obvious gesture of refusal.[34]

Telephone and conference calls (teleconferencing) afford feedback immediacy, allowing communicators to clarify and discuss issues. A further affordance of telephone-mediated communication is accessibility. Because it allows people to be reached outside office hours, the telephone makes it convenient for them to stay connected, which is especially important when an immediate response is needed. Mobile telephony has, of course, increased this affordance. Ubiquity, measured in terms of continuity, immediacy, portability and searchability, has been referred to as 'one of the most important characteristics of mobile services'.[35]

Short message service (SMS or texting) is a service component of phone, web, or mobile communication systems that allows the exchange of short text messages between fixed line or mobile phones. SMS is the most widely used data application in the world, used by 78 per cent of all mobile phone subscribers in 2013. Most SMS messages are mobile-to-mobile text messages. They offer similar affordances to those of mobile telephony: they allow people to be contacted outside office hours and, because mobile telephones are now ubiquitous, the message is very likely to reach the intended recipient. Unlike a telephone call, however, the

> The following quote is from an interview given by Don Tapscott, a professor at the University of Toronto's Rotman School of Management:
>
> 'Email is sort of like what Mark Twain said about the weather. Everybody's talking about it, and nobody's doing anything about it. We have to get rid of email.'
>
> Do you agree? Why or why not?

SMS is text-based and does not require synchronous feedback. This can often make the SMS feel less intrusive than a telephone call. Finally, because SMS is so popular outside of work and because messages have to be short, it can afford a greater feeling of informality than email.

Instant messaging (IM) is a form of computer 'chat' that allows real time, typed 'conversations' with one or more 'buddies' while connected to the internet. 'Instant messaging provides unobtrusive feedback immediacy and availability information. It is seen as less intrusive than a telephone call; it also supplies present availability and absent availability information. Such availability information supports unplanned [communication] and is not afforded by either email or telephone/teleconferencing.' [36]

Many predict that IM usage will eventually outstrip email usage, especially 'because it has been transformed into a multi-functional communication medium with the recent additions of file transfer, audio- and video-conferencing'.[37] Many organizations permit their employees to use it because it has benefits such as providing 'immediate' contact with remote employees, customers and vendors, though most also have rules about its use because it also has dangers of importing worms and viruses (computer programs that copy themselves to other computers across the internet) into systems, of leaking confidential information and of legal compliance issues.[38]

> *To learn more about the conditions that many organizations require for IM use, visit the companion website... 1.3.1.*

Teleconferences (conference calls) are live exchanges among several persons and machines remote from one another but linked by a telecommunications system. Such a system may support the teleconference by providing one or more of the following: audio, video and/or data services by one or more means such as telephone, computer, teleprinter, radio or television. Unlike ordinary telephone calls, conference calls have to be set up in advance to ensure that all participants are available:

> **"** I find them slightly worse than meetings for getting things done. They are often confused and they go on a long time without achieving anything. Usually when I do take part in them it's because a client wants to do it that way. Occasionally it's because I'll suggest a call to a client and then they may ask for one of their colleagues to join in.
>
> I think some clients like them because they mean that one individual does not have to take responsibility for a buying decision. As a rule of thumb, you know that if you are on a call with five people, it will be harder to make a sale. If there's just one of them it's more likely to go through.
>
> Some of my colleagues use video-conferencing – I don't myself. They tell me that it's better than the phone or conference calls because you can tell when the other person wants to interject.
>
> (Author's interview with an executive from a
> media organization)

Video-mediated communication is becoming a more common and effective means of interpersonal communication, including for work-related activities, distance education, telemedicine and access to public information.[39] Accessibility, flexibility and utility are important positive aspects of video-conferencing as perceived by users, though it does also have drawbacks: for instance, the interruptions caused by the technology, such as network outages or delays, are a notable distraction.[40]

Voice over internet provider services allow users to communicate by voice using a microphone and by video using a webcam. Some also provide simultaneous IM, file transfer and video-conferencing.

> ❝ We can have this setup on our PC called Windows NetMeeting where we can run an application and they can see what I am doing here. So I can give a demo to them. It's quite good. Anytime they can take over control of the application. So if they want to show me something, sometimes it's very difficult for them to tell me over the phone what they have done and what problems they have encountered. So they can simulate and we can see on the screen after which step they will hit this problem. It's a very good tool. We use the speaker, we can just talk like that.[41]

Social websites present and juxtapose messages that are generated by different authorial sources: central messages posted by a web page's proprietor, and user-generated content that other readers contribute.[42] There is evidence that social media facilitate virtual spaces where individuals can, for instance, co-construct third cultures, develop cosmopolitanism, and transfer cultural and **social capital**.[43]

In communication terms, social websites are complex. They not only contain proprietor content (the messages composed and displayed by the primary author or proprietor of a webpage) and user-generated content (the messages that social websites invite, capture and display from non-proprietary visitors), but also deliberate and incidental aggregate user representations (computer-generated descriptive statistics that a web page displays representing accumulations of users' ratings, votes or other site-related behaviours). Users can include business customers, whose online content can broadcast dissatisfaction with an organization. Users' comments can be more influential in shaping observers' impressions of a proprietor than proprietors' own comments because they possess **warranting value**. Many companies proactively manage these relationships, though others monitor and respond to these messages as best they can.[44]

These six forms of mc – email, fixed line and mobile telephony, SMS, IM, audio and video-conferencing, VoIPs and social websites – are the predominant forms currently used in organizations, where they are now often found to be indispensable. There are, however, problems for organizations that arise from employee misuse of the technologies, as Section 11.1 will explain. Cyberloafing (time-wasting on the internet), cyberslacking (using the internet at work for personal purposes) and cyberdeviancy (illegal or risky online behaviour) are growing problems and can negatively affect an organization's performance.

In addition to the forms of mc that are widely available there are also a growing number of applications of cmc that are tailored to the demands of work and the needs of organizations. These include basic groupware, group decision support systems, argumentation support systems, computer-supported collaborative software and virtual worlds.

Groupware is a set of tools for computer-supported cooperative work which attempts to create for physically dispersed groups the kinds of opportunities for collaboration that are normally only available when people meet ftf. Collaborative idea-organizing tools and group editors of various kinds are examples of groupware. For instance, in one case:

> *Look at the Glossary for the meaning of 'warranting value'.*
>
> *On two or more typical work or study-related days, log the amount of time you spend using email, fixed line and mobile telephony, SMS, IM, audio and video-conferencing and social websites for work or study-related purposes. Repeat the process for the time spent on non-work-related or non-study-related mc. Compare with a colleague, fellow student or friend.*

❝ Each group member sat at a networked workstation. On the screen a set of scrolling message display areas was arranged vertically, one for each group member. The message area was large enough to accommodate ten lines of text. By the side of each message area was a button labelled with a name of a group member, signifying to whom the message area belonged. Messages would appear on the screens of all group members in the message area identified with the name of the sender. Visual feedback of actions (i.e. key strokes and button presses) appeared simultaneously on all workstations within a group, thereby enabling participants to monitor one anothers' activities.[45]

With more sophisticated groupware, users can also share files or calendars with whole groups.[46]

Group decision support systems (GDSS) are a class of collaboration technology designed to support meetings and group work. GDSS are focused on task support and provide scheduling, documentation and brainstorming support features as well as communication functions.

Argumentation support systems 'record, organize, regulate and coordinate argumentation processes in organisations and enable managers to argue about decisions, issues, and goals'. They claim to be able to 'understand' arguments (by simplifying them and identifying the main elements), to enable the human user to present arguments electronically to others, and to have rules of thumb (e.g. simplicity, relevance) for estimating the strength of arguments. Such systems can 'see' their human users or opponents or collaborators by means of a simplifying model (in the form of a list of previous claims and premises used by that person). They represent debate in the form of a diagram shown on the computer screen, in which arguments are arrows from premises to claims:

> **"** The argument diagram is updated as new evidence is added, and the user is prompted when vital evidence is missing. Given a claim to substantiate, an argumentation support system searches for necessary premises from a database. Given premises in a database, it searches for all supportable claims. And given premises which are inadequate to support or attack a claim, it says what extra premises are needed. To do debate planning it suggests the best order in which to present claims and premises, where particularly strong arguments should be emphasised, and where particularly weak arguments should be bolstered or disguised. It gives a 'current score' of the strength of the user's case. The system spots gaps in an opponent's case, finds the weakest part of the opponent's case, and identifies where the opponent has to give more evidence.
>
> The context in which such systems currently operate is as electronic meeting support systems.[47]

Computer-supported collaborative software (also known as virtual work-places or collaborative tools) supports project management – for example by providing task assignments, time-managing deadlines, shared calendars and shared documentation of project plans and deliverables. This software can be used by co-located teams as well as geographically distributed teams.

Virtual worlds (also known as virtual environments) are online graphical three-dimensional representations of an environment. Systems track the verbal and non-verbal signals of multiple interactors and render those signals onto **avatar**s (three-dimensional digital representations of people in a shared digital space) or **embodied agents**. Unlike in telephone conversations and video-conferences, interactors (people or avatars that interact) in virtual environments have the ability to filter the physical appearance and behavioural actions of their avatar in the eyes of their conversational partners, amplifying or suppressing features and non-verbal signals in real time for strategic purposes. Avatars interact with other graphical representations, including those of other users. As a result, virtual worlds may be useful tools to overcome the limited interactivity of most cmc.

Virtual worlds may also provide '**situatedness**' (a feeling of being physically present in a situation or **context**), which plays an important role in learning and decision-making. Most cmc technologies are limited in the amount of situatedness that they can provide. Because virtual worlds provide open, three-dimensional platforms for creating and designing real life-like spaces and allow for interaction between users in the form of avatars in that space, they do accommodate situatedness. They facilitate designing real life-like spaces and rich many-to-many interactions, allowing users to feel that they are 'situated' or present in the context in which they interact.[48]

" You need to have a new collaborative suite where, rather than receiving 50 emails about a project, you go there and you see what's new. All the documents that are pertinent to that project are available. You can create a new subgroup to talk about something. You can have a challenge or an ideation or a digital brainstorm to advance the interests of that project. You can cocreate a document on a wiki. You can microblog the results of this to other people in the corporation who need to be alerted.[49]

Finally, IT-based networking trends such as distributed problem-solving networks, crowdsourcing and electronic networks of practice 'enable a profoundly different way' of working, collaborating and doing business.[50]

Distributed problem-solving networks (DPSNs) are 'network-enabled' distributed problem-solving organizations. In this context being network-enabled means that the emergence of the organization and its sustained functioning depend upon the use of cm telecommunication networks in recruiting, mobilizing and coordinating spatially distributed knowledge resources.[51] DPSNs are in principle decentralized because the participants are both spatially distributed and peers: they operate and are ruled by 'bazaar **governance**' (controlled by market factors), although the findings of case studies show a significant degree of management centralization.[52]

> *Which of these technologies – groupware, GDSS, argumentation support systems, computer-supported collaborative software and virtual worlds – do you use in your work or studies? What, in your experience, are their strengths and weaknesses?*

Crowd sourcing internet marketplaces enable computer programmers to coordinate the use of human intelligence to perform tasks that computers are unable to do yet. Complementing conventional working environments such as organizations, online working websites provide a new channel for exchanging labour and money. On these websites, people can ask for others' help by posting tasks with a promise of providing monetary rewards as the payment for the task completion, or provide help to others by fulfilling the posted tasks with the potential of obtaining the promised monetary rewards.[53] Crowd-sourcing, though a useful addition to ways of working, does have its limitations as the following comment shows:

❝We have just got a contract from a business that claims to do web research through crowd sourcing. In practice, they can't do it that way because the 'crowd' is too unreliable and the quality of their work is too uneven. So while they are selling their research as crowd sourced, they actually have to use another firm to do the work.

(Author's interview with an executive from a web research business)

Electronic networks of practice are computer-mediated social spaces where individuals working on similar problems self-organize to help each other and share knowledge, advice and perspectives about their occupational practice or common interests. They facilitate **knowledge sharing** among geographically dispersed members.[54]

Sustained through generalized exchange, they are supported by a critical mass of active members who develop strong ties with the community as a whole, rather than interpersonal relationships. Knowledge contribution is significantly related to an individual's expertise and length of time in his or her occupation, the desire to enhance reputation and the availability of local resources. In most electronic networks of practice there is high member turnover.[55]

Together these applications (distributed problem-solving networks, crowd sourcing and electronic networks of practice) have come to be known as the network economy. In the network economy multiple parties contribute to innovations and entrepreneurship according to their specific strengths. The network economy has emerged as a result of ubiquitous information technology allowing access to information at any time and anywhere. Although cost reduction is a typical primary objective of sourcing, other benefits derive from allocating functions to other parties according to their respective strengths, such as quality and innovative strength.[56]

Summary

Work interactions regularly take place ftf, but also by telephone, conference calls, video-conferencing, email, instant messaging, SMS, listservs and social media. Other cmcs used in the workplace include groupware, group decision support systems, argumentation support systems, computer-supported collaborative software and virtual worlds. Additionally, there are new networking trends that can change how people work and collaborate; these include distributed problem-solving networks, crowd sourcing and electronic networks of practice.

Ftf is sometimes considered to be optimal for interaction because it allows the greatest number of ways of sending and receiving messages, some verbal and some non-verbal. It has some drawbacks, such as the fact that individuals need to be co-located (in the same place).

Affordances are design aspects of cmcs that facilitate communication. Affordances of email, for example, include digital storage (people can document their communication) and the rapid transfer of information (several multi-media documents can be attached to a single email). Each form of cmc also has properties that impede communication – for example, email does not afford non-verbal communication, so that messages can be ambiguous and therefore misunderstood.

This section has described a number of different forms of cmc which now predominate in organizational communication. Vital though they are, they can also be misused. The section also described applications of cmc that are specifically tailored to the demands of work and the needs of organizations, as well as IT-based networking trends that are enabling entirely new ways of working, collaborating and doing business.

1.4 SKILLED INTERPERSONAL COMMUNICATION: ITS IMPORTANCE AND COMPLEXITY

In a list of ten employability skills given by the United Kingdom's National Science, Technology, Engineering and Mathematics Network in 2011, 'communication and interpersonal skills' were quoted as no. 1, before problem-solving, using initiative, working under pressure and so on.[57] In most contemporary work, communication skills are a necessary underpinning for many other employability skills, as work is often carried out by teams and decisions are often made in meetings, while communication is intrinsic to negotiating, organizing and managing. However, all communication is complex:

❝ Communication is a complex process. It is dynamic, consisting of numerous stages and many dimensions. Unconscious and subconscious processes are intertwined with the conscious (and often unconscious) act of sending and receiving messages. The studies of non-verbal communication suggest that many non-verbal cues are manifestations of the cognitive and affective processes resulting from eons of learning ingrained in the genetic codes.[58]

However, 'studies ... suggest a strong influence of learning on perceptions, and on the interpretations of the signs and symbols that constitute a message'.[59]

Work-based interpersonal communication is made more complex by: the constraints of the work context; the technical demands of tasks; the presence, 'interest' or pressure of multiple stakeholders; the history and anticipated future of relationships; individuals' differing and sometimes conflicting overt or covert motives, emotions and attitudes; cultural differences; environmental influences such as increasing emphasis on **ethics**, diversity and international issues; and the demands of cmc. To communicate effectively in these (often rapidly changing) circumstances, a high level of skill is needed. The communication skills we have learned during our upbringing and education need to be adapted and polished to cope with the requirements of interacting with suppliers and customers, cooperating on tasks, integrating our specialist knowledge with that of others, team-work, leadership, negotiating and so on.

Ongoing changes in the way organizations function also require employees to hone their communication skills: as organizations shift from manufacturing to service jobs, expand their operations overseas, manage "talent" more strategically, and alter traditional bureaucratic structures, business communication is becoming increasingly intercultural, virtual, horizontal, strategic, and change focused'.[60] These changes in the economic environment have led to an increased demand for employees to be skilled communicators; organizations know that unskilled interaction can lead to a lack of internal **cooperation** and **coordination**, inability to take decisions, undermining of strategies, internecine conflict and even the break-up of companies.

Although communicating with skill is a challenge, it is rewarded. In fact, communication skills are usually at the top of the lists of skills employers ask for. On the job, being a skilled communicator is closely linked to career progress in most organizations. Whether measured by job level, upward mobility, performance appraisal ratings or current salary divided by age, communication abilities help people progress in organizations.[61] Moreover, frequent skilled communication with others can make people more likeable, and likeability in turn helps them perform better, while those who are disliked by others are less likely to achieve a good performance rating, even when they have positive personality traits such as conscientiousness, emotional stability or **openness to**

Find examples of: constraints of the work context; technical demands of tasks; the presence, 'interest' or pressure of multiple stakeholders; the history and anticipated future of relationships; individuals' differing and sometimes conflicting overt or covert motives, emotions and attitudes; cultural differences; environmental influences such as increasing emphasis on ethics, diversity and international issues; and the demands of cmc that add complexity to work-based interpersonal communication.

To learn more about factors that increase the complexity of communication at work visit the companion website... 1.4.1.

Find examples of intercultural, virtual, horizontal, strategic and change-focused business communication

experience.[62] This book, and those listed in the Further Reading, will help you to improve your interpersonal work communication skills.

> **❝** Hester was a very experienced banking employee specializing in regulatory reporting. However, although she would very much have liked a permanent job, all she was ever offered was temporary work, often as a maternity leave or illness replacement. She would work to the end of her contract, sometimes a month or two more, but was never offered a permanent post. There was never any criticism of her performance, but when Hester asked her agent why this kept happening, the agent said there had been reports that Hester was not a good team member. She kept herself to herself, never socialized or ate her lunch with the others, eating sandwiches at her desk instead. As a result colleagues felt they could never ask her to help out in a difficulty; they also felt she did not want to share the benefits of her expertise. Hester had seen her attitude as one of devotion to her work; but that was not how her colleagues saw it.
>
> (Author's interview with a bank regulatory reporting specialist)

Summary

All communication is complex, and the workplace can increase its complexity, for example by the constraints of the work context, the technical demands of tasks, the presence of multiple stakeholders, cultural differences and the demands of cmc. Effective communication at work requires a high level of skill. Recent changes in the way organizations function have made skilled workplace communication even more important, with, for example, increased intercultural and virtual communication and a larger number of service jobs. Skilled communication is closely linked to career progress in most organizations and can help improve performance.

1.5 ABOUT THIS BOOK

The book is divided into three parts. Part I, which consists of Chapters 1 and 2, introduces interpersonal work communication, demonstrates its importance, describes alternative ways of working – that is, the different communication modes and technologies of the modern world – and explains why the subject requires study. It then turns to the important question, effectively a new one, of choice of mode. It outlines the different affordances of different modes and explicates the factors that influence how people decide what mode to use, with a particular focus on work-related factors.

Part II turns to a consideration of the processes involved in communication and the social and psychological influences on it; without an understanding of these processes interpersonal skill development can only be superficial. Chapter 3 deals with the vital antecedent to effective communication of social cognition; Chapter 4 deals with making a contribution, self-presentation and impression management; Chapter 5 with the dynamic processes involved in interaction. These processes are universal; that is, they apply to all communication and all communicators.

Part II then moves on to explain the factors that produce differences in how we communicate, which are the influences of two sets of factors: social factors, such as demography, culture and situation (Chapter 6), and psychological factors (Chapter 7). In the context of situation, Chapter 6 explains the central theories that have developed to predict how mode affects communication. Chapter 8 covers three applications of communication that are of great importance at work: influencing, handling conflict and negotiating.

Part III of the book relates mediated interpersonal communication directly to major concerns of modern organizations and businesses: cooperation, coordination and knowledge sharing (Chapter 9); teamwork (Chapter 10); management and leadership (Chapter 11); organizational structures and processes (Chapter 12); and inter-organizational relations (Chapter 13).

At all points throughout the book four matters are highlighted: the work context, cultural differences, the impact of different communication modes and ways to perform skilfully using different modes.

Quotations from interviews undertaken by the author and from published sources are supplied as illustrations; in some cases readers are left to interpret their significance for themselves. Questions and small exercises are provided throughout the text to help the reader with learning and self-development; and a set of cases and exercises is given at the end of the book for group or class discussion or role playing. Terms that are included in the Glossary and not fully explained in the text are emboldened on first introduction. The book is accompanied by a Student Companion Website which contains suggestions about how to use the book, links to videos on topics of interest, further guidance on how to develop particular work communication skills and more in-depth material on selected aspects. Using this Website will add considerably to the reader's understanding of work communication and, it is hoped, their enjoyment of the subject.

2 WORK COMMUNICATION MODES

This chapter introduces a major issue that arises because we now have a wide range of alternative modes for communication, especially at work: how people choose a communication mode. The chapter also suggests how such choices should be made, following this argument: 'The goal in using a particular communication medium is not to replicate identically that which can be easily achieved when interaction partners are face-to-face. Rather, it is to find ways to provide participants with a means to achieve all the interactions that are necessary to complete the defined task in a productive and efficient manner.'[1]

On completing your study of this chapter, you will be able to explain and apply the implications of:

- The alternative modes available for work communication, presenting their characteristics and their advantages and disadvantages.
- The main considerations other than media characteristics that influence who uses the different forms of communication and how intensively they use them.

You will also be able to make a choice of communication mode for a particular work-related purpose and justify your choice.

Figure 2.1 shows the main communication mode alternatives and the factors that influence how people choose a mode.

The chapter has two sections: the first analyses media affordances, the second describes the factors other than media characteristics that influence media choice. The exercises give you an opportunity to practise media choice.

Figure 2.1 Choosing a communication mode

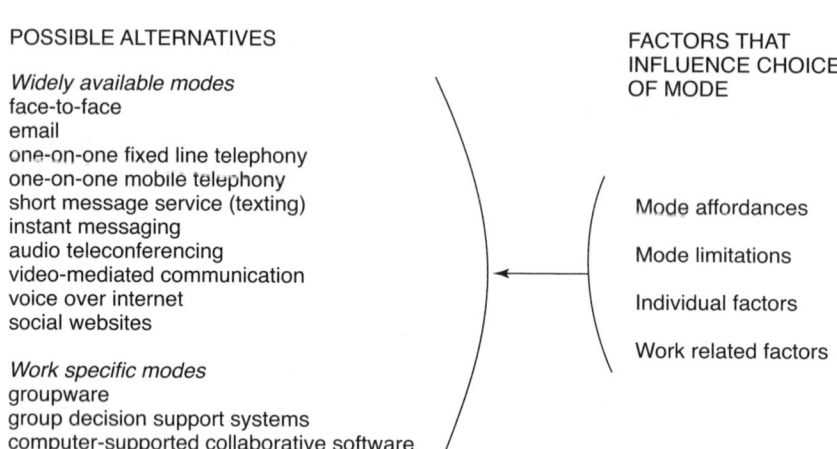

POSSIBLE ALTERNATIVES

Widely available modes
face-to-face
email
one-on-one fixed line telephony
one-on-one mobile telephony
short message service (texting)
instant messaging
audio teleconferencing
video-mediated communication
voice over internet
social websites

Work specific modes
groupware
group decision support systems
computer-supported collaborative software
virtual worlds

FACTORS THAT INFLUENCE CHOICE OF MODE

Mode affordances

Mode limitations

Individual factors

Work related factors

2.1 AFFORDANCES OF DIFFERENT WORK COMMUNICATION MODES

Communication modes vary in the properties that enable or constrain interaction: these properties are called **social affordances**. Chapter 1 introduced the concept of affordances. Social affordances are an important category of affordances for understanding different communication modes; this section will demonstrate their importance and then analyse the most important of them. Social affordances of interactive communication technologies (ICTs) include their technological capabilities, such as their ability to transcend space and time, but also their potential for social enhancement, as they can expand users' local and global connectivity and provide them with an additional means for social interaction. Not all digital affordances are specifically social: those of search engines, for instance, are not.

Technological properties and social contexts are 'matched' in social interaction, because people are likely to use a certain kind of computer-mediated communication (cmc) only when its capabilities are able to fulfil their interaction purposes and are suitable for the social contexts in which communication occurs. On the one hand, ICTs provide technological capabilities facilitating communication and social interactions in various ways. On the other hand, the social contexts of interactions and users' knowledge of and skills for using ICTs shape the way users perceive and employ ICTs in actual communication practice.

" Consider a communication episode of a friend of mine, Bill, who works at an advertising agency. Bill sent an urgent IM [instant message] to the members of his work group to call off the weekly routine meeting at the last minute. However, when Bill sent the message, he did not notice that none of his colleagues were logged on to the IM service. As a result, while Bill successfully sent the note to everyone, they did not receive it and got together in the meeting room due to the miscommunication. In this extreme instance, Bill clearly knows how to use IM to initiate an 'instant' communication, but he may not understand completely how IM supports his communication with others and under what circumstances he can initiate interaction through IM successfully.[2]

Individuals' knowledge of the properties of cmc technologies is an essential component of the social affordances that allow cmcs to support social actions and achieve interaction goals. In the episode in the example above, IM did not afford Bill prompt communication with his colleagues, as the fact that he sent out his alert when everyone was logged off the service shows. However, if Bill had been aware of the online status notification and knew that such functionality can provide information about the availability of his colleagues, then he might have decided to use an alternative mode to alert them. In other words, knowledge about how to use cmc features appropriately to sustain communication for a certain purpose plays a crucial role in enabling their affordances to support intended interactions.

The old adage 'horses for courses' applies to media choice. For instance, for transferring knowledge in groups, net-based methods have three advantages and three disadvantages: the strengths of permanent storage (correspondence can be stored in an easily organized archive), representational flexibility (diagrams and photographs can be inserted in emails and some media afford the use of avatars) and computational power; but they also have the drawbacks of cluttering of content, lack of interpersonal information and lack of sequential structure.

> *Give examples to show how knowledge of the properties of text messages (SMS) allow or constrain their use at work.*

- Cluttering of content occurs when communicators try to make references to several different things, such as earlier messages, during an interaction. Because net-based communicators are not physically together, they are not able to point to the things they want to discuss.
- Lack of interpersonal information means not being supplied with enough social, behavioural and cognitive cues about the other participants to adjust communication appropriately.

> *To learn more about the technical problems of knowledge transfer by IT-based methods and their solutions, visit the companion website... 2.1.1.*

- Lack of sequential structure refers to an inability to overcome 'coordination barriers' by restricting interaction (as **turn-taking conventions** do ftf) or providing scaffolding mechanisms (such as the signals that ftf interactors use when they want to take over the speaking role).

There are ways to overcome these drawbacks:

- Content elements can be represented in ways that can be easily integrated and/or cross-referenced, to solve the problems of disjointed chat discussions.

> *Look at the Glossary for the meaning of turn-taking conventions.*

- The interpersonal barrier to net-based knowledge communication may be overcome by using 'communication media that transmit visual and/or acoustic cues' such as videoconferences or audio chats.
- The lack of sequential structure may be overcome by using 'scaffolds'; that is, when participants create a new message in an online discussion they can choose among a predefined set of message types like 'My theory is...' or 'I need to understand...' or 'Different opinion ...' that help to structure the contents of a group discussion.[3]
- Cooperation scripts can be used and have in fact become more common in net-based scenarios where structuring is an even more pressing problem than it is in email correspondence.[4] They involve sequencing large parts of the interaction, an approach known as scripted cooperation. A cooperation script is a procedural sequence of collaborative, tightly interwoven events that participants are either requested or obliged to carry out. For example, a cooperation script might specify:

(1) All participants in turn state their understanding of the issue; this is recorded and distributed. (2) Participants question one another about their understanding of the issue; again, the answers are recorded and distributed. (3) Participants in turn contribute 'new' information that has not or appears not to have been taken into account in the earlier formulations of the issue. (4) The issue is reformulated and agreed. And so on.[5]

Box 2.1 sets out eight affordances on which media differ in ways that affect an important aspect of interpersonal communication – **grounding**, or reaching a clear understanding of one another's meaning. Other affordances of media that are important for interpersonal work communication include mobility, ubiquity, high/low attention getting, user identifiability, user privacy, synchronicity/asynchronicity, interactivity, propinquity, tele-/social/copresence, information control and media richness.

Mobility: the ability to communicate while moving around or travelling is a highly valued affordance, and for organizations an important aid to efficiency.

BOX 2.1 GROUNDING AFFORDANCES ON WHICH COMMUNICATION MODES VARY

1. *Copresence: A and B share the same physical environment.* In ftf conversation (ftfc), the participants are usually in the same surroundings and can readily see and hear what each other is doing and looking at. In other modes there is no such possibility.
2. *Visibility: A and B are visible to each other.* In ftfc, the participants can see each other, but in many other modes they cannot. They may also be able to see each other, as in video teleconferencing, without being able to see what each other is doing or looking at.
3. *Audibility: A and B communicate by speaking.* In ftf, on the telephone, and with some kinds of teleconferencing, participants can hear each other and take note of timing and intonation. In other modes they cannot. An answering machine preserves intonation, but only some aspects of utterance timing.
4. *Cotemporality: B receives at roughly the same time as A produces.* In most conversations, an utterance is produced just about when it is received and understood, without delay. In modes such as letters and electronic mail, this is not the case.
5. *Simultaneity: A and B can send and receive at once and simultaneously.* Sometimes messages can be conveyed and received by both parties at once, as when a hearer smiles during a speaker's utterance. Simultaneous utterances are also allowed, for example, in the keyboard teleconferencing program called Talk, where what both parties type appears letter by letter in two distinct halves of the screen. Other media are cotemporal but not simultaneous, such as the kind of keyboard teleconferencing that transmits characters only after the typist hits a carriage return.
6. *Sequentiality: A's and B's turns cannot get out of sequence.* In ftfc, turns ordinarily form a sequence that does not include intervening turns from different conversations with other people. With email, answering machines and letters, a message and its reply may be separated by any number of irrelevant messages or activities; interruptions do not have the same force.
7. *Reviewability: B can review A's messages.* Speech fades quickly, but in media such as email, letters and recorded messages, an utterance stays behind as an artefact that can be reviewed later by either of the partners – or even by a third party. In keyboard teleconferencing, the last few utterances stay visible on the screen for a while.
8. *Revisability: A can revise messages for B.* Some media, such as letters and email, allow a participant to revise an utterance privately before sending it to a partner. In ftf and telephone conversations, most self-repairs must be done publicly. Some kinds of keyboard teleconferencing fall in between; what a person types appears on the partner's screen only after every carriage return, rather than letter by letter.[6]

Ubiquity (reachability): as with mobility, the ability to reach others and be reached by them wherever you are is a highly valued affordance, and for organizations an important aid to efficiency.

Attention gaining: getting other people's attention, for instance when working in a group, is a precondition for getting a message across. Though not entirely unproblematic ftf, it is generally more difficult in mediated communication. In ftf, conversation partners signal each other in a number of different ways, using gestures, sounds, facial expressions and body movements. Some of these means are either not available at all or are of only limited availability when participants interact in other ways, including by video-mediated communication such as that used in video conferences. In these, communication partners must often rely on strategies such as waving their hand in front of their face. These strategies may be inappropriate in the context of work-related conferences and are often more awkward to employ than the signals that can be used ftf.[7]

> **"**I do use texting a bit, mainly when it is urgent to get someone's attention without disturbing them with a phone call. However, I use email far more. When you are out and about you always have your smartphone with you and you send an email. The client is usually either by their computer and checking their emails or often they'll see it come through on their smartphone, so you do get their attention and you can say far more.
>
> (Author's interview with an executive from a media and information company)

User identifiability: for emails and chat systems people can adopt usernames which permit their identity to be disguised. Usernames allocated by organizations do not usually permit people to disguise their identity, but some chat systems used at work allow anonymity.

Anonymity is seen as appropriate for some organizational purposes and not others, survey data shows. Anonymity is most appropriate for organizational surveys and/or assessments, then decreasingly for formal evaluations, use of technology, informal evaluations, general use and firing. Using anonymity appropriately is significantly related to the quality of relationships that people have with their colleagues.[8]

Some organizations allow staff a degree of anonymity because it increases participation in discussions, especially of sensitive issues. Maintaining people's motivation to participate in anonymous discussions can, however, be problematic because of the fact that they cannot be rewarded for their contributions. There are ways that allow rewards to be allocated without identifying their recipients, but anonymous rewards do not motivate as well as identified rewards. People work harder at tasks when it is known who received rewards and especially when it is known what rewards they each received so that comparisons are possible.[9]

User privacy: privacy is related to anonymity but differs in that a communication that is available only to the intended recipient is private but not anonymous if the recipient can identify the sender. Thus encrypted communication by email is private even when it is not anonymous.

The use of mobile telephony in public places has demonstrated that many people have fewer privacy concerns than once seemed the case. Nevertheless there is evidence that privacy is an issue, for instance for women in their use of SMS. Text messages cannot normally be encrypted and so, research has shown, a significant number of women have concerns about using them for intimate or personal communication, despite their affordances of mobility and ubiquity that they value.[10]

A study of employee preferences regarding management communication found that employees perceived it as critical to receive human resource information that is private (confidential), personal or sensitive ftf; whereas information not seen as confidential – meeting times, training times, policy changes, system problems and information with numerous details – were seen as just as productive and sometimes more so to receive through email.[11]

Synchronicity/asynchronicity: communication modes are synchronous when they allow two or more people to communicate at the same time. 'Chat', or instant messaging, is considered synchronous; email is asynchronous. However, 'synchronous' when applied to cmc is misleading: in spoken conversation listeners hear the other's message as it is being produced; in cmc they only receive it after it has been produced.[12]

Although the general assumption has been that asynchronous communication is more formal than synchronous, this may not be so when asynchronous communication is used as if it were synchronous. In a forum discussing sport, 'very short messages' and 'bursts of activity followed by hours of negligible activity' suggested that users 'use the normally asynchronous medium of a forum as if it were a synchronous chat'. Other features of this asynchronous forum that resembled synchronous chat included 'lack of topical coherence' – that is, people would digress or wander off the subject. Additionally, few users quoted others' messages. This suggests the participants 'simply rely on the temporal immediacy of the messages to create short-term coherence, as happens in chats'.[13]

Asynchronicity such as that afforded by text messages (SMS) can be as highly valued as synchronicity in some circumstances because it allows senders to communicate at a time of their choosing without interrupting the receiver in the way that a telephone call, for instance, may do. Furthermore, asynchronicity can improve performance: groups working by asynchronous communication, such as email, performed a deeper problem analysis and generated more inferential ideas than groups using synchronous group communication, as represented by group support systems.[14] On the other hand, asynchronous cmc may not work well for collaborative writing projects; synchronous alternatives, such as 'netmeeting', may work better.[15]

Interactivity: a dictionary definition of interactivity is 'allowing or relating to continuous two-way transfer of information between a user and the central point of a communication system, such as a computer'. Some understandings of interactivity consider it a purely technological attribute: 'interactivity can be conceptualised as technological attributes of mediated environments that enable reciprocal communication or information exchange, which afford interaction between communication technology and users, or between users through technology'. However, it is also usual to acknowledge that interactivity has subjective aspects: one model incorporates interactive attributes, user perceptions (such as perceived interactivity) and individual differences (such as confidence in using the internet).[16] Perceived ease of use, usefulness and the flow experience of a medium, which are elements of interactivity, affect people's attitude to and intention to use a computer medium, whether their purpose is to perform a task or be entertained.[17]

Propinquity: some forms of electronic communication induce a feeling of nearness, despite users being physically distant from one another; this feeling is known as propinquity. Electronic propinquity has been linked to the level of satisfaction experienced by users from their communication. Research has now shown that high media bandwidth (the range of senses impacted on by the medium), feedback immediacy, low complexity of a task or of the information being transmitted, lack of media alternatives and skilled communication by users are linked to propinquity and satisfaction. Being constrained to use one medium leads people to compensate by exerting more skill to get their message across and making this greater effort in itself leads them to experience greater satisfaction and a greater sense of propinquity.[19]

> According to Klein (2002) 'Businesses are spending millions of dollars to add interactivity to their Web sites, in the form of games, animated pictures, and personalization tools, without knowing exactly what impact this has on their customers.'[18]
>
> How would businesses find out what impact interactivity has on their customers?

Telepresence/social presence/copresence: related to propinquity, though distinct, is the concept of telepresence or social presence. This has been defined as the feeling a person has that other people are involved in a communication exchange. Communication partners can have the sensation of being continuously available to one another; this is copresence.

User control and media richness both contribute to creating a sense of telepresence. Moreover, through telepresence, these media characteristics influence people's cognitive responses, such as the beliefs and attitudes of consumers about products.[20] The dynamics of virtual interaction may cultivate virtual copresence. For example, in IM relatively speedy interaction and the ability to track what people are doing in real time (at least to the extent of knowing when they are online) may promote users' sense of virtual copresence.[21]

It has been suggested that experienced presence can be higher during a virtual interview than in a real world simulation. When a comparison was made between an immersive virtual reality (VR) job selection simulation and a real world simulation that was identical to its VR counterpart (same interviewer, same questions) but without technological mediation, self-report data and subjective anxiety scores, but not objective (skin conductance) scores suggested that experienced presence was higher during the virtual interview. This finding would tend to run counter to the widely held view of presence as 'disappearance of mediation' that implies that technology is a barrier, a mediating tool, that can only reduce the level of presence experienced in an interaction.[22]

Media with high social presence allow users to experience interpersonal warmth, friendliness and satisfaction with the interaction.[23] Social or copresence is not advantageous for all purposes, however. For multimedia customer services such as planning a holiday or choosing a property and arranging an appropriate mortgage, teledata is more highly valued by users than telepresence as provided by video links. A comparison of telepresence (provided through video conference communication links between users) and teledata (supplied by multimedia systems which provide video data) showed that, while the perceived quality of the telepresence and the teledata were similar, teledata was rated higher in terms of what was most useful, what was the most important feature to preserve and what was the most important to improve.[24]

Information control: this refers to how the use of a medium amplifies or attenuates an individual's ability to perform actions that allow him or her to regulate or restrict the flow of social information during interactions. A channel such as email affords an individual with greater control over an interaction than ftf because the feature of asynchronous, or non-immediate, message exchange allows greater time to plan and edit messages, providing the individual has the necessary knowledge and ability.[25]

As this last affordance implies, the contemporary view is that while the capacity of a medium to convey information has an effect, different individuals have different degrees of control over social information exchanged during interactions over different interpersonal media. Some individuals may have lesser abilities to manage their needs for expression and privacy in a social encounter even when that channel happens to have features that allow for more social cues. It is how those individuals are able (or unable) to use those features that affects this.[26]

Table 2.1   Affordances of different communication modes

Affordance	Communication modes that most easily provide the affordance
Mobility	mobile telephone, sms, email
Ubiquity/reachability	mobile telephone, sms, email
Copresence	ftf
Visibility	ftf, VoIP (partial), video teleconferencing (partial)
Audibility	ftf, telephone, VoIP, teleconferencing
Cotemporality	ftf, VoIP, teleconferencing, (IM provides near cotemporality)
Simultaneity	ftf, VoIP, teleconferencing, *Talk* IM
Sequentiality	ftf, telephone, teleconferencing, IM
Reviewability	Email, voicemail
Private revisability	Email, voicemail, IM
Attention gaining	ftf, SMS, email*
High user identifiability**	ftf, most intra-organizational email
User privacy	ftf, telephone
Synchronicity**	ftf, telephone, video
Interactivity	ftf, telephone, VoIP, teleconferencing
Propinquity	ftf, VoIP, virtual worlds
Tele-/social/copresence	ftf, VoIP, virtual worlds
Information control	Email, SMS, IM
Media richness	ftf, VoIP

    * Ftf requires copresence, SMS and email require the technology to be turned on.
  ** Anonymity and asynchronicity can also be desirable affordances.

Media richness: this is a term for a combination of affordances. Rich media have high feedback capability, support the transmission of several cues, the source of the message is human and the language used can have high variety (express a wide range of ideas).[27] Media richness perceptions are considered to be an important influence on channel choice. Section 6.3 describes media richness theory, which purports to explain how media richness influences communication. Table 2.1 shows which communication modes most easily provide different affordances.

> *Assume you need to let a colleague know that your train has been held up and you will be late for work. What mode or combination of modes would you use and why?*

Summary

Communication modes vary in their social affordances, which are the properties that enable or constrain interaction: mobility, ubiquity, visibility, audibility, cotemporality, simultaneity, sequentiality, reviewability, revisability, high/low attention gaining, user anonymity/identifiability, high/low user privacy, synchronicity/asynchronicity, interactivity, propinquity, telepresence/social presence/copresence, information control and media richness have been explained in this section. Many of these affordances depend not just on the technology but also on the skill and approach of the user.

2.2 FACTORS THAT INFLUENCE PATTERNS OF MEDIA USAGE

Quite soon after cmc became widely available at work, researchers were studying how people choose what mode to use. (Access is far from universal, but that question is not part of this discussion.) The researchers' findings gave rise to a number of models of media choice that emphasize different influencing factors.

> **"** In contact with clients (I'm in a business-to-business selling role) you have a kind of sixth sense about what is the right way to communicate at this point. Perhaps you've sent several emails with information and the relationship is becoming a bit impersonal, a bit distant, so you'll arrange a visit to make it more human again. Clients usually like the fact that you take the time and trouble to go to see them – so long as you don't do it too often.
>
> (Author's interview with an executive from a media and information company)

People undoubtedly perceive significant differences in communication channels, but the hierarchy of preference is not clear. For example, some authors report a general preference for ftf and telephone over computer-based conversations, while others find that people choose media based on convenience.[28] In a study of working groups, ftf conversation was preferred for negotiating and reaching consensus, whereas email was preferred for coordinating schedules, assigning tasks and making progress reports.[29] Again, in a high-tech computer manufacturing company, although technology was used to communicate, it did not replace ftf interaction. Instead, 'mundane, commonplace, "informal" activities performed by employees ... [were] not only prevalent but also critical to the achievement of collaborative problem solving'. These informal problem-solving meetings were 'ad hoc' and spontaneous, often not affiliated with a formal meeting or group.[30]

> **"** These preferences can be explained in terms of the costs associated with each medium relative to the participants' purposes. Sometimes the participants want a reviewable record of a conversation – as for schedules, task assignments, and progress reports; and other times they do

not. Sometimes speakers want to get a hearer's full attention, and sometimes they want to avoid interrupting. Sometimes people want their reactions to be seen, as in negotiating and reaching consensus, and sometimes they do not.[31]

The 'costs' referred to in this extract are not necessarily or even usually financial: time and effort are the important costs here.

" I use email much more than the phone; that's mainly because wo have to communicate quite a lot of data. I use the phone when I need to discuss or explain something, especially with someone in, say, Japan or Switzerland. Then we would talk but we would both be looking at the same documents on our screens.
(Author's interview with a bank regulatory reporting specialist who has worked on a series of temporary contracts)

According to Trevino et al. (1987), media choice can be related to three independent variables: the degree of ambiguity of the message, the symbolic cues carried by the mode and situational constraints, such as time pressure and distance. They argued that the level of ambiguity (or equivocality) of a given message leads to different interpretations and that different modes increase or decrease such ambiguity. Ftf allows immediate feedback, provides multiple cues and uses natural language. Therefore it can decrease ambiguity more quickly than any other mode. However, messages not only carry content but also symbolic meaning. For example, a reprimand from a manager to a subordinate may have more significance if it is put in writing than spoken, even if the wording is identical. Situational constraints are often linked to convenience; geographical distance makes ftf too costly, time of day differences lead to using email instead of IM if the intended recipient is not likely to be awake.[32]

" You have to think through how your communication mode will appear to others. For example, if you generally use email with someone, it can suggest that you have a problem with them and can't talk to them face-to-face.
(Author's interview with a bank regulatory reporting specialist who has worked on a series of temporary contracts)

The argument of Trevino et al. (1987) and other scholars who take a similar view is essentially that media choices are rational: people decide what mode to use according to the purpose of the communication and the features of the media; subsequently, however, attention focused on the social determinants of media choice. According to this perspective, the richer a medium is perceived to be, the more likely it will be chosen to communicate any message, whatever its purpose and whether it is ambiguous or not, subject, of course, to availability and convenience. Later studies have concluded that both rational and social factors should be included in models of modal choice. Findings such as the following suggest a mixture of factors:

- Choosing a ftf meeting is often decided by how equivocal the message seems to the sender.
- Symbolic cues are the most influential factor for letters.
- Email use by peers is the most influential factor for email.
- Rational choice factors such as message equivocality, distance between communication partners and the number of message recipients significantly influence all media choices, but so does **social influence**.[33]

Further research by the same scholars suggested that a number of factors differentiated among media choices, including medium symbolism, message equivocality, distance between message partners, perceived media richness, number of message recipients and perceived message recipients' attitudes. General attitudes towards the different media were influenced most consistently by perceived medium richness. New media attitudes were also influenced by person/technology interaction factors. General medium use was influenced by different factors for the different media.[34] Not only do different factors imply different choices but the relative importance of choice factors depends on the medium. Social influences may be more important for some media, but the content of a message may be more important for others.

> Social influence, the idea that attitudes and behaviours are partially determined by the social context, is explained in Section 2.4.

Following a meta-analysis of the research into situational influences on the use of communication technologies, van den Hooff et al. (2005) created a model to describe whether email is used for a specific task. This had the following elements:

- The user's age, expertise and skill, innovativeness, organizational position and experience with the medium all directly affect email use and affect it indirectly through the range of tasks for which they think email suitable (ranging from lean to rich communication tasks) and how useful they perceive email to be for their work.
- The medium's geographical reach, speed, perceived richness, perceived ease of use and compatibility directly affect email use, while perceived richness and perceived ease of use also affect it indirectly through the range of tasks and perceived usefulness.
- The task's geographical distance (how 'distributed' it is among non-co-located workers), its equivocality (complexity plus social presence requirement – that is, whether or not it is clear what needs to be done

and so how much discussion is needed) and its time frame (such as urgency) affect whether email is used indirectly through task range and the perceived usefulness of the medium.
- The social environment, analysed into co-worker evaluations (of task-medium fit), co-worker use and critical mass affect email use directly, and in the case of co-worker evaluations indirectly through the range of tasks and the perceived usefulness of the medium.[35]

Thus, for example, if the potential user was young, skilled, innovative, had experience with email and held a mid-level or above position in the organization; if the task involved people who were geographically separated, was able to be clearly defined in advance, and did not require an immediate decision; if co-workers thought email suitable for the task, tended to use it themselves, and enough people in the organization were regular users of email (there was critical mass), email would be a likely communication mode because of its geographical reach, its perceived ease of use and its compatibility (email's lack of perceived richness and relatively slow speed would not, in this case, be important).

Figure 2.2 shows the factors deciding whether email is the chosen communication mode, according to the van den Hoof (2005) model.

Overall, two points seem fairly clear. First, in common with most human behaviour, the choices people make about which communication mode to use is multifactorial; second, different media are both complements and substitutes.

While findings on the substitutability and complementarity of modes apply to private life, and work communication patterns would no doubt be subject to different influences, it nevertheless seems likely that at least some of these findings apply.[36] We know, for instance, that managers who search for authentic knowledge in the public domain are most likely to use formal methods such as management systems, company **intranets**, email applications and search engines, while managers who look for implicit knowledge, such as individuals' personal perspectives, are most likely to select online audio or video communication applications, telephone conferencing or customer online community websites: in other words informal and interpersonal sources.[37]

> *Using the van den Hoof (2005) model, set out the conditions in which a conference call would be the preferred mode for a task.*

> *To learn more about the factors that influence choice of mode and why different media are both complements and substitutes, visit the companion website... 2.2.1.*

Figure 2.2 Factors influencing whether email is the chosen communication mode

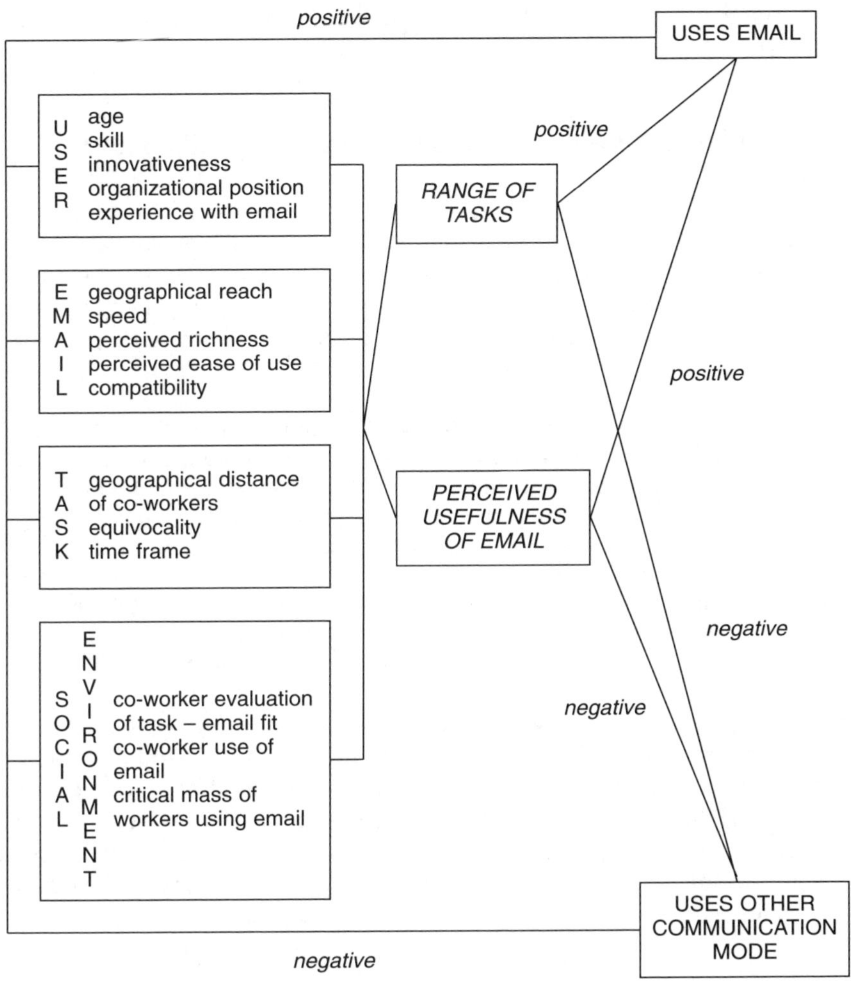

Based on van den Hooff, B., Groce, J. and de Jonge, S. (2005) 'Situational influences on the use of communication technologies: A Meta-analysis and exploratory study', *Journal of Business Communication* **42**(1)

Summary

Early models of media choice presented it as based on the purpose of the communication, the features of the medium and the communicators' own preferences. Later models introduced other variables, including character-istics of the communication task such as the geographical dispersion of the communicators and social influences.

The next section will discuss users' characteristics in the sense of individuals' reasons and psychology; Section 2.4 will consider the influence of elements in the users' environment such as co-workers and the organizational background.

2.3 FACTORS RELATING TO INDIVIDUALS THAT INFLUENCE MODE CHOICE

According to the findings of a longitudinal study, people at work are 'incredibly adept at evaluating and judging when and how communication media need to be adapted to support either a particular plan, the relationship atmosphere or to manage or promote perceptions of past, present or future events'. For instance,

> **"** For information exchange the speed of response required ... the content and the importance of the information affected the media chosen ... As Company A and Company B interact, the procedures that were in place ... are translated into communication practices that become common to both companies. The actors, through individual communication episodes both within their own organization and between organizations ... changed and developed the procedures to ensure the aims of the relationship were met, iteratively allowing new plans to emerge. Different task-media fit judgments were made as the relationship unfolded.[38]

As the above finding illustrates, we now know that which mode people use to communicate is affected not only by the affordances and limitations of the mode but also by other factors, such as the kind of message or task involved, the age, gender and probably the culture of the user, individual preferences and attitudes, the type and stage of the relationship between the communicators, and organizational support and **norms**. This section explains some of these factors and how they affect media usage.

Demographic and cultural factors

There is some evidence that **demographic factors** influence internet use; two of these factors are age and gender. A third factor is culture, and there are some interactions between culture and demographic factors.

Age

Ageist assumptions are common in relation to information technology in general. However, employee reactions to the implementation of a new IT initiative challenged ageist assumptions.

> *To see some survey data about email usage, visit the companion website... 2.3.1.*

Younger workers reported less satisfaction than older workers; this effect was more, not less, pronounced in departments where most staff were relatively young.[39] Again, contrary to **stereotypes** of older workers, skilled older workers such as accountants negotiate the various pressures associated with technological innovation strategically: they deliberately comply with some and refuse others; in general they resist typification either as excluded older workers or as continuous learners, while being focused on what, when and how they engage.[40] Further, age was unrelated to the use of social media by research scientists, a study found, though it was correlated to factors such as connectivity, research style and awareness of social media.[41]

Gender

There are differences between men and women in terms of actual use of the internet and communication technologies, with women being slower to adopt cmc but then using it more intensively. Gender also affects attitudes to and evaluations of cmc, though not consistently.

> *To learn more about how gender affects internet usage, visit the companion website... 2.3.2.*

There are gender differences in IM usage. Some differences reflect gender distinctions in face-to-face (ftf) spoken conversation, such as women using it 'predominantly as a tool for facilitating social interaction', whereas men 'are more prone to use it for conveying information'. Other differences indicate gender-based attitudes towards the importance of language standards in speech and writing: women use fewer contractions and more standard punctuation and capitalization.[42] Among IM users, significant gender differences emerge in 'every communication', a study found. 'Females rated their IM interactions significantly higher in communication quality and more valuable than did males'.For both sexes, 'interactions with males produced less perceived control than did those with females'. Again, for both sexes, 'interactions with same-sex partners were perceived as being higher in communication quality than were those with cross-sex ones', while 'interactions with opposite-sex partners were rated as more valuable and change-producing than with same-sex ones'.[43]

Culture

Although we know that **ethnicity** is currently linked to access to cmc through its link to income, we have, as yet, limited information on how culture affects cmc use. It might seem that culture-based differences in **communication style**s would affect how much members of certain cultures use cmc. However, a study in Singapore found evidence to the contrary:

❝ Monochrons (originally associated ... with the cultures of Northern Europe and North America) prefer to organize their time in a linear, 'one thing at a time' manner, in contrast with polychrons (originally associated with the cultures of Latin America and the Middle East) who are more relaxed about deadlines, etc. Polychrons are more likely to be multi-taskers, capable of handling several responsibilities simultaneously. [Thus] the internet would seem to be the ideal medium for multi-tasking polychrons: its famous collapse of traditional boundaries of time and space and multiple channels of communication would seem perfectly suited to multi-taskers who prefer nonlinear approaches to time. Somewhat surprisingly, however, the Singapore survey results did *not* show a strong correlation between polychronicity and internet use.[44]

These findings are significant because they show that actual behaviours in relation to cmc do not always follow what we might predict on the basis of earlier cultural analyses.[45]

Some cultures, such as those of Greece and Japan, are characterized by **'high-context' communication** in which much of the communication is expressed non-verbally or interpreted from a shared understanding of the context. High-context cultures would seem to have a 'handicap' in the **low-context**, non-verbal-deficient world of cmc (specifically text-based email). Language may present further obstacles to cmc use in some countries. In a setting of participants with diverse linguistic backgrounds (a randomly selected 6.5 hour chat session which elicited 3,092 contributions from 185 participants), the dominance of English was very strong. This feature may reduce participation by people with limited English language competence.[46]

If, however, there is a handicap, it is probable that users of different languages and people from different cultures learn to communicate within the restrictions of the medium. Users in a developing country (Saudi Arabia) view cmc as an important business communication medium, used with both their managers and their equals; many notice that they use other communication media less than before. Furthermore, the factors that influence the adoption of electronic services in Saudi Arabia are similar to those applying in other countries (see Figure 2.3).

The perceived importance of different media varies across different groups in society, a Korean study found: IM, SMS and mobile phone are 'important' media for students, mobile phone for homeworkers, and email for organizational workers. Moreover, mobile phones tend to be used in reinforcing strong social ties, and text-based cmc media tend to be used in expanding

> *Consider whether these findings are likely to be universal – that is to apply in all or most nations – or to be specific to Korea.*

Figure 2.3 Factors affecting e-service adoption in Saudia Arabia

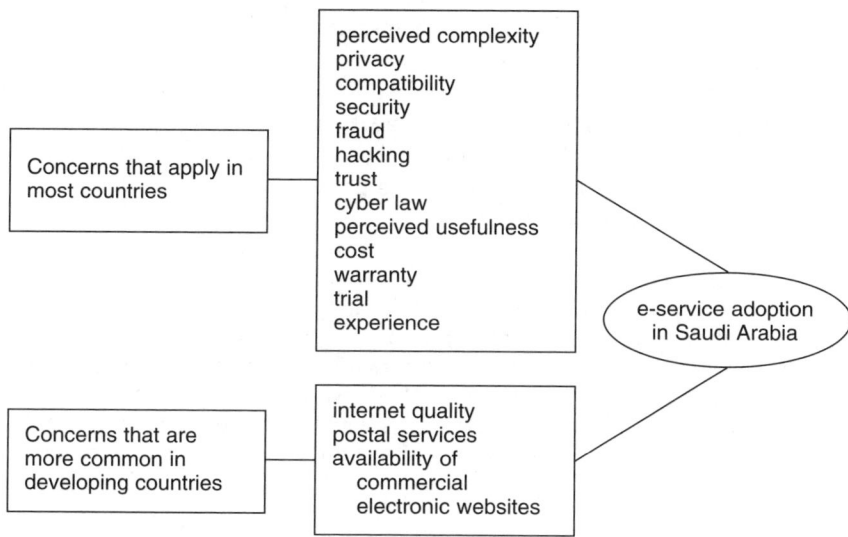

Based on Algahatani, M.A., Al-Badi, A.H. & Mayhew, P.J. (2012) 'The Enablers and disablers of e-commerce: consumers perspectives', *The Electronic Journal of Information Systems in Developing Countries*, **54**.

relationships where ties are weak. Finally, ftf seems to be a universal medium without significant differences across respondents' occupational categories.[47]

Individuals' reasons and psychological factors

As noted in Section 2.2, media-use patterns have been attributed to objectively rational choices that are based on evaluating communication options and selecting an appropriate medium to match the communication requirements of the task. Such an approach does undoubtedly explain some choices: for instance, instant messaging, with its capabilities of rapid but unobtrusive communication, is widely used for relational maintenance and everyday communication.[48] Attitudes towards using text messaging depend on how effective and easy to use it is seen to be.[49] Again, the reasons people give when asked for their choice of mode are generally 'rational': for example, influential factors in the choice of text messaging for communication include concern for conflict avoidance and privacy protection:

> To see other findings that show a 'rational' approach to choice of mode, visit the companion website...
> 2.3.3.

when people are concerned with conflict avoid-ance or privacy protection and they perceive SMS to be an effective communication means, they will have a positive attitude towards SMS.[50]

Despite the rationality of the reasons people give for their choice of communication mode, using cmc is associated with individual psycho-logical differences, for example in the personal-ity trait of **extraversion**.[51]

> *To see other findings that show psychological influences on choice of mode, visit the companion website...*
> *2.3.4.*

" Some people use email to avoid confrontation; some people use it because they want to confront but not face-to-face; people also use it to comment to trusted colleagues on things that happen in the office, as in 'What did X think he was up to with that daft idea about Z?' It's actu-ally risky, because of course it's all on the record, but people just seem to ignore that. I don't think they would ignore the risk face-to-face.

(Author's interview with an executive from a media and information company)

In the context of work there is evidence of nega-tive employee attitudes towards digital commu-nication methods: they reveal 'a negative stream of opinion on the use of digital communication when compared to face-to-face communication', according to a 2010 study. Specifically, employ-ees said, 'face-to-face contact is the best way to interact at work', 'digital communication meth-ods interfere with face-to-face relationships', 'digital messages can be misunderstood' and 'the loss of non-verbal cues is relevant'.[52] There is also evidence that user preferences do not always support the optimal system. Research by Nowak et al. (2009) found that while user satis-faction and preference for systems are impor-tant, neither directly predict outcome success or the ability of a system to facilitate collaboration. Despite users' reported preferences for media requiring less effort and time, the expenditure of effort better predicts outcome success than do user preferences.[53]

> *Do you think people are less risk-averse when they communicate by email as against ftf? If that is so, why would it be? If not, why not?*

> *O was ten minutes into a work-related videocall with Y when he received a text from Z asking him to call Z urgently. What factors would influence whether O excused himself and called Z or waited until he had finished his videocall with Y?*

Summary

Age has less effect on media usage than is widely believed, especially at work. Gender differences in internet usage generally seem to be time-related: women were in the main later to adopt cmc than men but subsequently came to use it more. Evaluations of media do not differ by gender in relation to affordances, but gender does affect socio-emotional evaluations. There is, as yet, a lack of evidence on how culture affects cmc usage and attitudes, but it is likely that people adapt to enable them to use a medium when other factors are in its favour. Users are generally able to give good reasons for their choice of mode but preferences are also influenced by psychological factors such as personality.

2.4 WORK-RELATED FACTORS INFLUENCING MODE CHOICE

At work, in comparison with in private life, people may, on the one hand, have ready access to a wider range of communication modes: for instance, few people, probably, set up conference calls with their relatives and friends. On the other hand, there are constraints on employees' choice of media that do not apply in private life. This section explains how organizational adoptions, organizational support, use by a critical mass of colleagues, rules and norms, social influence, and task requirements affect employees' media choices.

Organizational adoption

Use of any medium at work depends, necessarily, on its being adopted by the organization. Anticipated savings in time and money, quality issues, and in developing countries the availability of expertise, are often critical factors for adoption by organizations. For instance, in four Swedish media companies, the main force driving companies and individuals to consider meeting at a distance were time and financial savings. The appropriateness of the technology, the infrastructure required and personnel confidence in using and handling the equipment were also necessary before adoption.[54]

Finally, organizational adoptions and use of information and communication technologies are linked to organizations' 'self-perceptions' of themselves as leaders or as scanners of the environment and emulators of leaders. Early adopters also tend to have organizational decision-makers with the expertise to enable adoption and use.[55]

To see other factors that influence organizational adoptions of cmc technologies, visit the companion website... 2.4.1.

In 2012 a *McKinsey Quarterly* survey of the state of networking in organizations found the following:

Use of social networking, blogs and video-sharing by organizations was a substantial 53%, 43% and 41% respectively and in each case usage was up significantly over the previous ten years. 2012 was the first time that online video conferencing and collaborative document editing were surveyed. At 60% and 43% of respondents whose companies use each technology they immediately entered at first and third.

The respondents rated the top five benefits of technology use as follows: Internally: increasing speed to access knowledge (72%), reducing communication costs, increasing speed of access to internal experts, reducing travel costs, increasing employee satisfaction (42%). With customers: increasing marketing effectiveness (65%), increasing customer satisfaction, reducing marketing costs, reducing travel costs, reducing customer support costs (34%). With partners, suppliers and external experts: reducing communication costs (63%), increasing speed to access information, reducing travel costs, increasing speed to access internal experts, increasing satisfaction of partners, suppliers and external experts (42%).

On the networked status of their organization, in 48% of the sample the network was 'developing', 13% were internally networked, 29% were externally networked, 10% (up from 3% in 2011) were fully networked.[56]

Other organization-level factors affecting the use of cmc at work

Beyond mere adoption, the amount of use of a communication technology by an organization's employees depends on other factors at the organizational level: the amount of support given and the quality of training where needed, the presence of a critical mass of users, and organizational rules and norms.

Organizational support and training

Perceived organizational support has a strong influence on people's motivation to use IT in general at work, as well as their acceptance and enjoyment:

- Acceptance of new IT reflects intrinsic, rather than extrinsic, motivation and perceived organizational support rather than a belief that using IT will be rewarded;[57]
- The size of the support network as well as the strength and density of the information network significantly predicted employees' adaptation to a new IT-based system, according to a survey of 371 employees working in 133 different branches of an organization;[58]
- In a developing country, proper training, informative documentation, awareness campaigns and good maintenance were seen as the most important factors in encouraging or limiting cmc use.[59]

Critical mass of users

Critical mass represents an important factor for the success of any cmc in the workplace. People will use what enough of their colleagues are using in order to be 'in the loop'.[60]

> *In 1989, the author was provided with email at work. From then until she left the organization six months later, she received a total of four emails. She did not actually send even one herself.*

Organizational rules and norms

At the individual or group level, one strong influence on how to communicate (whether ftf or by cmc and if by cmc then which media to use) are the rules and norms of the organization. Rules on media use produce a mandatory force for using computer-based media, though employees generally prefer guidelines to restrictive policies for email communication.[61] Even where explicit rules are not applied, organizations have dominant norms about which media to use for internal communication. These norms influence employees' choice of which media to use and can be reflected in higher performance ratings for employees who use the normative media, a study of IM and email in a large high-tech organization found.[62] Acceptance of cmc (the perception that it is useful and the intention to use it) are strongly influenced by whether the system provides information process support, whether there are norms about its use and user experience.[63]

> **"** I'm sure my organization does have rules and policies about internet use and so on but I don't know what they are. That is, I read them once, realized I was unlikely to be in breach of them, and haven't referred to them since. We do, though, just 'know' what is acceptable or unacceptable here. For instance, we know that if the phone rings we should take the call.
>
> (Authors' interview with an executive from a media organization)

Social influence

One view on media choice is based on the idea that attitudes and behaviours are partially determined by the social context. People who work together often come to have similar beliefs and attitudes about communication technology. A study of electronic mail use among a group of scientists and engineers found confirmation of this view: the more individuals were attracted to their work group, the stronger were the social influences on their attitudes and behaviour towards cmc. People who were only weakly attached or attracted to their work group conformed to the prevailing patterns but did not internalize them as beliefs and attitudes, in contrast to people who were strongly attracted to their work group.[64]

Markus (1994) found that there could be drastic variations in the usage and acceptance of cmc between units within the same organization. These variations, which stem from norms, values and standards engendered by the institutional environment, in turn reshape these norms, values and standards.[65]

To see the findings that show that norms have a strong influence on cmc usage, visit the companion website 2.4.2.

Groups within organizations or even those that are composed of people from different organizations often have their own norms about media; members' media preferences are influenced by group norms and over time these effects grow stronger.[66] More particularly, organizational norms have a strong influence on attitudes towards email messages, on whether superiors comply with requests from subordinates and on employee performance ratings.

Task requirements

In specific cases, the task influences the mode that people choose for communication at work. When the task is highly complex or important, managers select their mode by extensively appraising information. However, if the task is urgent, they base their choice of mode on limited information, even though this limiting of their appraisal results in their actual choice being worse than optimal.[67] Again, noting that fast-paced organizational environments and growing needs for permanent and fast connectivity have steered the adoption of technologies such as IM for organizational communication, Pazos et al. (2013) found a significantly greater use of IM for tasks requiring collaboration.[68]

Summary

Organizations' adoptions of new communication technologies tend to be governed by assessments of their effectiveness and efficiency, together with the organization's capacity for technological leadership. Organizational support, including training, affect use by employees at least up to the point where a critical mass of them are using it. In some cases organizational rules decide the choices of individuals and group. Social influences of colleagues and group norms are often influential, though the requirements of the task play a part.

PART II
Core Processes in Work Communication

Part II of the book considers the core processes involved in communication and the social and psychological influences on it; without an understanding of these processes interpersonal skill development can only be superficial. Chapter 3 deals with how we can and do understand other people through the processes of social cognition; Chapter 4 with what happens when we contribute in speech or writing to a dialogue or multi-party interaction, self-presentation and impression management; Chapter 5 with the dynamic processes involved in interaction. Chapter 5 also explains what we know from research about skill in interpersonal communication. Part II goes on to explain the influences on how we communicate two sets of factors: social factors such as demography and culture as well as the situation (Chapter 6), and psychological factors (Chapter 7). In the context of situation, Chapter 6 explains the central theories that have developed to predict how communication mode affects communication. Chapter 8 covers three applications of communication that are of great importance at work: influencing, handling conflict and negotiating.

3 SOCIAL COGNITION AND IMPRESSION FORMATION

Social cognition is the overall process of observing and trying to make sense of other people, especially those with whom we communicate. It consists of trying to understand their overt behaviour, including what they are intending to communicate, but often it also involves trying to understand more than this – for example, their motives or attitudes, or whether they are telling the truth. Research has shown that people interpret behaviour by making inferences about others' intentions, mind and personality. They do this in an order that is consistent across individuals and stable across verbal and visual presentations: from intentions to desires to beliefs to personality.[1]

On completing your study of this chapter, you will be able to:

- Analyse the central processes involved in social cognition.
- Describe, recognize and work on reducing biases and other errors that lead to misunderstanding others and so to miscommunicating with them.
- Explain and apply the implications of how mediated communication affects social cognition.

Topics include: the importance of social cognition; how we perceive people; inferences; how we perceive groups, perceptual errors and biases, including stereotypes and prejudice; and how to achieve skilled social perception. Section 3.1 covers how the basic elements of social cognition lead us to perceive other people's behaviour; Section 3.2 describes how we build on these perceptions to form impressions and make judgements about individuals and groups; Section 3.3 explains how we make inferences about events and how we perceive and judge environments, including work environments. A major focus throughout is how different communication modes affect all these cognitive processes.

Social cognition is the foundation of all interpersonal communication. It is also a major source for acquiring knowledge: we learn by observing others within the context of social interactions and from our own interactive experiences.[2] At work, social cognition is particularly required for some roles, such as those of selection interviewer, international negotiator, supervisor or manager, but everyone needs a grasp of the values, motives, assumptions and attitudes of their colleagues.

3.1 SOCIAL COGNITION

This section is concerned with the interpersonal processes of perceiving others, such as observing cues, and with the intrapersonal processes, such as linking observations together, which are involved in making sense of what we observe about other people. The section further shows how perceptions are integrated with memory and thought to generate beliefs and attitudes. These processes include attribution to situations or dispositions and judgements of responsibility and justice.

Accuracy in social cognition is extremely useful, indeed vital: without accuracy in our social cognition we are likely to respond inappropriately, leading to miscommunication. We know, for instance, that the more accurately the members of a group (category of people) perceive the values endorsed by members of another group, the better the quality of their social relations with those outgroup members.[3] Unfortunately, though, there are many sources of bias and hence inaccuracy in the way we perceive others: we tend to select, distort, over-interpret and judge too rapidly. While generating meaning from an interpersonal exchange, the brain needs to synthesize information from a wide range of both internal sources such as memory and from external cues; this complexity adds to the perceptual errors we make.

When using cmc, people less known to each other perceive each other less accurately; however, this finding mirrors more general research on person perception, which has tended to find that individuals are more accurate at perceiving known than less known targets.

> **"**I exchanged 15 to 20 emails with someone from a company we were considering investing in. The company employed several Indians, and I built up a picture of my respondent as male, around 40 and Indian. The name was too unfamiliar to give any clues. Finally we met; and she was female, around 30 and Irish. Although I have not gone back through my emails to check, I feel sure that my assumptions about her will have slanted some of my communication.
>
> (Author's interview with a fund manager)

Inputs to social cognition processes

We have two primary external sources of information for reaching an understanding of other people: their messages and their non-verbal behaviour.

Messages

Probably our first thoughts when we consider interpersonal communication concern spoken or written messages – what a communicator intends to convey. Artefacts such as drawings or diagrams are also messages when a communicator intends them to convey meaning. However, meaning cannot be transmitted – it must be encoded in symbols by senders and the symbols must be decoded by receivers who must also infer the meaning of the message. Unfortunately, though, there are barriers to decoding accurately the symbols of messages and they may have been inaccurately encoded in the first place – not be an accurate representation of the individual's intention. They are also often intentionally ambiguous or contain multiple meanings, as the following example shows:

BOX 3.1

In a selection interview for a role in a medium-sized company, the candidate, whose previous experience was in large organizations, was asked, 'What made you apply for this position?' To answer this question appropriately she needed to understand that the interviewer wanted to find out whether some problem with her current job was causing her to need to shift to a smaller company.

We do learn from experience in understanding others' meaning, so that we are much less likely to make interpretive errors about messages from people we know well than about those from new acquaintances; similarly, the work context, by reducing the range of likely topics, cuts down on interpretive errors.

The understanding of messages is potentially reduced, however, when people communicate electronically, because of the lack of cues from non-verbal behaviour. For instance, electronically mediated groups have been shown to have more difficulty in establishing the meaning of information and in managing feedback in discussions.[4] People sometimes compensate for the lack of cues by over-interpreting features of text messages and so compound the problem. For example, in emails technical language violations, such as spelling and grammatical errors, and etiquette errors such as short messages lacking a conversational tone, lead receivers to form negative perceptions of the sender's conscientiousness, intelligence, **agreeableness**, extraversion and trustworthiness. Although most of the negative perceptions resulting from technical language violations are reduced when receivers know that the sender is from a different culture, this is not the case for etiquette violations; these lead receivers to negative perceptions even when they know the sender is from a different culture.[5]

Non-verbal behaviour

Although spoken and written messages are an important source of the information about other people, in their presence there are many others. We observe their voice loudness and tone, speed of speech and the variations in all of these, their nods, gestures, shifts of posture, their smiles and frowns, gaze and eye contact – in other words, their body language. We also do this not only while being spoken to but while speaking ourselves: 'during face-to-face interaction (dialogue), both or all parties are almost continuously engaged in trying to understand one another. Speaking and listening together form a joint activity. Speakers monitor not just their own actions, but those of their addressees, taking both into account as they speak'.[6]

All mediated communication reduces the amount of cues available from non-verbal behaviour. Text-based communication, such as email, almost eliminates these cues; although when they want to, senders can replace non-verbal behaviour with, for instance, smileys, the cues that come from non-verbal behaviour that is not intended to communicate are not replaceable.

> *Visit the companion website... 3.1.1 for a link to a video about video etiquette. What are the main points it makes?*

> *To interpret messages more accurately: do not draw too extensive inferences from a small sample, especially of text messages; stimulate more information with questions and prompts; ask yourself if the choice of medium is part of the message; be aware of ambiguities and alert to possible alternative meanings; be neither too little nor too much emotionally aroused; see the message from the sender's point of view; and do not judge the sender by technical violations.*

> *Visit the companion website... 3.1.2 for a link to a video about body language. How valid are its assumptions and how useful are its recommendations?*

Social cognition processes

To comprehend messages and make sense of others' non-verbal behaviour we go through a set of processes: paying attention, observing cues, applying cognitive schema and making attributions.

Paying attention

Our awareness of others' messages and non-verbal behaviour comes to us via sensory impressions of objects, people or events and these are, of course, based on stimuli. Since we are bombarded with more stimuli than we can deal with, we are selective in attending to them. What gets our attention depends on the following:

- Characteristics of the stimulus, especially its salience (that is, its importance to us or how much it sticks out in its context).
- Whether it is inconsistent with how we already think, is over-familiar or is a detail (all of which we tend to ignore). Moreover, we are less likely to pay attention to, and later recognize, the faces of older or younger people than those of people of our own age.[7]
- Our motivational state: people who feel that they may be socially excluded – for instance, somewhat ignored at a meeting or party – are faster to pay attention to and so to identify smiling faces within a crowd of faces and to stay attuned to them.[8] We also 'close out' new information once we are satisfied that we know enough for our purpose. For instance, people who are working on a problem in a group pay less attention to new information that is given out once they have been made aware of the others' preferences. As a result, groups composed of people who know one another's preferences for solving a problem are less likely to solve it correctly than groups whose members are not told about their fellow group members' preferences.[9]

Social cognition processes are affected by the communication mode from this very earliest stage of paying attention: for instance, when people communicate by textual chat or audio, they pay significantly less attention to their interaction partner than they do face-to-face (ftf);[10] occupied with constructing, sending and receiving messages via computer-mediated communication (cmc), they are also distanced and distracted from the social context.[11]

> *For other findings that show that cmc affects attention, visit the companion website... 3.1.3.*

Selective attention is one kind of perceptual bias that reduces the accuracy of our perceptions; there are many others, as this section will show.

Observing cues

Cues are a kind of stimulus of our senses – a kind from which we infer meaning. Cues about people often include their appearance, what they say and how they say it, and their body language, as well as possibly the reactions to them of others who are present; prior beliefs based on earlier experience with them or things we have heard about them can also be activated (brought to mind) and serve as cues. We infer meaning both from messages and from unintended transmissions. In the case of messages, we have first to decode the symbols – the language or the visual signs – that the person is using. In the case of unintended transmissions we have to decide whether an apparent cue is in fact one or is without significance. Although the contention of this book is that interpersonal communication itself concerns messages, that is, it is limited to intentional behaviours, there is no doubt that people infer a great deal about others from the cues that those others emit unintentionally and that these inferences strongly influence how they themselves communicate in turn. Senders unintentionally transmit a good deal of information that sometimes contradicts or negates the overt message. Moreover, most people seem to have an unconscious knowledge of this because ftf they seldom derive meaning solely from message contents.[12]

Although 'slips of the tongue' can occur, most unintended cues are non-verbal. Interpreting non-verbal cues accurately is more difficult than accurately interpreting content cues. For instance, familiarity with the situation increases people's ability to tell when others are lying or telling the truth. This is achieved partly because when they are familiar with the situation they rely more on verbal content cues but when they are not they use more non-verbal cues.[13]

In general, in fact, we are not very good at perceiving accurately in the case of unintended transmissions, especially concerning others' feelings: 'although there is a positive correlation between what people intend to display by non-verbal cues of affect (emotion) and what others perceive when the intention to communicate is made clear, when the display occurs spontaneously or naturally without an explicit intention to communicate, the chances that the cue will be accurately perceived are very low'.[14]

Our ability to make accurate evaluations based on inferences from non-verbal cues is further limited by cultural difference. For instance the same facial expressions express similar emotional states cross-culturally, but are less accurately recognized when the perceiver and expresser are from different cultures. This is probably because people are

> Eliot nodded at Adam, smiled at him, leaned towards him, moved a little closer and increased the amount of eye contact with him. Mark stepped back, shifted his gaze away, and raised his hand to his mouth. *Honestly write down how you would interpret these behaviours in a natural setting. Then think through whether your interpretation might be biased.*

more motivated to process faces of people from their own culture accurately.[15]

Clearly the opportunity for misinterpreting unintentional transmissions in text-based cmc is reduced because senders in principle have more control and because of the absence of non-verbal cues. However, we do not at this stage know the extent to which they do in fact occur. We do, though, know that behaviours can still be misperceived as emotionally charged in cmc: for instance, resolute behaviour (sticking to your point) is interpreted as a display of anger and flexible behaviour as a display of happiness.[16] How long people take to reply to an email is also often interpreted as expressing an attitude, though delays may often occur through overload, network failure or, in developing countries, power outages.

Applying cognitive schemas

Once a cue has been observed, the processes of social cognition are internal to the individual. At this point we apply cognitive schemas to our observations. Cognitive schemas are inductions from past experiences, introspection, drawing analogies and believing things that we have read or been told. They are integrated mental networks of knowledge, beliefs and expectations concerning a particular topic or aspect of a topic.

Cognitive schemas vary in strength and accessibility. Consider production scheduling: a production manager would have a strong and accessible cognitive schema about it, a human relations (HR) manager would have one of middle strength and accessibility, while a receptionist might be expected to have only a weak and rather inaccessible one. Men have better developed schemas than women for thinking about football and women have better developed schemas than men for thinking about women's fashions.[17] People generally have better developed schemas for thinking about individuals than for thinking about groups. The stronger and more accessible our cognitive schema about a topic, the more it is likely to influence our behaviour.

Cognitive schemas include personal **identification rules** that draw on the categories that we have in memory from earlier experiences and

During a ten-minute conversation between Rebecca and Judith, Rebecca looked at Judith most of the time, but Judith frequently looked around, particularly when Rebecca was speaking. When Rebecca replied to Judith, there was often a pause before she began speaking, but then she spoke fairly continuously; Judith, however, began her replies to Rebecca immediately Rebecca finished speaking, but then often paused or hesitated during her reply.

Honestly write down how you would interpret these behaviours in a natural setting. Then think through whether your interpretation might be biased.

that lead us to link one observation with another cognition – for instance, that someone who smiles at us is pleased to see us, that someone who frowns is annoyed. As this second example suggests, our identifications may be faulty – quite often people frown because they are concentrating.

We all have cognitive schemas about interacting – including, for instance, that more formal terms of address are suitable in business meetings than with friends – and most people now would have cognitive schemas that include the difference between interacting ftf or by cmc.

Making attributions

A key process in social cognition is attribution. Because we are motivated to make sense of what we observe, we try to assign a cause to other people's observed behaviour. This is attribution. Although there are many different ways behaviour can be attributed, they generally fall under two headings: we either attribute it to some aspect of the person's situation (situational attributions) or to some aspect of themselves – their mood or their personality for instance; these are dispositional attributions. For example, a supervisor in a bank might attribute an error in a subordinate's data entries to carelessness (his disposition) or to his being overworked (his situation). The attributions we make are very important at work. In the words of some scholars, 'attributional processes appear to affect virtually all goal and reward oriented behaviour in organizations'.[18]

Attribution is an error-prone process. Biases that can lead to errors include the fact that people see the preferences of those who agree with them as more rationally based than the preferences of those who disagree with them. The more important the issue, the more this attribution bias applies. In groups it is also increased by the sense of being in a majority.[19]

For more findings that show that attribution is error-prone, visit the companion website... 3.1.4.

The effects of attribution biases are usually negative. For instance, the tendency of some subordinates to attribute their problems wrongly to abusive supervision is likely to affect their attitudes to work. Again, when followers attribute their leader's emotional expressions (of anger or sadness) to the leader's disposition, their perceptions of the leader are negatively affected, but when they attribute them to the leader's role (which is part of their situation), this effect may be attenuated.[20]

The loss of visual cues in some forms of cmc tends to bias attributions towards dispositions rather than situations. For instance, when a hypothetical woman was presented as having negative attitudes towards strangers, people who only received text-based cues were more likely to make a dispositional attribution, whereas those who were given the same information through an avatar of the woman were more likely to say that the female's situation caused her attitudes towards strangers. It is 'possible that the participants could identify more... with the female when they watched the avatar's frown, facial expressions, and dynamic body movements while those who only received text messages could not get beyond these negative impressions'.[21]

At work, an important influence on the attributions co-workers make about one another is whether they are located in the same place or geographically distant – and this, of course, is important for how cmc affects their mutual understanding. Separated team-mates are significantly more likely than co-located team-mates to make dispositional attributions rather than situational attributions for the negative behaviour of their colleagues; this is probably because the colleague's situation is not evident. These dispositional attributions in turn affect relational outcomes such as satisfaction and cohesion. Since mediated work often involves team-mates working at a distance from one another, this is unfortunate. However, when it is possible to explain the other person's situation the impact of situation invisibility is reduced.[22]

> To improve your skills in perceiving other people you need to attend to more cues, become more aware of your own **association rules** and stereotypes, become aware of your own attribution biases and correct for them, and when communicating by cmc avoid the tendency to over-attribute to dispositions by finding out about or at least thinking about the other person's situation and environment.
>
> To learn more about person perception skills, visit the companion website... 3.1.5.

Summary

To understand the other people we communicate with we decode their messages and observe their non-verbal behaviour to provide ourselves with cues, then identify the cues with behaviours, beliefs, emotions or moods and attribute causes to the observed behaviours. There are numerous sources of error, especially biases, which reduce the accuracy of our initial perceptions of others. However, theoretical accounts that suggest that the accuracy of interpersonal perceptions is undermined in cmc are contradicted by a study that found that it did not differ substantially between cmc and ftf interactions.[23]

Beyond the core processes described in this section, several sets of processes in the course of social cognition enable us to form impressions, perceive groups, frame events and form judgements. These are the subjects of Sections 3.2 and 3.3.

3.2 FORMING IMPRESSIONS AND PERCEIVING GROUPS

When we interact with people we usually form an overall impression of them – we go beyond the particular behaviour and make judgements about their traits or personality; we also often categorize them as belonging to a particular group. There are biases that may distort these impressions and perceptions and they may be affected by the communication mode through which cues reach us.

Forming impressions

People form impressions of each other all the time, whether consciously or subconsciously, and use this interpersonal 'knowledge' for a variety of purposes in their daily life. In an organizational setting, such as at work, impressions take on an increasingly crucial role because organization by definition requires interpersonal socialization. Whether it is assigning work, asking others for assistance or deciding whether to interact with them personally or not, people at work need to make judgements that rely on impressions of others.[24]

An early stage in forming impressions is to generalize from one or more examples of observed behaviour and to pass a trait judgement, such as that someone is kind or dishonest. Correlations have been weak when researchers have tested trait variables against observed behaviour;[25] these findings are unsurprising when it is considered how small are the samples that people often use for making these judgements.

Certain traits have been shown to possess the property of 'centrality' – that is, we subjectively deem them to imply other traits by applying our own ('lay') inference rules. Which traits have centrality varies from individual to individual, so that it is not a property of the trait itself that gives it central-ity.[26] People also usually categorize the people they meet in a relatively automatic way, based on available cues such as appearance or tone of voice; they give more elaborate thought to their impression only under certain circumstances, such as when they particularly want to have confidence in their judgement and are not too occupied with thinking about other things.

> To learn more about trait inferences, visit the companion website... 3.1.6.

An example of interviewer bias

Non-verbal behaviours may not influence interviewer evaluations, accord-ing to a field study in Taiwan; physical attractiveness, though, does influ-ence them, particularly when jobs require substantial customer contact. This effect of physical attractiveness was weaker when the applicant's gender was inconsistent with the interviewer's sex-type belief relative to the job.[27]

As the preceding point suggests, impression formation is a bias-prone process. For example, people form more positive trait impressions of the people whose faces they see clearly than of those they only see in a blurred form, as, for instance, in a grainy photograph, through misted up glasses or at a distance; similarly, they are more likely to think someone is honest if they can see him or her clearly and less likely to think someone is intelligent or truthful if they see only an indistinct image of them.[28] Again, people see others as less likeable when they use abstract language to describe the negative actions of others ('Kim was aggressive' instead of 'Kim hit John') but more likeable when they use abstract descriptions of others' positive behaviours ('Kim was generous' instead of 'Kim gave John a gift'). This may be because abstract language implies a judgement, and the judge who reaches a negative assessment is disliked, whereas a judge who reaches a positive assessment is liked.[29]

At work, supervisors often form generalized impressions of their employees and then rely on those images in making evaluations of them. As a result, supervisors sometimes recall behaviours that would be 'typical' of an employee even though they do not actually observe the behaviour.[30]

Culture influences the impact of impressions. Although people can reliably infer how other members of their own culture will respond to perceived traits, in relation to people from other cultures they will tend to judge according to their own unless they have considerable knowledge about the target's culture.[31]

Forming impressions in cmc

When people interact from the beginning by text-based cmc, elements of an impression of the other person, such as their age or gender, may have to be deduced rather than being 'obvious' as they usually would be ftf. To form impressions of senders, email recipients often rely on symbolic cues, such as all-through capitalization of letters, emoticons, the time lag of a response, email signatures, punctuation marks and spelling or typing errors. However, the receivers' own personalities also influence their perceptions of the email sender.[32] In ftfc silences and hesitations affect our impressions of other people; similarly, in asynchronous cmc the length and frequency of messaging have significant effects on our impressions, especially our impressions of the emotional responses of the communicator.[33] In fact, time-related cues such as pauses, conversational rhythm or time of day play an important role in cmc, substituting for the non-verbal cues available in ftfc and influencing online interaction, according to Kalman et al. (2013):

" For instance, imagine you are having a conversation over Instant Messenger (IM) with a colleague about the next stage of a project. If the conversation feels like it has a 'flow' to it, you might feel that you are making progress, or that you and your colleague work well together. You might pose a question to your colleague who responds quickly, which may give you the sense that your colleague is attentive, prepared or decisive. Then imagine that your colleague's responses take longer to arrive, and are punctuated by long pauses. Is your colleague suddenly distracted and neglecting your conversation? Or did you say something wrong, making your colleague unsure of how to respond?[34]

The possibility is, however, that the longer pauses are the result of technical delays, and that you are wrong to attribute meaning to them.

Impressions formed in the cmc environment are more intense but less comprehensive and detailed than those formed ftf and are less likely to refer to specific traits such as extraversion or **neuroticism**. While the low level of reference to extraversion may be because it is 'highly visible' and so 'undermined in a text-based cmc interaction', there is no clear explanation of the difference in perceptions of neuroticism, which is 'the least observable trait'. This suggests that 'factors other than visibility must be involved in ratings of neuroticism, factors that are available in a single ftf interaction but not in a single cmc interaction'.[35]

Some research has suggested that impressions of others formed while interacting over cmc are more favourable than impressions formed ftf, while other research has suggested that the pattern is in the opposite direction. To resolve this question, an examination of impressions formed via each of the two modes while controlling for the other was undertaken. It was found that participants interacting by cmc formed less positive impressions of their partner than did those interacting ftf.[36] When cues to identity – information about an interactor – are given in cmc, they have a positive effect on how the other person is perceived but not on how the interaction is evaluated. People actually feel more certain about their performance in an online task and more satisfied with the medium when no such cues are provided.[37]

> *To see the earlier research on the favourability of impressions formed by cmc, visit the companion website... 3.2.1.*

In addition to the sources of bias that occur in interpersonal cognition generally, there are some that affect it only when communication is at least partly mediated. Inconsistencies between self-presentations online and offline can have a negative effect on the impressions we form of other people, though this varies according to the relationship of the observer and the target. The inconsistencies of acquaintances are rated more intentionally misleading, more hypocritical and less trust-worthy than those of friends. People also explain their own online behaviour more favourably than that of both friends and acquaintances.[38]

Overall, however, the conclusion from the large body of research into impression formation and communication mode is that impression formation occurs more slowly by cmc as against ftfc,[39] that is, it is the rate of impression formation that distinguishes them, rather than the fullness or accuracy of the impression formed.[40]

We have some findings about who is better at accurate impression formation online, though the evidence is inconclusive:

- Personality affects accuracy levels: extraverts among both experienced and inexperienced cmc users assumed, often wrongly, that their interaction partner's personality was similar to their own.[41]
- Male and female judges are equal in both accuracy and confidence in their judgements about the gender of an anonymous sender, based on the communication style of text-based messages.
- Accuracy does not improve with more experience of cmc: following internet-mediated chat, experienced users showed no greater accuracy in perceiving their interaction partner's personality than internet novices.

Impression formation in distributed work

For purposes of distributed work, where people working jointly on a task are located apart and communicate mainly by cmc, complex and individuated impressions can help to avoid breakdowns common in these settings, such as misattribution, mistrust and consequent conflict. Forming impressions of distributed co-workers can be more challenging than forming impressions of co-located co-workers. Dispersion not only reduces the amount of information available about co-workers but also decreases people's motivation to form impressions. The greater the distance that separates co-workers, the more their reliance on technology for communication and interaction, the more heterogeneous co-workers' culture and nationality are and the more structural change occurs in the virtual teams to which they belong, the less information and motivation they have for forming accurate impressions.[42]

Forming impressions of groups and stereotyping

We do not only perceive people as individuals: on occasion we also perceive them as members of groups, especially as either members of our ingroups (groups in which we are members ourselves) or of our outgroups (groups of which we are consciously not members). This process is referred to as social **categorization**; it means classifying people, usually on the basis of individuals' similarities to and differences from other people, particularly ourselves. For example, if an important part of someone's self-concept (what kind of person they think they are) is that they are intelligent, they will tend to categorize other people as similarly, more or less intelligent than themselves. However, people's self-concepts are partly influenced by the stereotypes of the groups to which they accept that they belong. Thus categorization of others and of ourselves both causes us to perceive ourselves as having the same social identity as other members of the category – it places us in the relevant social category, or 'places the group in our head' – and leads us to behave in ways which are consistent with our stereotypes of the categories to which we accept that we belong. Social categorization is the process that transforms our perceptions of individuals into perceptions of a group, and self-categorization is the process that makes us members of groups in our own view of ourselves.

Biases introduced by social categorization

Social categorization can introduce bias into social perception:

- Categorization compromises accuracy for ease and speed of processing and analysis. When people (or objects) are categorized into groups, differences between members of different groups are accentuated, while those between members of the same group are minimized. Furthermore, these similarities and differences are often viewed as inherent to the nature of the groups and generalized to additional dimensions, such as character traits, beyond those facets that originally differentiated the categories.
- Recognition of one's own membership in some groups (ingroups) but not others (outgroups) arouses, often spontaneously, fundamental psychological biases. Cognitively, people process information about ingroup members more deeply than about outgroup members, and individuals have better memory for information about the ways in which ingroup members are similar and outgroup members are dissimilar to them than the reverse. Emotionally, people feel more positively about ingroup than outgroup members. They place a lower value on outgroup members than ingroup members. Individuals are also more generous and forgiving in their attributions about the behaviours of ingroup members relative to outgroup members. Thus it is not surprising to find that social categorization is a major determinant of intergroup tensions and potential conflict between groups.[43]
- Perceptions of groups differ in their **entitativity**, which means the degree to which we see them as a unit or as a collection of separate individuals, and the degree to which we see their members as like one another. Across several different group types, it has been shown,

people's perceptions of their ingroup are more entitative than those of their outgroups, while for similarity of members, the finding was the reverse – outgroup members are perceived as more similar to one another (less easy to distinguish from one another) than ingroup members.[44]

- People generally perceive their ingroups as having more desirable attributes than their outgroups; this is usually harmful for social relationships.

Stereotyping

Social categorization gives rise to stereotypes. Stereotypes are whole complex images consisting of a number of characteristics, usually of a group of people. Quite different characteristics may be linked in a stereotype – 'cunning' and 'cowardice', for example. Stereotyping is now considered an ordinary cognitive process in which people construct schemas to categorize people and entities in order to avoid trying to absorb too many cues simultaneously.[45] It is over-reliance on stereotypes which is now considered to prevent perceivers being accurate, and the uncritical use of negative stereotypes which is linked to prejudice.

Stereotypical expectations are implicitly reflected in language and are thereby subtly communicated to message recipients. For example, people use more negations (e.g. 'not smart' instead of 'stupid') in descriptions of stereotype-inconsistent behaviour; receivers of messages infer from the fact that a sender used this expression that this behaviour was considered by the sender to be an exception to the rule and that it was more likely to have been caused by situational circumstances than by dispositional factors.[46]

At work, negative stereotypes, when perceived by the people who are stereotyped, are harmful to them: criticism of task performance, blatant stereotypical statements, contextual cues such as stereotypical cartoons and simply being in the numerical minority in a stereotyped domain are all experiences that induce stereotype threat, which impacts on performance. Chronic stereotype threat, which occurs when people believe that some people think that they have less ability because of, for instance, their ethnicity, can result in them disidentifying from or leaving their organization. It is, for example, one cause of student drop-out from their university.[47]

Stereotyping tends to introduce specific biases:

- Older workers are perceived as less competent but warmer than younger workers; these stereotypes interact with job requirements to predict age bias. Older candidates are discriminated against, even if the job primarily requires warmth-related qualities, because of the negative stereotype of their competence.[48]

- People with faces that have features thought relevant to stereotypes tend to be over-allocated to the stereotype category by perceivers. For example, men seen as having 'feminine' faces tend to be allocated to the category of homosexual, even though they are heterosexual. This bias applies to perceivers of all kinds, not just prejudiced perceivers. Prejudiced people over-allocate according to negative stereotypes to a greater degree but under-allocate more according to positive stereotypes.[49]

Across cultures, there are both similarities and differences in stereotypes. There is substantial agreement among cultures about gender stereotypes. Across 30 countries, the content of the male stereotype turned out to be more active and more associated with strong feelings, but not any more favourable. On the other hand, stronger male stereotypes were found in cultures with lower levels of literacy and socio-economic development and with a lower proportion of women enrolled in college.[50] Another study found cultural differences in stereotypes, in this case of older workers. UK respondents saw older workers as more effective but less adaptable compared with how they were seen by a Hong Kong sample.[51]

How does cmc affect stereotyping? The question is contested, as follows:

- Research by Epley and Kruger (2005) found that text-based cmc inherently inhibits the reduction of stereotypes. This may be explained by the reader assuming or filling in what is not written, using what the person thinks he or she knows about the sender or can deduce from the message.[52] However, a later study challenged both their logic and their findings, and found that cmc is functionally equivalent to vocal communication in its ability to reduce negative stereotypes and that it can be superior in creating and/or retaining positive impressions.[53]
- A further study found that email correspondence between people from Iran and Canada who initially held unfavourable stereotypes of the other country fostered more favourable attitudes of participants towards people from the other country, even though the judgements of the similarities between the two cultures remained unchanged. Negative stereotypes changed towards more realistic ones. Attitude change was affected by the quality, topic and frequency of email exchange. Knowledge of participants about different aspects of the other culture became more complex and realistic over time. However, for many aspects of each culture, there was no consistent relationship between raising the level of knowledge and a change in attitude.[54]

Thus it may be that stereotype alteration can occur through cmc, though more gradually than it does through ftf contact. Where stereotypes do exist, however, their impact may be similar online to offline: for instance, ethnic stereotypes deter helping behaviour online just as they do ftf.[55]

Evaluating

Our impressions of others are often judgemental. Core dimensions on which we judge are warmth and competence. Whereas warmth relates to qualities such as friendliness, kindness and trustworthiness, competence concerns efficiency and capability. There is an evolutionary explanation for the primacy of these two dimensions: warmth indicates whether someone's intentions towards us are beneficial or harmful, that is, whether they present an opportunity or a threat, and competence indicates whether they have the ability to fulfil anything they undertake to do.

During the early data-gathering phase of impression formation, people seek warmth information more frequently than competence information; warmth information also influences overall conclusions on others to a higher degree than information on competence. Warmth, though, has two components: sociability, such as friendliness and likeability, which is predominantly linked to cooperation and forming connections with others, and morality, which is predominantly linked to characteristics such as honesty, sincerity and trustworthiness. Of these two components, it is morality which has most effect on evaluations of others, probably because it affects how threatened by others people feel.[56] In fact, impressions of people are better predicted from beliefs about morality-related traits than from beliefs about competence-related traits, and attitudes towards others are based more on the morality than the competence of their behaviours.[57]

One kind of judgement of people that has been shown to be important in a work context is judgements of fairness. Fairness judgements applied by people can affect whether they decide to support a decision made by those in **authority**. How they decide depends on how knowledgeable they feel about the issue: when they feel very knowledgeable they decide according to their prediction of how the outcome of the initiative is likely to affect them, but when they feel less knowledgeable, they decide according to their perception of the fairness of the decision maker.[58]

Another significant judgement of persons is identifying others as free riders (those who fail to contribute out of an intention to benefit themselves at the expense of people they are supposedly cooperating with). We know that people make these assessments, but how they do it is not fully understood. One study eliminated various possibilities – differences in contribution levels, general tendencies to categorize and mechanisms that track a broader class of intentional moral violations do not predict how people identify someone as a free rider. Thus, the researchers suggest, identifying free riders involves the operation of an evolved concept with features tailored for solving the collective action problems faced by ancestral hunter-gatherers.[59]

Forming judgements, like forming impressions, takes longer by cmc. Since there is evidence that delaying judgement of others increases understanding of them, this consequence may be beneficial, although as the benefits of delay accrue to gathering more information, the slower pace of receiving information by cmc may reduce or outweigh the gain in understanding. Somewhat surprisingly, cmc may lessen the tendency to rely on stereotypes when evaluating others. Interviewers' evaluations of job applicants are less stereotyped and more valid when visual cues are removed. This may because the removal of irrelevant stimuli improves impression accuracy.[60]

Summary

As well as ascribing individual traits to other people, we form overall impressions of them. These can be inaccurate because, for instance, we have learned to link one trait with others, although they may not always be associated in reality. Impressions take longer to form by cmc than ftf, and are sometimes less vivid but usually no less accurate.

Allocating people to groups through social categorization, stereotyping and judging whether people are warm, competent, sociable, moral, fair or free riders are further processes of social cognition. Like impression formation more generally, they are subject to biases. Whether cmc leads to more or less use of stereotypes than ftf is contested. Forming judgements takes longer by cmc.

> **To increase the accuracy of your impressions of other people when you interact ftf or by cmc:**
> - Make sure you concentrate on what they are saying or on the email you are reading; do not be distracted by thinking of your reply before you have understood their message.
> - Concentrate on the cues; look out for cues you might have missed (most people over-use a few cues and neglect others).
> - Use contextual cues: if others are present or taking part in a cmc dialogue notice how they respond to the target individual (but remember they may be inaccurate perceivers).
> - Encourage the output of information from the target — ftf by active listening; by cmc with well-framed questions or short prompts. Check that you understand – ask 'Did you mean...?'.
> - Make sure that what you infer from the target's face at rest, clothes, accessories, hairstyle, position, voice, voice tone, speed of speech, gaze, eye contact, facial expression, body movement, gestures,

postures and verbal expression can be inferred validly. For example, if someone stumbles over words and uses awkward syntax, it may mean that they are inarticulate but it may be a sign that they are anxious or fatigued. By text-based cmc do not read too much into how long they take to answer, whether they write grammatically or spell correctly.

- Do not assume that the target will act in the same way in other situations – that is, do not jump to a dispositional judgement.
- Do not jump to a holistic judgement, assuming that because someone is attractive he or she is clever or kind, or that because someone is awkward in expressing him or herself that he or she is not well-informed or intelligent.
- Be aware as to whether your impression is being distorted by stereotypes and correct for the distortion.
- Do not let your judgement be influenced by the comfortable sense of familiarity when you learn you have things in common – shared interests, sport, from the same country – as the target.
- Do not be biased by what the target represents to you – for instance, if he or she is a newly appointed manager and could be a threat to your position, don't be over-influenced by their negative points and ignore their positive ones. Or vice versa.
- Postpone evaluation as long as possible; first impressions are often wrong but tend to exert undue influence. Think description – 'soft voice', not 'nice voice'; 'sits still', not 'seems laidback'; and if the initial meeting is by text-based cmc, 'writes in short sentences', not 'writes well'.
- Accept that forming an accurate impression will take longer with people when you interact only by cmc, but do not give up.

3.3 PERCEIVING EVENTS AND ENVIRONMENTS

Our work-related communication is influenced not only by our impressions of other people, but also by how we perceive the events that occur and the situations and environments within which we work. As with impressions of people, these perceptions often result in judgements. An important process in forming these judgements is the process of social comparison.

Perceiving events

To interpret events, people use 'frames'. For instance, an interaction observed between two or more people who are standing by a car in a dealer's showroom might be framed as a buyer and sales representative negotiating about the car. However, different people taking part in the same event may frame it differently[61] – for example, a sales representative may frame making a telephone call to a customer as a courtesy, but the customer may frame it as a nuisance interruption. Equally, the same person may frame similar events differently at different times: someone might usually frame taking a telephone call from a sales representative as an opportunity to learn about a new product, but if they are under intense pressure of work they might frame it as a nuisance call.

How events are framed affects subsequent behaviour. When people are presented with, or can see for themselves, two sides of an issue (two different frames) they are more willing to talk and to seek information; information seeking is a possible strategy to cope with ambivalence, uncertainty or anxiety, especially when the individual is motivated to be accurate. Social influence has a strong impact on event appraisal: the way an individual appraises and the extent to which he or she feels anger, happiness or fear about an event is influenced by the way other individuals appear to appraise and feel about the same event.

BOX 3.2

In Spiro and Co., the processing of customer orders is being delayed as documentation moves back and forward among four different departments. How are people's responses to the situation likely to differ according to whether their manager describes it as A, B, C or D?

A 'Things just aren't in sync. A lot of things are fouled up. You've got to fix things fast.'

B 'We can do better than we have been doing. We need to improve our performance, building on the strong foundation we've put in place.'

C 'We've stayed with our old system too long. It's time to leave that behind and go on to a more modern operation.'

D 'It's time we woke up to reality... we need someone who can help us to create a new vision of the future, and get us out of the box we're in.'

A highly significant type of event for people's social cognition is the interactions in which they are themselves involved. In particular, they are concerned to detect deceptions. They are also concerned to infer others' goals in their interactions with them (this topic is discussed in Section 7.1).

Detecting deceptions

A number of high-profile cases in the banking world where individuals lost billions and then lied to cover up aroused considerable interest in how to tell whether someone is lying or not telling the whole truth. Clearly this question is important in organizational life: people do practise deception, and costly wrong decisions or lack of corrective action can follow.

Unfortunately research has shown that people distinguish truths from lies at a rate only slightly better than chance.[62] There are a number of explanations for this low rate. Firstly, most receivers assume that their interactions with others are truthful more often than not and take others' statements at face value. This bias acts as a heuristic (rule of thumb) to judge everyday interactions.[63] In addition, the demeanour of a sender explains as much as 98 per cent of the variation in how well people detect that a deception is being practised. As demeanour is independent of actual honesty, this finding helps to explain the relatively low rates of detection of deception.[64]

To add to the problems caused by low detection rates, it has been found that, although people feel angry when they realize they have been deceived, the attitudes inculcated by the false information often remain uncorrected; it seems that while they are motivated to correct for inaccuracies they have difficulty in doing so.[65]

How to tell when someone is being deceitful

- Asking strategic questions designed to increase sender transparency can significantly improve the rate of detecting deceptions from the near-chance level found by research, because it is 'relatively more difficult to credibly maintain a lie under strategic, direct, sustained, and unanticipated questioning'.[66]
- Detection accuracy rates are higher when people judge the truthfulness of message content by using contextual knowledge, such as explicit contradictions, information about what is normal or possible in a given situation, or idiosyncratic knowledge that points to a higher probability of deception occurring. For example: 'A number of shortages have occurred at a bank. The shortages stop when one of the employees goes on vacation and begin again when the employee returns. When questioned about the shortages, the employee's statements may not explicitly contradict what the interviewer knows, normative information may not suggest that the employee's statements are implausible, but idiosyncratic knowledge about the starting and stopping of the shortages may still cause the interviewer to believe that the employee's statements are deceptive.'[67]
- Typographical error ratios are higher in the messages of deceitful cmc senders.
- Deceivers use more sentences, verbs, modifiers and noun phrases, and show less variety of vocabulary and content.
- Deceivers show more informality and negative emotions and refer less often to themselves and more often to groups.
- Ellipses, being wordy, using the passive voice, second person address and the possessive form are linked to deceptive behaviour.
- People who are being deceptive about hidden agendas experience higher tension than those without hidden agendas;[68] this tension can show in their non-verbal behaviour.

- However, offensive language, incomplete sentences, jargon and run-on sentences are not used more by deceivers, nor are there any differences in expressiveness or specificity.[69]

Ftf conversational partners do change their behaviour during deceptive conversations – they ask more questions with shorter sentences and match the liar's linguistic style, suggesting that they perceive something is amiss; nevertheless they seem unable to use these perceptions to improve their detection accuracy.[70] In cmc, 'inundated with massive amounts of textual information ... people remain largely unsuccessful and inefficient in detecting those messages that may be deceptive',[71] though experimental research has found that people are better at detecting lies in cmc than ftfc.[72]

There is, in fact, evidence that people are more truthful online, but because there is greater uncertainty attached to cmc, especially initially, cmc users are often sceptical about the legitimacy of others' online self-presentations. One explanation for this scepticism is **signalling theory**, which explains that some signals cannot be manipulated deceptively: an example would be the way the heavy horns of a bull signal strength because unless the bull was strong it would not be able to support the weight of the horns. Other signals, however, can easily be manipulated deceptively: words are a prime example. In a purely verbal system, therefore, even though in fact people do not behave more deceptively, the likelihood that they will is greater, and people, rightly, judge by the probabilities.[73] Of course, some impressions given verbally are hard to manipulate: if people write on their résumé that they write well in a language but their personal statement about themselves in that language is ungrammatical and ill-spelt, their assertion about themselves will lack credibility. Signalling theory helps explain why people who interact on social networking sites have more trust in what others say about third parties: the ability to contact other individuals in a social network reduces the chances that people will deceive, because of the increased risk of exposure, and users take this different probability into account.

As a consequence of online scepticism, in internet communication perceivers' judgements about a target rely more heavily on information that the targets themselves cannot manipulate than on self-descriptions. This has been labelled the '**warranting principle**'. In an experiment concerning physical attractiveness judgements, a person's friends' comments had more influence than his or her own comments, supporting warranting theory; but in an experiment concerning extraversion perceptions, although warranting theory was supported, rival explanations also applied. These results show that warranting theory has both validity and limits: whether people using the internet prefer to rely on information about others that is given by a third party varies.[74] There is evidence that they should so prefer: verbal behaviours typically correlate better with others' ratings of someone's personality than with his or her own self-ratings.[75]

Perceiving situations and environments

How people perceive their work environment strongly influences their work behaviour. Aspects of their perceived work environment that affect employees' behaviour include their perceptions of policies and the organizational structure, and here we have evidence that these perceptions are often biased. People process information about hierarchy more easily than they do similar amounts of information which is non-hierarchical. For instance, participants in a study found it easier to make decisions about a company that was more hierarchical. They also thought the hierarchical organization had more positive qualities, probably because they found the information about it easier to process. This characteristic of social cognition might, it is suggested, contribute to the construction and maintenance of hierarchies.[76] People also exhibit a bias in favour of policies labelled 'status quo', partly, at least, because they have another bias that makes losses from unknowns loom larger than gains. The magnitude of status quo enhancement is predictable from a quantitative model that measures aversion to potential losses.[77]

An important aspect of people's perceptions of their work environment concerns fairness or justice. Fairness judgements are made not only about people but also about events and about abstractions such as procedures and policies. Several different types of justice perceptions have been identified and shown to influence factors such as employees' feelings of commitment towards an organization. These different types include procedural, informational, distributive and interpersonal justice. Procedural justice concerns how fairly decisions and judgements are made, informational justice to the fairness with which information is made available, distributive justice to the fairness of reward allocations, and interpersonal justice to the even-handedness of judgements between contending or competing individuals.

Justice perceptions have an impact on work behaviour:

- High perceived distributive and procedural fairness enhance employees' identification with their organization, and perceived interpersonal and information fairness enhance the quality of their relationship with their supervisor. These two factors – organizational identification and relationship with supervisor – in turn increase effective work-related learning behaviour, including voluntary learning behaviour in the employee's own time, and so improve job performance.

- On the other hand, employees who perceive that they have been mistreated – subjected to injustice – may indulge in counter-productive work behaviour. They often direct this against the perceived source of the mistreatment, which tends to be the supervisor in the case of inter-personal or informational perceived injustice and the organization in the case of perceived procedural injustice. Desire for revenge often, but not always, mediates this relationship between counter-productive work behaviour and perceived injustice.[78]

Perceptions of overall fairness predict how people respond to managerial actions more closely than any one type of justice, and are also used to infer trust when certainty about the trustworthiness of management is low. However, overall fairness perceptions themselves are more strongly influenced by perceived distributive and interpersonal justice than by procedural or informational justice.[79] When forming justice judgements, unconscious thought can lead to more accurate justice judgements than either conscious thought or immediate judgement, experiments have shown.[80]

Fairness from authorities is more salient to the members of cmc groups, because a lack of information surrounding their work-related interpersonal interactions makes them feel a higher level of uncertainty. Thus they tend to react more negatively to 'unfair' events than people who work ftf. Moreover, the difference between the members of cmc and ftf groups, in reactions to unfair events, increases over time.[81]

Social comparison

People commonly compare their own abilities, performances and treatment with those of others in a process labelled social comparison. At work, they perform both upward and downward social comparisons, i.e. they compare themselves both with colleagues whom they perceive as doing better and with those who seem to be doing worse than they are themselves. Workers experience 'positive emotions' when making downward comparisons, and 'negative emotions' when making upward comparisons.[82] Related changes in behaviour follow these emotional reactions. Upward comparisons can negatively influence self-evaluations and people actively employ various protective strategies, such as telling lies about their performance, to mitigate the effect of such comparisons.[83] Upward comparisons also tend to lead to reduced job satisfaction and emotional commitment to the job or the organization and to an increase in searching for another job; downward social comparisons in contrast are significantly positively related to job satisfaction and emotional commitment and negatively related to searching for another job.[84]

People are particularly likely to compare their own achievements in the domains of promotions and salary increases with those of colleagues.

These social comparisons damage trust – when they are made with colleagues doing 'better' than themselves, they damage feelings-based trust (affective trust) and when they are made with colleagues doing 'worse' than themselves, they damage cognitive trust, that is, their thoughts about the colleague's competence and so on.

Assessments of fairness on the job are also comparative. This is clear from 'all ... forms of organizational justice'. People judge fairness 'by comparing themselves to others in two ... ways – the procedures by which they and others obtain rewards, and the manner in which they and others are treated in the course of enacting those procedures'. Social comparison processes also 'play a key role in the performance evaluation process but they do not always enhance the validity of the evaluation process'. In traditional 'top-down evaluations', 'comparative information may be rejected and/or ignored in keeping with the tendency to bias information in a self-serving manner'. Furthermore, social comparison processes 'are involved with stress in a cognitive capacity. Comparisons with others help people assess the extent to which they have the resources necessary to perform a task. And this, in turn, is a primary step in the assessment of stress'.[85]

Working by cmc affects social comparison. When workers 'are physically distant, special challenges emerge as people endeavour to compare themselves to others'. The 'limited availability of local comparisons leads workers to compare themselves to others who provide less-than-ideal sources of relevant comparative information, such as those who are dissimilar along key dimensions (e.g. people working in other organizations, or who do highly different work)'. However, people working by cmc 'may attempt to overcome such limitations by being highly proactive in their efforts to collect information in alternative ways (e.g. by posing questions in emails or phone calls). Such effort enables workers in virtual environments to remain "in the loop", thereby overcoming the limitation imposed by environmental conditions'.[86]

Summary

'Frames' are used to interpret observed events; the frames vary from individual to individual and from occasion to occasion. Interactions in which someone is participating are particularly significant events for them: they try to understand their interaction partner's goals and to detect if others are being deceitful.

People are generally not very successful in detecting deceptions, though there are ways of improving. Though still poor, performance at detecting deceptions by cmc is better than ftf, partly because people are more sceptical online, and partly because they (unknowingly) apply signalling theory and warranting theory more effectively online.

How people perceive their work environment affects their behaviour. Research has shown that these perceptions can be biased. Fairness judgements are particularly important influences on positive and negative work behaviour. People who work mainly by cmc react more negatively to events that they perceive as unfair than those who work mainly ftf.

Social comparison helps explain key areas of working life, such as perceptions of organizational justice, performance appraisal and stress. It also helps account for some problems that can arise in virtual work.

4 CONTRIBUTING TO COMMUNICATION, SELF-PRESENTATION AND IMPRESSION MANAGEMENT

However fully we understand interaction partners we have not communicated with them unless and until we have sent them a message ourselves. Therefore Section 4.1 examines what it is we do when we contribute to communication. Unfortunately, the English language does not have a general term for the forward act of communication; 'speaking' and 'writing' are at once too specific and too narrow (they exclude body language), 'expressing' is transitive, 'sending messages' is ambiguous and does not comprehend some views on what we are actually doing; 'communication' implies successful reception of a message. So this chapter will use the terms 'contributing to communication' and 'communication contribution(s)', although I recognize that other writers use a different terminology.

On completing your study of this chapter, you will be able to:

- Explain what is involved in making an appropriate communication contribution.
- Explain the significance and meaning of self-presentation and impression management.
- Explain how different communication modes affect communication contributions, self-presentation and impression management, and how to adjust for these differences.

You will also:
- Know how to make an effective contribution by email.
- Know how to use text messages at work.
- Know what you can do to help make your self-presentation match your intention.
- Know the guidelines for effective impression management.
- Know how to self-present skilfully by cmc.

To avoid mistrust, misattribution and conflict, and so to work effectively and productively, co-workers must both understand one another and form accurate and useful impressions of each other; the same applies to all the other stakeholders who interact at work. While, as Chapter 3 has shown, this partly depends on the perceiver, the person perceived can contribute significantly by his or her self-presentation. Sections 4.2 and 4.3 cover self-presentation and impression management. A major focus throughout is how different communication modes affect all these communication processes.

4.1 CONTRIBUTING A COMMUNICATION

Different views on the essentials of making a contribution in an interaction emphasize messages, intentions, rules and reciprocity. Although none of these is a complete account, they contribute to our understanding. These approaches all construct communication as a cooperative endeavour, as it usually must be to function at all. There is a major exception, however, and that is when the speaker or writer intends to deceive the hearer or reader.

Encoding/decoding models

One view on communication is that it means getting messages across and understood. The process involves one information processing device (usually a person) turning an internal representation into code (which could be words, a picture or even music) and transmitting it; then another information processing device (another person) receiving it and decoding it. The receiver decides a response and the process is repeated in reverse. 'Noise' such as a distracting environment or psychological resistance can prevent messages from being received, so effective communicators try to ensure that the person they are addressing is not likely to be affected by noise.

Thus for encoding/decoding models, meaning is a property of messages. However, the literal meaning of a word, phrase or sentence and the meaning the communicator intends to convey by using it are often different. Irony is the clearest example – 'I love getting up early' means something quite different if spoken or written ironically than if the sender intends to convey the literal meaning. People often signal verbally, non-verbally or by symbols that they mean something other than the literal meaning.

Many messages (greetings are an exception) contain content, and communicators try to get this content understood, accepted and believed. To do this they avoid ways of expression that will make the receiver defensive, such as wording that suggests a sense that the sender perceives him or herself as superior or hostile. Messages that are 'receiver-oriented', or ask questions or seek information, are more likely to lead to being understood as well as conveying a more positive impression of the speaker, especially in terms of empathy, than other kinds.

How cmc affects messages

Email messages have their own characteristics. For instance, users of email appear to be generally unconcerned with formalities. Although a sample of email texts was lucid, a study found, writers often dispensed with traditions (greetings) when opening their email, and their closings were informal. Social emails involved the most creative sort of communication. The increased informality and lack of consistency of email texts has been attributed to the 'newness' of the medium; often no clear guidelines exist.[1] Again, online **self-disclosure** occurs in an accelerated manner compared to offline. This is particularly so when the person has a positive attitude towards forming relationships online. However, evidence suggests that it is the quantity of online exchanges that is enhanced rather than the quality, as self-disclosure initially occurs only for superficial information about personal matters and interests,[2] and a review of research findings published in 2012 found that disclosure is not consistently greater in online contexts. Factors such as the relationship between the communicators, the specific mode of communication, and the context of the interaction appear to moderate the degree of disclosure.[3]

There is some evidence that, compared with face-to-face (ftf) communication, computer-mediated communication (cmc) reduces fluency and increases the burden on senders relative to receivers. In one study electronic communication media posed obstacles to complex communication between collaborators when compared with the ftf mode; cmc led to an increase in cognitive effort of about 12 per cent and in communication ambiguity of 19 per cent. Those obstacles were met with 'compensatory adaptation', whereby electronic communication users attempted to make up for the obstacles by modifying their communication behaviour; unfortunately, however, this effort led to a reduction in communication fluency of 90 per cent. Most of the effort to make up for the obstacles posed by electronic communication media was exerted by those attempting to convey information as opposed to those receiving it.[4]

In contrast to these negative findings, Tu (2000)[5] found that in educational settings email, bulletin board, real time discussion and listservs enhance as well as inhibit online interaction. Users are better able to optimize their communication, online image and online impression than

> *In 1964, Marshall McLuhan proclaimed, 'The medium is the message'. At that time, of course, he was not talking about cmc but broadcast media. How far does it apply to cmc?*

in ftf encounters that require the simultaneous use of all communication channels.

Research has shown that people actively try to be understood – or at least to have their message understood. 'People not only speak, but nod, smile, point, gaze at each other, and exhibit and place things. Gestural acts like these are often tied to what people are doing as they are talking ... It is the vocal and gestural acts together that comprise their talk.'[6] As explained in Chapter 3, ftf receivers of messages use the speaker's non-verbal behaviour as well as the spoken words to draw inferences about the speaker's meaning. From this point of view the disadvantage of cmc for making communication contributions is obvious: it removes the possibility of supplying certain cues. For instance, as Kruger et al. (2005) noted:

> ❝ Without the benefit of paralinguistic cues such as gesture, emphasis, and intonation, it can be difficult to convey emotion and tone over electronic mail (email) ... This limitation is often underappreciated, such that people tend to believe that they can communicate over email more effectively than they actually can ... Because email communicators 'hear' a statement differently depending on whether they intend to be, say, sarcastic or funny, it can be difficult to appreciate that their electronic audience may not.[7]

The loss of the visual channel has been blamed for informal speech (mildly uninhibited behaviour) and flaming (the hostile communication of emotion) online; both may present higher rates in cmc than in either videoconferences or ftfc. Siegel et al. (1986) found 34 episodes of uninhibited behaviour in cmc, and none in ftf conditions. Although some instances of perceived flaming

To see more findings that show that cmc has disadvantages for making communication contributions, visit the companion website... 4.1.1.

may arise from verbal messages that would not have been abrasive in ftf but turned face-threatening in cmc due to lack of non-verbal cues,[8] Siegel et al. (1986) considered that the distraction from the social context in cmc means that people are less concerned with what others will think, which presumably leads to uninhibited behaviour.[9] On the other hand, Hiltz et al. (1989), in a study done with corporate managers as subjects, reported that about half the cmc groups had no incidence of uninhibited behaviour. Even when a certain amount of anonymity was created by assigning pen names, the likelihood of uninhibited behaviour was not much higher.[10] Furthermore, there is evidence that employees exercise self-discipline regarding email – a thematic analysis of data produced two rules employees cited for email usage: be careful what is committed to writing (because of loss of message control and fear of being monitored) and maintain an appropriate, professional communication style (free of emotion, sent only to the appropriate people, and used for topics not needing ftf interaction).[11] These findings suggest that the work context may create an important difference in how email users behave.

The disadvantage of the loss of available cues can be overcome, according to Riordan and Kreuz (2010) who found that cmc users do use a non-verbal system of communication, which consists of using words or symbols that are cue-laden. These cues are used to express a feeling, to strengthen or increase the impact of a word, (for example, 'you should NEVER do that') to regulate the interaction by, for example, suggesting insight ('I _think_ that's right'), cause ('<Because> it's a terrible song'), discrepancy ('There {should} have been four files there, but one got lost'), tentativeness ('I *might* be able to get there by ten'), perception ('I {feel} like you're making the wrong choice'). Messages can be clarified by, for instance, indicating a quantifier ('_Some_ people think it's a great song, but I disagree'), describing cognitive mechanisms ('I <know> I put it somewhere'), indicating inclusion ('I got the interview _and_ I got the job!'), and indicating exclusion ('The song would work better {without} the guitar riff').[12] This study suggests that people are adept at overcoming the limitations of a medium.

Words and symbols that substitute in cmc for non-verbal behaviour:

- Capitalized words: for example, 'I can't BELIEVE you said that'.
- Vocal spelling: for example, 'Ohhhh I see' or 'mhmm'.
- Repeating punctuation: most commonly exclamation marks, question marks or a combination – for example, 'I've found the answer!!!!!!!', 'Where are they?????', 'What did you say?!?!?!'.
- Emoticons: for example :-) or, more rarely, 'extra-mouth' emoticons, for example :-))))).
- Asterisks: for example 'I'm not *entirely* sure'.
- Angled brackets: as in '<Maybe> the next album will be better'.
- Underscores surrounding words: for example 'Try downloading the file _without_ saving it first'.
- Tildes: for example 'I've been ~extremely~ busy'.
- Curly braces: for example 'I {thought} it was next week'.

Modern email programs also give individuals the option of using different fonts, font sizes and colours, all of which may be used to communicate paralinguistically and to enrich lean text-based communication.[13] There are simple-to-use technologies available, such as smileys for communicating emotional tone, system architecture for time and date tracking, and translation, to overcome language barriers possibly more effectively than they often are ftf.[14]

Conveying an intention

Communicators can have one or more of a range of intentions, including informing, requesting, disagreeing, qualifying, ordering, promising or a number of other possibilities. This intention is fundamental to communicating. If the receiver does not understand what the speaker's intention is, the communication will fail. For instance, if, when Person A emails Person B, 'Let me have a look at the Y file', B does not realize that A intends to ask him or her to send the file, B is unlikely to send it, and the communication will fail.

Speech-act theory identifies what it takes to have an intention understood; its label dates from before writing was used for everyday interactions, but it applies quite well to cmc. The theory states that there are guidelines for how to use speech to accomplish a particular intention. For instance, if A wants to be given some information, he or she asks a question and does it in a form which B will understand to obligate him or her either to answer it, give an excuse or ignore it; in speech the question form is usually both verbal and paralinguistic (in British English often using a rising intonation), in writing both verbal and symbolic (indicated by a question mark).[15]

> Selection interviewers sometimes ask questions such as: 'How many aeroplanes landed in Delhi airport in 2002?'. Interviewees are not expected to know the answer; they need to understand that the intention behind the question is to see whether they can think through a logical process that might give a rough answer.

Conveying an intention by cmc

It is often useful to classify emails according to the intention of the sender (e.g. 'propose a meeting', 'deliver information'). Taking this idea as a starting point, systems based on the speech-act perspective have been used to build tools for coordinating joint activities. While such systems have been useful in limited contexts, they have also been criticized as cumbersome: by forcing users to conform to a particular formal system, they constrain communication and make it less natural. Users often prefer unstructured email interactions. An alternative approach is to devise a system for classifying naturally produced emails. One such uses the following categories:

- A 'request' asks (or orders) the recipient to perform some activity. A question is also considered a request (for delivery of information).
- A 'propose' message proposes a joint activity, i.e. asks the recipient to perform some activity and commits the sender as well, provided the recipient agrees to the request. A typical example is an email suggesting meeting up.

- An 'amend' message modifies an earlier proposal. Like 'propose', the message involves both a commitment and a request, but is associated with an already proposed task.
- A 'commit' message commits the sender to some future course of action, or confirms the sender's intent to comply with some previously described course of action.
- A 'deliver' message delivers something, e.g. some information, a PowerPoint presentation, the URL of a website, the answer to a question, a message sent 'FYI', or an opinion.

> To learn more about emails and intentions, visit the companion website... 4.1.2.

The intention behind other emails might be to refuse, greet or remind.[16]

How to use text messages at work:

- Decide on the purpose of your text (your communicative intention). If you simply need to confirm a time or place, writing the entire message will provide clarity and hardly takes any time. If you need to write out a very long text, some shorthand can save time and money.
- Evaluate your relationship with the person whom you are texting and the capabilities each of you has for sending and receiving messages. If you are unsure of using abbreviations, or if the person receiving the text message might not understand abbreviations, spell out all the words.
- Address the recipient as you would in any other context. Although, if it is someone you know well, it is common to sign off the text message with an 'X' resembling the common symbol for a kiss, this is inappropriate in a work text message. If you are texting from a work phone or in a professional context, type your name as a sign off.

Conversational maxims (or rules)

Even when their purpose is to dispute, criticize or insult, communicators must cooperate to the extent of shaping their messages to be meaningful to their addressees by following four basic rules or maxims. Messages are meaningful when they are consistent with the maxims of quality (truthful), quantity (containing neither more nor less information than is required), relation (relevant to the ongoing discussion) and manner (brief and unambiguous). Moreover, because senders of messages usually are cooperative, receivers will usually assume that they are, and so will be able to infer the intended meaning, even when these maxims are violated. Even where, for instance, the answer to a question seems irrelevant, as in an exchange such as 'Where's the meeting?' or 'It's Friday', the cooperative principle allows the receiver to infer something such as 'It's where meetings are always held on Fridays' – i.e. in Room X. The cooperative principle also means that speakers 'monitor their own speech and, when they discover problems, make repairs. Speakers also monitor addressees for understanding and, when necessary, alter their utterances in progress; and addressees co-operate by displaying and signaling their understanding in progress'.[17]

Conversational maxims and cmc

To a large extent, the cooperative principle applies in cmc. For example, when people engage in online discussions, they respect the maxim of quantity by inserting hypertextual links into messages, explaining a topic and adding a link to a more in-depth article or website on the topic. Then, 'if the message is seen as informative enough ... a recipient does not consult a complementary document by clicking on the hypertextual link. If the message is seen as not informative enough ... a recipient is able to find more information by clicking'. Furthermore, receivers of online communications explicitly evaluate whether the maxim has been respected or violated by their interaction partner through 'calls to order', as in 'You give too much detail ... it is not going to be easy to help you' or 'Would you care to elaborate?'. Equally, senders apologize when they feel they have broken a maxim by comments such as 'Sorry to be so long-winded' or 'I think I have approached the question clumsily... I have not been overly explicit'.[18]

Reciprocity

The social pressure on people to produce equivalent responses[19] (for example to self-disclose at a similar level)[20] has been described as one of the defining features of social life. It 'has profound effects on the emergence of integrative bonds of trust and solidarity'. Reciprocal exchange enables communicators to 'overcome the divisions created by power and to develop the trust and affective bonds that promote productive exchange relations. As a result, power and trust need not be mutually exclusive'.[21] Reciprocity, it is argued, explains how people behave better than dominant theories built on the assumption that all actions are either self-interested or altruistic. Reciprocal exchange draws individuals into a relation of recognition: many social actions that solicit a return-action seek to neither profit nor benefit, but rather express a desire to draw others into social life and relationships.

Reciprocity and cmc

Pelaprat and Brown (2012) argued that reciprocity underlies much online activity. Three kinds of online activity (web forums, social networking sites and online games) illustrate the presence of reciprocity; for instance 'the online forum (the message board) is, among other things, a space structured to facilitate encounters... and hence recognition. Strangers recognise each other in a manner that preserves and discloses their status as others – thus, initial posts by one is not only a call for support, or a response to an article, but also an invitation to dialogue'.[22]

Deception

Although in general people actively try to get their message across, have their intention understood, behave cooperatively and reciprocate, there is a significant exception – and that is when they are lying. Lying is a common aspect of interpersonal relationships,[23] so common that it has given rise to a theory, interpersonal deception theory, which predicts that language choice in deceptive messages reflects strategic attempts to manage information through non-immediate language:

> **❝** Senders display greater verbal non-immediacy when deceiving, but also adjust their linguistic behaviour when they believe the person they are addressing has relevant information or expertise; deceiving senders use more verbal non-immediacy with novice receivers. It seems probable that these findings reflect deceivers' strategic attempts to bolster credibility.[24]

Not surprisingly, people do better at detecting deceptions when their suspicions are aroused; this occurs either because they have been warned or because their prior experience makes them suspicious. According to interpersonal deception theory, however, deceivers are often alert to and good at detecting when their interaction partner is suspicious, and this, in turn, 'can clue the deceiver on whether the attempted deception is working, leading to behavioural reactions on the part of the deceiver'.[25]

Deception by cmc

Is deception more common in ftfc or cmc? One study found that respondents displayed higher levels of deceptive behaviour when interacting ftf than by cmc; this applied to both Korean and American respondents despite significant differences in culture, suggesting that the tendency to be more truthful online is cross-cultural.[26] Again, interacting through avatars can reduce deceptive behaviour. People who perceive their online avatars to look similar to themselves are less likely to try to deceive, while avatar similarity in attitude and behaviour heightens self-awareness, which in turn reduces deception.[27]

On the other hand, people are more willing to lie via email than via pen and paper and feel more justified in doing so, even though both are text-only. The findings are consistent irrespective of whether participants are told that their lie either will or will not be discovered by their counterparts. The researchers suggest that people are more likely to lie via email because email may feel less permanent (more like ftf) than pen and paper and because people may feel more anonymous online:

- 'Email is often treated as a substitute for verbal communication' so that 'people may transfer perceptions about face-to-face communication to email' feeling that they are 'talking', not writing, to others through email.
- 'Electronic text inherently permits the deletion of words, sentences, or even whole documents with the touch of a button, potentially making people feel less attached to the words that they use in this medium. The impermanence of online written text can leave the writer feeling less ownership of the words and diminished concern for the moral and ethical implications of what is written.'
- 'People may unconsciously feel less of a personal connection with their communication partners via email than via pen and paper. People seem to feel more removed from both their own behaviours and the effects of their actions over email. This psychological distance may make people more likely to lie to another in this medium than in pen and paper.'
- There is a greater ambiguity about appropriate behaviour online.
- At work, 'given that few organizations have specific policies to date on what is appropriate (form or content) for email, ambiguity about what is permissible may allow ethical or moral violations to be perceived as more justifiable in email than they might be in less ambiguous and better established media'.[28]

How to make an effective communication contribution by email:

- Consider your message and style from the perspective of the recipient.
- Think about whether and how to replace body language by your language and/or symbols.
- At work, bear in mind the organizational norms for email.
- At work, bear in mind the importance of appearing business-like (even if you do not work in a business).
- At work, ask yourself: 'Does my email ask the reader to do anything? If not, why am I sending it?'
- Can the reader tell from the subject line and first sentence what I'm writing about without going further? If not, why are you insisting that they guess?

- Am I relying on what the audience knows or what I think they ought to know? Am I hiding anything from the reader? If so, why do I want to surprise them later on?
- Is my email giving my opinion and options for the reader to respond to? If not, why am I making them try to read my mind?[29]
- Avoid flaming.

When initiating a correspondence:

- Think carefully about how to gain attention by your subject line – especially when you are writing to a busy person who may have many emails in their inbox.

When responding to an email:

- Think about when to respond: how delays of different duration will be interpreted;
- Decide whether to increase, decrease or maintain social distance by converging towards or diverging from the sender's style and tone.

Summary

Messages encode meaning and have to be decoded for the meaning to be understood. Messages that take into account the perspective of the receiver are more likely to be understood and accepted. Ftf, non-verbal behaviour is widely used to help others understand; this strongly suggests that people do usually want to be understood. The absence of non-verbal cues in cmc constrains the ability to express ourselves fully and clearly, leading sometimes to uninhibited behaviour; however, there are multiple ways of circumventing this constraint and research has shown that people do in fact succeed in doing so.

Conveying an intention (performing a 'speech' act) is a core function of contributing a communication; it seems likely that it can be performed as effectively by cmc as ftf.

Cooperating by usually following rules of quantity, quality, relevance and ambiguity together with producing equivalent responses (that is, reciprocating), whether ftf or by email, are important for smooth communication both socially and at work.

There are stylistic patterns that occur more frequently when people are lying. People lie more readily ftf than by cmc, but more readily by cmc in the form of email than in letters.

4.2 SELF-PRESENTATION

Being concerned with one's self-presentation is, in the words of one scholar, necessary: 'far from being a sign of insecurity, vanity, or shallowness, a certain degree of concern for one's public impressions is essential for smooth and successful social interaction'.[30]

In any case, we cannot avoid being perceived and so giving an impression, and we cannot have total control over what impression we give. For instance, we often act in ways which are consistent not with our own attitudes, beliefs or feelings, but rather with the perceptions and stereotypes which others hold of us and our attributes; again, when we are distracted by having to attend to several cues, our self-presentations are more positive, even when we would prefer them not to be (perhaps because we are trying to discourage someone who is too attentive).[31] However, we do have some influence over the impressions we create. With this in mind, the purpose of this section is to give a brief outline of self-presentation through explaining communicator style and how 'face' and 'politeness' affect self-presentation, including the impact of different communication modes on these factors. A further note covers additional points about cmc and self-presentation.

> Visit the companion website... 4.1.3 for a link to a video about the best way to communicate in business.
>
> Do you agree with the interviewee about this? Why or why not?

Communicator style

Communicator style has been defined as 'the characteristic way a person sends verbal, paraverbal and non-verbal signals in social interactions denoting (a) who he or she is or wants to (appear to) be, (b) how he or she [in]tends to relate to people with whom he or she interacts, and (c) in what way his or her messages should usually be interpreted'. This definition 'focuses explicitly on interpersonal communication behaviors; it excludes intrapersonal communication behaviors, such as purely cognitive interpretations of other people's utterances or internal affective states as a reaction to these utterances'.[32]

De Vries et al. (2009) identified seven bipolar dimensions of communicator style:

- Expressiveness reflects a mix of talkativeness, certainty, energy and eloquence.
- Preciseness consists of a mix of clarity, conciseness, efficiency and (business-like) composure.

- Niceness consists of friendliness, uncriticalness, modesty and cheerfulness.
- Supportiveness: 'in contrast with ... niceness ... supportiveness ... can be characterized as a relational response factor, consisting of mainly verbs that denote how one responds to a specific person'. Thus, niceness seems to reflect a general communication attitude, while supportiveness reflects the actual communication behaviours in response to someone else. Supportiveness consists mainly of accommodation, admiration and stimulation.
- Threateningness consists mainly of abuse, threat and deceptiveness.
- Emotionality seems to reflect the components sadness, irritability, anger and tension.
- Finally, 'the ... reflectiveness factor is clearly a smaller factor consisting mainly of the components engagement, analytical reflectiveness and philosophical or poetic communication behaviors'.[33]

These dimensions, found through lexical research, are closely, although not wholly, aligned with dimensions uncovered in personality research. Expressiveness, preciseness, emotionality and reflectiveness seem to be communicative versions of extraversion, conscientiousness, emotional stability and openness to experience. Honesty-humility, which has been found in personality research, seems to divide itself among two communicator style factors: threateningness (with deceptiveness as a facet) and niceness (with modesty as a facet).

According to the trait perspective advocated by McCroskey et al. (1998),[34] communicator styles have a biological and temperamental origin. However, because communicator styles are probably more 'statelike' (less stable) than personality traits, the demands of the situation play a role: for instance, to avoid conflict, people will refrain from posing critical questions or remarks; again, group norms that support disinhibited and threatening communication will lead to an increase in this kind of communication from group members. Consequently, how someone communicates may be to some extent a function of the group he or she identifies with.[35] Nevertheless, although it is likely that there will be variations in personal communicator styles according to the context, people will tend to rely on the style of communication that is most natural for them. Consequently, their personality traits and personal identity will be expressed to a considerable extent through their communicator style.[36]

Communicator style and cmc

There is little research as yet on the extent to which personal communicator style is reflected in text-only formats such as email. The format itself of course has its own conventions, such as its jargon, etiquette, symbols, even vocabulary and ways of creating impact or visual variety; however, what we know about mediated communication behaviour does suggest that people will not be so constrained by these conventions as to be unable to use their own preferred communicator style. We do know that there are style differences between, for example, business email messages, which appear to follow the normal conventions for standard written business English, while academic users appear to view the medium as a pseudo-conversational form of communication, conducted in extended time and with an absent interaction partner.[37]

> **"** My style in emails is quite formal. Not chatty. The most informal I get with the opening is 'Hello'. Usually I just open with the person's bare name, as in 'Derek'. Generally I respond at the same level of formality as the person who emailed me used. I got burnt once sending an email to the wrong person. It wasn't important, but I decided then that I would never send an email that could not be printed and left on my desk.
>
> (Author's interview with an executive from
> a media organization)

> **"** Managers here [in the European bank where I am working now] send emails that strike me as unprofessional. For instance, one opens his to this department of 15 people with the words, 'Hello, People.' And there are bits of personal content that are meant to be funny; for example, when there was a system problem and he needed to stay until IT had fixed it, he wrote, 'My wife has gone to her mother's house so I can stay until 9 p.m.'
>
> (Author's interview with a bank regulatory reporting specialist
> who has worked on a series of temporary contracts)

Facework

Self-presentation, like all behaviour, reflects our needs. One set of needs that has a strong, though often unrecognized, influence on self-presentation is known as **'face'** needs. Meeting our need to maintain 'face' depends on perceiving that others respect us (a positive face claim) and also that they respect our right not to be interfered with, to be allowed personal space and privacy (a negative face claim). People 'lose face' if their face claims do not seem to be honoured by others; for instance, if someone 'corrects' them about an organizational rule that they should have known about, they will suffer a loss of face; to overcome or avoid this, they undertake **'facework'** such as making excuses or ensuring that they do know the rules. People may also be concerned to help others maintain face (though sometimes they may deliberately or unintentionally threaten others' faces) and this too involves them in facework such as showing support for the others' ideas. Facework is performed by communicating: for instance to support a positive face claim of being accepted by a group, a new member might gradually transition from using 'you' to refer to the group to using 'we'; to support a negative face claim of the right to privacy, someone might refuse a request to show another person their work, but often they would at the same time support the other person's 'face' by being tactful, using an excuse such as 'It is still too early a draft to be readable'.

Erving Goffman's model of self-presentation

The American sociologist Erving Goffman originated much of the study of face and self-presentation. Goffman (1959) wrote:[38] 'when an individual appears before others, he knowingly and unwittingly projects a definition of the situation, of which a conception of himself is an important part ... When an event occurs which is expressively incompatible with this fostered impression, significant consequences are ... felt'. For example, an applicant for a first-time-buyer mortgage (home loan) during an interview with a bank manager might self-present as naïve about, for instance, interest rates, self-presenting in this way because it seems appropriate and more likely to be successful. There may be no deliberate intention to deceive and no lies may be told. Suppose at some point in the discussion our home loan applicant reveals that he or she does in fact run a successful small business and has had a business loan and regularly paid the interest on it. There need be no absolute contradiction with the applicant's 'definition of the situation', but an event will have occurred which is 'expressively incompatible with this fostered impression'. Then, according to Goffman (1959), 'the social interaction may come to an embarrassed and confused halt; the situation may cease to be defined, previous positions may become no longer tenable, and participants may find themselves without a charted course of action'. Furthermore, this disrupted interaction is likely to have wider ramifications and future consequences: for example, the applicant might so dread the possibility of a future 'exposure' of the same kind that he or she never again applies for a home loan.

As Goffman (1959) put it, 'while the likelihood of disruption will vary widely from interaction to interaction, and while the social importance of likely disruptions will vary from interaction to interaction, still it seems that there is no interaction in which the participants do not take an appreciable chance of being slightly embarrassed or a slight chance of being deeply humiliated'.

The interactors, then, must keep behaving in a way that sustains their initial 'definitions'. To sustain a self-presentation they have to regulate how much information they give out and control the level and type of contact they have with the other party. In Goffman's model, tact, or protecting other people's faces, is very important: 'few impressions could survive if those who received the impression did not exert tact in their reception of it'.

Furthermore, since reciprocity is a key characteristic of interactions, only by 'exerting tact' in the reception of others' self-presentations can people hope and expect to have their own face protected by others.

Unfortunately, if we are not giving our full attention to an interaction, are too self-conscious, over-aware of the other person or too concerned with the impression we are giving, we are likely to undermine our self-presentations by showing too much or too little attention, involvement, concern or emotion, by losing muscular control, for instance by yawning when our 'face' requires us to be interested, or by timing and other errors such as embarrassing silences or over-talking. All this means that self-presenting well requires not only skill, but also self-discipline. It is necessary to suppress inappropriate responses, such as desires to laugh about matters that are defined as serious or to take seriously matters that are defined as funny.

Facework in cmc

Some conceptualizations of face, such as that 'it comes into being when one person comes into the presence of another',[39] seem to exclude face as a factor in such media as email. However, asynchronous media have the advantage for facework of avoiding the effects of distraction that can undermine facework ftf.

We have few empirical findings that directly describe the consequences of cmc for face and facework. There are, however, one or two findings: most importantly, findings by O'Sullivan (2000)[40] suggested that individuals strategically prefer interpersonal channels with fewer social cues when threats to their self-presentation arise; that is, individuals will prefer to use mediated channels rather than ftf conversation in **face-threatening** situations because mediated channels allow for control over exchanged social information. Based on his findings, he asserted that when self-presentation concerns are threatened, individuals strategically prefer channels with fewer social cues.

This claim is contrary to several earlier approaches to mediated communication such as social presence, media richness or social context cues that argued that channels with features that allow for more social cues should be preferred in most situations, particularly those that pose some difficulty. Instead, it is now generally accepted that the information-constraining features of a less rich channel such as text-based cmc allows individuals to manage their self-presentational needs better and derive more positive outcomes during face-threatening situations. Two findings lend support to this idea:

- O'Sullivan (2000) noted that in an earlier study of interpersonal media and long distance relationships, respondents reported advantages with regard to 'the capacity to control the timing, duration, and nature of information exchanged during these interactions'. Mediated communication channels can therefore be seen as 'a tool for managing self-relevant information in pursuit of self-presentational goals'.[41]

- Feaster (2010) showed that people's communication mode choices are influenced by positive and negative face concerns. Different media allow different degrees of expressive information control and privacy information control. Expressive information control is the degree to which use of a medium affords an individual the ability to regulate the flow of information revealed/expressed (verbally or non-verbally) during an interaction, and pertains to addressing positive face concerns. Privacy information control pertains to the degree to which a use of a medium endows an individual with the ability to *restrict* or *halt* certain forms of information from entering into an interaction, and pertains to addressing negative face concerns. Choice of media is affected by which of these concerns is greater at the time an interaction is initiated.[42]

> *You have found that you made errors in the sales figures you submitted recently. What would O'Sullivan (2000)'s theory predict about what communication mode you would choose to report this?*
>
> *For other findings on facework in mediated channels, visit the companion website...*
> *4.2.1.*

Politeness

Consideration and politeness are very important in a work context. Experiencing incivility from co-workers and customers, and especially from both of these, reduces performance and increases withdrawal behaviours such as absenteeism and lateness for months afterwards, a survey of bank tellers found.[43] Group members get more satisfaction, though they do not necessarily perform better, from interacting in groups where the members have shared beliefs about how to communicate in terms of politeness or efficiency.[44]

There is a theory that builds on the concepts of face and facework and helps us to understand how we use politeness in communication. This is politeness theory, which asserts that people will use more politeness the higher the intrinsic level of threat in the communication. Threats in this context are **face-threatening acts** (FTAs) – a matter of how much someone thinks a communication imposes on the person they are addressing. This of course varies from individual to individual, but for many people expressing disagreement, for instance, imposes a degree of threat to the face of the other person; research has shown, though, that requests (to do something) are seen as the most threatening acts – worse than disagreements.

There are a variety of forms of politeness used to reduce face threats: most polite is not to perform the FTA – for example, instead of asking someone to fetch a file for you, fetching it yourself; next is to go 'off-record' – be so ambiguous that the intention to ask is unclear, as in 'Has anyone seen the X file?'; next is to use negative politeness, which respects the hearer's autonomy as in, 'I'd be very grateful if you would get me the X file'; then to perform the FTA but show solidarity with the hearer, as in 'We could really do with the X file – please get it for us' – this is positive politeness; and least polite is a bald on-the-record act: 'Get me the X file'.

> *Look ahead to Box 5.1. How should the bank regulatory reporting specialist have pointed out that the team she had newly joined had been making errors in its Bank of England procedure? What level of politeness should she have used and why?*

Politeness theory has received some support from research and there is also some evidence that it applies cross-culturally. For example, politeness increased, eight experimental studies found, when the addressees were construed not as individual people but as abstractions such as stereotypes, or were remote in time or space. Equally, increasing politeness produced abstract construals and a greater sense of temporal and spatial distance.[45] Despite this support, criticisms of politeness theory have been common. A major criticism is that people do not always aim for politeness – for mitigating the level of threat. Instead, on occasion, and depending on their interaction strategy, they may at times aim for impoliteness: they may, for instance, wish to rebuff someone and use an increase in threat to the person's 'face' to achieve this. Furthermore, people are not always trying to be either polite or impolite: they may aim only to behave appropriately.[46] Thirdly, evaluation of politeness or impoliteness may arise from different perceptions of what norms apply.

Politeness in cmc

Morand and Ocker (2003) posed the question, 'Is politeness present in cmc?' They answered it as follows:

> **❝** There should be little doubt that face and the remedial politeness behaviours used to defray face-threat occur with considerable frequency in computer-mediated environments. [A published] examination of transcripts from cmc sessions (synchronous and asynchronous) found the great majority of messages to contain instances of face-threat... mitigated through employment of linguistic politeness. FTAs are unavoidable in cmc no less than in ftf. Common interactional events such as disagreements, criticisms, requests for information or help, giving directives or even a simple request for clarification of a prior message – all these moves are charged with potential face-threat.[47]

However, although politeness is certainly present in cmc, politeness behaviour and expectations are found to vary across communication modes. For instance, there is one FTA that is common ftf that is not found in cmc: this is conversational interruptions, which are 'potentially dysfunctional or indicative of dominance'. On the other hand, electronic technologies give rise to FTAs of their own: interpersonal intrusions are actually facilitated by technology. 'It is easier to hit the "send" button than to walk down the hall.' Another example of an FTA that would be more likely by cmc than ftf is of an individual who violated protocol by sending the same request by email to five individuals representing different organizational units and different hierarchical levels.[48] Politeness behaviour also varies across communities. In an online community of practice, a unique set of norms of polite interaction was found. Deviation from these norms frequently resulted in conflict.[49]

> *Think about a situation in which you have found that your boss made errors in the sales figures he or she submitted recently. What would politeness theory predict about how you would report this?*
>
> *To see the arguments and research about politeness in cmc, visit the companion website... 4.2.2.*

In ftf interaction non-verbal cues play a substantial role in politeness. For example, a bald statement can be turned into a question by a rising inflection. However, people can learn to compensate for the lack of non-verbal cues in cmc.

> **"** Messages embodying politeness are certainly not static – senders continuously adjust their level of phrasing, based upon whatever trade-off they wish to make between clarity and consideration. One possibility is that senders will eventually gain awareness of which aspects of written messages make them vulnerable to misinterpretation and learn ways around this. One way to make up for the lack of non-verbal accompaniments would be to make messages more direct [in SMS]. A downside of this would be the appearance of rudeness. Therefore senders may take the trouble to provide explanations for those messages with dual interpretations. Or [they may] adorn with indices of positive politeness through use of emoticons, acronyms such as jk ('just kidding') and so forth.[50]

At work, people use linguistic markers in email to convey a willingness to yield to another's preferences or opinions as a sign of respect or deference. The greatest amount of deference is expressed laterally, between peers of equal or similar rank, rather than, as might be expected, from lower-ranked senders to higher-ranked recipients. Lateral deference is most frequently displayed by those individuals most concerned with preserving their status and rank, confirming that lateral deference may be used as a status-saving strategy designed to protect individuals from status loss associated with 'overstepping one's place'.[51]

❝ Most people – even senior people – do not understand that when it comes to communication, simplicity is key. They are concerned more with seeming expert than with actually getting their message across. And you get some extraordinary jargon, like 'We are planning to extend our platform', which actually means 'We are planning to recruit some more staff'.

(Author's interview with a former UK civil servant)

How to self-present skilfully by cmc:

Abel (1990) quotes a Xerox researcher mentioning rules developed at Xerox Palo Alto Research Center for effective videoconferencing between Palo Alto, California and Portland, Oregon:

❝ We have become sensitized to the different social protocols of the link. For example, we have adapted to the technology in giving cross-site demos in the following ways:

- Wearing bright colors to give more cross-site presence;
- Preparing ahead of time because glitches are much more difficult to deal with over the link (the communication mechanism and demo are using the same channel);
- Trying not to move too much so that the video compression doesn't dominate the conversation;
- Doing things 'on cue';
- Speaking loudly and choosing carefully when to speak, etc.[52]

- When choosing a communication mode, if you have self-presentation concerns, you may prefer channels that give fewer social cues; remember, however, that your choice may itself be interpreted.
- Especially if your work involves communicating with the public, in text-based cmc use text versions of interpersonal rituals such as greetings and closings, seeking or receiving reassurance, and so on.
- Do not be influenced by cmc technology into unintentionally making the FTA of interpersonal intrusion.
- Compensate for the effect on clarity of the lack of non-verbal behaviour in text-based cmc by providing explanations for those messages with dual interpretations.
- Where appropriate, compensate for the effect on solidarity and cohesion of the lack of non-verbal behaviour by suitable expressions of support: 'Well done', for example, or 'Can do'.
- Make sure your offline and online self-presentations are consistent with one another.

Summary

Individuals have communicator styles that reflect their personality, although these styles may be modified in some situations or influenced by group norms. A set of communicator style dimensions derived from lexical research identifies seven dimensions: expressiveness, preciseness, niceness, supportiveness, threateningness, emotionality and reflectiveness. Online self-presentation is more malleable and subject to self-censorship than ftf self-presentation. There is little research as yet on the extent to which personal communicator style is reflected in text-only formats such as email, but we do know that people vary their online style between social and business emails, and according to their goals in the online groups they are attached to. Online styles can transfer to offline styles, research into avatars has found. There are also cultural differences in how people self-present online.

When communicating, people feel a need to maintain the images both of the person they present themselves as being and, usually, of the person(s) they are interacting with; that is, they have face needs. To meet these face needs they engage in facework. Goffman (1959)[53] noted a number of ways in which people can easily undermine their own self-presentations; facework therefore requires having skill and being self-disciplined. In face-threatening situations people may choose cmc rather than ftf because the reduced social cues support negative facework; there is also evidence that they have strategies for meeting positive facework goals, such as building solidarity, by cmc.

Politeness theory asserts that people use more politeness when they are contributing a communication that they believe will threaten the face of the person they are interacting with. There are different levels and kinds of politeness that correspond to the perceived level of the FTA. Politeness theory has been shown to apply to cmc as well as ftfc.

4. 3 IMPRESSION MANAGEMENT

❝ People regularly monitor their impact on others and try to gauge the impressions other people form of them. Often, they do this without any attempt to create a particular impression, but simply to ensure that their public persona is intact. Under certain circumstances, however, people become motivated to control how others see them. This impression motivation process is associated with the desire to create particular impressions in others' minds, but may or may not manifest itself in overt impression-relevant actions.[54]

As this quotation suggests, although self-presentation is often subconscious, people do at times make explicit self-presentation efforts. When they do, we call their behaviour impression management. This is the 'goal-directed process of controlling information about the self in order to influence the impression others form of one by behaving in ways that communicate certain types of personal qualities'. For instance, people who say that they think others are more influenced than they themselves are by, for example, advertising are to a degree influenced by an impression management motive. They show a larger 'third-person perception' effect in public than in private.[55] There is evidence that impression management strongly influences responses in interviews and questionnaires.

Studies have also confirmed that impression management appears to work but needs to be well-judged: for instance, job applicants who use ingratiation are more likely to be evaluated positively and to get job offers than applicants who do not use such tactics; self-promotion, however, can be counter-productive.[56]

Quite apart from such impression management directed at a specific goal, people usually have the goal of presenting a favourable image of themselves. 'In short, people communicate favourable information about themselves … because the impressions they convey to others can significantly impact how others come to perceive them.' The urge can be a powerful one, for instance leading people to display comparative optimism to the degree that **accountability** allows,[57] while people experiencing threatening social comparisons dissemble personal information in order to portray a positive outward image.[58]

What people see as a favourable image varies, however, both across individuals and in the same individual at different times. For example, according to Bergsieker et al. (2010), in 'interracial' interactions the impression-management goals of people from 'racial minorities', such as Blacks and Latinos in America, are more likely to include being respected and seen as competent than are the goals of members of 'racial majorities' such as American Whites; on the other hand

> Look back at the selection interview question given in Box 3.1. This was the applicant's response (the role was for a permanent post and the candidate had only had experience of fixed-contract posts):
>
> 'I have learnt and gained a lot of experience from past contract roles and tried to enhance my knowledge by taking time out for studying my Masters. So now I would really like to consolidate all my years of experience, putting my knowledge to work in one company and continuing to develop myself as the company grows. Having spoken to my agent and through my own research I know this is a very good environment to work in and the role offers all the elements that I'm interested in. Of course a permanent job offers more security and stability in my working life.'
>
> What do you think of this response? How could it be improved?

the goals of Whites are more often those of being liked and seen as moral. These different goals may originate in different 'pervasive representations' of Blacks and Latinos as unintelligent and of Whites as racist. Divergent impression-management goals can produce misunderstanding and poor communication. For example, 'relative to Blacks, Whites tend to perceive people who engage in self-promotion more unfavorably, deeming them less trustworthy, and evaluating them negatively even when the self-promotion is truthful'. Black people 'may be likely to distrust Whites' display of overtly friendly behavior more so than other types of behavior. For instance, Whites' verbal friendliness in inter-racial interactions often does not lead their Black interaction partners to see them favorably.'[59]

To see other findings that show that impression management can be effective, visit the companion website... 4.3.1.

Visit the companion website... 4.3.2 for a link to a video that gives advice on the non-verbal aspects of impression management for job interviewees. What are the main learning points? Are they practical? Can you add any that are not mentioned?

Guidelines for impression management:

- Make sure that the image you project by your opening remarks and demeanour in ftfc or tone in cmc is one that you can maintain. Do not,

---

BOX 4.1

Imagine that you receive the following email from a distantly located colleague. This is your first contact with him or her. What impression might you form about him or her?

Subject line: Client seminar.

Here are the arrangements for the above seminar:

1. The list of names and numbers of people attending the course has not yet been finalized.
2. A client code is in the process of being set up specifically for this course.
3. We have requested that a cloakroom attendant be available from 8.45 a.m.

I hope that the above plus the booking form is clear, but if you have any queries please do not hesitate to contact me.[60]

for instance, imply that you know somebody well whom you have only met once or twice.

- Do not allow preoccupations or fatigue to lead to losses of attention; ftf be aware of the importance of and stay in control of your non-verbal behaviour; in cmc do not allow depersonalization to lead to uninhibited behaviour.
- At work, remember that roles, others' expectations and the need to convey the accepted attitude constrain impression management.
- Do not boast or put the other person down, especially in the presence of a third party.
- Bear in mind that the other people taking part in an interaction are likely to see the situation differently from how you see it.
- To increase the chances of a good match between how you define the situation and your role and how the other interactors define them, emphasize similarity with them and try to reduce situational ambiguity by, for instance, giving your business card on first introduction.
- Remember that all social interactions are essentially performances in which it is legitimate and reasonable to expect the cooperation of the other parties. They are more likely than not to help you enact your role, i.e. to be tactful, especially if you are tactful too: reciprocity is among the most common social norms.
- Most of this guidance applies equally or more to cmc as to ftfc; for example, if in cmc you make claims that are only partially true, others will be able to check them before responding. In addition, online, verbal immediacy is important. Verbal immediacy expressions include expressions of participation (*we* vs *you*), probability (*I will* vs *I could*), mutuality (*we met each other* vs *I met her*), proximity (*these* vs *those*), concern, openness, inclusiveness and a variety of other distance-reducing ways of expression. Verbal immediacy may substitute at least in part for the absence of non-verbal signals in cmc interaction. Participants in **virtual groups** that use more verbal immediacy report significantly higher perceptions of their group's communication effectiveness.[61]

> *A candidate for a post with a Dubai company was asked the following by an interviewer from Dubai: 'How would your previous managers describe you?'*
> *She replied: 'My previous line managers from (naming four companies) said that I am professional, reliable, very thorough and hardworking.'*
> *What do you think of this response? Can it be improved?*

> *Visit the companion website... 4.3.3 to read about a model of motivations for impression management.*

Framing, or managing impressions of events

Chapter 3 introduced framing as the way in which we form impressions of events. Here I consider framing as a tool for managing impressions of events and situations – 'a quality of communication that causes others to accept one meaning over another'. Within organizations, framing can be used to set agendas, generate consensus, give prominence to issues or focus staff on particular issues. Framing techniques include choosing the angle from which an issue is depicted: for instance, health and safety at work issues can be framed as welfare concerns, macro-economic concerns, micro-economic concerns (impact on the enterprise) or insurance concerns. As Figure 4.1 shows, Fairhurst (1993) showed how framing was used to communicate the vision of a Total Quality Program in work conversations between leaders and staff in five manufacturing plants during implementation.[62]

> *Look back at Box 3.2. How would you recommend the manager to frame the issue and why?*
>
> *For suggestions on how to frame when making or handling a complaint, visit the companion website... 4.3.4.*

Figure 4.1 How framing was used to communicate the vision of a Total Quality Program

FRAMING TECHNIQUES   COMMUNICATION OBJECTIVE

Positive spin
Articulating advantages associated with the vision and its solution to problems

Agenda setting
Identifying needs, next steps, challenges and issues

Personalization
Tying the vision to people's recurring activities and roles

Reconciliation
Linking the vision to old or existing visions' values, norms or political realities;
Clarifying seeming contradictions;
Rejecting the old in favour of the new

→ Communicating the vision of a Total Quality Program

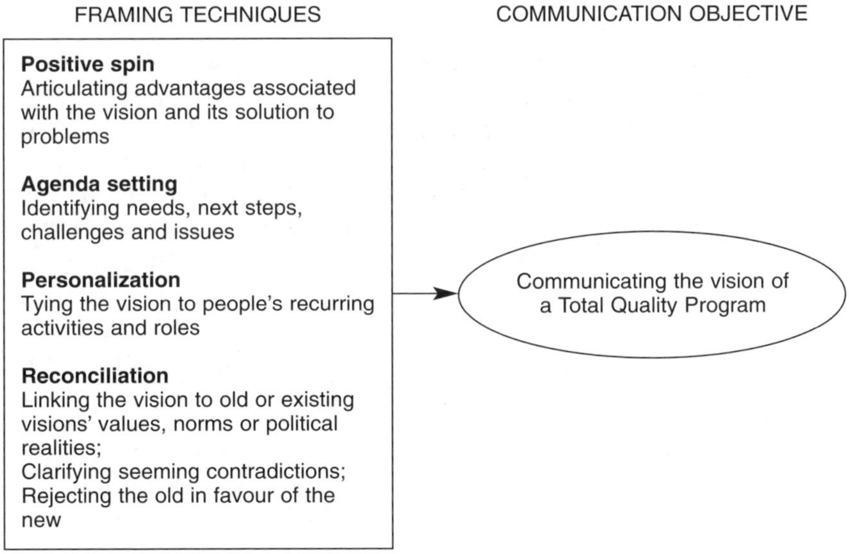

Based on Fairhurst, G.T. (1993) 'Echoes of the vision: When the rest of the organization talks total quality', *Management Communication Quarterly*, **6**(4): 331–71.

Impression management in cmc

Although there are disadvantages, on balance it appears that cmc has advantages over ftf interaction from the point of view of impression management. Cmc provides a greater possibility of strategically developing and editing self-presentation, enabling a selective and optimized presentation of one's self to others. Other advantages include a greater ability to manage ambiguity and clarity, at least in asynchronous text-based cmc like email because of the opportunity to revise and to avoid unexpected impression-marring encounters. In virtual work, distance reduces the probability of unexpected ftf encounters, which can destroy attempts at impression management. Working by cmc also increases individuals' ability to control the flow of information. However, social constraints allow individuals who interact ftf some control over information flow, and they can use language to explain their behaviour and maintain positive impressions, so that the difference in these respects between cmc and ftf are not as great as they might at first appear.[63]

When they can, people generally strategically choose their mode with the goal of impression management in mind; they also tactically self-present appropriately online. According to the impression management model of communication channel choice they also choose modes that support their impression-management goals.

Summary

Impression management is goal-directed self-presentation. The evidence is that it can be successful and useful at work. Research-based guidance suggests some ideas about how to create a favourable impression. Impression management can be directed at impressions of events or situations as well as at impressions of oneself; this is termed 'framing'. Impression management is as important and as practised in cmc as ftf; choice of mode is often an impression management choice.

5 INTERACTION

This chapter deals with the processes that cause interaction partners simultaneously to affect, and to be affected by, one another; that is, it discusses interaction, the interpersonal level of communication. Interactive behaviour is based on social perception, social cognition and self-presentation, but goes beyond these to the processes such as responding that are involved in the dynamics of communication.

On completing your study of this chapter you will be able to explain and apply the implications of:

- The dynamics of interaction.
- The meaning of communication competence and how to achieve it by following an accepted ethical code, applying facework and politeness to communication elements, and accommodating, grounding and managing uncertainty.
- How different communication modes affect the dynamics of interaction.

Also you will know:

- Ways of grounding whatever the mode or purpose.
- How to build shared **mindfulness**.
- How to make **intercultural communication** work.
- How to achieve competence in mediated communication.

In the words of Ellis (1999), 'there is a tremendous variety and complexity of interactions that one may engage in. Some of them are everyday and routine; others are new, creative and distinctive. Some involve asymmetries of various types, but all of them actualise one's membership in social networks and establish power, roles, and identity'.[1]

A number of theories have been put forward that try to reduce this variety and provide some general principles that describe how people do in fact interact and how to do it more effectively. One such theory, social exchange theory, asserts that people treat interactions in effect as trans-actions, which may on the surface deal with material matters but are also concerned with social resources such as enhanced **self-esteem**. Participants in interactions are self-interested, and power strongly influences who gets most from a social exchange. Another theory, equity theory, however, asserts that a fair balance is sought between what individuals bring to a social exchange and what they take from it. Interaction theory combines these ideas in a theory of how elements of a social-exchange context affect how individuals perceive their own positions relative to others and how these perceptions in turn influence the attributions they make for others' behaviour and so their communication during interactions with those others.

To learn more about these theories of how people interact, visit the companion website... 5.1.

When supermarket chains negotiate with small-scale producers, the price is likely to be more favourable to the supermarket chain than to the small-scale producers. Which theory about interaction explains this best?

Finally, there is a body of theory and research known as interpersonal theory. Its most important implications are that people in interactions use verbal and non-verbal cues to 'negotiate' the definition of their relationship along the following lines: dominant-friendliness invites submissive-friend-liness, and vice versa, whereas dominant-hostility invites submissive-hostility, and vice versa. Interpersonal theory also contends that people with rigid, inflexible personalities have more problems, even if such people are inflexible in a friendly direction, whereas people with flexible, adaptive personalities have fewer problems, even if such people are generally more hostile than friendly.[2]

These theories, though providing useful simplification of the 'tremendous variety and complexity of interactions' commented on by Ellis (1999), are generally considered reductive of people's motives for, and emotions and cogni-tions during, interactions; a more detailed consid-

To learn more about interpersonal theory, visit the companion website... 5.2.

eration of processes, functions and differences in interaction is needed before lessons on how to do it better can be drawn. Section 5.1 describes these functions and processes, Section 5.2 sets out what is involved in interacting skilfully; both sections consider the impact of mediated communication.

5.1 HOW WE INTERACT

This section of the chapter outlines different views on what interaction is and does and discusses how cmc affects interaction processes.

Communicating means constructing and transmitting, receiving, interpreting and responding to messages, whether verbal or non-verbal. Interaction requires communication and therefore involves all these processes as well as 'speech' acts, rules, collaboration and reciprocity, but it also implies taking it in turns (or turn-taking) to make contributions. Interactions vary in the number and size (length) of contributions, number of contributors, and level of interactivity – the percentage of contributions responded to or linked to other contributions. Contributions may propose (provide relevant information with ideas), argue (disagree, discuss, refine or clarify ideas or information in such a way as to advance the discussion) or agree (manifest implicit or explicit agreement with the other contributions). These stages can be repeated and interleaved in a collaborative process. 'Agreeing' contributions are also used for finishing the discussion.[3]

An interaction can be looked on as a unit of communication, somewhat akin to a rally in a game of tennis. It is of varying duration in time and varying length in terms of the number of sender–receiver exchanges. Completing a task or communication may require only one, or a large number of interactions; and in the case of tasks requiring multiple interactions, the time delay between them may be minutes, days, weeks or even longer. In general, despite exceptions, the same communication mode is used for an individual interaction; inertia means it is usually the mode chosen by the person initiating the interaction. A switch of mode

Identify proposing, arguing and agreeing contributions in the following dialogue:

CUSTOMER: Good morning.

REP: Good morning Mr Smith.

CUSTOMER: Take a seat. I've got a few questions on my mind, and I thought I'd ask you along and sort it out with your company. As you know, we've had one of your printers for the last four years now – we have rented the thing; I was looking at the figures and it struck me that four years on – now – we've paid for the machine about twice over. So I thought, we ought to be looking at the rental charges now.

REP: You said that you've had the machine for four years, and you've paid twice already for it – you do have to bear in mind that you never had to pay out the lump sum, the capital, which you would have paid to buy the machine.

CUSTOMER: Yes, well, can I just leave it there for now, because I've got to dash off to a meeting. What I'd ask you to do is send me the details and leave your phone number with my secretary and we can talk this over some more.

REP: Yes. I'll be happy to come in and see you again whenever it suits you.

usually requires one or the other interactor to request it: 'Drop me a line with those points, please, Paul' during a telephone call, or 'Can we meet on Wednesday to talk this over?' in an email exchange. A switch of mode usually creates a change of tempo and often of tone; it can be used tactically to alter the 'mood' in negotiations or discussions.

In principle the choice of mode is decided by its effectiveness and efficiency for the purpose, where effectiveness means the ability of the mode to convey the intended message or achieve the communication objective, such as to persuade or inform, while efficiency refers to the cost of meeting the objective by this mode. Often cost in this context means effort – so that a writing-based mode is of higher cost for most people than a speech-based mode – although it can mean time and money: if a communication initiator is located in another country from his or her interactor(s), face-to-face communication (ftfc) may be extremely high cost. Most organizations recognize this by at least imposing budgetary restraints, which mean that a whimsical preference for ftf meetings is not indulged without justification when it involves intercontinental travel.

BOX 5.1

'A switch of mode, especially from face-to-face to email, usually indicates a change of attitude on the part of the person who makes the switch. For instance, a team leader who was sitting next to me, and quite friendly, started sending me my work in very abrupt emails: 'Do this and this.' It turned out that a mistake the team had been making in its Bank of England procedure had come to light. I had pointed it out when I joined six months before but been over-ridden. The team leader wanted to blame me, but I had been able to show that it had been going on for two years, since long before I joined. So she was upset with me.'

(Author's interview with a bank regulatory reporting specialist who has worked on a series of temporary contracts)

In practice, choice of mode depends on other factors than effectiveness and efficiency, as we began to see in Chapters 2, 3 and 4. It is clearly not the case, and would be impractical for it to be the case, that every work-related interaction is preceded by a careful analysis of media alternatives and their pros and cons. Instead, habit, convention and individual preferences often decide the choice.

Ftf, interactions involve self-identification, turn-taking, interruptions, overlaps, back-channelling behaviour (a listener response providing the speaker with feedback that the message has been received, for example 'mmm' or 'yeah'), pauses, side comments, small talk, breaks and distribution of talk. Non-verbal behaviour, such as prox-emics, kinesics and paralinguistics, profoundly affect attitudes of communicators and so can affect the ultimate outcome of interactions. People's physical relationship to one another during the interaction, for example sitting across a table from one another, may unconsciously promote adversarialness and create a psycho-logical barrier to communication, recognition or agreement. Verbal pitch, rate, volume and tone of communicators strongly affect the outcome of ftf interactions.

Body language is present and significant in videoconferencing and in graphical avatar confer-encing. In one study involving highly collaborative tasks using videoconferencing, subjects did not prefer the collaborative side-to-side position; rather they preferred the more 'competitive' ftf position. Another study found that the further avatars were apart, measured in pixels, the more likely an individual would perceive the conversa-tion as appropriate. The closer avatars appeared to be on the screen, the greater the perceived social attraction between them.

Non-verbal behaviour is absent in text-based online interaction, so that the parties are more likely to respond to others' comments textually, whereas if the parties were in the same room together, the reaction would be likely to involve body language as well as or instead of verbal expression. Textual expres-sion may, however, be more accurate and authentic than a 'read' of ambiguous and culturally influenced body language. In text-based interac-tions, the sender has several options for sending paralinguistic cues, such as those described in Chapter 4, but cues given unintentionally through body language are absent; this may be beneficial or detrimental to effec-tive interaction, depending on the circumstances.

Time is an important consideration in many ftf work-related interac-tions. In a business meeting or negotiation, for instance, how long each party has to speak and the duration of the meeting may have a profound impact on the attitudes of the parties. If both parties do not receive equal time to state their position, the one receiving less time may feel slighted or unfairly treated. This in turn can lead to increased hostility and lowered cooperation. Since text-based online communication permits the parties to participate to the extent they desire, greater or lesser participation should

> *Compare the following three mediation scenarios:*
>
> *In scenario one, the mediator sits across the table from both disputants who are sitting next to one another.*
> *In scenario two, the mediator sits at the head of the table with the two disputants facing one another along the sides of the table.*
> *In scenario three, the mediator sits on the same side of the table as one of the disputants but opposite the other.*
>
> *How are the proxemics of these scenarios likely to affect the perceptions and attitudes of the parties to the mediation?*

raise fewer inherent equity and bias issues. In addition, online parties may avoid the time pressures to concede that can be experienced in ftf negotiations or meetings, although conference calls often have a pre-determined duration.

Responding

Responding plays an important role in interaction, allowing senders to know that a message has been received, understood and accepted; it may go further and indicate the receiver's positive or negative evaluation of the message and its consequences for the overall activity. Explicit responses are usually verbal as in expressions such as 'Sure', 'I see', 'I understand', etc. Ftf, response is often implicit as in the following exchange:

> Speaker 1: 'Do we have the report yet?'
> Speaker 2: 'No.' (Here the response is explicit.)
> Speaker 1: 'Tell Y to follow it up.' (Here although the part of the response that deals with consequences is explicit, the fact that the receiver has heard, understood and believed the message is only implicit – isn't stated.)

Implicit response in computer-mediated communication (cmc) is provided by a range of technical devices and their associated affordances: in some messaging systems a confirmation will automatically be sent to the sender that a message has been read; systems for marking messages for future access are ways of giving implicit responses in some cmc systems 'since, when the sender reviews the message, he or she can read the line "Marked by xx", and infer that the receiver intends to do something about the message'[4]; and there are forwarding systems that allow the original sender to see that a message has been forwarded or allow the receiver of the forwarded message to reply to the sender, thus making the sender aware that the original receiver did receive and act on the message.

Implicit responding, as against explicit, actually has a greater role in cmc compared to ftfc, due to the conditions for communication in this mode. These include the time delay, the fact that cmc allows for communication with large groups, and in those cases the need for an explicit response 'as a politeness gesture' is given less priority, and the fact that it is easier to provide 'no reply' in cmc than ftf. On the other hand, because 'participants in a dialogue are not mutually present' in cmc, explicit response may sometimes be used to create coherence in a

A fellow member of your six-person sales team reports that he or she has just made a 'mega' sale.
How does this make you feel? What factors might influence this? How do you respond? What factors might influence this?

dialogue, in the sense that 'it facilitates the resumption of a dialogue which may have been felt as terminated by one of the parties'[5]

Turn-taking

Turn-taking in a dyadic interaction is 'fundamental to conversation, as well as to other speech-exchange systems [such as] talking in interviews, meetings, debates, ceremonies'. There are both similarities and differences in how turn-taking is organized in these various systems; there are 'rules' which are complicated to explain but understood and generally adhered to by the participants. In the words of Sacks et al. (1974),

> **❝** Overwhelmingly, one party talks at a time, though speakers change, and though the size of turns and ordering of turns vary ... transitions are finely co-ordinated ... techniques are used for allocating turns ... and ... there are techniques for the construction of utterances relevant to their turn status [for instance, expressions which suggest that a speaker is willing to cede his or her turn], which bear on the co-ordination of transfer and on the allocation of speakership.[6]

For example, ftf, interaction obligations 'weigh most heavily' on the shoulders of the most recent contributors; those who contributed somewhat less recently remain engaged but have more latitude to take discordant positions; and those who have been quiet for longer periods are susceptible to 'alienation from topic', as a result of which re-entry is often accompanied by an attempt to change the topic.[7]

Mediation changes the dynamic of talk and turn-taking. When participants in a collaborative problem-solving task can both see and hear each other, the structure of their dialogues differs compared with dialogues obtained when they only hear each other. Audio-only conversations have more words, and these extra utterances often provide and elicit verbal feedback, which visual signals can deliver when available; however, even high-quality video-mediated communication does not appear to deliver the same benefits as ftf, copresent interaction.[8]

Groupware has a variety of turn-taking protocols: 'request-and-grant' (where a turn is held until explicitly relinquished) has been shown to be 'the most successful CMC condition'. 'Subjects learn quickly how to register their

In conference calls there are fewer interruptions, overlaps and pauses than there are in ftf meetings. Small talk is restricted to the end or beginning of calls if it happens at all, side comments do not happen among the participants but may occur with people outside the conference. Back channelling, however, 'occurs more frequently in work-related conference calls'.[9]

What features of conference calls might explain this finding?

turn-taking intentions, but these signals do not seem to engender the same quality of communication as the more familiar non-verbal counter-parts.' Free-for-all (in which subjects can send messages simultaneously if they wish) is a less successful condition. 'In the early stages, subjects found it difficult to co-ordinate the discussion, with the result that any conventional sequential structure broke down.' But as the task progressed 'a form of structure emerged': 'subjects would complete an individual message' and 'then pause to read the contributions of other group members'. In effect, the condition 'encouraged subjects to devise a form of delayed-action turn-taking'. Request-and-capture (in which subjects could take the turn from someone else whenever they wanted to) 'did least well'. In this condition, 'a group member could only get the turn by wresting it from another, thereby preventing the latter from proceeding. Delayed-action turn-taking was therefore impossible'. Additionally, as 'turn-giving was typically quite involuntary', 'instead of acquiescing to an involuntary change of turn subjects often tried immediately to recapture it'. This meant that 'turns of only one or two characters duration were common'.[10]

Berry (2011), on the other hand, argued that the absence of turn-taking can have advantages:

> **"** Temporal independence of communication (resulting from computer mediation) changes the patterns of work, decision making, and under-standings about the work and the relationships between the individu-als involved in the work. Temporal independence here refers to the fact that in cmc turn-taking, usual in ftf communication, need not be observed, so that multiple threads from different contributors can occur simultaneously. Some people enjoy this, others find it uncomfortable; it also changes understandings because a message is often read after comments from others have been read.[11]

Another aspect of temporal independence is that 'members can manage multi-thread dialogues over extended time frames. The process requires members to be cognizant of and incorporate past, posted information and decisions into current dialogue'.[12] One possible effect of these differences is an assumption of greater mutual understanding, which can sometimes be inaccurate.[13]

> **"** In the kind of conference calls I do, although there can be 12 or 13 people taking part, during the bulk of the call there is no problem about who should speak. That is because one person is the obvious expert on the topic and the rest of us are there to be informed by him or her. During the question-and-answer session at the end, two or three people can want to jump in with a question at the same time; then people just have to be self-disciplined and take it in turn.
>
> (Author's interview with a fund manager)

Ftf, communicators distribute communicative control, that is, determine how 'air time' is allocated. They may compete by sending messages implicitly designed to obtain control, or one participant may claim control and the other or others implicitly concede. Messages designed to obtain control include formal terms of address and pronoun usage, doing most of the talking, initiating topics, posing questions, asking further questions before the last one has been answered, interrupting more, determining the 'agenda' and when to end the encounter, and exhibiting a relaxed posture (arms akimbo, reclining or leaning backwards, legs open).[14] These control messages limit the options available to other participants. It is likely that communicators usually seek optimal control distribution rather than dominance, but there are exceptions.

It is likely that email, for instance, reduces the capacity for exerting communicative control, as several of the techniques used ftf are not available: doing most of the 'talking', asking further questions before the last one has been answered, interrupting, and exhibiting a relaxed posture are techniques that cannot be used in email. To date, research does not seem to have identified any alternative for these. Taking control in email requires explicit verbalization, and that is more likely to be challenged than the more subtle techniques used ftf.

Summary

Interactions can be regarded as units of communication that have their own structure and duration and vary in terms of how much initiative, creativity, elaboration and conformity characterize them.

Ftf and cmc interactions differ not only in the availability of non-verbal behaviours, but also in the implications of time constraints, the frequency of implicit rather than explicit responding, and in the methods used for and effectiveness of turn-taking and exerting communicative control.

5.2 INTERACTION SKILLS

To interact effectively at work in the many complex situations that arise in working life depends on overcoming communication barriers. This section describes those barriers and shows ways to overcome them and develop interaction skills. It covers competence in communication, ethical communication, achieving clarity, grounding, communication accommodation, uncertainty management, taking the perspective of others, developing shared mindfulness and sharing reality. Findings on the impact of cmc on communication competence, ethical communication, grounding, communication accommodation and uncertainty management are given under each of these headings; further findings on adapting for cultural difference and for different communication modes are given at the end of the section.

Communication barriers

For people to communicate fully, there are significant barriers to be over-come. 'Human communication is intrinsically fallible, whether we are aware of it or not.'[15] Miscommunication – not expressing what we really mean, not understanding what others are trying to express – is much more common than most people realize. Ironically, we tend to be more aware of the possibility of miscommunication, and therefore perhaps more likely to overcome the barriers, in unusual rather than everyday situations – for example, when interacting with someone whose first language is different from ours. The barriers are of three kinds:

- Barriers inherent in the basic processes: poor encoding by the sender, noise, channel distortion (common in videoconferencing) and percep-tual blocking or poor decoding by the receiver.
- Emotional and attitudinal barriers.
- In intergroup encounters (interactions between people from different backgrounds), barriers due to the differences in the importance of context, the accepted sequence of types of content, directness, relative emphasis on content or relationship, emotional display rules and body language, the cognitive difficulties of following the communication rules of other groups and understanding other groups' values, the tendency not to treat members of other groups as individu-als, and negative emotions provoked by inter-group encounters.

> To learn more about how physical and psychological factors can create communication barriers, visit the companion website... 5.2.1.

Furthermore, both physical factors (such as brain chemistry) and psychological factors (such as personality) can create communication barri-ers.

Competence in communication

When a researcher undertook a set of interviews with employees of an organization, the following emerged as the behaviours they perceived as competent or incompetent. Those most often mentioned are given first. What emerges clearly from a reading of the list is how few of the perceived competent behaviours are not either actual communication behaviours or dependent on them:

- Listening: 'strong listening skills', 'ability to paraphrase while listening' versus 'not listening to the other's point of view', 'formulates responses while you are talking', 'no empathic communication'.

- Friendly, personable behaviour: 'sense of humour', 'sensitivity', 'reasonable', 'warm'.
- Successful behaviour: 'dedicated', enthusiastic, persistent.
- Good leadership skills: 'works by example', uses innovation, successful delegator, maintains authority without distance, effective goal-setting abilities, knows how to hire competent people versus 'can't implement the concept', 'makes promises he can't keep', 'doesn't hire super employees because afraid for own job'.
- Understands human nature: consistency, dealing with people versus can't work with women, is racist and is sexist.
- Motivation: ability to motivate self and others – can energize people, creates positive environment, is a team player/builds team spirit.
- Professionalism: maintains a professional demeanour, has a professional air, versus brash, rude, intimidating, manipulative, jokes are offensive.
- Organizational involvement: willingness to learn, knowledgeable about the job, values training for self and employees versus doesn't go beyond the job, doesn't take chances, doesn't seize the opportunity to grow professionally.
- Organized: pays attention to details, complete preparation.
- Feedback: responds with positive before negative statement, uses compliments and constructive criticism well, keeps others informed of the progress of the project, gives information without getting into minutiae and telling more than they need to know versus can't see the value of telling others what you see and hear, no positive feedback, telling others what they want to hear, not aware of others' feedback.
- Interaction skills: ability to negotiate and coordinate; also to socialize; 'ease at communication, communication focuses on the situation, no games playing'; versus 'little or no interpersonal skills, socially inept, "doesn't know how to talk to people", doesn't convey changes in the contract to those who would carry them out'.
- Effective verbal style: comes to the point, articulate, clear and concise, doesn't raise voice, doesn't lose emotions, succinct in verbal style.
- Ability to demonstrate knowledge of the business to superiors.[16]

Communication barriers are overcome by competence in communication, which entails following basic rules that guide all social interaction, such as making yourself clear and being polite (which were explained in Chapter 4) and by acting ethically, grounding, accommodating, taking the perspective of others, adjusting for cultural difference, developing shared mindfulness, managing uncertainty, and communicating strategically.

Competence in communication can be understood in terms of effectiveness (achieving goals) and appropriateness (matching others' expectations and behaviours). These may apply to communication both within and between cultures. However, what counts as competent communication may differ from culture to culture and from organization to organization. For instance, skilled verbal behaviour is more highly valued by American workers than their Chinese counterparts.[17] At work, competent communication is adapted at least in part to the organization's preferred style. To adapt successfully, a person must understand the accepted guidelines. Research has shown that employees clearly recognize the rules for competent communication in their organization.[18]

Supervisor communicator competence accounted for 68 per cent of the variance in subordinate communication satisfaction and nearly 18 per cent of the variance in subordinate job satisfaction, a study found.[19] Call centre agents' sales effectiveness is linked to their communication competence: the most effective agents speak at an appropriate rate, emphasize important points with changes in pitch and volume, acknowledge or paraphrase what the customer said, use short, affirmative words and sounds to indicate that they are listening to the customer and use language the customer can understand.[20]

Interviewees' communication competence has also been shown to be critical to recruiters' hiring decisions. General interpersonal skills, self-confidence and taking an active role, together with interview presentation skills covering positive language, future career goals, verbal fluency, self-awareness, preparation and giving focused answers, are all strong influences on recruiters' view of candidates' hireability. However, when candidates show weaknesses in general interpersonal skills, the recruiters attribute it mainly to the interview situation. When they appear to lack interview presentation skills, on the other hand, recruiters blame it on a lack of ability or effort of the candidate.[21]

A study in two multinational companies (MNCs) that have BPO sites in India and the Philippines revealed a problematic stakeholder understanding of what to look for in language ability when recruiting staff; it also revealed the problematic use of language assessment tools and practices in terms of validity, reliability, practicality, and fairness. It was argued that this unfortunate combination may be resulting in unreasonable language assessment 'gatekeeping' to BPO industry employment.[22]

In general, people who are competent communicators in ftf interpersonal communication are also competent in mediated interpersonal communication, a study comparing mobile phone, instant messaging and ftf communication found, although in the case of mediated communication, media efficacy (confidence in using the medium), social presence and the level of concern to maintain a relationship played a role.[23] However, collaborative communication and global interconnectivity create a need for new communication competencies that encompass technology, intergroup relations, non-verbal and chronemic awareness, relational competence and more, according to a content analysis of articles from popular press and practitioner-oriented business periodicals. These new competency requirements are as follows:

- Relationship and interpersonal communication, which refers to 'communication skills that assist individuals in initiating, maintaining, or disengaging from work-related relationships'. These include 'networking, conflict management skills, communication in relationships with a power differential, small talk and rapport building'.
- Mediated communication, which refers to 'individuals' ability to use communication technologies appropriately and effectively'. Examples include 'willingness and ability to participate in online training, using interactive media (e.g. podcasts, blogging, video), following the rules of etiquette when using technology, using online social networking appropriately to facilitate work, and balancing stress and productivity while digitally connected'.
- Intergroup communication, which refers to skills that help people to communicate 'within and across groups'. These include 'intergenerational communication skills, cross-cultural communication ability, team effectiveness, bilingual skills, and sensitivity to the global nature of organizing'.
- Communicating enthusiasm, creativity and entrepreneurial spirit 'enable individuals to communicate their enthusiasm and passion for their jobs, companies, and products or ideas'. These competencies include 'engaging others to embrace ideas; demonstrating a positive attitude and willingness to innovate; and the ability to motivate others'.[24]

Non-verbal communication skills also have a place in the requirements for contemporary interpersonal communication competence, presumably because most people still work in 'workplaces', even though they may communicate as much or more with people in other places. Non-verbal skills 'assist individuals in managing a diversity of non-verbal behaviours important in the workplace' and include 'the ability to use time appropriately (time management and punctuality)', 'appropriate dress', 'physical arrangement of the workspace' and 'the use of humour'. Speaking and listening skills 'assist individuals in public presentation and active listening tasks in the business context'. These include 'facilitation (either of group discussions or meetings)'; 'public speaking'; and 'listening to others' ideas'.[25]

Ethical communication

An agreed set of ethics governing communication enhances mutual understanding and reduces the scope for misunderstanding and conflict. At work, however, people are not always able to be 'autonomous moral agents, acting on the basis of their own values alone'. Organizational and small-group influences are strong. 'As an administrative and functional structure established to facilitate group activity, an organization by its nature places restrictions on individual autonomy.' There are several dimensions of organizational influence, including 'explicit policy directives from the management' and the influence of the small group in which people perform their work tasks. This influence consists of norms (social rules) for ethical behaviour. Other types of social influence that limit individuals' autonomy in ethical matters at work include 'competitive', 'occupational' and 'legal' pressures.[26] In determining whether an act is right or wrong, whereas the powerless focus on the consequences, the powerful focus on whether rules and principles are violated; except, that is, when rule-based decisions threaten the self-interests of the powerful.[27]

According to a study, if an ethical issue is perceived as important, the majority of people say they would probably not behave unethically, but that they would be more likely to if the issue was perceived as unimportant. Evaluations of importance, however, are significantly affected only by awareness of the consequences of the behaviour and not by other factors.[28]

Attitudes (favourable or unfavourable evaluations) towards a behaviour and personal normative beliefs (sense of moral obligation) are significant predictors of intention to behave ethically or unethically when using information technology. Computer-mediated group discussion impacts on an individual's ethical behavioural intention, though it depends on the situation: in some situations, discussion increases individuals' ethical intentions but in others it decreases them. An individual's attitude (toward ethical behaviour), personal normative beliefs, ego strength, **locus of control**, perceived importance and gender also affect them.[29]

Both moral and circumstantial factors influence cmc ethics, studies have shown. The concepts of justice, fairness and moral rightness influence Japanese students' ethical judgements in all ICT-related ethical dilemmas; legal obligations and benefits to society have a weaker impact.[30] A further influence is personality: traits such as agreeableness, conscientiousness and emotional stability are significantly and negatively correlated with unethical internet behaviour in university students.[31]

Achieving clarity

Clear communication is often an important communication objective, especially in work-based situations where the requirements of the task demand it. If, for instance, instructions are unclear, the person giving them depends on the person they are being given to second-guessing their meaning, and that can lead to them not being carried out fully or well.

In all modes, clear communication requires the sender of a message to state his or her points concisely and precisely, adjust to the other person's level of understanding without being demeaning, simplify language, explain or avoid jargon, avoid slang, start from where the other person is 'at', use progressive approximations, divide explanations into smaller, more specific units, repeat in alternative ways, get the other person to ask questions, give short answers, stop after a partial reply and wait for their response and check understanding to ensure messages are communicated clearly and completely: for example by asking 'Am I being clear?', 'Will you say it back to me in your own words?', 'Let me show you what I mean', 'Why don't you give it a try now?'.

In speech, clarity can often be improved by slowing down, but not speaking louder, and by using gestures and facial expressions that match the words. (Where clarity is less of an issue, a greater richness of expression can be achieved by gestures and facial expressions that complement rather than reinforce the words.)

In writing, checking for the appropriateness of language in different situations and editing to clear up mistakes or imprecision are needed for clarity. Robbins (1990) comments that the ability to write clear communications is a skill: 'people who have this skill know the particular sequence of action to be taken to propose a project or summarise a report. They can separate primary from secondary ideas. They can organise their thoughts in a logical manner. They can simplify convoluted ideas'.[32]

Clarity and consideration are opposing communicative principles. They often clash, for to be polite often entails being ambiguous, while to be straightforward can be offensive. For example many tactics water down the intent behind speech acts. Thus the imperative 'I want the report by 3 p.m.' is clear but brusquely offensive, but the alternative 'If it's not too much trouble, could you get me that report by around 3 or so?' is so vague as to diminish the likelihood of the report being done on time. 'This clash between message clarity and consideration is particularly

People who use IM on a frequent basis often use bad grammar, poor punctuation and improper abbreviations in formal writing. According to Lee (2002), 'papers are being written with shortened words, improper capitalization and punctuation, and characters like &, $ and @. The ability to separate formal and informal English declines the more people use instant messages, while heavy IM use actually changes the way people read words on a page.'[33] Carlo and Yoo (2007) responded more favourably, describing cmc as a 'different form of life' (set of daily practical interactions and activities) than ftfc. This new online form of life shapes people's sense making and the way they use language, resulting in emerging new grammars of cmc.[34]

What examples of these changes have you noticed?

crucial in organizational contexts – where many applications of cmc exist ... given organizations' intrinsic emphasis on productivity and performance goals, the likely tendency is for efficiency constraints to eclipse the need for consideration, but with dysfunctional consequences.'[35]

Moreover, important though clarity and politeness are, they are not by themselves enough for communication to be really effective. Additional competencies and skills are needed.

Grounding

Grounding is an important process for communicators' ability to achieve mutual understanding. To coordinate or cooperate or even to communicate effectively, interactors need and assume a vast amount of shared information or **common ground** – that is, mutual knowledge, beliefs and assumptions: 'to co-ordinate on process, they need to update their common ground moment by moment. All collective actions are built on common ground and its accumulation'. In effect, communication is not possible without a minimal stock of common ground. Because people know that understanding can never be perfect, they use what is known as the 'grounding criterion': the belief that they both or all have understood what the person speaking or otherwise contributing means, at least sufficiently for current purposes. For a question, sentence or other contribution to be grounded, it must be both presented and accepted and in addition an expression of acceptance must be given; that is, people often use a higher grounding criterion than negative evidence, looking rather for an acknowledgement, a further contribution that shows that the receiver has understood their contribution or that they are still paying attention.[36]

> *A team leader sent an email to one of her team, with copies to the other four members. It read: 'We need to do some more work on the wording of the "Our Services" part of the corporate brochure. Please let me have your thoughts.' Only the person to whom the email had been sent, not those copied in, responded, although she had intended her instruction to be acted on by all members of the team. She had sent it to the person up to then responsible for the section in question and copied it to the others with an idea that that would make clear that he was still primarily responsible, but her intention had been misunderstood. How should the team leader have communicated with her team on this?*

Grounding can often require a process of repair, where there is evidence that a contribution has not been understood, or even where there is a lack of evidence that it has been understood.[37] For instance, to make sure that they have fully understood, people will ask, 'Do you mean x?', whereas to make sure that they have heard the exact words used, they will say, 'Could you say that again?'

People try to ground with as little combined effort as possible. What takes effort, however, changes a great deal with the communication mode. Differences such as in copresence, visibility, audibility, co-temporality, simultaneity, sequentiality, reviewability and revisability impose different effort costs on the grounding process. For instance: starting a communication 'costs' more effort in email than ftfc; delaying a response (in order to plan or revise) 'costs' more in ftfc than email because of the way delays are interpreted (though delays in both media are interpreted, the 'normal' time lag is much longer in email); making an error probably 'costs' more in email than ftfc because people make more allowances for the way the demands of ftfc lead to errors.

> *A contract worker received a call from her agent to tell her that she had succeeded in a job application.*
> *'They want you to start straight away.'*
> *'Do you mean tomorrow?'*
> *'No, not quite that soon, but on Monday.'*
> *(Source: overheard by the author)*

Ways of grounding whatever the mode or purpose:

- Both parties should take responsibility for achieving grounding, not leave it to the other party.
- Both should be aware of the possibility of misunderstanding and take action: the speaker or sender should test for it; the receiver should ask appropriate questions.
- The parties must coordinate on process, so that each person only contributes when the other party is attending to, receiving and trying to understand what is said or written. The receiver must guide by giving evidence of this.

Research on managers' use of cmc in natural settings suggests that having common ground with the recipients of their communication may be an important factor influencing how effectively they communicate. Managerial communication was shown to be more effective when the recipients already knew what managers were referring to. Other influences on managerial communication effectiveness were using traditional modes (ftf, telephone and written memo) to build or share understanding of an issue, using leaner media, and complying with communication procedures by choosing the expected mode of communication.[38]

Turn-taking, which was explained in Section 5.1, is important for grounding. For example, turn-taking helps to coordinate the speaker's action with the listener's attention. Communication settings such as instant messaging that disrupt the regulation of turn-taking impede grounding, both by undermining the construal of meaning and by increasing how often purpose-designed signals are needed in order to coordinate the speaker's action with the listener's attention. Hancock and Dunham (2001) argued that in task-oriented, text-based exchanges, an explicit turn marker is needed to facilitate the construal of meaning and reduce the number of verbal coordination devices required to ground communication.[39]

Communication accommodation

In interactions people constantly make adjustments in order to create, maintain, increase or decrease social distance from an interaction partner. To decrease social distance, they adjust to be more like the other person, to increase it they adjust to be more unlike them. Accent, speed, loudness, vocabulary, grammar, voice tone and gestures are all among the aspects they may adjust in ftfc. These are ways for speakers to signal their attitudes toward each other – to gain approval or identify on the one hand or to distinguish themselves or accentuate their own group membership on the other;[40] alternatively they may make these adjustments to try to achieve smoother or clearer communication. Again, to varying but considerable degrees people using cmc match linguistic styles, word counts, pronoun patterns and verb tenses when they want to identify with or gain approval from the person they are communicating with.

Several points show how powerful the tendency to accommodate can be:

- First, almost immediately after a social interaction begins, verbal and non-verbal behaviours become synchronized.
- Second, even in asocial contexts, individuals tend to produce utterances that match the grammatical structure of sentences they have recently heard or read.
- Third, **convergence** occurs even when people are speaking on the telephone to an answering machine: individuals modify their language choices as well as some message features in order to display similarity to the recorded message.
- Finally, in a study to test whether linguistic style matching occurs naturally in written formats, students were found to match the language style of questions they were responding to; the researchers concluded that 'the behavior seems to be automatic': participants could not deliberately increase how much they matched the style or content of the questions.[41]

The importance of accommodation is suggested by findings that the cohesiveness of groups engaged in an information search task is related to how closely the members match linguistic styles. This applies to both ftf groups and those working via text-based cmc. In the ftf groups, but not the cmc-using groups, matching linguistic styles also predicts how well the group performs the information search task. Again, successful negotiations are associated with higher aggregate levels of linguistic style matching compared to unsuccessful negotiations. This is due to extreme variations in the level of linguistic style matching during unsuccessful negotiations, with negotiators unable to maintain the consistent levels of rapport and coordination that occur in successful negotiations.[42]

When they interact with strangers, people have expectations about the optimal amount of accommodation they expect from particular others or in general; these expectations are based on stereotypes about outgroup members as well as prevailing social norms. When an interaction partner does not accommodate – when their communicative behaviour is inappropriately adjusted for the other participants in an interaction – how those others evaluate the interaction depends on what attribution they make: if they infer a negative motive for the problematic behaviour, their evaluations of both the interaction and the speaker are less positive than if they infer either a positive motive or a lack of intentionality. Under-accommodation is consistently evaluated less positively than over-accommodation, probably because of the inferred motive.[43]

There are cultural differences in expectations about communication accommodation. Some participants in international business meetings involving both native and non-native speakers of English show an awareness of the need to adjust language for an international audience and an intuitive understanding of some of the ways this can be achieved through normalization and convergence strategies. Normalization strategies aim to make talk appear meaningful, orderly and normal 'in the face of sometimes abnormal and extraordinary linguistic behavior'; for instance participants may concentrate on content, ignoring linguistic anomalies, and refraining from correcting them.[44] However, such adjustments are not always easy. For example, one study found that although native speakers of English attempted to accommodate non-native speakers during negotiations, there was significant variation in the way that individual participants chose their strategies and approached accommodation. Although the native speakers understood the need for adapting in intercultural communication they found it difficult to accommodate effectively for non-native speakers.[45]

Accommodation is quite 'normal' in cmc. Groups who communicate by email display growing accommodation in both content and style.[46] Similarly, there is a general tendency toward convergence in both message length and response time of individual contributions in instant messaging,[47] while people alter their

> *Enjoy a video about how not to accommodate for people from another culture: visit the companion website... 5.2.2.*
>
> *What are the learning points it makes?*

rates of communication by cmc to match those of a correspondent who responds at a consistently slower pace, an experiment showed.[48]

Uncertainty management

As Chapter 3 explained, to interact effectively people need to predict others' attitudes and behaviours; if they are uncertain about these factors, they are less effective and may experience considerable anxiety. To reduce uncertainty, they collect information about or from the other person. An important theory, uncertainty reduction theory,[49] predicts that people use passive, active and interactive strategies to reduce uncertainty: a passive strategy means watching people as they interact with third parties, an active strategy means finding out as much as possible from outside sources and an interactive strategy means seeking the information directly from the 'target' person during the exchange. Which of these strategies are used and when depends in part on politeness and the requirements of behaving appropriately in particular situations. Interactive strategies for uncertainty reduction require direct and obtrusive exchanges with targets: the uncertainty reducer can expect to have to identify falsifications, distortions or omissions of information, ask questions and self-disclose in order to induce the other to reciprocally self-disclose. Directness and obtrusiveness tend to mean that interactive strategies are considered impolite ftf, and so are often avoided or ineffective.

In general, people feel greater uncertainty about people they interact with by cmc than they do about people they meet ftf. As uncertainty reduction theory would predict, the greater level of uncertainty experienced in cmc leads people to undertake more uncertainty reduction strategies. For example, people interacting by a form of cmc similar to IM exchange more personal information in initial interactions than those interacting ftf. They use a greater proportion of self-disclosure and question-asking and as a result gain more in attributional confidence over the course of initial conversations. These direct strategies lead to the partners judging one another's conversational effectiveness as higher.[50] Again, both ftf and video-mediated speakers use visual cues to check for mutual understanding. When they cannot see each other, such checks need to be conducted verbally, which leads to widely observed effects: dialogues are prolonged and participants interrupt one another more. However, although video supplies visual cues in much the same way as ftf, it still leads to prolonged and interrupted dialogues. Users of video also gaze far more overall than ftf communicators. These findings suggest that when speakers are not physically copresent, even though they can see their interaction partners, they are less confident in general that they have mutual understanding. This uncertainty leads them to compensate by trying to obtain more information about the other person.[51]

Uncertainty reducing strategies may, however, be limited by cmc settings. Passive strategies require public settings and so are not always available by cmc. Active strategies, too, can be more difficult to deploy in cmc than ftf, as they require certain resources that may be less available online. Specifically, for the purpose of asking third parties for information, cmc relationships offer a more limited network of people to ask than ftf associations. Verbal interrogation and self-disclosure, however, are uncertainty reduction strategies that are as readily deployed in cmc as ftf. Thus in cmc people use more interactive strategies and, research has shown, unlike in ftf, in cmc interactive strategies are generally considered polite (thought by their partners to be appropriate) and effective.

In the words of the researchers, 'the restrictions of cmc prompt users' adaptation to the medium through modification of uncertainty reduction behaviour. Bereft of most non-verbal cues, cmc partners forgo the peripheral questions and answers that mark the normal superficial exchanges among new acquaintances in ftf encounters. Instead, cmc interactants appeared to employ a greater proportion of more direct, interactive uncertainty reduction strategies'.[52]

Figure 5.1 shows how people tend to choose different uncertainty reduction strategies when interacting ftf or by cmc.

Figure 5.1 How different modes affect choice of uncertainty reduction strategies

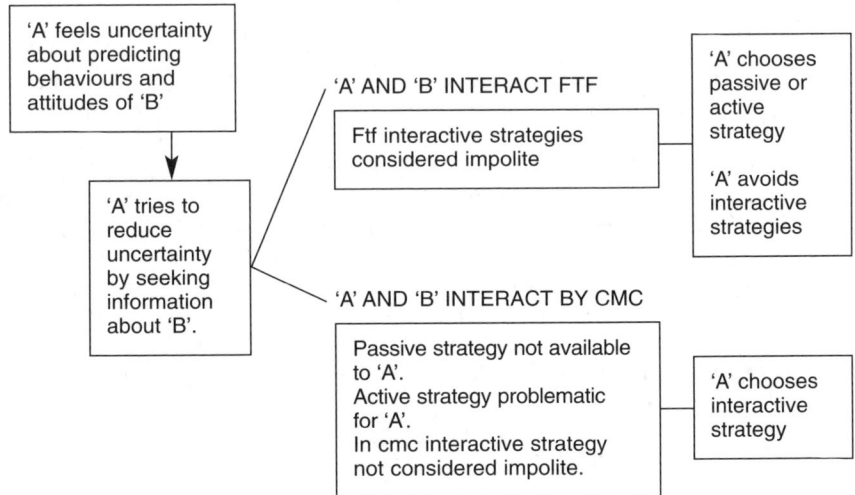

Taking the perspective of others

Perspective taking is 'the process of approaching an interaction from another's point of view'. According to perspective-taking models, full communication requires that communicators identify or create shared contexts or points of view. Shared contexts are constructed, at least in part, through a process of reciprocal perspective-taking: both speakers and hearers must try to experience the situation as it is experienced by the other participants. By means of this reciprocal process, the shared communicative context is continuously expanded and refined. Communicators generally do tailor their speech or written words to their addressees, and doing so is required for communication competence.[53]

Developing shared mindfulness

Shared mindfulness is defined as 'a state of mindfulness achieved conjointly, whereby, in the communicative interaction, the individuals involved are in an active state of attending, responding, and perceiving information correctly. As a result, they are continually updating, attuned, and open to incoming data that are unexpected, disconfirming, improbable, implicit, and/or contested'. Mindfulness is defined as 'a psychological state in which individuals engage in active information processing while performing their current tasks such that they are actively analyzing, categorizing, and making distinctions in

---

BOX 5.2 HOW TO BUILD SHARED MINDFULNESS

- Seek the input or opinion of partner, and identify/verbalize new, missing or discrepant information.
- Reason from a positive perspective, presenting thoughts, ideas, input, and opinion from a perspective of what is available and possible, noticing and accepting discrepant and disconfirming information.
- Perceive multiple perspectives and alternative courses of action.
- Project thoughts and feelings, for instance by using diagrams, figures, or body movements to accurately translate verbal messages.
- Use non-verbal projection, including puzzling looks, furrowed brow, scratching head.
- Acknowledge partner communication either via metacommunication (e.g. yes, uh-huh, right) or by a verbal response that indicates the information was received and critically processed.
- Use participative and conditional terminology, such as 'What if...?', 'Suppose we ...?'.
- Demonstrate fluid turn taking.
- Show agreement.[54]

data'. 'If mindfulness represents the active information processing at the individual intrapersonal level, shared mindfulness represents this activity at the interpersonal interaction level.'[55] Shared mindfulness has been shown to lead to better decision-making by two interacting people, including in crisis situations. There are specific communication behaviours associated with the construction of shared mindfulness in an interaction: Box 5.2 gives a list based on a study of an aeroplane cockpit crisis simulation; these methods seem applicable with both ftfc and cmc.

Sharing reality

Over time, research suggests, members of groups develop shared reality. As long ago as the 1930s, Sherif (1935) demonstrated convergence in group members' judgements of ambiguous perceptual stimuli.[56] More recently a similar coming-together has been demonstrated for group members' strategic **orientations** (attitudes and intentions) for solving problems, that is their tendency to seek and adopt risky or conservative solutions.[57] Figure 5.2 shows how reality sharing is understood to function.

An example of reality sharing would occur if two colleagues in a work-place were discussing a new employee and, noticing that the first colleague expresses liking for the new employee, the second colleague tuned her message by describing the employee's recent work in a favourable light. Later, she may remember the new employee's work more positively as a

Figure 5.2 Shared reality theory

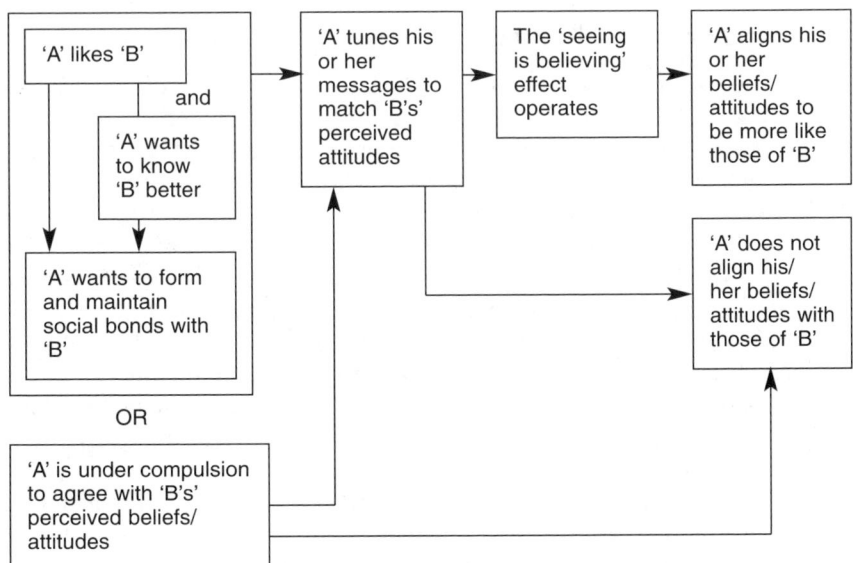

consequence of her audience-tuned message: when people tailor a message to suit an audience, as they often do, their subsequent memories and impressions about the communication topic change to correspond to what they said in the message. This is known as the 'saying-is-believing' effect. The effect occurs both with one-person audiences and in group contexts when the audience explicitly validates communicators' messages.[58] However, the communicators' motives affect whether this memory bias results: it is more likely when they make the adjustment because they want to develop common ground with the audience, less likely when they do it to comply with a blatant demand.[59]

Social tuning and shared reality

Because sharing reality fosters social bonds, it follows that people experience a heightened desire to develop shared reality with another person to the extent that they are motivated to get along or foster social bonds with this person (i.e. they possess what is called affiliative motivation toward this person). One way for individuals to achieve this shared understanding is to 'tune' their social beliefs toward the views of the other. That is, when affiliative motivation is high as opposed to low, individuals may attempt to achieve a sense of shared reality with others by adjusting their views, including their view of themselves, to the apparent views of others.[60]

> To learn more about social tuning, visit the companion website... 5.2.3.

Adapting for cultural difference

To work successfully with people from diverse backgrounds, communicators need to achieve intercultural communication competence. That means they need to perceive 'different' others accurately, use inclusive language, manage their own anxiety that may be aroused by intercultural encounters, communicate openness and avoid ethnocentrism.

Ethnocentrism is defined as using one's own set of standards and customs to judge all people, often unconsciously. Since most people dislike the feeling of being judged itself, and since ethnocentrics usually are negative in their judgements of people from other cultures or ethnicities, ethnocentricity disrupts communication. Ethnorelativity means the opposite of ethnocentricity; it refers to being comfortable with many standards and customs and to having an ability to adapt behaviour and judgements to a variety of interpersonal settings.

Knowledge and motivation have been identified as important components of intercultural communication competence, together with listening skills, prior cross-cultural experiences, having a global outlook as opposed to an ethnocentric one, and an 'other-centred' style of communication.[61]

Adapting for different communication modes

Among new users of different kinds of cmc media, perceptions of communication outcomes – perceived satisfaction, decision confidence, immediacy, effectiveness and system ease of use – differ by cmc medium. Slow feedback rates and the lack of automatic message notification systems in some cmc lower new user satisfaction and may hinder the perception of the medium's capacity to facilitate smooth interaction. In fact 'the simultaneity of messages and interaction are essential to satisfaction'.[62] However, novice users of text-based cmc, though initially performing less well than spoken interaction partners on collaborative problem-solving tasks, achieve effective communication and collaboration after a 'relatively modest' amount of experience.

> To learn more about these and other ways to work successfully with people from diverse backgrounds, visit the companion website... 5.2.4.
>
> Why and how do intercultural communication and intercultural communication competence differ according to the context (business, medicine, law, religion or politics)? Answer for your own field of study.

A 1997 synthesis of the experimental literature on computer-mediated literature on ftf versus cmc found that 'in general, discussions on CMC take longer, but produce more ideas, and have greater equality of participation. There is reduced normative pressure and poorer comprehension of the discussion in CMC'.[63]

To adapt for different modes, communicators change how they give instructions, use a mixture of modes, adjust similarly to how they would adjust between spoken and written communication outside of cmc and use a wide range of strategies when using cmc for learning:

- In cmc, communicators change the way they give instructions and interact, adopting a precise, highly specified style of giving directions which require little interpretation by addressees. This concise style of communication is rarely found in ftf or spoken interactions.[64]
- Dixon and Pantelli (2010) argued that technology-mediated interactions do not substitute for but rather complement ftf interactions: that most teams, for example, use a mixture of ftf and mediated interactions. In an in-depth case study of an inter-organizational centre of excellence, they found evidence that the formation of 'virtual continuities' mitigated the effects that create discontinuities or boundaries; these are perceived boundaries created by differences in physical location, time-zone difference, language and cultural differences, professional and organizational affiliation in virtuality. That is to say, by combining ftf and

    technology-mediated interactions rather than by technology-mediated interactions alone, people mitigate the subjective impression of boundaries within the team.[65]

- Rettie (2009) in a study of mobile phone communication, which permits both synchronous (voice) and asynchronous (text) communication, found that interactional norms, rather than the technology, determine the important distinction between synchronous and asynchronous interaction. That is to say, people adjust their communication behaviour according to their usual norms for synchronous and asynchronous interaction in the same way as they would for the differences between conversational (ftf) and written communication (by letters). This means that some, at least, of past findings about the differences between these modes of communication may well apply to mediated communication.[66]

- Learners use a wide array of communication strategies during task-based cmc; and the cmc environment shapes this use. Learners also employ various strategies to compensate for the limitations of cmc.[67]

According to St. Amant (2002) online communication technology makes intercultural communication faster and more direct than was ever before possible, but, in doing so, it may also amplify cultural rhetorical differences.[68] Research has found that differences in ftfc between cultures – specifically, between people from high-context and low-context cultures – also appear in cmc. For example, Indians (from a high-context culture) disclose less private information and rely more on non-verbal communication (emoticons) than Germans (from a low-context culture). This suggests that intercultural communication skills for ftf interactions can readily be adapted for cmc.[69]

Summary

This section of the chapter shows that there are barriers to communication which can be overcome through the use of clarity and politeness. It also demonstrates that skilled interaction is ethical and responsible and uses techniques such as grounding, communication accommodation, management of uncertainty, perspective taking, the development of shared mindfulness, sharing reality and adjusting for cultural difference and the communication mode.

6 DEMOGRAPHY, CULTURE, SITUATION AND MODE AS INFLUENCES ON COMMUNICATION

Chapters 3, 4 and 5 have explained the processes 'universally' involved in interpersonal communication; the next two chapters highlight the effects of difference, distinguishing difference that originates in factors external to the individual communicator's psychology in this chapter from intrapersonal factors, which are discussed in Chapter 7.

BOX 6.1

'The particular mechanisms by which cognition is accomplished are themselves important determinants of the outcome of the process. For example, particularities of the structure of human memory, and of the processes of encoding and retrieval, can affect what will or will not be recalled.

Prof Francisco J Varela, a renowned French scientist in the field of neurodynamics ... said that even while visualizing the same object, like a piece of paper, different people report "differences in brain function". If people's brains have "different" ways of perceiving a seemingly innocuous object like a piece of paper then what tricks do the brains play while generating meaning from complex constructs or stress-inducing face-to-face interactions?'[1]

As Box 6.1 suggests, there are significant individual differences in social cognition; these in turn lead to individual differences in self-presentation and interaction. Demographic differences among people – differences of age, sex and gender, education and ethnicity – and cultural differences undoubtedly affect how they communicate, though there are still many unanswered questions about precisely how these differences affect it. Section 6.1 will discuss the communication effects of sex/gender (as an example of a demographic variable) and culture (as an example of a social factor); Section 6.2 explains social influence theory, which is an important theory about how these social factors have their

On completing your study of this chapter you will be able to explain and apply the implications of:

- How demography, culture and the situation act as influences on communication processes.
- Social influence theory.
- Leading theories about how communication mode impacts on communication.

You will also be able to:

- Give examples of how sex/gender and culture affect communication
- Describe issues in intercultural communication that arise from differences in how people communicate that are related to demographic and cultural differences.

effect. Section 6.3 analyses the effect of different situations and modes and presents mainstream theories about how mediation impacts on communication.

6.1 DEMOGRAPHY AND CULTURE AS INFLUENCES ON COMMUNICATION PROCESSES

'The groups to which people belong, whether by assignment or by choice, will be massively significant in determining their life experiences.'[2] A group in this sense is any collection of individuals who categorize themselves (and whom, usually, other people categorize) similarly. Membership of demographic groups or categories is largely assigned, not chosen: our sex, age and ethnicity are outside our own control but they significantly affect many processes in communication. Culture and social class are also important influences that are only partially controllable.

This section discusses the influence of sex/gender and culture on social cognition, self-presentation and interaction and considers how these influences vary with the communication mode.

Sex and gender

Sex is biologically determined; gender, however, is culturally constructed. Both sex and gender influence communication behaviour in sometimes similar, sometimes different, ways. Voice pitch, for instance, is primarily determined by sex; other aspects of voice, such as tone or pace, are just as strongly influenced by gender. Most research into communication behaviour has not, however, distinguished sex and gender. Subject to this limitation, we do know a good deal about how sex and gender affect communication, including social perception and self-presentation.

Sex/gender and social perception

A majority of studies have found significant sex and gender differences in how people perceive others:[3] for instance, when male and female participants attempt to identify facial emotion, males consistently find it harder to recognize emotion 'correctly', so that men are less likely than women to identify the presence of emotion in facial expressions.[4]

> For more findings that show that there are significant sex and gender differences in how people perceive others, visit the companion website... 6.1.1.

It is likely that men and women notice different cues, which then affect their overall perception of a situation. In addition to these differences in general perception, expectations can affect the way men and women perceive each other. While some studies have found that people can use cues to predict another person's gender accurately,[5] others have shown that people often make judgements based on gender expectations rather than situational cues, leading to perceptual errors: for example, how both men and women perceive women in the workplace is affected by their expectations about women's abilities to cope with certain roles,[6] and these stereotypes can persist despite evidence to the contrary.[7]

Sex/gender and self-presentation

There are significant differences in how men and women self-present, for example in body language. Some women use body language to express submissiveness – making less eye contact, for example, or standing in the background. Furthermore:

- Women smile more than men in most situations.[8]
- While both men and women use smiling as a self-presentation strategy, the situations in which they use this strategy differ, with both men and women smiling to show friendliness and approachability but women also smiling in response to gender expectations.[9]

Self-presentation differences between men and women are not confined to body language, however. When conversations are written down and all reference to gender removed, people are still very good at identifying the gender of the speakers, because language differences are easy to recognize.[10] A 1997 meta-analysis found that the language women use when they present ideas or attempt to influence others is consistently different to the language used by men, with women using less assertive language and hedging or qualifying their statements more frequently than their male counterparts.[11] A later meta-analysis did find that the use of tentative language in females is only negligibly more common than in males, except in situations with high uncertainty such as in large groups rather than pairs;[12] however, at work such situations are significant.

Certain behavioural differences in self-promotion can be attributed to women's fear of a backlash if gendered expectations are not adhered to. Fear of social penalties inhibit women's ability to self-promote; assertiveness and competitive tactics are hedged, resulting in lower outcomes.[13] Self-promotion in men, and peer-promotion in women, however, seem not to be affected by such fears.[14] While gender differences in self-presentation often result in dominating behaviour from males, it is unlikely that the cause of such behaviour is an active intention to dominate. Rather, it is possible to observe gender differences from a cross-cultural approach,[15] viewing masculine and feminine styles of discourse as two distinct cultural dialects rather than as inferior or superior ways of speaking.[16]

More recently an increase in equality may have brought about a reduction in gender-based differences in self-presentation: a 2007 meta-analysis of studies into gender and self-presentation found that the more recent the study, the less pronounced the differences are between men and women.[17] It is also hard to isolate gender as a distinct variable. Some recent studies have questioned the categorization of participants by gender in earlier research; it has been suggested, for example, that 'masculine' language could actually be language particular to a specific career or working environment, rather than to the gender of the speaker.[18]

Sex/gender and cmc

There are significant gender differences in online perceptions; for instance, when single-sex and mixed-sex pairs interact through both video and IM, the female participants report higher levels of trust in both media than men,[19] suggesting that women are more likely to perceive trust-based cues even in cmc.[20]

The question of whether cmc reduces some self-presentational differences is contested, with some studies, but not others, claiming that cmc promotes more democratic interactions, as Chapter 5 explained. However, a number of studies indicate that many gender-based self-presentational differences are carried over from face-to-face communication (ftfc) into computer-mediated communication (cmc); for instance, a

> For more evidence that there are significant gender influences on online perceptions, visit the companion website...
> 6.1.2.

direct comparison of messages from men and from women in two professional listservs found that male users were more likely to dominate discussions;[21] women showed more apologetic and self-revealing behaviour than men and men showed more assertive, authoritative and adversarial behaviour in a variety of asynchronous communication media.[22]

> *For more evidence that gender-based differences in self-presentation carry over from ftf to cmc, visit the companion website... 6.1.3.*

The online self-presentations of men and women do, however, differ from their ftf equivalents in one way: they are more affected by the sender's perceptions of the status of their sex. In enduring task groups men are more likely to seek ways to make computer-mediated interactions more like a ftf interaction, whereas women are more likely to employ strategies that maintain the reduced social cues of cmc and afford them greater potential influence in mixed-sex interactions. Women aim to 'minimise the status differentials typically present in face-to-face interactions'. Evidence that women recognize and enjoy the social benefits afforded them through reduced social cues includes the facts that women enjoy anonymity more than men and that many women perceive their contributions to be accepted more readily when working with anonymous group technology; on the other hand men exhibit a greater desire to divulge personal information that reveals their sex.[23]

Sussman and Tyson (2000) found that even though cyberspace is a context where the gender of communicators is not salient, it retains a male-dominated atmosphere, where gender differentiation and power displays in communication persist, as in other modes. Men used more words, women communicated more often than men and men tended to write more opinionated communications.[24] Herring (2008) also found that gender differences tend to disfavour women in online communication. In mixed-sex public discussion groups, females post fewer messages and are less likely to persist in posting when their messages receive no response. Even when they persist, they receive fewer responses from others (both females and males) and do not control the topic or the terms of the discussion except in groups where women make up a clear majority of participants. The lesser influence exercised by women in mixed-sex groups accounts in part for why women-centred and women-only online groups are common, whereas explicitly designated men-only groups are rare.[25]

Other studies, however, suggest that in cmc the context is a major influence. Gender-stereotypical behaviour is only found within single-gender groups (that is, when pairs of men or pairs of women interact).[26] Affiliative behaviour, too, is associated with single-gender groups, either male or female, rather than with just females.[27] These studies suggest that what changes interactive behaviour by cmc is not gender per se, but individuals' perceived importance of, and alliance with, their gender group: as gender becomes more important, so interactive behaviour conforms more to perceived gender differences. A recent study on gender and cmc confirms this, showing that when gender salience (that is, the importance of gender) is used as a variable, those strongly identifying with their gender show the most gender-stereotypical self-presentation.[28]

A further limitation on the extent of gender differences in cmc is that the expression of computer-mediated affective communication varies with the particular medium: for instance, online chat expressions vary according to whether the user is visible (via webcam) or not, as well as by gender. Men in a webcam condition used significantly less active words than men in a no-webcam condition and less than women in a webcam condition. Women in a webcam condition used significantly more emoticons than women in a no-webcam condition or men in either condition. Men and women did not differ in their use of emoticons in the no-webcam condition.[29]

Finally, gendered language in cmc discussions may be more closely related to the topic under discussion than to the gender of the participants. Gender-neutral topics were found in studies to lead to less gender-preferential language being used than gender-stereotypical topics, regardless of the gender of the participants.[30]

Culture

Culture is one way – a very important way – in which societies differ from one another. Culture can be understood primarily in a number of different ways:

1. In terms of values shared by the members of the society. A major distinction here has been drawn and partially supported by research between **collectivism** – cultures which place most value on the group – and **individualism** – cultures which place most emphasis on the independent individual. Individualist cultures are mainly Western and have been estimated to constitute less than 20 per cent of global populations. Other cultural value differences that have been identified are between 'masculine' and 'feminine' value cultures, high- and low-**uncertainty avoidance** cultures, **long- and short-term orientation** cultures and high- and low-**power distance** cultures. A refinement of the collectivist/individualist classification uses a variable seen as orthogonal to it and so distinguishes 'horizontal individualistic' people who desire to be unique and to 'do their own thing' from 'vertical individualistic' people who not only want to do their own thing but also strive to be the very best. People who are 'horizontal collectivists' cooperate with their in-groups. In contrast, 'vertical collectivists' submit to the hierarchy defined by their in-groups and are willing to sacrifice themselves for their in-groups.

2. As whether members' self-concept is highly interdependent – they see themselves primarily as members of a group – or highly independent – they see themselves primarily as individuals. This distinction corresponds to the collectivist–individualist distinction in cultural values.
3. In terms of their shared ways of viewing the world.
4. As a historically transmitted system of symbols, meanings and norms.
5. As how members of the society communicate: either assuming that their interaction partner shares most of their understanding of the context and so not stating it – 'high-context' – or not assuming that and so stating it – 'low-context' – or in a number of other ways.

Although the fourth and fifth of these ways of understanding culture are themselves theories of how culture and communication are linked, communication has also been associated with the other ways. For instance, in the 'culture as values' theory that distinguishes collectivist from individualist values, high-context communication has been linked to collectivism and low-context communication to individualism.

Broad ethnic and cultural divides are important, but culture can also be defined in much more local terms. Sociologists have studied numerous subcultures, including professional, regional, youth and class subcultures, as well as subcultures associated with hobbies, such as hiking, knitting and mushroom hunting. Cultural and subcultural differences in communication have been found in person perception, what is going on in a conversation, how situations are interpreted and responded to, whether the role of speaker or listener is more emphasized, communicator styles, messages, codes, verbal and non-verbal communication, communication rules, information-seeking, directness, facework and politeness, among others. For example even something as seemingly self-evident as what cues are relevant when determining another person's sex can vary subculturally: transgender people often view the human body in light of the possibility of transitioning between the sexes, a unique perspective that heightens their awareness of both the similarities between male and female bodies and their key differences – the body parts that are the most common barriers to 'passing'.[31]

The values-based and high- and low-context-based analyses of cultural difference have been widely criticized, primarily as over-simplifications. They 'run the risk of essentializing national culture as something fixed... Moreover, such frameworks give us, at best, a crude set of tools for analyzing culture: ... five or six dimensions vis-à-vis the 50–70 elements of culture identified by anthropologists and others interested in cross-cultural communication'. Critics also argue that these frameworks are not well-suited

To learn more about cultural and subcultural differences in communication, visit the companion website... 6.1.4.

for a range of important foci of cmc research: the multiple minority cultures within a given national culture; the third cultures and hybrid identities facilitated by intercultural flows online; and culture as something fluid and dynamic.[32] Unfortunately, however, while we have many findings based on the values and high/low-context approaches, we have as yet almost no empirical findings for interpersonal communication based on an alternative framework for culture.

Culture and social perception

Cultures can differ in what types of information are available about people in the first place. Whether normatively withheld, disregarded or simply unavailable, our perceptions of others are in part a reflection of the particular details of appearance and behaviour that we *cannot* access. 'For instance, without information about a person's skin colour, blind people's perceptions of race are significantly different from the typical sighted experience. And the type of personal information one provides to others in a knitting circle no doubt differs substantially from the type of information one provides to other members in a swingers club.' Norms regarding the acceptance of gossip, and whether it is appropriate to talk about absent individuals, may also vary substantially between subcultures, with significant influence on the impressions we form of others.[33]

Another way in which culture affects person perception is by influencing attribution: Shweder and Bourne (1982) argued that 'many non-Western cultures inculcate a holistic world view that promotes context-dependent, occasion-bound thinking', leading attributions made by members of non-Western cultures to be more external/situational (less dispositional) than those made by Westerners.[34] This is supported by Kashima et al. (1995), who 'found non-Westerners less likely to believe that others' behaviors are consistent with internal loci such as attitudes'.[35]

Again, judgements are culturally influenced. A study found that while people from Hong Kong tended to absorb the judgements of other people into their private self-definitions, especially when those judgements were made public, people from the United States showed a studied indifference to these judgements of their peers, regardless of whether those assessments were public or private, were positive or negative, or were made by qualified peers or unqualified peers. The researchers interpreted these findings in terms of face cultures (Hong Kong) and dignity cultures (USA).[36]

One explanation of how knowledge such as cultural knowledge comes to be shared is that

> *Visit the companion website... 6.1.5 for links to videos that give practical examples of how cultural differences affect business meetings.*

there is evidence that stimuli which are assumed to be experienced by one's social group are more prominent in cognition; this effect only occurs when other members of a person's social group are thought to be experiencing different stimuli.[37]

Culture and self-presentation

Examples of cultural differences affecting self-presentation include paralinguistics. Turn-taking, voice tone, speed of speech and how long one person speaks vary cross-culturally. People from collectivistic cultures distribute their turns and speaking time more evenly than those from individualistic cultures.[38] Again, for some groups, touching another person is proscribed. These groups include the people of China, Indonesia, Japan, the Philippines, Thailand, Australia, England, Germany, the Netherlands, Norway, Scotland, America, India and Pakistan. Contact groups, who use 'touch' with less inhibition, include the people of Iraq, Kuwait, Saudi Arabia, Syria, the United Arab Republic, Bolivia, Cuba, Ecuador, El Salvador, Mexico, Paraguay, Peru, Puerto Rico, Venezuela, France, Italy and Turkey.

Non-verbal expression varies from country to country; for instance, cultural display rules govern how people display emotions such as grief. Culture may also determine how individuals use personal space. People from contact cultures, such as those of the Middle East, choose closer distances, maintain more direct eye contact, touch each other more frequently and speak more loudly than those from non-contact cultures. Although the work context can over-ride cultural variations in communication,[39] there are also work-specific cultural variations. For instance, Germans expect formal work attire, terms of address and seriousness, and there is a tendency for everything to be put in writing (email flourishes), while use of the telephone is inhibited; in France there is an emphasis on written reports rather than oral presentations and on formality in work communication; in Italy there is extensive use of all personal channels of communication, including telephone and email, that can be used to bypass the formal structure. In Spain, communication is mainly oral, ftf and one-to-one, especially with the boss.

Intercultural communication

Cultural differences lead to intercultural communication issues. We know that at a level beyond their immediate control, people are influenced by whether someone they are perceiving comes from a different ethnic group. In general, people are worse at recognizing the faces of people from a different ethnicity than of those from their own 'race'. This lower recognition rate may help explain the discomfort some people feel in the presence of people from other 'races' and so contribute to poor inter-ethnic communication. (The effect is attenuated, however, when the perceiver has experienced high levels of inter-ethnic contact).[40] Again, people are more likely to recognize others' facial expressions of emotion accurately when the perceiver and expresser are from the same cultural group. Across the whole range of cultural relations between the perceiver and the expresser, people are better at identifying emotions from facial expressions of others from their ingroup than from outgroups.

Both inter-ethnic and intercultural deficiencies in social perception can be explained by studies that show that automatic forms of cognition rely heavily and uncritically on culturally available schemas and that people are more motivated to process ingroup than outgroup faces, leading to less automatic processing of ingroup than outgroup faces. We have distinct processing modes for ingroup and outgroup faces, resulting in differential identification accuracy for facial expressions.[41]

Culture, intercultural communication and cmc

There are different views on how cmc affects the cultural influences on communication and so how difficult or easy intercultural communication by cmc is. At one extreme there is a possibility that a digital culture can obliterate cultural biases, since people are totally enmeshed with the rules and roles of the digital environment. Consequently, the meanings of values, beliefs and artefacts in the digital world differ from their meanings in the real world, since digital culture eradicates real world culture. People will tend to act and behave with values and beliefs constructed in the online environment and according to its etiquette. The bias of external culture is minimal. This extreme is only likely to be reached in virtual world environments using avatars, since lack of interactivity and situated-ness prevent it in most cmc, while in media such as videoconferencing or the telephone, the individual communicator has a relatively high level of social presence.

A less extreme view is the idea that imported culture may be aligned with digital culture. As a consequence, the dialectic between external and internal culture may result in forms of integration. Therefore, the mean-ings of values, beliefs and artefacts in the digital world are somewhat simi-lar to the meanings in the real world, since there is a degree of compatibility between digital and real world culture. Cmc's internal culture is partly developed from external culture.

Finally, there is a view that digital culture may be too weak to replace the external one at all. People will act and behave online in the same manner as in the real world. Thus, the meanings of values, beliefs and artefacts in the digital world replicate the meanings in the real world, since digital culture is superseded by real world culture.[42]

Unfortunately, we have as yet very little actual evidence of the extent to which these different levels of real-world cultural displacement are occurring, though the following example suggests that it is limited. Noting that Facebook has struggled to achieve high penetration in Japan, Nozawa (2012) argued that Japanese virtual communicators seek a level of anonymity that social networking sites of Western origin make difficult. On 2ch, a Japanese discussion board, participants are oriented to anonymity – not only do 2ch participants never use actual-world names when posting their messages on a thread, there is a widely held expectation that they avoid even using *kotehan*, that is, pseudonyms. Nozawa (2012) described the character of Japanese virtual communication as having 'opacity' but contended that it is situated in local ideologies of communication. 'In the Japanese virtual, opacity is simply normal and ordinary.'[43]

We do know that culture influences individuals' media choice for deception. Figure 6.1 shows the relationships found by research between cultural values and choice of mode for deception.

Figure 6.1 Cultural values and choice of mode for deception

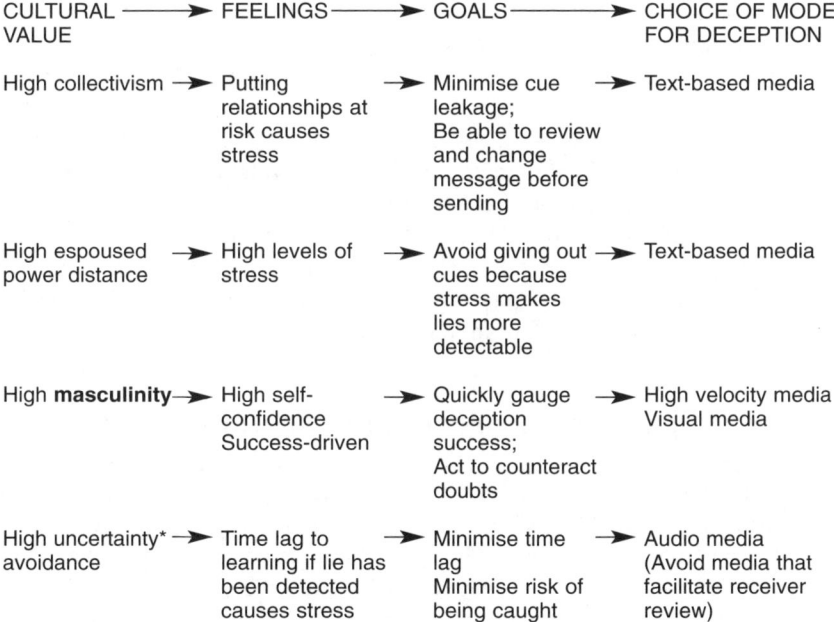

CULTURAL ⟶ FEELINGS ⟶ GOALS ⟶ CHOICE OF MODE
VALUE   FOR DECEPTION

High collectivism ⟶ Putting ⟶ Minimise cue ⟶ Text-based media
relationships at   leakage;
risk causes   Be able to review
stress   and change
                    message before
                    sending

High espoused ⟶ High levels of ⟶ Avoid giving out ⟶ Text-based media
power distance   stress   cues because
                                  stress makes
                                  lies more
                                  detectable

High **masculinity** ⟶ High self- ⟶ Quickly gauge ⟶ High velocity media
confidence   deception   Visual media
Success-driven   success;
                    Act to counteract
                    doubts

High uncertainty* ⟶ Time lag to ⟶ Minimise time ⟶ Audio media
avoidance   learning if lie has   lag   (Avoid media that
                   been detected   Minimise risk of   facilitate receiver
                   causes stress   being caught   review)

* Tests of this hypothesis did not support it

Based on Furner C.P. and George, J.F. (2012) 'Cultural determinants of media choice for deception', *Computers in Human Behavior*, **28**(4): 1427–38.

Summary

There may be differences in how women and men perceive other people ftf, with women being more aware of expressions of emotion and men more aware of conflict. Gender stereotypes distort perception in both sexes and both ftf and online.

Self presentation is influenced by gender effects on both body language and verbal language. Women are less likely to self-promote, with adverse effects in some cultures. These differences may lessen as gender equality increases. Online, some topics are seen as gendered and these perceptions affect tentativeness in both genders and conformity in women. The status of their communicator affects women more than men; the gender of their communicator affects men more than women. In cmc men are more likely than women to dominate and interrupt. Identifying strongly with their gender leads people to show the most gender-stereotypical self-presentation.

Cultures can be differentiated on the basis of values, world views, ways of communicating and other variables. The kinds of information available as cues about others vary and so affect person perception; attribution and judgements are examples of culturally influenced social cognition processes. Paralinguistics and contact are aspects of self-presentation that culture influences. At work, cultures differ in their expectations of aspects of self-presentation such as dress code and preferred communication mode.

Cultural differences give rise to issues in intercultural communication such as worse face recognition. How cmc affects cultural differences in communication and intercultural communication is contested and, except in relation to deception, there is little empirical evidence.

Demographic and cultural factors affect communication but neither alone determines it: they interact with one another, with psychological factors, and with the situation.

6.2 SOCIAL INFLUENCE THEORY AND INTERACTION

Since we know that external factors such as demography, culture and group memberships influence how people interact, the question arises as to how they do this. Social influence theory is an explanation, and in fact the theory goes beyond helping to account for communication differences to helping to explain behaviour more generally and some important beliefs and attitudes as well as how persuasion works.

There is clear evidence that people have a tendency to act or think like others and that this 'social influence' extends beyond obedience (a change in behaviour that is the result of a direct order or command from another person) and compliance (a change in behaviour that is due to a request or suggestion from another person), both of which are motivated by a desire to gain rewards or avoid punishment. Other forms of social influence include:

- Adopting opinions or beliefs based on a relationship with another person; this occurs particularly in groups because individuals want to maintain membership in the groups to which they belong, so they are susceptible to the social influence of other members of that group. This influence is likely to be quite strong in a work situation.
- Accepting social influence because of the desire to reduce uncertainty by believing what others believe.
- Accepting influence because it is congruent with one's value system. This last is likely to be the strongest and longest-lasting of the social influence effects.[44]

There are various 'mechanisms' which transmit social influence to individuals. These include the expectation of accountability, inferring others' opinions, behavioural mimicry and legitimizing some behaviours and deligitimizing others:

- The **expectation of accountability** is an 'explicit or implicit constraint on virtually everything people do'.[45] People ask themselves, 'If I do this, how will others react?' This is one mechanism by which norms and roles, which will be explained further in Chapter 7, affect individual behaviour. Bystanders communicate to the 'perpetrator' of a norm transgression that his or her action is socially unacceptable (this is called exerting social control). It is the behaviour's level of deviancy, rather than its frequency of occurrence, that is likely to provoke this reaction. People will exert social control when they feel personally implicated by the uncivil behaviour.[46]
- Strongly and widely agreed perceptions and beliefs act normatively to influence behaviour in various communication situations.[47] However, people do not primarily infer one another's views on particular issues by discussion. Rather, it appears that they infer opinions in part by relying on stereotypes of their friends and in part by projecting their own views. This can mean that there is a gap between real and perceived agreement and that people may be socially influenced to believe something that the 'influencer' does not.[48]
- **Social contagion** is pervasive in human interactions; it underpins interpersonal coordination. By the largely automatic processes of behavioural mimicry, verbal and emotional contagion, and attitudinal convergence, people adapt how they manage their communication and relationships. Behavioural mimicry is the automatic imitation of

gestures, postures, mannerisms and motor movements. The amount of behavioural mimicry that occurs in an interaction is affected by various motivations, social, emotional and personality factors. For instance, an ambitious teenager who frequently uses street-speak terms with her friends, when she begins work with older colleagues in an office will probably, even without noticing, talk differently with them. Behavioural mimicry in turn has unexpected influences on individuals, affecting for instance their cognitive processing style, attitudes, consumer preferences, self-regulatory ability and academic performance.[49]

- Social influence in the form of socially constructed norms has its effect in part by legitimizing some behaviours and delegitimizing others. For instance, during transitional periods managerial networking intensity (i.e. developing and maintaining relationships that may be used for business purposes) declines markedly over time, whereas the importance of market-based strategies increases. These findings have led researchers to conclude that these changes in strategy are driven by socially constructed norms; during transition periods these legitimize new ways of competing and delegitimize old ones.[50]

Social influence is exercised on individuals at work by a wide range of groups, particularly cultural and gender groups. Social influence is fundamental to culture, and so to the cultural differences that shape the nature of management and leadership. Gender characteristics, too, as opposed to biological sex characteristics, are essentially transmitted by social influence.[51]

Social influence and cmc

There is a version of social influence theory that deals specifically with its online effects. Social influence affects individuals' technology-related attitudes and behaviours; these converge with those of important communication partners, especially co-workers in someone's own organizational unit. What people think about their combined network partners' attitudes and behaviours in using electronic mail predicts their own attitudes and behaviour. Social influence in relation to cmc is stronger for co-workers than for supervisors.[52] Perceptions of others' thoughts concerning the use of ICTs for multi-tasking during a meeting, in conjunction with perceptions of organizational norms, explain a considerable amount of variance in how individuals use ICTs to multi-task electronically in meetings.[53]

In cmc communication, style can influence how effective social influence is. How self-confidence is expressed affects how people of different genders respond: when it is presented in quantitative form its effect on conformity is greater among men than women; the reverse is true when confidence is expressed verbally.[54]

Social influence helps explain a number of communication phenomena including group norms and the effect of culture. As well as obeying orders and complying with requests out of hope of gain or fear of punishment, people often adopt the opinions and beliefs of others with whom they have a relationship they want to maintain, as for instance, membership in a group. The desire to reduce uncertainty, internalization, the expectation of accountability and behavioural contagion also lead people to accept social influence.

Social influence may be particularly powerful over which cm media to use and how, though social pressures to conform to majority judgements have less effect in cmc than ftfc. Communication style influences the effectiveness of social influence in cmc. (See Box 6.2 on page 146).

6.3 THE SITUATION AND MODE AS INFLUENCES ON COMMUNICATION: IMPORTANT THEORIES

It is clear that the situation in which communication takes place has a very strong influence. For instance, among other things this book has noted that being in a competitive situation biases attributions, that familiarity with the situation increases people's ability to tell when others are lying, that in face-threatening situations people may choose a different communication mode, that the nature of a task also affects mode choice, and that power and status affect how people communicate both ftf and by cmc. Of these aspects of situation, the effect of the mode of communication is of central importance for this book. It has also attracted significant attention and debate from scholars, and a number of theories have emerged.

Write the following emails:

- *To follow up on an invitation to a customer to attend a conference. The customer has not replied to the invitation and you need to know whether they intend to attend.*
- *To a customer whose bill is overdue for payment.*
- *To a supplier of a printer which is not performing satisfactorily.*
- *To inform a customer that you will be unable to deliver to them on the day promised.*
- *A holding communication following a complaint from a customer.*
- *A listserv to inform customers of a price increase.*

Take these points into account:

- *What will you put in the subject line? (This is critically important as if you get it wrong they may not even open the email.)*
- *What greeting will you use?*
- *What font will you use? In what font size?*
- *How will you introduce your request?*
- *What will you say to persuade them to commit/pay up/replace the printer or give you a refund/accept the delay in getting their complaint resolved/accept the price increase?*
- *How will you conclude and finish?*

BOX 6.2

On 26 April 2013 Christa Carone, Chief Marketing Officer of Xerox, wrote a blog on leading by example in social media. Here are some extracts:

A year ago I decided to become an active content creator and social media contributor.

Here's what I've learned:

Don't boil the ocean. I.e. begin with a single platform. It's better to be active on a single channel than to have a sporadic presence across several.

Be conversational. Initiate or amplify conversations with clients, prospects, media players and employees.

Be prepared to move quickly. One day, comments I made during a speaking engagement appeared in *Click-Z*, a marketing publication. The headline was misleading – and some of the comments that followed the story were off base. I jumped to the head of the comment thread to put my quotes in context. Don't forget that conversations continue after a speech is delivered or a tweet is posted.

Don't sell. If you want to sell, buy an ad or an advertorial or, perhaps, sponsor tweets.

Enlist a team. Chatter on digital media outlets is 24/7. So be open to asking trusted advisors to watch your blog and social media feeds while you're 'dark' and alert you when it's important that you respond.[55]

There are significant differences in how different modes are seen in terms of their impact on communication in general and at work. There are, for instance, findings that indicate that while email is seen by the members of an organization as having a significant impact on how individuals communicate within it, voicemail is viewed as only a supplement to the telephone and as having little impact.[56] Again, although employees regard IM as much less rich than ftf, they use it not only as an additional method for reaching others but also as a replacement for other modes. With IM, employees engage in polychronic communication; they view IM as informal and privacy enhancing, but see its interruptive nature as unfair.[57]

A major issue concerning the use of cmc is the question of whether it makes communication more or less impersonal than it would be ftf. Clearly this issue is more salient for some work roles than others – more for healthcare professionals than software engineers, for instance. However, because, as Chapter 1 has shown, good relations are important in all walks of life, the issue has significance for everyone at work. Other concerns have been with whether and how strongly cmc constrains the behaviour of those using it, whether communicators using cmc are psychologically distant from one another, whether social influence is greater in cmc than ftf and whether status differences are decreased or increased. These issues have been addressed and to some degree answered by a range of theories and empirical studies.

The social presence model, reduced social cues theory and media richness theory

In the early days of studying cmc, scholars believed that it strongly constrained the behaviour of the participants – that there was a 'technological imperative' operating. Three such models are the social presence model, reduced social cues theory and media richness theory.

Social presence model (SPM)

High social presence, the sense of 'being there' that obtains between two ftf communicators and can be created by some media, has been found to enhance performance on tasks which are wide ranging, complex and uncertain. Tele-operations, where personnel need to adapt their responses to another physical environment, is one such setting. Communication media differ in their degree of social presence, and these differences play an important role in how people interact. The psychological state of being present is a function of the quantity and quality of the cues a person receives with the communication. Thus, the fact that all media filter out cues implies that to varying degrees mediated communication is lower in social presence than ftfc. In particular, since text-based modes of communication like email do not support non-verbal codes such as facial expressions and gestures, they are low in social presence: that is, senders are not fully aware of the presence of a receiver (who, of course, may well not be 'present' in any meaningful sense at the time an email is being written). According to SPM, lower social presence results in lower social influence: cmc, it asserts, can often diminish the effects of social pressures to conform to majority judgments.[58] Later research, however, associated the low social presence of a medium with a high capacity to influence others, undermining this theory.

Cmc researchers used SPM to explain that cmc was inherently impersonal because non-verbal and relational cues, which are common in ftfc, are filtered out of cmc. However, later researchers argued on the basis of empirical findings that participants in online discussions, using text alone, are able to project their personalities into online discussions and to create social presence.[59] Thus, users' personal perceptions of social presence and the behaviours they use to make up for the cues that are filtered out matter just as much, if not more, than a medium's supposed capabilities.

In addition, as more research was conducted it became apparent that the value of a visual channel was more situational than originally thought. For instance, research began to show that how people evaluate a communication medium depends largely on the task at hand. They might want a less intimate or immediate communication medium for certain tasks – those where they anticipate conflict or embarrassment, for instance.[60]

Reduced social cues theory (RSC)

Even before the internet became available, it was contended that the fewer social cues, the greater the psychological distance between two communicators. Social cues are both visual and given by physical presence and were shown to decrease from situations using closed-circuit television, which supplies visual cues, to those using a curtain and wooden screen, which removes the visual cues, to audio only, which provides neither visual nor physical cues. Further, this early theory argued that the greater the psychological distance between two people the more likely it is that communication will be task oriented and depersonalized.[61]

A corollary of this theory is that the relative anonymity provided by text-based cmc tends to reduce the attention people give to social relationships and supportive interactions, behave in an uninhibited and non-conforming way and overestimate their own and underestimate others' contributions. At work, the results of these differences would mean that interactions were more task-oriented, that upward communication increased, and that information exchange increased, with a large part of what is exchanged being information that would not be exchanged without email.[62]

Media richness theory (MRT)

MRT is another 'cues-filtered-out' approach: richness is defined as 'the potential information-carrying capacity of data'. Very slight communications, such as a wink, can be rich if they substantially increase understanding. As Chapter 1 noted, media richness is a function of a medium's social affordances. MRT states that rich media have high feedback capability, support the transmission of several cues, the source of the message is human and the language used has high variety (can express a wide range of ideas). According to MRT, communication media can determine the richness of information: a 'medium's capacity for immediate feedback, the number of cues and channels utilized, personalization, and language variety' all influence its degree of information richness. Thus ftfc has the highest richness whereas numeric communication (e.g. sending a spread sheet with numbers) has the lowest.[63]

MRT proposes that different communication media support various levels of ambiguity reduction, which is a function of a medium's richness, that is its capability of facilitating feedback, communicating multiple cues, presenting individually tailored messages and using natural language to convey subtleties.[64] Many forms of cmc are limited in their ability to transmit cues and this has negative consequences for reducing ambiguity. Email and other forms of text-based cmc limit communicators' perception of the social context due to their narrow bandwidth. Email attenuates both dynamic social context cues (non-verbal behaviour such as nodding to show agreement or frowning for displeasure) and static social context cues (the appearance of people and the communication setting). For example, emails from unknown senders do not show cues about their geographical location, organizational department, hierarchical position, sex or age. The richer the medium, the greater its capability to reduce ambiguity. This characterization of communication media would seem to argue for using the most cue-rich medium. However, richer media and the increase in completeness may cost more (both financially and in terms of time and effort) than less rich media. Thus, if the task involves lower levels of ambiguity, leaner media will accomplish the same task more efficiently.

At work, it was argued, the more the complexity and variety of the information needed, the richer the medium used. Members, rationally, adopt the technology that fits with their task. According to MRT, therefore, organizational members use richer media to face complex situations, reduce equivocality of information and increase coordination and task performance. In hierarchical organizations, middle and top managers have to face increasing levels of equivocality and uncertainty. Higher hierarchical ranks imply roles that are more and more in contact with the environment, which is the main source of uncertainty and equivocality. Lower-level participants, in contrast, are faced with more routine tasks and defined goals and technologies: in MRT these members therefore are expected to use poorer communication media. It is questionable, however, whether an increase in the amount of cues and language complexity leads to a reduction of equivocality and uncertainty of information and thus to better decisions.

Some scholars have argued that media richness is a social construct rather than an objective fact; if so, as individuals receive influences from other people about cmc, their perception of the media richness of any technology and their satisfaction with online communication will tend to grow. Schmitz and Fulk (1991) found that the social influence of colleagues had pervasive effects on how people at work assessed a medium. They also found that experience with a medium increased a user's satisfaction with it.[65]

Critique of the social presence model, reduced social cues theory and media richness theory

As noted above, these 'cues-filtered-out' theories have received a measure of support from research. However, critics have pointed out that many of these supporting studies were one-shot studies of extremely short duration in which the parties had neither the time nor the motivation to create a positive impression. A criticism of all these 'bandwidth' models is that they assume that the 'channel' effects of internet communication are similar across all contexts. There is evidence, however, that it varies according to the context or domain within which communication takes place: for instance, whereas in negotiations trust is lower by cmc than ftf, in romantic relationships it is higher.[66] Again, people with stigmatized social identities (such as homosexuality is in some countries) are motivated to join and participate in internet groups devoted to that identity because of the relative anonymity and thus safety of the internet compared to ftf participation and the scarcity of such groups offline.

As new insights emerged from research, by 2002 a review concluded, 'while social science commentators agree that the singular difference between computer-mediated communication and face-to-face communication is that non-verbal cues are reduced or eliminated in cmc, there is no agreement on the effect that this has on the communicative process'.[67] As evidence began to accumulate that how cmc affects communication could not be predicted from the affordances and limitations of the technologies alone, new theories began to emerge, built on our understanding of social cognition, impression management and interaction. These are social information processing theory, hyperpersonal theory and the social identity model of deindividuation effects.

Social information processing theory (SIPT)

SIPT is a theory of how people understand one another and manage relationships, especially online. Pointing out that 'several theories and much experimental research on relational tone in computer-mediated communication (CMC) points to the lack of nonverbal cues in this channel as a cause of impersonal and task-oriented messages. Field research in CMC often reports more positive relational behaviour', Walther (1992) put forward the theory that communicators 'develop individuating impressions of others through accumulated cmc messages. Based upon these impressions, users may develop relationships and express multidimensional relational messages through verbal or textual cues'.[68] Thus, according to SIPT, cmc can be very personal.

Walther (1996) argued that human social nature is the same in cmc and ftf environments: given enough time people would find ways to compensate for any social cues that are filtered out in cmc.[69] Previous research tended to put time restrictions that made interpersonal and relational communication unlikely. A 1994 review of past research had already found that the degree of social interaction in cmc is greater and proportionately higher in relation to ftf where interaction is not time-limited and that having interacted previously led communicators to more social- and less task-oriented communication online.[70]

Walther (1994) made a further point: when people anticipate that they will be interacting long-term in the future they behave differently, particularly with more intimacy and composure. This effect is stronger in cm than ftf groups, though it is the anticipation rather than the communication mode that is the stronger influence.[71] Later, Walther et al. (2010) found that cmc is 'functionally equivalent to vocal communication (by telephone) in its ability to ameliorate expectancies and that in some cases it can be superior in transmitting positive impressions'.[72] In sum, bandwidth is an insufficient predictor of cmc effects on the nature of social interaction. 'The more often an individual spends time communicating with others on-line, the more easily s/he can adapt to the lack of non-verbal and contextual cues and the more satisfied s/he becomes with a relationship.'[73]

Thus SIPT's main hypothesis regarding cmc is that, in contrast with previous theories, 'the difference between ftf and cmc is a question of rate, not capability'. The problem with the early experiments assessing the effects of cmc is that they involved zero-history virtual groups interacting for a short time with no anticipated future interaction. 'The underlying social processes in ftf and cmc settings are the same, but the limited bandwidth of cmc retards the relational development ... Given sufficient time and message exchanges for interpersonal impression formation and relational development to accrue, and all other things being equal, relational (communication) in later periods of cmc and face-to-face communication will be the same.'[74] SIPT findings suggest that 'the interpersonal effects that are expected to accrue quickly over time in ftf interaction can indeed occur in cmc, but require extended time interactions'.

Hyperpersonal theory

On the basis of findings such as those just described, hyperpersonal theory contends that users exploit the technological aspects of cmc in order to enhance the messages they construct so as to manage impressions and facilitate desired relationships. Just as some cues are filtered out, other cues are filtered in and therefore cmc has some affordances that ftf communication does not and that allow more personalization in cmc. Communicators adjust message composing time, editing behaviours, personal language, sentence complexity and relational tone for different presumed targets, thus exploiting the technology to achieve their goals.

Research partially supports this theory, and has also found unanticipated effects suggesting behavioural compensation through cmc when people address partners whom they do not wish to encourage.[75]

The social identity model of deindividuation effects (SIDE)

SIDE is a model derived from social identity theory that directly criticizes the main assumptions of RSC theories. SIDE rests on the concepts of social categorization, which was explained in Chapter 3, social identity and deindividuation; it will be helpful to introduce these last two before explaining the theory:

- Social identity is the aspect of an individual's identity derived from membership in a social group. The social identity approach argues that groups, which in this case refers both to small ftf groups or an entire social category, such as an ethnic or national group or a gender, strongly influence individuals' experiences in life, their identity or self-concept, and how they behave. Categorization of the self and other people is at the heart of this effect. Depending on the situation, people think of themselves primarily as distinct individuals or primarily as members of a group. When salespeople are talking to a client on behalf of their company, their group self, in this case their 'company' self, is likely to be uppermost; this group self places in the foreground those aspects of an individual that are interchangeable with others; as a member of a sales team, a salesperson's identity is similar to that of the other team members. However, when the same salesperson is emailing his boss about a recent successful sale he has achieved, his individual self will predominate – he'll distinguish himself in his own mind from the rest of the sales team. His uniqueness will be foregrounded.
- Deindividuation is a temporary loss of self-awareness. In some social situations, deindividuation theory asserts, people 'lose' themselves. In large crowds (in football crowds, mobs or on demonstrations) people can lose their sense of themselves as individuals and think and act as one of the crowd, for better or worse. There has been a debate about whether people are deindividuated when they use cmc.

SIDE rejects the idea that cmc is necessarily less social than ftfc or that the processes of social categorization do not operate in cmc. Spears et al. (2001) distinguished two different social cues: interpersonal cues that identify and individuate communicators and cues to social features such as group identity and category membership.[76] While the first can be filtered out by cmc systems, they asserted that the latter types of cues, 'that are communicated relatively independently of bandwidth considerations, are thereby given more opportunity to influence interaction, and the definition of the self and situation'. Thus, factors such as the relative anonymity of cmc, group immersion and inter-acting with a computer rather than a person (the factors traditionally causing deindividuation) are not a cause of unregulated behaviour, polarization or status equalization.

> To learn more about the social identity theory perspective on communication media, visit the companion website... 6.3.1.

Deindividuation does, the theory asserts, affect how people process arguments, but this only increases social influence. 'Although CMC gives us the opportunity to traverse social boundaries, paradoxically, it can also afford these boundaries greater power, especially when they define self- and group identity.'[77]

> For more findings that support, and one more that contradicts, the SIDE model visit the companion website... 6.3.2.

Findings that support the SIDE model include a review of research which showed that cmc by no means always breaks down social boundaries or liberates individuals from social influence, group pressure, and status and power differentials that characterize much face-to-face interaction. When communicators share a common social identity, they appear to be more susceptible in anonymous cmc to group influence, social attraction, stereotyping, gender typing and discrimination.[78]

There have been one or two research findings that contradict aspects of the SIDE model, for instance experimental research found that no statistically significant differences emerged between identifiable and anonymous users of cmc. As SIDE hypothesizes that in a group context where social identity is salient, anonymity, as available through cmc, will facilitate influence among group members, this finding contradicts the model.[79]

Summary

Early theories of the impact of cmc depicted it as making communication impersonal, due to lack of social presence and reduced social cues, and as unsuitable for equivocal messages due to lack of media richness. These theories were criticized for assuming a technological imperative, and because some empirical findings did not support them.

Gradually new theories have emerged which contradict earlier views that communication by cmc is more impersonal and that social influence is reduced in cmc. They can perhaps be best summarized in the words of Thompson and Nadler (2002): 'people are not passively affected by technology, but actively shape its use and influence'.[80]

SIPT asserts that, given enough time, people compensate for the lack of social cues available online and are able to manage online relationships as successfully as they do offline; the linked hyperpersonal theory asserts that by using cues that are not available offline more intense relationships can be and are created online than offline.

SIDE argues that anonymity in cmc does not, as was previously asserted, eliminate social influence: when people's social identity is fore-grounded in their mind, social influence can be just as powerful or greater in anonymous as in fully identified communication. All the later theories have received some support from empirical research, but other research has pointed out boundary conditions.

7 INTRAPERSONAL INFLUENCES ON COMMUNICATION

The factors described in Chapter 6 – demographic and cultural background and the communication situation – are important for how people communicate, but they only have their effect through influencing the communicator's internal (psychological) processes. Communication is a type of human behaviour; as such, it is affected by a combination of psychological variables; and these in turn, through social influence, are affected by the social categories or groups of which we are members, including, for instance, gender, age and culture. This chapter is concerned with the 'internal' psychological influences.

Some behaviour, such as blinking or 'flight or fight' reactions to threat, is semi-automatic. Most behaviour, however, is experienced as resulting from thoughts (although neuroscientists are beginning to find that we sometimes act first and think later); psychologists have studied what factors and processes underlie our actions – both those that result in action and those that do not. They have identified sets of factors with

On completing your study of this chapter you will be able to explain and apply the implications of the psychological constructs and processes underlying communication at work, especially:

- Motives, motivations and goals.
- Affect (emotions and moods).
- Cognitions (thoughts and beliefs).
- Attitudes.
- Values.
- Intentions.
- Personality.
- The self.

You will also be able to explain and apply the implications of how different communication modes interact with psychological factors to affect communication.

varying components, but which usually include motives, motivations and goals, affect (emotions and moods), cognitions (thoughts and beliefs), attitudes (cognitions with affect attached), values, intentions, personality and the self. These factors, which are really constructs that we have devised to explain our psychological experiences and our own and others' behaviour, result from the social cognition processes described in Chapter 3 in conjunction with abilities such as memory, and from drives and needs. These constructs and the linked communication behaviours at work, both online and offline, are the subject of this chapter. It can give you only the briefest of introductions to these vast subjects.

> *To learn more about psychological constructs and behaviour, follow up on the Further Reading given at the end of the book.*

7.1 MOTIVES, MOTIVATIONS AND GOALS

Motives

Humans experience needs; motives are their internal responses to those experienced needs. People have biological needs – for food, sex and air – but also learned needs, such as to feel that others respect and esteem them, for self-fulfilment, or for power and control. They also have needs which are intermediate between the biological and learned; these include the needs for security and for affiliation. When needs are unfulfilled they create a state of tension: for example, when we need food we experience hunger; when we need safety we experience fear. Innate drives lead us to respond to our needs; they activate behaviour to change our situation. If the action succeeds in reducing the tension, then the drive is de-activated. If the tension is not reduced and the need remains unfulfilled, the drive is re-activated, causing us to take further action to meet the need.

Drives are generalized – they do not determine the specific actions we take in response to a need. The combination of particular needs and drives are what we term 'motives'. For example, a conflict with a colleague is likely to arouse a drive to resolve the situation: one person, motivated by a need for control, might respond by reporting the issue to a manager; another, motivated by a need for affiliation, might instead discuss the issue with the colleague directly. Motives can be specific responses to particular needs, or they can be chronic, in which case they are often called motivation.

> *What different motivations might make someone very ambitious?*

Motivation

Motivation influences our work-related behaviour. Values, cognitions and feelings as well as needs and drives influence work motivation; goal-setting, social cognition, organizational justice, national culture, job design and person–environment fit also impact on it indirectly. Stable work-related motivations include the motivation to attain mastery of one's environment, which has been shown to influence how persistent someone is with a difficult task, and **epistemic motivation** which describes the willingness to expend effort to achieve a thorough and rich understanding of the world, including the task or decision problem at hand. Higher epistemic motivation induces more systematic information processing. As Chapter 5 pointed out, when communicators have high epistemic needs, they tune their messages to suit their audience's attitude about what they are discussing; in this condition, tuning gives them a confident view about the subject. In some circumstances the fact of having undertaken this adjustment biases their subsequent memory of the subject.[1] Group creativity, too, is linked to the members' level of epistemic motivation; when members have high rather than low epistemic motivation, they produce more ideas, especially when they also have a pro-social rather than pro-self motivation.[2]

During interactions, people often experience competing motives – they want both to assimilate and to seem unique.[3] Assimilation motivation describes people's desire to be similar to others, to ensure that they do not feel isolated or disconnected from a group. Uniqueness motivation, contrastingly, describes the desire to be perceived as a unique individual. People can try to meet both these motivations by ensuring that they remain somewhere between complete similarity and complete uniqueness. If people feel they are too similar to others, for example, they may try to increase their uniqueness in order to redress the balance. If they feel they are too dissimilar, they may try to increase their similarity to others.[4]

BOX 7.1

In a telecoms company, the sales staff have been asked to cooperate with the credit department to work out a better system of identifying bad payers. At the same time, however, they blame the credit department for customers lost when they are wrongly refused goods because they were erroneously recorded as bad payers. How is this situation likely to affect the behaviour of the sales staff?

Goals

Motives affecting communication behaviour can be interpreted in terms of goals that people are trying to reach, although goals are more complex than the outcome of a simple needs-drives process. 'Goals are rooted in a value system and a sense of personal identity, so invest activities with meaning and purpose ... Goals embodying self-engaging properties serve as powerful motivators of action.'[5] People tend to give weight to a goal's positive aspects (its desirability) when making decisions for the long-term, and to the goal's negative aspects (its difficulty) when making decisions for the short-term.[6] Goal incongruence, which can follow from differences in local and professional knowledge, reduces the satisfaction of clients with their agencies, such as advertising agencies.[7]

A theory which has received some empirical support asserts that a motivational system regulates goal-directed behaviour: this system is termed **regulatory focus**, and consists of either a promotion focus or a prevention focus. Table 7.1 shows how a promotion and a prevention focus differ. The strength of promotion and prevention focus varies both chronically across individuals and momentarily across situations.

Studies based on regulatory focus theory have shown that regulatory focus affects a person's commitment to goals and the means to reach them, whether people use their manager as a role model, and how leaders' vision motivates followers. Regulatory focus also affects people's beliefs about the outcomes of actions and the self-defined conditions under which people believe they perform best: one study showed that people primarily concerned with growth and advancement preferred optimistic forecasts and performed better when adopting an optimistic outlook, whereas those primarily concerned with safety and security preferred pessimistic forecasts and actually performed better when adopting a pessimistic outlook.[8]

Interactional or conversational goals are particularly important for this book. These goals are 'integral to interaction because, when people engage

Table 7.1 A comparison of types of regulatory focus

Type of focus	Concerns	Goals	Strategy	Response to success	Response to failure
Promotion focus	Gain	Growth Accomplish-ment	Approach strategy	Cheerfulness	Dejection
Prevention focus	Safety	Fulfilment of duty and responsibility	Avoidance strategy	Quiescence	Agitation

in interaction, they typically do so with some purpose or objective, whether it be something significant, such as to persuade, or something trivial, such as passing idle time ... Goals and their pursuit during an interaction can guide people's behavior, alter their impressions of others, influence their thought processes, and alter their perception of events during the interaction'.[9]

Among the most widespread of these interactional goals are to understand what is going on in the interaction and to be able to explain the behaviour of the others taking part, to control the outcome of the interaction for themselves and to enhance self-esteem. Other goals that people attempt to realize in their interactions are to belong and to trust their ingroup. These relational goals – which may be for disaffinity rather than for affinity – affect information seeking (especially in relation to ongoing discussions), conversational behaviour and attitudes towards both the topic and the conversational partner. Individuals express affinity–disaffinity through arguments, agreements and disagreements with their interaction partners; these behaviours lead to changes in their own attitudes.[10]

Interactors also attempt to discover their partners' goals. Communication competence is enhanced by accuracy in goal detection; however, there are differences in how accurately and quickly people perceive the interaction goals of their partners. Unsurprisingly, certainty about others' goals is higher in unambiguous than ambiguous contexts; inferences about goals are also made more consistently by observers when the communication tactics of the person observed are more compatible with the context.[11] For instance, in business an interaction goal of informing someone about a change to a marketing plan would be more easily inferred than a goal of informing them about an historical fact. Furthermore, the more specific and concrete one interactor's goal is and the more efficiently they pursue that goal, in general the more quickly and accurately the other interactor infers what the goal is. Being high in perspective-taking ability generally increases goal detection accuracy and speed, whereas scepticism reduces it because it tends to lead people to infer more malicious goals and so to be inaccurate when their interaction partner's goals are benign.[12]

When a perceiver interacts with a partner whose behaviour implies that he or she is pursuing a particular goal and the perceiver accurately infers

> *To see the details of the other findings on regulatory focus visit the companion website... 7.1.3.*

> *When you ask someone why they did or said something, do you expect their answer to be their reason or their motive?*
> *When you ask yourself why you did or said something, are you more likely to find an answer in your reason or your motive?*
> *When you think about why someone else did or said something, are you more likely to think in terms of their reason or their motive?*

the partner's goal, they may sometimes proceed to pursue that goal. This behaviour has been labelled goal contagion.

> ❝ 'Goal contagion is consequential for communication processes. Having shared mental states, such as a goal, can increase affinity and be a means to cultivate a positive relationship between partners. Goal contagion, therefore, can foster favorable relationship development and maintenance ... Goal contagion arguably might account for, at least in part, reciprocated behaviors in the context of conflict and other arenas. Negotiators might be able to encourage less tension during conflict by efficiently pursuing cooperative goals, which the negotiation partner could in turn infer and likewise adopt.[13]

Motives and cmc

Assimilation and uniqueness motives continue to affect behaviour in mediated as they do in face-to-face (ftf) interactions. An experiment using virtual self-representations showed that uniform virtual appearance, while encouraging group identification, made individuals perceive a strong threat to their uniqueness, leading them to disagree more often with others as a way to assert their uniqueness. When their visual representations differed from those of other members of their group, however, they tried to find any cue to allow them to bond with the others and so meet their need for assimilation.[14] Relational goals also affect online behaviour: people who do not want a close relationship with their present conversational partner use the web to seek information for discussions more than those who do have an affinity goal.

Summary

Motives result from drives acting on felt needs; chronic patterns of motives, or motivations,

I had a problem with the way people treated email. For example, I would have to send my drafts to the relevant policy team. I would send it to the right person for them to check it, but they would then copy it to everybody they could think of. They would copy in people in their team who were 'experts' in the subject, their immediate boss, the Director General, Special Advisers. Many of these people would then send me comments on my draft – an avalanche of opinions – and I would have to reply to their comments or, rather, battle to fend them off. The individual I sent it to would be trying to evade responsibility; that's a natural human instinct but email made it easier. It's a very effective way of spreading responsibility. (Author's interview with a former UK civil servant)

What underlying motives might be influencing the person described here as 'copying it to everybody they could think of'?

affect work behaviour in general. Among the motives and motivations that particularly affect communication behaviour at work are mastery, epistemic, assimilation and uniqueness motives.

Goals are conscious motives influenced by a person's value system and identity. Goal-directed behaviour may be regulated by either a promotional or a prevention focus which has in turn been linked to a range of work attitudes and behaviours.

In interactions people have a range of goals concerned with the interaction itself. They also want to discover their interaction partners' goals. Accuracy in goal discovery increases communication competence and is linked both to the behaviour of the seeker and to that of their target.

Online behaviour, as well as ftf behaviour, reflects relational goals.

7.2 AFFECT: MOODS AND EMOTIONS

'Affect' is a psychological term that denotes general moods (happiness, sadness) and specific emotions (fear, anger, envy), states that contain degrees of evaluation and arousal. Affect should not be confused with attitude, which refers to the overall degree of favourability a person has towards something (another person, an object, or an event).[15]

Moods

People experience 'diffuse, slow-moving feeling states that are weakly tied to specific objects or situations'; these are moods. Moods affect social perception: when perceiving a target person's emotions, happy people are more influenced by the context than sad people are.[16] Mood can also influence trust development, though it is not as simple as a positive mood enhancing trust. People in a positive mood increase their trust in another person when available cues promote trust; when cues promote distrust, people in a positive mood decrease their trust.[17] Negative mood increases, and positive mood reduces, concern with fairness. This suggests that positive mood leads to more internally focused processing that promotes selfishness, while negative mood induces more externally oriented, accommodative thinking and greater concern with social norms.[18]

Emotions

Emotions are quick-moving reactions that occur when organisms encounter meaningful stimuli that call for adaptive responses.

To learn more about what emotions are, visit the companion website... 7.2.1.

Emotions, like moods, have important effects on the way we behave at work: for instance, middle managers' emotional responses in radical change situations in large firms affect the outcome of those change attempts. Low emotional commitment to change by middle managers can lead to organizational inertia, whereas high commitment to change with little attention paid to the emotions of those affected can lead to chaos. An intermediate level of emotional commitment to change by middle managers, however, can facilitate organizational adaptation, supporting change, continuity in providing quality in customer service, and development of new knowledge and skills.[19]

Particular emotions whose work-related effects have been studied include anger, fear and anxiety, feeling accepted and respected and feeling powerful.

Anger

Anger can affect people's communication behaviour, from the way they perceive things to the way they negotiate with others. There is evidence that anger affects recognition of objects. In a series of five experiments, participants experiencing different emotions were asked to make rapid judgements about whether target individuals were holding guns or neutral objects. Results showed that anger increases the probability that neutral objects will be misidentified as ones related to violence.[20] Anger can even prevent people from protecting their own perceived worth and propel them toward self-inflicted pain. Compared with both sad and emotionally neutral participants, in five studies angered participants rated painful activities as more desirable, showed greater mental accessibility of pain, were more likely to choose a painful-sounding sweet (a 'jawbreaker') when given a choice between two sweets, gave themselves more electrical shocks and scored higher on a clinical survey used to measure self-inflicted pain.[21]

Anger also affects how people respond to each other. Research has shown repeatedly that emotional expressions tend to be reciprocated. Expressions of anger are perceived as expressions of dominance, hostility, accusations of wrongdoing and a more aloof and arrogant stance by the expresser; all of which are likely to produce angry responses in the other person. As a result, when participants in mediation express anger, the chances that they will find ways to bridge their differences are reduced and, it has been shown, the resolution rate is lower. These effects may be especially pronounced in email-based mediation. Anger has also been found to raise the perceived importance of competitively oriented goals in negotiations, so making integrative ('win–win') negotiation less likely.[22]

Fear and anxiety

Although the terms 'fear' and 'anxiety' are often used interchangeably, they can be differentiated. Fear is a response to an unambiguous threat, whereas

---

BOX 7.2

'There are times when using an email can be seen as rude. In one bank, for some reason there was a shortage of rulers. I can't work without a ruler as I have to read across long lines of data. One day when someone had borrowed my ruler and disappeared with it, I waited and waited, and then I had to go to lunch. So I dropped her a very polite email asking if she could please return my ruler. She was angry, saying to use email for that was rude, and she complained to our boss.'

(Author's interview with a bank regulatory reporting specialist who has worked on a series of temporary contracts)

---

anxiety is a response to an ambiguous one and involves risk assessment. Perkins et al. (2012) have shown that anxiety and fear are expressed by different facial expressions. Observers are able to distinguish which of these another person is experiencing from their facial expression.[23]

Certain kinds of fear relate particularly to interaction; these are **communication apprehension**, computer apprehension and writing apprehension:

- Communication apprehension (CA) is the fear that interactions will become uncomfortable or even hostile. People feel CA particularly in situations which contain stimuli that are new, atypical or conspicuously different. CA reduces the ability to communicate orally, and people experiencing CA tend to ask few questions during the first minute of an interaction, to engage in high levels of self-disclosure, and to be considered less competent by their interaction partners.[24] There is evidence to suggest that CA levels can have an effect on career type and enjoyment, with one study finding that the people most satisfied with their jobs may be low in CA and have jobs with high communication requirements.[25] CA can also reduce people's ability to think critically and affect how well their level of extraversion and emotional stability is reflected in assessment scores. This can influence their chances of being selected for a job.[26] Increased CA is weakly associated with decreased frequency of use for new communication technologies, especially those involving oral communication.
- Computer apprehension (CompA) is 'a fear of impending interaction with a computer that is disproportionate to the actual threat presented by the computer'. Individuals with CompA often choose not to use a computer when given the option. High CompA is linked to low frequency of use for new communication technologies, especially those that are more technical or mathematical. However, CompA is found at a lower level in most people than either CA or writing apprehension.[27]

- Writing apprehension is 'a situation and subject-specific individual difference concerned with people's general tendencies to approach or avoid writing'.[28] It includes fear associated with writing situations, a tendency to avoid such situations, frustration, and low productivity while writing, although it does not influence whether or not people use IT.[29] In fact there is some evidence that compared to doing so ftf, collaboratively planning documents on email enhances the process for subjects who are high as well as for those who are low in writing apprehension.[30]

Feeling respected and accepted

A feeling of being respected and accepted improves performance. When people feel that their co-workers in a team respect them they are more engaged with the team. This works through two psychological processes: perceived inclusion of the self in the team and perceived value of the self for the team are separate psychological consequences of respect. Perceived inclusion facilitates the development of a positive team identity (how the individual feels about the team), while perceived value elicits the willingness to invest in the team (what the individual is willing to do for the team). Reports of individual team members about positive team identity and willingness to invest in the team correlate with supervisor ratings of the team's action readiness.[31]

Feeling powerful

Feeling powerful (or powerless) should be distinguished from actual power, which is the ability to influence the outcomes of other people; although actual power and feelings of power are correlated, the fit is not one-for-one. Regardless of its validity, feeling powerful increases an individual's ability to judge others accurately, decreases judgements when making decisions, and affects how consistently they pursue their goals. Feeling powerless increases how submissively people behave and how motivated people are to seek information about people with higher status.

> *To learn more about how feeling powerful or powerless affects work behaviour, visit the companion website... 7.2.2.*

Emotional transitions

The switch from one emotional state to another leads to consistently different outcomes than their corresponding steady-state emotions.

Negotiators facing partners who appear to be becoming angry accept worse negotiation outcomes, yet form better relational impressions of their partners than negotiators facing partners who display steady-state anger. In reverse, when the negotiating partner seems to change from angry to happy, there are no significant differences in negotiation outcomes but the negotiator forms lower relational impression ratings than perceivers of steady-state happiness. These findings apply in both cm and ftf negotiations. Attributional and emotional contagion seem to be the operative processes in these behaviours.[32]

> *Although embarrassment is experienced as an unpleasant emotion, it serves useful social functions – in particular it fosters trust in others and signals to them that the person is 'prosocial'.[33]*
>
> *Do you agree? Why or why not?*

Culture and emotions

There is a general tendency for people to react more emotionally when they are thinking about themselves, as opposed to neutral topics or other people. Research has found, however, that this response varies cross-culturally. When the relational self is primed (that is, when individuals are encouraged to think about other people), people with interdependent selves, such as Asian Americans, react more emotionally than people with independent selves, such as European Americans. When the independent self is activated (that is, individuals are encouraged to think about themselves), the reverse is true: European Americans react more emotionally than Asian Americans do.[34] These findings are consistent with what we know about cultural differences, which Chapter 5 has explained.

BOX 7.3 EMOTIONAL LABOUR IN SERVICE ENCOUNTERS

In the words of Ashforth and Humphrey (1993), '*emotional labor* is the display of expected emotions by service agents during service encounters. It is performed through surface acting, deep acting, or the expression of genuine emotion. Emotional labor may facilitate task effectiveness and self-expression, but it also may prime customer expectations that cannot be met and may trigger emotive dissonance and self-alienation'.[35]

Korczynski (2003) noted that the customer can be 'a key source of both pleasure and pain for service workers. Irate and abusive customers, who are systematically part of the social relations of the service workplace, may occasion real pain to service workers'. However, Korczynski's (2003) research in four call centres in Australia and the USA showed that service workers may form 'communities of coping' with informal, dense cultures that limit managerial control.[36]

Affect and computer-mediated communication (cmc)

Cmc can have an impact on emotions during interpersonal communication. For instance, in general, social anxiety is lower when interacting online than ftf.[37] Communicating about work by cmc leads people to perceive tasks as less difficult and so to have reduced anxiety about them. Psychological distance or 'the different ways in which an object might be removed from' the self along dimensions such as 'time, space, social distance, and hypotheticality' can reduce the subjective experience of difficulty caused by task complexity. Since this effect is produced by even quite small amounts of physical distance, working virtually by teleworking or in a virtual team can significantly reduce task anxiety.[38]

When the topic of an email dialogue has emotional overtones and the emotional cues transmitted between senders and receivers are few, however, it tends to create misunderstanding and cause emotions such as anger and anxiety to increase.[39] Moreover, there is some evidence to suggest that emotions are commonly communicated, both accurately and inaccurately, by email at work. Despite widespread advice to avoid doing so, email senders intentionally and unintentionally communicate emotion. Email characteristics make miscommunication likely, and receivers often misinterpret work emails as more emotionally negative or neutral than intended.[40] Furthermore, even in task-oriented instant messaging in the workplace, negative emoticons can cause a negative response in both men and women.[41]

As these findings show, users of cmc do express and transmit emotion but in the absence of non-verbal cues they use linguistic features such as evaluation devices (emotive adjectives, adverbs, verbs and nouns) and quantity devices (expressions of measure, duration and frequency) to express how strongly they feel about a topic. Unfamiliarity with using this format to show emotion can lead to 'ranting' or over-heightened expression.[42] There is some evidence that in cmc individuals are affected by the mere presence of aggression regardless of its level. However much or little actual aggression is displayed in a mediated communication, if it stimulates excitation in the receiver, this in itself is likely to lead to subsequent aggressive behaviour from the receiver.[43]

On the other hand, cmc can alleviate social fear. Research suggests that people who fear ftf interactions feel more comfortable participating in electronic discussions, becoming more likely to contribute and to initiate topics of conversation. Fear of being isolated (the only person advocating a position) can strongly inhibit people from expressing their opinions but this effect is attenuated when they communicate through cmc instead of ftf.[44] On average, women tend to be less anxious after a cmc interpersonal interaction than after a ftf interaction. However, this is related to personality: while introverted and neurotic participants tend to be more anxious ftf than using cmc, extraverts and stable participants tend to experience low amounts of anxiety irrespective of the interaction type.[45]

Higher-status employees generally are less likely to send positive emotional content in emails. In a study of employees at a telecommunications company, Ku (1996) found that socio-emotional content, defined as using email 'to get to know someone, to keep in touch with someone in another location, and to send notes that contain sociable or non-work-related content', was less likely in emails sent to lower-status employees and that employees with high absolute status in the organization were the least likely to use email for socio-emotional purposes.[46]

Furthermore, higher-status employees may not only be less likely to express positive emotions, they may be more likely than lower-status employees to express negative emotions. Research has shown that employees are more likely to express negative emotions to those of lower, rather than higher, status. In reviewing research on emotional expression and status, Gibson and Schroeder (2002) found evidence that those with more power express a wider variety of emotions, including anger and other negative emotions. 'Lower status [organizational] members, however, are not free to express negative emotions upward.'[47] Although the expression of negative emotion downward in organizations may have fewer sanctions than the expression of negative emotion upward, however, this by no means implies that higher status senders can do so without fear of reprisal. Organizational norms, too, may discourage power abuse by higher-status employees.

Summary

Moods and emotions, together called 'affect', influence behaviour. Positive and negative moods influence social perception, trust development and concern with fairness. Anger, fear and anxiety (especially CA), feeling accepted and respected and feeling powerful are emotions that influence work-related communication.

In general, people feel less social anxiety in online than offline interactions. Higher-status senders may be more likely than lower-status senders to express negative emotion in emails.

7.3 COGNITIONS: THOUGHTS AND BELIEFS

Thoughts and beliefs are the result of the mental processes that were described in Section 3.1. The term 'thoughts' carries no implications as to whether a cognition is believed, whereas beliefs are cognitions to which at least some degree of credence attaches. Behaviour is influenced by thoughts other than beliefs, as when someone says, 'I have an idea; why don't we do x?' and acts accordingly; however, the greater credence attached to beliefs makes them stronger influences on behaviour in general. Other kinds of cognitions, such as daydreams or even perceptions, may entirely lack this element of being believed.

Thoughts

As the introduction to this chapter noted, the influences on behaviour that we are most often aware of are our thoughts, and these, according to most psychological theories, are influenced by motives and affect. While there is evidence of unconscious causation and automacity, however, so that behaviour cannot be fully under our conscious control in the way everyday intuitions suggest, there is also evidence that the contrary view, that conscious thought has little or no impact on behaviour, is wrong. Studies show that mental practice and simulation, anticipation, planning, reflection and rehearsal, reasoning, taking contrary views, perspective-taking, self-affirmation and framing, as well as overrides of automatic responses, do affect how we behave. However,

❝ conscious causation is often indirect and delayed, and it depends on [an] interplay with unconscious processes. Consciousness seems especially useful for enabling behavior to be shaped by nonpresent factors and by social and cultural information, as well as for dealing with multiple competing options or impulses. It is plausible that almost every human behavior comes from a mixture of conscious and unconscious processing.[48]

Beliefs

Beliefs certainly affect behaviour, though not as much as common sense would suggest. 'Personal and contextual factors combine to increase or decrease the accessibility of different kinds of beliefs, with potentially important ramifications for evaluative judgments and behavioural decisions.'[49]

Six kinds of beliefs are of special interest for understanding work-related communication: assumptions, **self-efficacy** beliefs, expectations, norms, stereotypes and fairness beliefs. Stereotypes and fairness beliefs have been described in Chapter 3. Assumptions, efficacy beliefs, expectations and norms are explained here.

Assumptions

Assumptions are unquestioned, often unconscious beliefs. They are pervasive in both social life and at work. Speakers make assumptions about what others know and take it into account in what they say.[50] At work, examples include the following:

- The well-known Theory X and Theory Y assumptions that managers make, which lead them to think either that only reward and punishment (Theory X) motivate their subordinates or that intrinsic rewards such as responsibility and interesting work (Theory Y) are equally motivating.[51]
- Nurses and doctors make assumptions about the heteronormativity of their patients and these assumptions 'communicated unconsciously by nursing staff, contribute to ambivalent attitudes and feelings of insecurity that prevent communication and easily lead to misconceptions'.[52]
- Intercultural negotiators make assumptions about negotiations that are often erroneous for the people they are negotiating with. Table 7.2 compares the usual assumptions of Western and non-Western negotiators.

Table 7.2 A comparison of Western and non-Western negotiators' assumptions

Type of assumption	Western negotiators assume	Non-Western negotiators assume
How to persuade	Rational argument	Emotional appeals are more persuasive
Negotiators' motives	Economic gain outcome	Building 'relational capital'
Attributions	Dispositional	Situational
Most effective procedure	Ask about opponents' preferences; Reciprocate with equivalent information; Build an understanding of the trade-offs; Formulate multi-issue proposals	Draw inferences about the other party's preferences from their proposals and counter-proposals; Formulate both single and multi-issue proposals
Best way to resolve negotiation breakdown	Talking and confronting the issues	Using silence

Based on Brett, J.M. and Gelfand, M.J. (2006) 'A cultural analysis of the underlying assumptions of negotiation theory', in Thompson, L. (ed.) *Negotiation Theory and Research* (Madison, WT: Psychosocial Press), 173–201.

❝ Here are a few assumptions that tend to drive poor communication: I send ... [someone] an email and then assume that they got it. I don't bother to verify that they got it. I don't call to confirm, or ask them in my email communication to verify receipt by replying to me ...

I got an email this weekend from a client that simply said 'Please call me on Monday'. My first thought was, oh great, they are unhappy and going to complain about something. But in thinking that, I was assuming that this client's intent in talking with me is negative when it very well may be just to touch base or to clarify something about the project.[53]

> To learn more about work-related assumptions, visit the companion website...
> 7.3.1.

Self-efficacy beliefs

Efficacy beliefs are beliefs in one's ability to perform an action effectively. Efficacy beliefs have three important dimensions. These are magnitude (how taxing are the tasks people believe they can handle), generality (whether their sense of efficacy extends well beyond the particular task) and strength (a weak sense of efficacy is easily extinguished by disconfirming experiences, a strong one leads to continued striving in spite of disconfirming experiences).

These self-efficacy beliefs influence individuals' actual performance, emotions, choices of behaviour and the amount of effort and perseverance they will expend on an activity. According to the originator of self-efficacy theory, Bandura (1986), individuals assess their own self-efficacy using information from four principal sources: actual experiences, vicarious experiences, what others say to them and bodily symptoms. Individuals' own performances, especially past successes and failures, offer the most reliable source for assessing efficacy. Watching peers performing a task conveys to observers that they too are capable of accomplishing that task. Being encouraged to believe that they possess the capabilities to perform a task (e.g. being told 'You can do this') can increase someone's self-efficacy. Finally, individuals might interpret bodily symptoms such as increased heart rate or sweating as a sign of anxiety or fear, so diminishing their self-efficacy belief.[54]

Job-related self-efficacy, together with perceptions of being able to influence their working environment so that it becomes more rewarding or less aversive, helps to give employees political skill, which in turn reduces their level of physiological strain or stress.[55] Efficacy beliefs can affect teams as well as individuals. Teams that have positive beliefs about their capability tend to perform more effectively. Most significant for performance is the belief that they can achieve a good result; the belief that they work with a good process is more closely linked to citizenship behaviours (treating one another well).[56]

Self-efficacy beliefs in cmc

Computer self-efficacy is a positive factor for cmc use. Through an influence on computer self-efficacy, culture influences the adoption and use of new technologies. Cultural values of low power distance and high uncertainty avoidance have been shown to affect the perceived ease of use of new technologies such as **enterprise resource planning systems** through a positive influence on computer self-efficacy.[57]

Self-efficacy beliefs affect people's use of cmc. Individuals' synchronous cmc self-efficacy can be measured by their own rating of how confident they would feel doing any of the following: providing a nickname within a synchronous chat system (if necessary), reading messages from one or more members of the synchronous chat system, answering a message or providing their own message in a synchronous chat system (one-to-many interaction) and interacting privately with one member of the synchronous chat system (one-to-one interaction). Individuals' asynchronous cmc self-efficacy can be measured by their own rating of how confident they would feel doing any of the following: logging on and off an email system, sending an email message to a specific person (one-to-one interaction), sending one email message to more than one person at the same time (courtesy copy or one-to many interaction), replying to an email message, forwarding an email message, deleting messages received via email, creating an address book, saving a file attached to an email message to a local disk and then viewing the contents of that file, attaching a file (image or text) to an email message and then sending it.[58]

> *Look at the Glossary for the meaning of power distance and uncertainty avoidance.*

Expectations (or expectancies)

Expectations, or in American English expectancies, are beliefs about the future. They are beliefs about how people do and should behave and what will and should happen. They colour interpretations of behaviour and so affect responses to other people during interactions. We know, for example, that when a supervisor is from an **ethnic minority** and their subordinate is from the dominant majority, more problems arise than when the situation is reversed; this has been explained by 'normal' expectations being contravened.[59] Expectations derive from beliefs about demographic characteristics, such as age, gender and ethnicity, and from more individuating characteristics, such as personality traits, previous actions and past experiences; more often than not these beliefs are stereotypical.[60]

Expectations affect communication. For instance, when people antici-pate or expect a long-term series of interactions rather than a one-off single interaction, they are more likely to adopt a more intimate, open, calm interpersonal tone of communication almost from the start. These aspects of the tone of communication are more affected by expectations of future interaction than by the communication mode.[61]

We rarely interact with others without at least some expectations about how they will act or perform. Our own behaviour, too, may be affected by others' expectations; we may conform to others' visions of who we are rather than to our own, perhaps not even realizing that our own self-presentations have been influenced by the expectations of others. When people work with others at a task they tend to give priority to what they think are others' expectations over their own, even when the two conflict, as they might, for instance, if someone believed she was of higher status than her interaction partner, but also that the partner thought the opposite. These second-order expectations are important during an initial interac-tion, although they rarely transfer to new groups and tasks.[62]

In interactions 'the expectations that a receiver brings ... are crucial toward how the receiver interprets the sender's behavior'.[63] More than this, though, one person's expectations about a person they are interacting with can be powerful enough to affect the behaviour of that other person in a process called behavioural confirmation or the self-fulfilling prophecy. 'When individuals (as perceivers) hold expectations about other people (as targets), they can elicit from these targets behaviors that are consistent with their expectations, even if these expectations are independent of the target's real characteristics.'[64] One person (the perceiver), having adopted beliefs about another person (the target), acts in ways that cause the behaviour of the target to appear to confirm these beliefs. For example, the behavioural styles used by selection interviewers tend to confirm their first impressions of job applicants. Interviewers follow up positive first impressions by showing positive regard toward applicants, 'selling' the company, giving job information and gathering less information; they follow up nega-tive impressions by doing the opposite. Applicants respond to these behaviours and their own communication style and rapport with inter-viewers adjusts to confirm the positive or nega-tive impressions.[65]

Positive expectations can be 'an important component in the development and maintenance of competent communication patterns'.[66]

> *Imagine you are a line manager interviewing candidates for a supervisory job in which being able to tolerate stress is important. Should you try to evaluate how well the candidate withstands pressure by aggressive questioning, interrupting, appearing annoyed or restless, or other similar methods? Why or why not?*

Uncertainty and negativity can result, however, when positive expectations are disconfirmed (or violated). This could occur, for example, if one person expected an immediate response to an email and this expectation was not fulfilled; the person who was expecting an immediate response might well feel 'decreased control of one's social environment' and so feel uncertain about what is going on and feel negative towards the other.[67] When job applicants violate expectations by not replying to emails, selectors' evaluations of them are lower and they are also rated as less credible and attractive.[68] When customer expectations are violated, communicators may complain, usually to the person responsible for having 'enabled or failed to prevent the offensive event'. A significant proportion of online complaints make explicit reference to the complainer's expectations not being met.[69]

> *Selection interviewers sometimes ask candidates what television channel they watch. As they know the candidate is trying to self-present favourably, they expect them to name a news or documentary channel. If instead candidates name a game show channel, the selector gives them a lower rating.*

There can be significant discrepancies in employees' and managers' expectations concerning the emotional support that the managers give to the employees: 'employees treat caring as part of the managers' role that requires no reciprocation, whereas managers see such help-giving as discretionary extra-role behavior that requires reciprocated commitment'. Discrepant expectations concerning emotion-helping can lead to negative outcomes when managers feel disappointed at the lack of reciprocity.[70]

The evaluation of a violation is often a function of our assessment of the person who committed it. For example, if a person who is highly rewarding, attractive and appealing to us moves closer to us than we expect, their behaviour is more likely to be judged as positive than the same action by a low-rewarding person whom we judge as unattractive or repulsive.[71]

Expectations about both work and communication behaviour are influenced by national cultural differences. For instance, individualism is reflected in expectations about how far to submit to authority figures as well as a preference for doing things in one's own way. Less individualistic people, such as Arabs, have a longer-range view and are more willing to take advice.[72]

Expectations in cmc

The question of whether cmc makes confirmation or disconfirmation of expectations more likely has exercised researchers. As Chapter 3 noted, Epley and Kruger (2005) found that pre-interaction stereotypes and expectations (in this case of the intelligence of an interactor) persisted in the post-cmc evaluations of partners, although they dissipated in voice communication.[73] However, their methodology was disputed by Walther et al. (2010), who found instead that post-cmc ratings indicated disconfirmation of expectations in cmc relative to voice.[74] By 2012 Tong and Walther were concluding that both confirmation and disconfirmation of expectations can occur even in communication media that lack non-verbal affordances.[75]

In text-based cmc, selectors who evaluate a candidate highly are less affected in their assessments of applicant credibility and attractiveness because the candidate is slow to respond to an email. The influence, however, is complex: in the case of the high-reward candidate, the social attraction of an applicant who responded after two weeks was significantly lower than that of an applicant who responded within a day, whereas the social attraction of the applicant who did not respond at all did not drop significantly. It seems the social slight associated with an applicant who responds after two weeks without any explanation or justification is significant, whereas an applicant who does not respond at all 'creates enough ambiguity as not to cause a significant drop in social attractiveness'.[76]

Norms

Norms are unwritten but understood rules of a group, organization, society or culture; they stipulate behaviours that are considered acceptable and expected. Norms that commonly affect work communication include norms of fairness or equity, reciprocity, reasonableness and roles. For example, a fairness norm might lead Michael, a better-qualified but younger person promoted over the head of Colin, an older colleague, to try to apologize or make amends in some way; a reciprocity norm might mean that if Carol supports Judith's suggestion in a meeting Judith would feel an obligation to openly compliment or privately thank her; a reasonableness norm can act as a brake on the exercise of power so that a company that has the power to make late payments to a small supplier in fact pays up on time; and work roles are norms because as well as job specifications they imply unwritten or unspoken rules about how to do the job and about related aspects of behaviour.

Research has shown that norms are significant elements of how organizations function in practice: in the absence of complete (fully specified) contracts, or, indeed, any contracts, social interactions within organizations are governed by

> *A consignment to an industrial customer sent by post has gone missing. The customer has not notified the supplier within the time stipulated in the contract but the supplier replaces it without a quibble. Do you think the customer will feel that they should reciprocate in some way? Why or why not?*

informal but mutually acknowledged norms of behaviour with which compliance is mutually expected. All organizations control their internal workings by using mixtures of (incomplete) contracts and informal social norms.[77]

Deference norms are prevalent in some cultures, such as those of Thailand and Japan, where as interaction partners get older younger adults linearly increase communicative respect and avoidance as well as beliefs about politeness.[78] Such norms, when they become salient, can be more powerful influences than goals, a study of deference behaviour in India found.[79]

Norms in cmc

There is evidence that when using a new communication medium people initially apply the norms and habits of earlier modes of interaction, including those of ftf, but gradually new norms evolve for the medium itself.[80]

In fact, group norms may emerge through interaction as a function of within-group accommodation to a prototype that is inferred from ingroup communications. Such processes are especially likely to occur in cmc groups in which certain features of the group (those identified by the social identity model of deindividuation effects described in Chapter 5) may reinforce the normative pull of the group.[81]

Norms may be particularly potent in cmc because of the lack of information on which to base trust: this leads interactors to use norms to reduce uncertainty and risk. Groups develop their own norms about cmc behaviour but there are also widespread norms that apply particularly to cmc. Kalman et al. (2006a) showed that email implies a widespread expectation of fairly rapid response to which most people conform: at least 70 per cent of responses are written within the average response time of the responders (though this, of course, means that some responses are very much delayed). These findings persist across various users, contexts and even traditional as well as online communication media.[82] Kalman et al. (2006b) also showed that there are norms about delays in responses to email questions: email responses under 12 days are normally perceived as latency, while delays longer than 12 days are perceived as silence.[83]

> ❝ There is no rule book in the civil service about what you can put in emails or how you express yourself, but if you transgress the unwritten code, you will get into trouble. A colleague who was given to firing off emails telling people what he thought of some action or policy got into serious trouble. You are expected to be diplomatic. You would never use the phrase 'This is rubbish' or 'This is unacceptable'. What you put on Facebook or Twitter is even more sensitive. That same colleague's profile was considered inappropriate, and came to the attention of the newspapers, so he got into trouble and had to delete it.
>
> (Author's interview with a former UK civil servant)

Norms that prescribe a particular use of technology and both the content and the form of communication are socially constructed over time at the level of locally bounded groups. Conformity to these norms increases over time but is limited to the boundaries of the group: communication outside the group is governed by different social norms.[84] A study of ten cmc learning teams found that group norms evolved from a generalized to an operationalized state. In a generalized state norms were 'expectations regarding what general values should be shared'; examples included: 'communicate frequently' and 'pull your weight'. In an operationalized state, however, norms were 'expectations regarding specific team behaviors' with 'clear/specific boundaries'; examples included: 'check and respond to email daily' and 'take initiative, don't wait to be told what to do'. The study proposed that general norms evolve into operationalized norms cyclically. The cycle runs: 'norm proposal'; 'discussion/negotiation of norm boundaries'; 'acceptance of norm'; 'compliance with or violation of norm'; 'attention to differences in understanding of norm boundaries'; 'norm proposal'; etc. The more times the cycle is repeated, the less fuzzy the norm's boundaries become.[85]

Summary

Thoughts and beliefs do influence behaviour, though not as much as or always in the way that our intuitions suggest. Assumptions – unquestioned, often unconscious, beliefs – permeate our lives. Work related assumptions include managers' assumptions about worker motivation, nurses' assumptions about patients' sexuality and negotiator's culturally influenced assumptions. Making wrong assumptions can drive poor communication.

Efficacy beliefs affect an individual's or team's actual performance, emotions, choices of behaviour and the amount of effort and perseverance they will expend on an activity; they can be derived in various ways.

Expectations, or beliefs about the future, including the future behaviour of other people, colour interpretations of behaviour and so affect responses to other people during interactions. A person's expectations can trigger confirmatory behaviour in their interaction partner. Positive expectations support good communication but when they are violated negative outcomes can follow.

Norms of fairness or equity, reciprocity, reasonableness and roles are common in working life; these unwritten but understood rules often complement or substitute for formal controls in organizations.

Communication mode impacts on these cognitions in various ways: for instance both widespread and local norms may be particularly potent in cmc.

7.4 ATTITUDES AND VALUES

Attitudes are favourable or unfavourable dispositions towards objects, people and events or towards attributes of any of these; they are usually composed of beliefs, affect and action tendencies, though some lack much belief content ('I like bananas') or have limited implications for action. 'Good-bad, harmful-beneficial, pleasant-unpleasant, and likable-dislikable' are common attitude dimensions. People can simultaneously hold two different attitudes towards a given object: one habitual and implicit, the other explicit.[86] Values are individuals' stable attitudes that suggest general patterns of behaviour; they can also be seen as favourable evaluations associated with abstract concepts such as freedom and equality,[87] or broad tendencies to prefer certain states of affairs over others.

Attitudes

Attitudes vary in strength, accessibility and ambivalence:

- Strong attitudes are relatively stable over time and resistant to persuasion; they are more likely than weak attitudes to predict overt behaviour. However, attitude strength is a problematic concept: different measures of it – by extremity, stability, certainty, vested interest, involvement, **affective-cognitive consistency**, knowledge about the issue and frequency of thinking about it – are only weakly related.
- Accessibility refers to how easily and quickly an attitude is brought to mind. It is greater for attitudes formed under conditions of high involvement, that is, when the person cares about the issue or object to which the attitude relates.
- When someone has an ambivalent attitude to something it points to their having either conflicting beliefs or conflict between their beliefs and affect. For instance, if someone has an ambivalent attitude towards smoking cigarettes, it may well be because they believe the evidence that smoking kills but enjoy doing it. In general, someone's attitudes are not all that likely to predict their behaviour. However, recent evidence suggests that in some cases ambivalence is more likely to predict intention and behaviour than non-ambivalence is, possibly because it leads to more central or systematic processing of cues.

Attitudes express values, support our sense of our identity and self-esteem, and help us adjust to the social circumstances that we find ourselves in. Positive attitudes incline us to approach people and situations, negative attitudes to avoid them. Attitudes tend to bias memory: we are less likely to remember something if it is not consistent with our attitudes.[88]

Two important types of attitude for how people communicate at work are trust and prejudice; attitudes to cmc, which were discussed in Chapter 2, are also important.

Trust

On the basis of a literature review of organizational trust, Mayer et al. (1995) defined the concept of trust as 'a willingness of a party to be vulnerable to the actions of another party based on the expectation that the other will perform a particular action important to the trustor, irrespective of the ability to monitor or control that party'.[89] Trust is based on a belief – for instance, that a partner is dependable, cares for your interests, is competent and/or will act with integrity. Trust is distinct from other relational variables such as group cohesion (the attractiveness of a group to its members), friendship (the close pre-existing ties between individuals) and familiarity (specific knowledge about another person). Trust and distrust may represent two distinct psychological processes that are associated with different antecedents and consequences. In the study of the influence of emotions on negotiation goals described earlier in this chapter, it was further shown that while distrust but not trust mediated the effect of anger, trust but not distrust mediated the effect of compassion.[90]

The degree of trust an individual has in a work partner directly or indirectly affects a number of work outcomes, such as work performance, **organizational citizenship behaviour**, organizational commitment, turnover intentions, satisfaction and group performance. Trust also influences group-level performance and citizenship behaviour.[91] Trust is reciprocally related to group process and performance – as people work together more efficiently and with better results, they come to trust one another more and that in turn leads them to work together more efficiently and perform better.

In interactions, trust influences levels of disclosure, openness and (in)formality on the part of speakers, and willingness to listen, believe and be persuaded on the part of receivers. Trust has been shown to promote open and influential information exchange, reduce transaction costs and conflict, and improve performance in inter-organizational collaborations.[92] In business settings, trust is required for partner organizations or co-workers to work together effectively. Without trust, partners will not share information openly, and transactions must be carefully contracted and monitored to prevent exploitation. Without trust, co-workers may avoid close coordination with others, thus limiting their productive capacity. If high degrees of trust can be established, organizations can work more efficiently and adapt more quickly to changing circumstances.[93]

Having high status leads people to trust others more because status alters how they perceive others' intentions towards them. So, for instance, high status people are more likely to think that others' intentions towards them are benevolent.[94] People are more likely to regard someone as trustworthy if he or she seems to have higher self-control; this applies with strangers as well as in established relationships. Perceivers not only detect another person's trait of self-control but do so quite accurately.[95]

Trust and cmc

Trust is a particularly important consideration when work or transactions are conducted by cmc because mediated interactions carry increased risk. As users might be placed in different contexts or cultures, misunderstandings become more likely and enforcement of agreements and regulations becomes more difficult. As risks increase and become more difficult to evaluate, users of collaborative technologies face more complex decisions. Trust helps to reduce this complexity – it is a shortcut for a full-scale, laborious evaluation of the risks and benefits involved. Because it fosters knowledge exchange and so team effectiveness, in new product development teams trust is particularly important for globally dispersed and nationally diverse teams using cmc.[96]

Unfortunately, research shows, it can be more difficult to develop trust in an online setting than ftf. Thus, as communication technologies replace ftf encounters, there is the danger of a proliferation of low-trust interactions. In the long run, low-trust interactions are more costly than trust-based interactions due to the increased need for contractual agreements and external enforcement.[97]

Trust was inhibited when three-person groups interacted via email rather than ftf (although in this study the effects diminished over time). This is consistent with other experimental studies of cmc, which have shown that text-based interaction increases the sense of social distance between participants, reduces pressure to conform, and may encourage uninhibited behaviour. These characteristics make trust harder to create and maintain. Text chat too produces lower perceived intimacy, co-presence and emotionally based trust than other communication modes such as audio, audio–video and avatar.[98] Again, studies of synchronous communication with chat, or other forms of cmc such as audio and video, show that when virtual teams need to establish trust at a distance, it is advantageous for them to use rich media to communicate. Ftf, video and audio all showed significant improvements over text chat in terms of trust development. Video and audio conferencing groups were nearly as good as ftf, but both did show some evidence of delayed trust (slower progress toward full cooperation) and fragile trust (vulnerability to opportunistic behaviour).[99]

❝ The fact that emails leave an audit trail makes them the perfect civil service tool. In conjunction with the Freedom of Information Act this creates a brake on candour. Civil servants are now aware that everything they put in writing, however minor or at however early a stage, or however just an idea, may be opened up for scrutiny. They feel threatened. So they won't put it in writing if they have any doubts – they'll phone instead. (As far as I know, internal calls within the civil service are not recorded – unlike the bank where I work now.) Or they'll say 'Shall we go and have a coffee?' and you know they want to speak about something that might be sensitive. Once a Minister wanted to meet me face-to-face before I did some work for him, although it was not normal procedure; I think he wanted to know if he could trust me.

(Author's interview with a former UK civil servant)

As with other consequences of using cmc, although trust is generally slower to develop in cmc than ftfc, over time trust in cmc can increase to levels comparable to that in ftfc. When people undertake projects via cmc, high levels of trust can be maintained by engaging in continuous and frequent interaction, being more efficient in moving through the phases of the project, focusing on the work content, and achieving enough social penetration during the first part of the project to increase work effectiveness through to the project's conclusion.[100]

Communication through technology-mediated sales communication tools such as video-conferencing systems, mobile phones, web sites and electronic data interchange systems have significant positive direct effects on industrial buyers' future intentions, especially when trust in and commitment to the seller is high. However, a person's trust in the intentions of a stranger met during a business transaction is affected by choice of communication mode and trust in turn influences how that person behaves. Media richness positively influences both trust based on feeling (affective-based trust), which in turn influences whether the individual lies (practises deception), and trust based on cognitions (cognitive-based trust), which in turn influences whether the individual defects (behaves uncooperatively).[101]

Prejudice

Prejudice is a 'negative attitude toward a person or group based upon a social comparison process in which the individual's own group is taken as a positive point of reference'. Social-cognitive explanations for the tenacity of prejudice stem from the assumption that categorization based on group differences (e.g. age, race, gender) is an automatic and universal process which inevitably leads to differential evaluation of group members (i.e. prejudice). Two kinds of prejudice have been identified: implicit prejudice, based on an unconscious, automatic association between group members and negative evaluation; and explicit prejudice, or affect that is consciously apathetic. There is strong evidence of implicit prejudice based on religion (Jewish vs Christian), age (young vs old) and nationality (American vs Soviet) as well as gender and ethnicity. Because implicit prejudice operates without individuals' conscious awareness, it may unintentionally influence judgements and behaviours in ways detrimental to members of stigmatized groups. Importantly and unfortunately, social-cognitive research has been recording the universality of implicit prejudice at the same time as survey research is documenting dramatic decreases in explicit prejudice and stereotypes.[102]

Fortunately, a positive shift in attitudes can follow contact with members of minority groups. The idea that bringing people from different groups into direct contact and interaction reduces stereotyping and prejudice has been extensively tested and supported. Contact can also be indirectly associated with attitudes to secondary outgroups, via attitude generalization. For instance, a person who is prejudiced both against people with a particular different ethnicity and against people with a particular sexual orientation may, through contact with members of the ethnic group, come to lose their prejudice not only against people with that ethnicity but also their prejudice against people with the sexual orientation that they previously disliked or despised.[103]

Prejudice and cmc

Prejudice may be more likely to be expressed openly in internet-based communication when it is anonymous, spontaneous, impersonal and disinhibited. Compounding this is the possibility that people expressing such attitudes will be reinforced by those who write in support, perhaps creating an 'illusion of large numbers'.[104] Furthermore, the enhanced ingroup identification that SIDE research has shown may occur in cmc could, in turn, contribute to stronger prejudice above and beyond the disinhibiting effects of anonymity.

On the other hand, because potential targets are also able to remain anonymous, perhaps concealing group-identifying cues, many forms of discrimination may be less common in cyberspace. It is also possible that the internet, with its ability to promote communication across physical and cultural boundaries, has the potential to reduce intergroup bias. However, such interactions are qualitatively different from the types of ftf contact that have typically been involved in studies on this topic. One scholar has questioned whether some cmc is 'contact' at all.[105]

Unfortunately, we have as yet rather limited empirical work on prejudice online, but there is some that shows that implicit prejudice extends to the online environment and some that automatic racial bias is not reduced by embodying a person of a disfavoured racial group. Dutch participants immersed in a virtual environment in which they encountered virtual persons (avatars) with either white or Moroccan facial features maintained more distance and showed an increase in skin conductance level when approaching Moroccan avatars as opposed to white avatars; it was concluded that prejudiced implicit associations may unintentionally lead to impulsive discriminatory responses and that these prejudiced impulses persist even though people know that the avatar is not a 'real' person.[106]

Values

It is important to society that individuals behave in certain ways and avoid behaving in other ways, and most members of any given society interpret its values as positive and endorse behaving in accordance with them. General values influence evaluations of specific objects and events. For instance, the values of communalism and the work ethic predict attitudes toward welfare,[107] power values are linked to competitiveness, benevolence values to cooperative behaviour. People are able to explain their choices in terms of values, emphasizing those that are important to them and relevant to the situation.[108]

Work values

Work values are a subset of values that suggest general patterns of behaviour that individuals expect to exhibit at work; they influence communication and other aspects of work behaviour. Research by Ravlin and Meglino (1987) suggests that the four work values of achievement, helping others, honesty and fairness are the most prominent for individuals, though these findings probably exhibit a cultural bias. They found that work values affect both individuals' perceptions and decision-making in organizations.[109]

A study of 411 team members from 72 Taiwanese corporate teams showed that the performance of individual team members and their level of satisfaction with cooperation in the team were positively related to having shared work values with team-mates. These relationships were, however, mediated by the perceived trustworthiness and trustfulness of the individual. When trust in the individual by his or her team-mates was low, the influence of shared

> *Selection interviewers sometimes ask this question: 'You are driving along a lonely road late at night. You see three people waiting beside the road, all obviously needing a lift. You can only take one of them. One is an old woman who is very ill, one is your best friend and one is your lover. To which of them would you give a lift?' What would your answer be? Why do you think they ask this question?*

work values on the team member's performance was reduced and vice versa when trust was high; when the individual had low trust in his or her team-mates, shared work values had less effect on his or her satisfaction with cooperation.[110]

Relationship values

Interpersonal values – those that concern relations with others – affect assumptions about how similar another person is. People with stronger communal values were more likely to assume self–other similarity with liked others, romantic partners and ingroup members but not with disliked others and outgroup members. These effects replicate across different cultures (India, Korea and the United States) and remain significant when controlling for self-esteem, national identification and attribute desirability.[111]

Managerial values

Managerial values vary across cultures, even within country groups that generally exhibit low **cultural distance** from one another. For example, Canadian managers show greater deference to authority than Australians do; Canadians are less 'assertive' and more embracing of a 'humane orientation' than Australians and Americans; Australian managers are less 'obsessed with profit maximization' than Americans, and so place a correspondingly lower perceived value on high achievement and individual success; Americans place greater importance on the value of 'competence' relative to Canadians, which underscores the American emphasis on 'individual achievement'.[112]

Cultural values

As Section 6.1 explained, fundamental values are considered to be at the core of cultural differences. These values affect communication; for instance, individualistic values tend to lead people to use low-context communication, and collectivistic values tend to lead people to use high-context communication.[113]

Values and cmc

Values affect media choice. For example, individual employees' personal values affect their choice of media: a 1999 study found that 'new' media such as email were used more by individuals with an orientation to innovation rather than reactivity or entrepreneurship. Relationship-orientation rather than task-orientation was also associated with email use, suggesting that the amount of feedback plays a role in the process of telecommunications media choice.[114]

Summary

Attitudes are dispositions to phenomena; values are highly stable attitudes. Attitudes predict behaviour less than is commonly believed, though stronger, more accessible and possibly more ambivalent attitudes have more impact.

Trust is an attitude that affects several work outcomes including group performance. Because it fosters disclosure, openness and informality, trust is vital for overcoming barriers to effective working by cmc, but also slower to develop than in ftfc.

Prejudice is a negative attitude towards a person or group based on taking one's own group as a positive point of reference. In many countries explicit prejudice is decreasing but implicit prejudice increasing. Contact counteracts prejudice. Anonymity in cmc allows more overt expression of prejudice but also concealment of targets' identity; the distance implied by cmc does not, however, reduce prejudice.

Values help to explain choices including choice of mode for communication; work values, relationship values, managerial values and cultural values are all important.

7.5 INTENTIONS, ABILITIES AND COMPETENCIES

The combination of motives, affect, cognition and attitudes can result in an intention to perform or not perform an action. Abilities may enable or impede the carrying out of an intention.

Intentions

An intention represents a planned course of action. Intentions are derived from attitudes, subjective norms and perceived behavioural control. Intentions do play an important role in guiding human action, but intentions are not translated into actual behaviour in a straightforward way. For instance, people are better able to follow a diet when they have not only formed an intention to do so, but have also formulated an implementation plan. A further complication is that most human pursuits involve other participating agents. Such joint activities require commitment to a shared intention and coordination of interdependent plans of action. The challenge in collaborative activities is to meld diverse self-interests in the service of common goals. These complications reduce the impact of intentions on behaviour. On average, intentions account for only 28 per cent of the variance in subsequent behaviour.[115]

Abilities and competencies

Abilities are capacities for doing things. They are a function of aptitudes, which are inherited dispositions, and environment (including learning or training). In organizations competencies, or the ability of an individual to do a particular job effectively, have recently been given more prominence than general abilities. Competencies can be seen as a combination of practical and theoretical knowledge, skills, behaviour and values.

Managers need to be able to assess others' competencies in order to be successful in employee selection, promotion and deployment, in deciding on training needs, adjusting the style of briefing or on-the-job instruction and assessing subordinates' performance.

The ability that perhaps is most widely valued in organizations in the modern world is intelligence, though it is hard to define or measure. Recently concepts called fluid and crystallized intelligence have attracted the interest of researchers. Fluid intelligence is the capacity to think logically and solve problems in novel situations, independent of acquired knowledge; crystallized intelligence is the ability to use skills, knowledge and experience by accessing information from long-term memory. Crystallized intelligence improves somewhat with age, as experiences tend to expand a person's knowledge.[116] Fluid intelligence is linked to short-term memory capacity, working memory capacity and neural processing speed, though working memory capacity seems to predict general fluid intelligence better than the other variables.[117]

In the 1990s much interest was aroused by a concept called emotional intelligence, which its originators call an ability. They defined the concept as 'an ability to recognize the meanings of emotions and to reason and problem solve on the basis of them'.[118] Unlike traditional views of emotion and intelligence, research based on emotional intelligence theory has 'demonstrated the symbiotic nature of the relationship between these complementary ways of apprehending and understanding the world'.[119] Emotional intelligence is, clearly, an ability particularly relevant to interaction skill and one in which there are individual differences.

In 2011 a meta-analysis showed that emotional intelligence has correlations of between 0.24 and 0.30 with job performance.[120] Emotional intelligence is also positively associated with constructive conflict management, for both leaders and subordinates, but more strongly for subordinates.[121] Côté and Miners (2006) found support for the hypothesis that task performance is more positively associated with emotional intelligence when cognitive intelligence is low; in other words, high emotional intelligence can help compensate for low cognitive intelligence so far as task performance is concerned.[122] Lindebaum and Cassell (2012) found, however, in the UK construction industry, that 'there are enduring, albeit changing, characteristics of the industry' and that the way project managers in the industry understand the concept of emotional intelligence 'renders the construct, at least for the time being, of limited utility'.[123]

Abilities and cmc

Obviously, being able to use cmc – possessing the necessary skills – determines whether it will be a communication mode option. Conversely, using cmc may affect more general abilities. Nearly one in five internet users reported changes concerning their memory or ability to concentrate as a result of internet use, with skilled computer users and non-workers, in particular, perceiving the change. Respondents identified age-related differences and exposure to potential **information overload** (difficulty in understanding an issue and making decisions that can be caused by the presence of too much information) to explain the perceived change.[124]

Summary

Intentions are planned courses of action derived from attitudes, subjective norms and perceived behavioural control. Intentions are carried out to a surprisingly low extent; lack of ability and other factors often intervene.

Abilities are capacities for doing things; intelligence, emotional intelligence and competencies, which combine abilities with practical and theoretical knowledge, skills, behaviour and values, are considered particularly important in modern work. Lack of relevant abilities, such as keyboard skills, can constrain media choices.

7.6 TRAITS, PERSONALITY AND THE SELF

Traits and personality

Traits are stable predispositions to act in a certain way, or habitual responses to situations. Honesty, competitiveness and cooperativeness, self-control and industriousness are traits. 'Personality' is often used to refer to a bundle of traits. Traits have attracted more interest from work psychologists than, for instance, moods or emotions, which pass quickly, because the qualities that traits ascribe are enduring ones and the behaviours they imply are recurring. This feature of trait judgements has led several psychologists to develop trait personality measures.

A theory of personality called the 'five-factor theory' identifies the traits of extraversion, neuroticism, openness to experience, agreeableness and conscientiousness as predominant in most personalities.

Trait-based approaches to personality do not explain how it develops or why it is what it is, but, according to Digman (1990), 'while deeper causal analysis may seem to account for the structure of personality, the structure that must be explained is, for now, best represented by the **five-factor model**'.[125] However, as Bond and Smith (1996), pointed out, the five-factor theory is a theory of implicit personality theories, the beliefs that people hold that certain traits tend to go together in the same individual: 'studies of implicit personality theory in any language studied to date indicate that a five-factor model can describe the organization of perceived personality. The apparent universality of the broad categories of extraversion, agreeableness, **conscientiousness**, emotional stability and openness to experience may arise from their importance in directing universal types of social behaviors such as association, subordination, and formality'.[126]

> To learn the meaning of the terms used in the five-factor model look in the Glossary.

Individuals' implicit personality theories significantly impact on how they behave towards others. Countering a common belief that the big five personality traits do not predict how people actually behave when faced with real pressures and real consequences of their actions, a meta-analysis of 20,000 reports of trait manifestation behaviours found that self-reported traits predict individuals' behaviour to a significant degree.[127] For example, in ftf interactions, extraverts show greater desire to communicate and initiate interactions, use a greater total number of words, talk more and initiate more individual and group laughter, have a higher speech rate in formal and informal situations and show less hesitation, although they also make a higher proportion of semantic errors.[128]

Traits and personality are linked to work behaviour and effectiveness: for example, employees with high agreeableness establish trustworthy and cooperative interactions with others, which in turn increases job satisfaction because of the positive relationships that are fostered.[129]

There are similarities in personality traits across cultures, but there may be additional personality factors specific to individual cultures, and some factors may be of greater or less importance in different cultures. Within the general framework of the five-factor model, culture accentuates certain of the dimensions over others. In free-response trait descriptions of themselves or of others, Chinese people, for example, use the category of conscientiousness more often and the category of agreeableness less often than Americans do. Moreover, the rated importance of each of the five categories varies among cultural groups, and these categories are differentially weighted in guiding social behaviour.[130]

> To learn more about the links between traits and work behaviour, visit the companion website...
> 7.6.1.

Traits, personality and cmc

Although the internet allows people to play with their identities, it would still seem that online behaviour tends to mimic the behaviour that corresponds to someone's offline personality.[131]

A 2010 review article drew the following conclusions on personality and patterns of internet consumption:

- Introverts are more drawn to online communication (specifically anonymous-style interactions) than extraverts; being high in extraversion is associated with levels of participation in computer conferences working on a problem-solving task. Extraverts 'still participate in online social activities' but may prefer to use activities that 'most saliently reflect their off-line identity'; both extraverts and introverts 'are receiving enhanced social support from cmc'. Online, extraverts respond more quickly to others' posts or messages.
- People who are highly neurotic 'value online communities, yet dislike online discussions'. They 'may use the Internet to escape feelings of loneliness': this applies especially to highly neurotic females, 'who use personal blogs as a form of online therapy'. High scorers on neuroticism 'may not fully benefit from the Internet because of apprehension associated with certain activities (e.g. forums)'.[132]

Problematic internet use (PIU) is a multidimensional syndrome that consists of cognitive, emotional and behavioural symptoms that result in difficulties with managing one's offline life. First, PIU is negatively associated with broader psychosocial well-being. Studies report significant correlations between PIU and loneliness, shyness, introversion, depression, aggression and social skill deficits. Second, the cognitive and behavioural symptoms of PIU appear to be especially related to online social interaction.[133] Consistently with PIU theory, Neo and Skoric (2009) found that oral CA and perceived inconvenience of using offline means are significant predictors of problematic IM use, whereas polychronicity (engaging in more than one conversation at a time) and trait procrastination are not.[134]

The self

Identity

Identity is a person's conception and expression of their characteristics, either as an individual or as a member of a particular social category or group. Identity strongly influences how people relate to one another, both at work and elsewhere. We construct our identities on the basis of social comparisons, how others respond to us and how we interpret our own thoughts, feelings and actions. There is evidence that people try to manage their identities by, for instance, regulating their interactions with others.

Members of complex organizations may have multiple social groups with which they identify; for instance, work group, organizational and professional identities.[135] Again, there may be significant cultural differences in identity, especially between cultures that inculcate independent and interdependent views of the self. These differences can have profound effects on individuals' motivations and interactive work behaviour.

Some individuals self-construct their identity online. Making a public presentation online has led people to internalize a trait that they presented – extraversion or introversion – to a greater extent than making a private presentation in a text document. Public self-presentations online also contained more certain and definite forms of language than private self-presentations, suggesting that audiences evoke a more committed form of self-presentation.[136]

Self-evaluations

According to one theory, core self-evaluations or the 'subconscious conclusions that individuals reach about themselves', influence 'all other appraisals of the self, others, and the world'. These self-evaluations, or self-assessments as they are also called, relate to aspects of the self as broad as moral worth or attractiveness and as narrow as how a recently completed task was performed. These self-evaluations change; for example, someone reading through an email they have just written and sent might judge it as succinct and cogent and evaluate themselves as an effective email communicator; then reading through the history of that correspondence they might notice some important points they had omitted and re-evaluate their competence.

There is substantial evidence that people err in their self-assessments, particularly of performance. These preconceived notions about their abilities with a task distort individuals' self-assessments of how they actually performed the task, a study reported. For instance, even assessments of an objectively measurable performance indicator – time taken to completion – was influenced by the individual's prior beliefs about their ability.[137]

People tend to see themselves as better than the average in abilities, that is, to self-enhance. However, contrary to the popular assumption that self-enhancement improves task motivation and future performance, both inflated and deflated self-assessments of performance are linked to an increased likelihood of practising self-handicapping (preferring to work under distraction and withholding preparatory effort), having relatively poor performance in future tasks and reporting a relatively low level of subjective well-being. These consequences follow from misperceiving actual performance, no matter at what level that actual performance was.[138]

Figure 7.1 Self-evaluation traits and job performance*

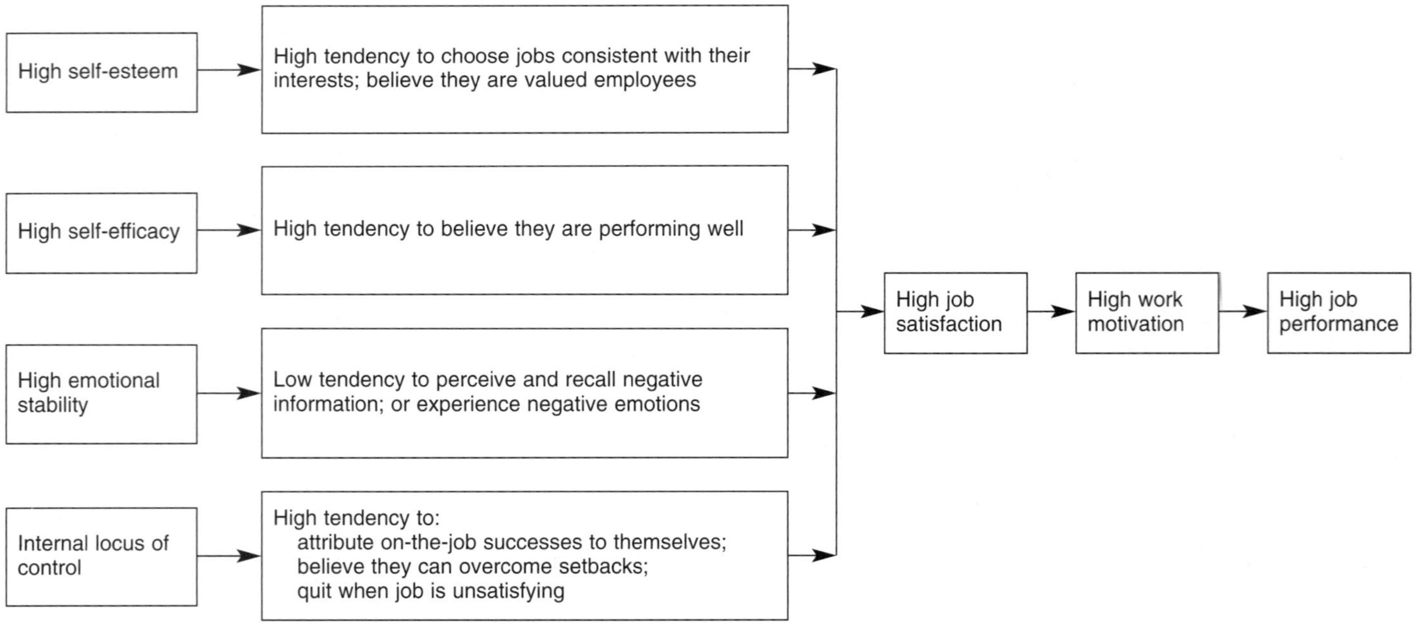

| High self-esteem | → | High tendency to choose jobs consistent with their interests; believe they are valued employees |

| High self-efficacy | → | High tendency to believe they are performing well |

| High emotional stability | → | Low tendency to perceive and recall negative information; or experience negative emotions |

| Internal locus of control | → | High tendency to: attribute on-the-job successes to themselves; believe they can overcome setbacks; quit when job is unsatisfying |

High job satisfaction → High work motivation → High job performance

Based on Stinson, D.A., Logel, C., Holmes, J.G., Wood, J.V., Forest, A.L., Gaucher, D., Fitzsimons, G.M. and Kath, J. (2010) The regulatory function of self-esteem: testing the epistemic and acceptance signalling systems', *Journal of Personality and Social Psychology*, **99**(6): 993–1013.

Judge, T.A. and Bono, J.E. (2001) 'Relationship of core self-evaluation traits – self-esteem, generalized self-efficacy, locus of control and emotional stability – with job satisfaction and job performance: A meta-analysis', *Journal of Applied Psychology*, **86**: 80–92.

Erez, A. and Judge, T.A. (2001) 'Relationship of core self-evaluations to goal setting, motivation and performance, *Journal of Applied Psychology*, **86**: 1270–79.

* Low values for self-esteem, self-efficacy and emotional stability and an external locus of control have the reverse effects on job performance

While people tend to see themselves as better than the average in abilities, in terms of personality they tend to view themselves less favourably than others do. For example, 'people see themselves as more neurotic and open to experience compared to how they are seen by other people. External observers generally hold a higher opinion of an individual's conscientiousness than he or she does about him- or herself. As a rule, people think that they have more positive emotions and excitement seeking but much less assertiveness than they seem to have from the vantage point of an external observer'.[139]

Core self-evaluations allow the identification of certain dispositional traits and help explain the effect that these traits have on employee job satisfaction and a number of other work-related issues. These traits are listed by Judge and Bono (2001) as self-esteem, generalized self-efficacy, emotional stability and internal or external locus of control.[140] Figure 7.1 shows how these self-evaluation traits affect job performance.

A process involved in the construction of the 'self' is self-regulation (or self-control). People undertake self-monitoring, performance self-guidance via personal standards and corrective self-reactions, and so self-regulate their motives, feelings and behaviour. One view is that the main motive for self-regulation is the fundamental need to belong. Being accepted – belonging – requires that we self-regulate and so alter or inhibit behaviours that would place us at risk of exclusion. In order to self-regulate, we need to self-monitor – that is, to be aware of our behaviour so as to gauge it against societal norms, to understand how others are reacting to our behaviour and to detect threat, especially in complex social situations. We also need to have mechanisms for resolving discrepancies between what we discover through self-monitoring and social expectations or norms; these 'mechanisms' consist of performance self-guidance via personal standards and corrective self-reactions.

The self-system allows self-regulation through self-reward and self-punishment – a possible basis of moral behaviour. Moral **agency** forms an important part of self-directedness. Moral reasoning is translated into actions through self-regulatory mechanisms, which include moral judgement of the rightness or wrongness of conduct evaluated against personal standards and circumstances, and self-sanctions by which moral agency is exercised.[141]

According to shared reality theory, which was described in Chapter 5, we understand the nature of the social world around us and our place in it from the messages that we receive from other people and their responses to us, particularly as we are growing up. In this way a shared reality is created between ourselves and others, particularly the significant others with whom we interact during socialization. The messages convey that the world has accomplishments to be promoted and dangers or mistakes to be prevented; these internalized messages create a balance that varies from individual to individual, from culture to culture and from time to time within the same individual. This shared reality becomes the basis for self-regulation – of whether we self-regulate by adopting a promotional or prevention focus, supporting an '**approach**' or 'avoid' attitude to life events. This is the basis of regulatory focus theory, which was explained in the context of motivation.

The self and cmc

Relative to an ftf comparison group, people using computer-mediation reported significantly higher levels of acute awareness of their 'private' self (personal feelings, attitudes, values and beliefs) and marginally lower levels of awareness of aspects that are sensitive to attention and evaluation by others, for example physical characteristics (their 'public' self). Cmc users who are low in public self-awareness are more likely to evaluate the social context negatively. The social evaluations of ftf subjects have not been found to be related to their levels of self-awareness.[142]

Summary

Traits are stable predispositions to act in a certain way; traits of extraversion, neuroticism, open-ness to experience, agreeableness and conscientiousness predominate in most people's implicit personality theories. Traits and personality are linked to work behaviour and effectiveness, patterns of internet consumption and, of course, communication behaviour.

Identity and self-evaluations are important aspects of the self, strongly influencing how people appraise the world and their consequent behaviour. Identity is a person's conception and expression of their characteristics; self-evaluations are the 'subconscious conclusions that individuals reach about themselves'. People tend to see themselves as better than the average in abilities but worse in terms of personality. People exercise self-regulation, including in the way described in self-regulatory theory.

8 INFLUENCING, HANDLING CONFLICT AND NEGOTIATING

This chapter examines influencing, handling conflict and negotiating, three uses of interpersonal communication that are somewhat different in nature at work compared with private life. Influencing is critical for personal selling, networking, making presentations, introducing change and subordinate–manager relations, business meetings and explicit negotiations. If conflict is handled so that it is constructive, then better decision-making and problem-solving can result from people advocating different solutions and arguing with each other. On the other hand, if conflict is mishandled and becomes destructive, worse, not better, solutions (or no solution at all) are the outcome and often lasting damage to working relationships also results. Negotiating takes place not only in the obvious situations of reaching agreements on inter-organizational contracts, industrial relations and international business, but also on the more mundane level of departmental budgets, salary settlements, holiday entitlements and timings and many other internal resource allocations and decisions.

On completing your study of this chapter you will be able to explain and apply the implications of:

- How influence is exerted through power and persuasion.
- How to exert power successfully.
- Factors that make sales calls effective.
- Techniques and strategies to increase the effectiveness of influencing by cmc.
- Different conflict-handling styles and the effect of the context, including culture and communication mode.
- How to work towards resolution of conflicts.
- Different approaches to negotiation and the effect of the context, including culture and communication mode.
- How to be a skilful negotiator face-to-face (ftf) or by computer-mediated communication (cmc).

8.1 INFLUENCING

Organizations are characterized by people's attempts to influence one another; supervisors, for example, often need to influence subordinates to work harder, longer or differently and accept change, to influence peers to adopt policies or strategies, to influence their own managers to support them, give them more resources (including power), pay them more or promote them.

Intentional influence – as distinct from, for instance, social influence, which can be unintentional – uses two methods: power and persuasion. Power relies on the ability to control others' outcomes, whereas persuading relies on the ability to change attitudes or beliefs. Both depend in practice on communication: power on conveying the message that the power holder wants his or her target to act in a certain way and that he or she possesses a relevant power source; persuading on providing new information or arguments to the target, or on appeals to emotion.

Although the most conspicuous of influence attempts in organizations are from managers to subordinates and, some would argue, the organization's effectiveness depends most directly on how successful those attempts are, upward influence attempts by subordinates to managers and laterally by colleagues to one another are also common and in some circumstances equally or more important. As earlier material in this book has shown, cmc has led to exponential growth in the amount of lateral communication in organizations; and with an increase in communication there is almost certain to be an increase in influencing.

Traditionally, managers' attempts to influence their subordinates depended on using power. However, using power may only produce compliance – an influence on behaviour that can be short-lived because beliefs and attitudes are either not affected or, in a process called **reactance**, negatively affected. Furthermore, in many organizations, the pervasive spread of information and knowledge via new media has undermined some bases for managing by exerting power or authority. Therefore managers, as well as organizational members who lack power over the person they want to influence, such as a lateral colleague, have turned increasingly to using persuasion, which aims for attitude change and so may be longer-lasting.

> *What arguments can you think of for and against the following two ethical principles that have been suggested for influencing?*
>
> 1. *Sharing influence is more ethical than exercising it unilaterally.*
> 2. *The ethics of advocacy differ from those of reporting, i.e. that objectivity is not required so long as the target clearly understands (and the advocate takes steps to ensure they understand) that what is in train is persuasion.*

Ethical issues arise in any attempt to influence others and must be considered; in particular they may infringe others' rights to autonomy, and they involve the influencer in responsibility for the outcome of the actions resulting from the influence.

Exerting power

In the words of Flynn et al. (2012):

> **"** limited resources, conflicting interests and task interdependencies make organizations fields for political activity... To understand organizational behaviour, then, one must understand power, which inevitably shapes how people make decisions, allocate resources and judge their colleagues ... To be effective leaders, managers must be able to diagnose who has power, how it is obtained and when it can be wielded effectively in order to advance their political goals and, in turn, benefit their constituents.[1]

Ensuring that subordinates comply with organizational policies and procedures is one of the responsibilities of team leaders, supervisors and managers. Carrying out this responsibility is one situation where power may be more appropriate than persuading, as subordinates need to understand that this compliance is mandatory, a lesson that may be undermined by the mere fact of their leader trying to persuade them. Even in these circumstances, though, care in the exercise of power is needed: compliance is impeded rather than supported by surveillance, when the person in authority is also seen by the subordinates as a member of their ingroup, such as a team member.[2]

It is generally agreed that power allows people to influence others but opinions vary on what power actually is. Structuralist theories of power are based on the view that it is a function of social positions such as organizational roles:

- One structuralist theory, deterrence theory, puts forward propositions about how the total amount of power and the power balance in a relationship affect how stable relationships are. Unequal power relationships are less stable than equal-power relationships and also more likely to lead to conflict escalation. This is because if they have any ability to 'punish' the higher power party, lower-power parties will resist efforts to coerce them into an agreement, resulting in more conflict.
- A second, network exchange theory, considers power in networks rather than dyads and proposes that weaker parties are less weak in circumstances where they are richly connected to their environment. The essence of 'strong' power lies in the absence of exchange opportunities for the weak and the exchange denials thus created. All else

being equal, higher connectivity provides more opportunities for people in weak positions to 'short-circuit' the structural advantages of the strong and thus a greater likelihood of small resource differentials, i.e. weaker power.

- A third theory, power-dependence theory, argues that A's power over B is a function of the netting out of B's dependence on A and A's dependence on B. Dependence itself is a function of a person's 'motivational investment' in the goals mediated by the other person and the ease or difficulty they would have in attaining those goals without the intervention of the other person.

An alternative to structuralist theories focuses instead on bases for social power. It argues that while reward, coercive and legitimate power are organizationally determined and designed to be equal for all supervisors or managers on the same hierarchical level, there are other bases for power: referent power (the power of an individual over others, based on their high level of identification with, admiration of, or respect for the person) and expert power (the power of knowledge) are 'idiosyncratic in character and depend upon an individual's unique role behavior'. These personal power bases have significant consequences: for example, in factories the expert power of a group's supervisor is related to a low accident rate, and both referent power and expert power are generally related to group production performance.[3]

These theories have implications for exerting power, because the structural power position and the possession or otherwise of power bases will affect the outcomes of attempts to exercise or restrain power, and therefore need to be realistically assessed; however, perceptual effects must also be taken into account. Some adaptations to structuralist theories specifically allow for cognitive intervening variables. One argues that people respond differently to the offensive and defensive use of punitive tactics, not just to the structural power position. Another is power-dependence theory, listed above, which argues that one person's power is a function of the other person's dependence, and considers depend-

> *Think again about the fact that when supermarket chains negotiate with small-scale producers, the price is likely to be more favourable to the supermarket chain than to the small-scale producers. Which theory about power explains this best?*

> *People sometimes voluntarily take on roles such as secretary of a committee or liaison officer between two departments or organizations because they see it as giving them influence. What power bases might these roles give?*
>
> *To learn more about social power bases, visit the companion website... 8.1.1.*

Figure 8.1 How having power may positively affect how people think and act

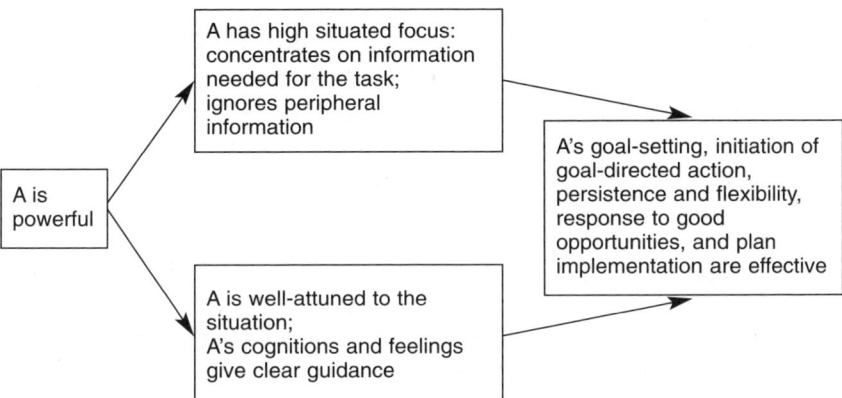

Based on Guinote, A. (2007) 'Power and goal pursuit', *Personality and Social Psychology Bulletin*, **33**(8): 1076–87; Guinote, A. (2007) 'Behaviour variability and the situated focus theory of power', *European Review of Social Psychology*, **18**(1): 256–95.

ence to be a function of the subjective value someone places on goals mediated by the other. For example if Eugene can determine whether Thomas will get a promotion, this still only gives him power over Thomas if Thomas wants the promotion.

Another theory argues that powerful individuals more easily gain their objectives partly because power makes them better at acting in a manner consistent with their goals, at receiving clearer guidance from mental processes and at being attuned to important rather than peripheral information. Figure 8.1 sets out the variables of this theory.

In this book the view is that different people have power in different relationships, and that power exists only when it is recognized by the target but, if it exists structurally, there is a real possibility that it will be so recognized. Therefore, having adequate and appropriate power bases relevant to a given relationship, such as position power or authority, reward and punishment power, knowledge or expert power, referent power or the power of connections, are necessary for asserting power successfully; assessing their strength and suitability is a first step to take when considering power exercise. Other factors also come into play, however. To exert power successfully, you need to believe that your case is strong; without that your communication is likely to be unconvincing. You also need to handle your own psychology of power, understand the motivational profile of the influence target and build the credibility of your power.

Asserting power can be both costly and risky. A failed power attempt can endanger important goals and relationships as well as damage the influencer's credibility. Therefore power exercise needs to be planned ahead, thinking in a systematic way about the various ways of mobilizing power, about the other party's probable responses, and about the benefits, costs and the circumstances in which to use each method. Successful power assertion by any mode

> To learn more about how to exert power successfully, visit the companion website... 8.1.2.

depends on skill in all the following: assessing the target and the costs and benefits of the exercise, choosing the appropriate power base and expressing the demand effectively.

Power can be increased by getting hold of more of its sources and/or by decreasing one's own dependence or increasing that of other parties, provided the changes can be successfully communicated to the influence targets. Strategies for retaining power include using it successfully, using it for information control, setting up regulations that preserve the individual's power base, fostering norms that make changes seem illegitimate, and rewarding supporters.

Even weak parties have powers of resistance, partly because it takes less power to resist than to assert. Short-run resistance measures include using persuasive skills and mobilizing the power-asserter's own behaviour norms against using power. In the longer run, alliances and building richer connectedness help low-power members to resist.

> To learn more about how to gain or resist power, visit the companion website... 8.1.3.

Power is usually associated with status, where status refers to 'the differentiation of prestige and deference among individuals'.[4] However, status and power have different consequences for the behaviour of the person possessing them. For example, status is positively associated with justice toward others, while power is negatively associated with justice toward others, although the positive effect of status on justice emerges when power is low and not when power is high.[5]

It is generally agreed that the naked display of power is counterproductive; it is more effective to use persuasive communication methods, allowing the relative power position of influencer and influence target to remain understood but unstated. That this is widely understood is suggested by a finding that 'communication of directives in organizations is done in a compact and incomplete way; subordinates are expected to fill in the implications of directives and behave

> A web editor wanted to tell the technical staff to stop uploading when the editors were downloading because editorial work had more urgency and was slowed up when technical staff were uploading. He decided to write them an email to avoid face loss – the technical staff had higher status than the editors and might well tell him to 'get lost'.

accordingly'.[6] In the words of Carli (2001), 'dominant behaviour, such as aggression or competitiveness, is relatively ineffective'. The use of non-verbal dominant behaviour, such as leaning forward across a table or making emphatic gestures, actually reduces a person's ability to influence others and is no more effective than displays of submission. Moreover, in group interactions, dominant people, whether men or women, evoke hostile and dominant reactions from fellow group members, are liked less than non-dominant members, and receive no particular gains from their dominance.[7] Instead, research has shown, consultation and rational persuasion are 'the tactics used most frequently, regardless of the direction of influence'.[8]

You are a team leader. You need to influence your team to take on an extra task. You know that they are already disgruntled, believing themselves to be overworked. How will you proceed?

There are gender differences in power that affect social influence. Men generally possess higher levels of expert and legitimate power than women do but women possess higher levels of referent power than men do. These differences are reflected, to some extent, in the influence strategies used by men and women. Women generally have greater difficulty exerting influence than men do, particularly when they use influence that conveys competence and authority.[9] Males in particular resist influence by women and girls more than females do, especially when influence agents employ highly competent styles of communication. Resistance to competent women can be reduced, however, when women temper their competence with displays of communality and warmth. The male advantage in influence is also reduced in domains that are traditionally associated with the female role and in group settings in which more than one woman or girl is present.[10]

Power concepts are an important element of culture and serve culturally relevant goals; studies have shown that how power is conceived varies across cultures. These studies provide evidence that cultures nurture different views of what is desirable and meaningful to use power for. For instance, individualism is associated with conceiving power in personalized terms (i.e. power is for advancing one's personal status and prestige), whereas collectivism is linked to conceiving power in socialized terms (i.e. power is for benefitting and helping others). Cultural variables predict beliefs about appropriate uses of power, memories about occasions involving power, attitudes in the service of power goals, and the contexts and ways in which power is used and defended.[11]

Exerting power by cmc

Although there is a large literature devoted to power in organizations, only a little of it deals with communicating power online. Panteli (2002) showed that text-based messages may be so constructed as to convey the social cues that are traditionally used to determine power and status differences in organizations; for instance, an email summoning people to a meeting at a certain time would clearly originate with someone in authority.[12] Another study found that people could successfully recognize and negotiate power differentials when communicating via emails. For example, people create a submissive identity by writing lengthy emails and using several 'want statements' and a humbling tone. To create an authoritative identity they use dialogic, informal, personal communication with an authority figure.[13] Perceived power affects the choices people make in deciding when to initiate email discussion and respond to others, and about decisions concerning whose messages they will read and when.

These findings suggest that power still operates in the online environment but there is evidence that status effects are reduced, weakening the influence of high-status individuals. The extent to which lower status individuals defer to the opinions of higher status individuals during group communication, that is the degree to which higher status individuals are able to influence lower status individuals, is higher among unsupported ftf groups than in cmc groups. Sustained influence (the extent to which the influence of higher status individuals is able to persist over time) and perceived influence (the level of awareness of influence attempts by higher status individuals on the part of lower-status individuals) are also lower in cmc. These differences between cmc and ftf appear to be cross-cultural; they were found in both Singapore and the USA.[14]

Persuading

To persuade is to influence by communicating information, feelings or reasoning, either separately or together. To a much greater degree than using power, persuading can get people to change their attitudes. It can also be more effective and have a more positive effect on how the influencer is perceived: managers who communicated using persuasive ('soft influence') tactics during the implementation of a change to self-directed work teams were both perceived to be more effective and had a significant positive effect on participation by team members, a study found.[15]

For persuasion, raising the level of dissonance that people feel between their attitudes and their other beliefs or behaviour can shift attitudes. Dissonance theory argues that, if a person has a high level of dissonance between their attitudes and their other beliefs or behaviour, they will change the attitude if doing so is easier than changing the other beliefs or behaviour. Understanding this can help in exerting influence. For example, if junior professionals such as lawyers regard filling in time sheets as a waste of time, it may well work better simply to insist that they do it, like it or not, rather than to try to get them to do it by persuading them of the usefulness of the information. Once they are completing the time sheets regularly they will usually be more easily convinced of their value, because then the pressure to preserve consistency is working in that direction.

Both giving targets a free choice and giving only low incentives to comply raise dissonance by giving them a sense of personal responsibility, without which they are unlikely to feel any dissonance between their actions and their previous attitudes. Increasing people's sense that they need to justify their action increases dissonance.[16] If people give in to extreme pressure they are likely to reason to themselves that they had no choice, whereas if they give in to moderate pressure they are likely to provide themselves with reasons for doing so and these reasons can shift their attitudes.[17] Again, because people feel a need for consistency between their attitudes to a person and an associated attitude object, influencers should pay as much attention to the target's attitude to themselves as to any attitudes of the target they want to influence.[18]

Experienced sales representatives who know that their company's products are more expensive than those of the competition will not wait for the customer to point this out. They will refer to it early on, before mentioning that their company has a more durable and reliable product, better delivery, less expensive spare parts and so on. Why is this approach effective?

How an influencer communicates a persuasive attempt is, of course, crucial. Messages intended to persuade can be based on an emotional appeal – consider the way advertisers use small children and puppies in their advertisements – but within organizations they usually contain an argument in favour of the advocated position. Two types of argument can be distinguished: argument by generalization and argument by analogy. To argue by generalization means to 'claim a general principle from a series of instances'; to argue by analogy is to compare two situations which are believed to have the same essential characteristics. Depending on the type of argument, either statistical or anecdotal evidence will be more persuasive. Statistical evidence is more persuasive when the argument type is 'by generalization' and again in the case of argument by analogy when the anecdotal evidence is dissimilar to the case in the claim. However, when the anecdotal evidence is similar to the case in the claim and the argument is one 'by analogy', anecdotal evidence is as persuasive as statistical evidence.[19]

The belief component of some attitudes can be changed by new information, while the affect component responds more to emotional appeals; trying to change values can be effective when message recipients are inclined to resist change.

For examples of argument by generalization and argument by analogy, visit the companion website... 8.1.4.

Finally, the receptivity of the target and the quality, appropriateness and method of delivery of the persuasive message influence how persuasive a communication will be:

- The communication goals of the target, whether they process the message systematically or heuristically, and whether they are multi-tasking when they receive the message, affect their persuadability;
- Repeating persuasive messages and positioning them successively further from the target's original position usually increase persuasiveness.

Culture and gender have an influence on persuadability and on the impact of the communication mode. Ftf, individuals from collectivistic cultures tend to conform more than their counterparts from individualistic cultures do, and women are least likely to agree in conditions of low social interaction, whereas men are least likely to agree in conditions that provide the most social challenge. However, the cultural difference in persuadability between collectivists and individualists occurs only in ftfc, being absent in cmc.[20] Again, women are less likely to agree with a persuasive message sent by email, compared with the same message delivered ftf; for men, however, the communication mode makes little difference to their persuadability.[21]

> To learn more about the factors that affect persuasion, visit the companion website... 8.1.5.
>
> A supervisor said to a subordinate, 'Working on anything interesting these days?'
> The subordinate replied, 'It's mainly routine.'
> Later in the conversation, the supervisor asked the subordinate to take on additional work.
> Why might the supervisor's approach be effective?

Persuasion and cmc

Research findings indicate that in cmc there is a negative relationship between perceived physical distance and influence; moreover persuasion is greatest when the time delay before a response is received is neither too short nor too long. These findings suggest that there are significant drawbacks associated with using computer networks to communicate persuasive messages over long distances.[22] Even in small group discussions there were fewer opinion changes after a persuasive message was introduced by cmc than ftf. This suggests that people in a discussion through cmc have more time to think in ways that could lead to resisting the effects of a persuasive message.[23] Again, the anonymity provided by some forms of mediated communication may undermine source credibility and influence. Receivers have been shown to attach lower value to sources and messages transmitted in, for instance, electronic meeting systems.

Even in anonymous cmc, however, contribution total and word total, assertiveness and exaggeration (but not emotional intensity and sensitivity), significantly predict who is perceived as directive and/or influential.[24] More specifically, the number of persuasive arguments and argument sources significantly and independently affect personal opinion change within a computerized communication environment.[25] Avatars support social presence, leading to increased message processing, which in turn increases both positive attitude and behavioural intentions toward an issue.[26]

It is more effective to switch between different information and communication technologies (ICTs) to deliver repeated messages when attempting to exert interpersonal influence. Switching between complementary ICTs, for instance between text-based media like email or audio-facilitating media like the telephone, increases receivers' perceptions of information effectiveness, attitudes and behavioural intentions compared to using the same ICT again. The use of complementary ICTs probably mitigates receivers' perceptions of overload ('Not again!') and in this way increases their persuadability.[27]

In addition, the persuasion strategies that are effective in text-based cmc differ from those that are most effective ftf, where 'using an emotional argument to get what you want' was found to be the most persuasive strategy, followed by 'using a logical argument to get what you want', then 'persuading others by offering rewards' and last 'threatening negative consequences'. All four persuasion strategies were found to be less effective in cmc, but their hierarchy of effectiveness was different to that in ftf: promising a reward was found to be the most persuasive in cmc, followed by the threat of punishment, then logic and then emotional appeals.[28]

Finally, a study found that upward influence strategies in virtual work contexts are different to those in physical contexts. Specifically, Steizel and Rimbau-Gilabert (2013) found that ingratiation is rarely used in virtual contexts, and rationality is more frequently used; they also identified a new tactic in virtual work contexts: intermediation. This term refers to using a third party to help define the best influencing approach to the target.[29]

> *Zeke is team leader of a team of three game designers who are working on a design to submit for a contract to build a new game. He knows that they are spending a great deal of time surfing the net and playing games they have downloaded. He feels that it is getting out of control and needs to be reduced, though he recognizes that at least some of this activity can be justified in terms of the project. How should he proceed? If he considers exerting his authority as team leader, what factors should influence his decision? In whatever way he proceeds, how should he communicate his influence attempt to the other team members?*

Combining power and persuasion

Successful influence often uses a combination of power and persuasion. The methods explained here need to be used strategically to have their best effect. Influence strategies are affected by the influencer's goals, perceived power, culture and ethical beliefs. For instance, if the goal is to give advice, explaining reasons for the suggestion is an appropriate strategy; if it is to ask a favour, persisting despite resistance or indifference is effective; if it is to enforce an obligation, exerting strong pressure and persisting despite resistance are strategies that have been shown to work. According to the user's and the target's culture, the use of punishment, moral pressure or modelling (influencing by example) may or may not be endorsed.

Summary

Structuralist power theories are based on the view that power inheres in social positions. Structuralist power theories such as deterrence theory and network exchange theory do not accept that power is mediated through influence targets' perceptions, although there are versions of structuralist theories that allow for the effect of cognitions and subjective values. Social power theories also do not take cognitive variables directly into account, although one contends that power affects outcomes by influencing the cognitions and behaviours of the powerful. In this book I take the view that the so-called 'bases of power', such as the ability to reward or punish, have information control or access to important people, and so on, have their effect by influencing both the influencer's and the target's beliefs about the latter having to comply with the former's demands. Stylistic factors, such as a convincing appearance of being authoritative, can also be effective.

Influence attempts based on power should be communicated persuasively, using consultation and reasoning. Gender and cultural influences on attitudes and responses to power should be taken into account. Power still operates in the online environment but there is evidence that status effects are reduced, weakening the influence of high-status individuals.

Persuading means influencing people by getting them to change their attitudes and beliefs. It relies on communicating reasons for these changes, as distinct from using power, which relies on the ability to control others' outcomes. Compliance can be produced by strong pressure but long-term attitude change requires more subtle methods. Adjusting the types of supporting evidence (statistical or anecdotal) for the kind of argument (by generalization or analogy), and using value-based messages, are techniques that can help to persuade. Using moderate pressure, adjusting for the characteristics of the target's existing attitudes, certainty about the influence object, intelligence and motivations underlie persuasive techniques. Being a credible source and fostering a positive attitude of the target to the influencer are important.

There are cultural and gender differences in persuadability, and these differences also vary between ftfc and cmc. In general, time delays, distance and in some cases anonymity reduce persuadability by cmc compared to ftf. There are, however, techniques and strategies to increase the effectiveness of persuasion by cmc, including repeating messages and varying the medium.

Text-based cmc may be less effective than other modes for persuading, though there are ways of writing that increase its effectiveness. The order of the impact of four persuasion strategies varies between ftf and cmc.

How to make effective sales calls ftf or by telephone:

- Sales calls are social interactions based on human communication behaviour; they are not a form of instrumental action based on technical rules.[30]
- Selling entails mutual adjustments by sellers and buyers.
- Sellers who are sensitive to buyers' motivational patterns are more effective.[31]
- The larger the number of cooperative responses that occur in a sales dialogue, the greater the probability of a sale resulting.
- The more similar the sales person to the buyer, the greater the probability of a sale resulting. Similarity of personal situation, attitudes, likes and dislikes, appearance and other symbols of social background, occupational status and professional/educational background, can all create an affinity which helps produce the sale.
- A friendly demeanour, showing interest in the buyer and implying reciprocity are positive for sales.
- Relevant expertise of a salesperson increases the buyers' trust.
- The main negative identified by research is behaving like a stereotypical 'salesman', though sales personnel should match buyers' role expectations of them.

8.2 HANDLING CONFLICT

No-one who has worked in an organization of any size can be unaware that conflicts among co-workers do arise and are often damaging both to them personally and to the organization. Arguing in favour of the benefits to organizations of conflict, however, Tjosvold (2008) argued that 'studies by diverse researchers have documented the contribution of conflict to making decisions', claiming that among other benefits it encourages innovation and reduces cost.[32] However, a 2008 literature review concluded that the evidence that workplace conflict is beneficial to the organization is rather weak.[33]

Lau and Cobb (2010) argued that the reason why interpersonal (relationship) conflict has a negative impact on job performance, as research has shown it to, is that the interaction between co-workers changes from being based on **relational trust** and reciprocity, instead becoming negotiated and '**calculus-based**'.[34] Conflict can lead to an employee experiencing social exclusion by co-workers, and this experi-

> To learn more about why Tjosvold (2008) believed that conflict is beneficial, and why a literature review concluded that it may not be, visit the companion website... 8.2.1.

ence actually causes people to behave aggressively, even towards others with whom they had no previous contact. Part of the explanation seems to be that excluded people develop a hostile cognitive bias such that, for instance, they rate the ambiguous actions of others as hostile.[35] Disputes over people's relative status in their group's social hierarchy are a type of conflict that have been shown to affect group task performance by undermining information sharing even more than other types of conflict do.[36]

Sexual harassment and bullying are two extreme examples of conflictual relations at work that have negative effects on organizations. Working in an environment characterized by bullying increases individual employees' turnover intentions. Importantly, employees report similarly high turnover intentions when they are either the direct target of bullying or when they work in units characterized by high bullying. In fact, the impact of unit-level bullying is stronger on those who are not often directly bullied themselves.[37] When a considerable level of bullying by email occurred in a large multinational company, it led to anxiety and intent to leave the organization as well as being negatively associated with job satisfaction and performance.[38]

Damaging conflicts can arise over a genuine conflict of interest – if, for instance, only one person can be promoted and two or more are desperate to get that promotion and each is convinced that he or she is the best person for the job. Many work conflicts, however, occur because of communication breakdowns. One person, in a bad mood that day, snaps at another and, as in private life,

> **❝** people reciprocate unpleasant behaviour in social interactions and get stuck in reciprocated contentious communications in negotiations. A change of perception can occur, leading to the other being seen as less moral than oneself, more different than previously thought, untrustworthy and an 'enemy'. If this change of perceptions occurs, then more aggressive behaviour towards the other is likely. Disliked others tend to receive more blame while liked others are given the benefit of the

doubt; ambiguous actions are more likely to be seen as threatening, inhibitions against retaliation are reduced, **avoidance** takes place, communication empathy is reduced.[39]

Conflicts easily escalate. One psychological factor promoting escalation is the way that people attribute exaggerated influence to others whom they consider enemies. They do this as a means of compensating for perceptions of reduced control over their environment, four studies showed. Perceiving oneself as having powerful enemies, although superficially disagreeable, may serve an important psychological function by bolstering feelings of personal control.[40]

Conflict handling styles include competition, avoidance, accommodation, compromise and collaboration. Table 8.1 sets out their characteristics. Compromise and, especially, collaboration are more effective than the first three.

The review that concluded that workplace conflict is on balance harmful also concluded that there is a need for cooperative conflict management (i.e. collaborative conflict handling styles) in organizations to prevent it from doing too much damage.[41] Cooperative styles of conflict management foster team performance, while competitive styles are negatively associated with it.[42]

Table 8.1   Characteristics of different conflict handling styles

Conflict handling style	Characteristics
Competition	Each party pursues his or her own interest with the aim of 'winning'; they conceal information and have negative attitudes toward alternative solutions. Competitive interactions involve the use of power and attempts to dominate.
Avoidance	This style is characterized by evasiveness and unwillingness to confront other parties. People acting in this way are generally apathetic about the conflicting points of view and the outcomes.
Accommodation	This style is characterized by an obliging concern for others at the expense of one's own rights or claims.
Compromise	The parties acknowledge differences in preferences and work to settle on an intermediate position. This style is characterized by intermediate concern for self and others.
Collaboration	People emphasize openness to others' points of view, consider all information objectively and share problem-solving, aiming for a jointly optimal solution.

Preferences for different conflict-handling styles seem to be culturally influenced: responses to receiving an offensive communication from a co-worker vary cross-culturally. Both Koreans and Americans are most motivated to reconcile (that is, take less offence) when the co-worker is seen as similar to themselves, but whereas Koreans are most motivated to reconcile when the offence targets them personally, Americans are most motivated to reconcile when the offence targets their group. These findings are consistent with the collectivist/individualist model of cultural difference, in which collectivists, such as the Koreans, identify most strongly with their group, while individualists, such as the Americans, self-identify. Further support for this analysis comes from a finding that Koreans (but not Americans) are more likely to avoid and to seek revenge on a co-worker whose offensive remark was group rather than personally directed.[43]

There are also cultural preferences for conflict resolution, with people from collectivist cultures preferring third-party interventions, while people from individualistic cultures opt for direct methods such as confrontation. Even in individualistic cultures, however, parties to interpersonal conflict often bring in third parties such as co-workers, friends or family, not to intervene, but to help them make sense of the situation. Talking, interaction, conversation, argument and dialogue with others assist individuals to make sense of problematic situations they find themselves in. The focus of the party initiating sense-making (usually, but not always, the person engaged in a conflict) helps decide whether emotional, cognitive or behavioural components of sense-making are most emphasized in the interaction with the third party.[44]

Intercultural conflict resolution may use 'universal' methods, such as offering unilateral initiatives, or may attempt to take cultural difference into account, as in an approach suggested for international **joint ventures**:

> **❝** although conflict management is often thought to be limited to the individualistic West, our studies conducted since the mid-1990s indicate that cooperative conflict management can be very useful for teamwork and alliance partners in China. Indeed, experimental and field studies have found that collectivist, compared to individualistic, values promote cooperative, positive conflict. Conflict management strengthens genuine harmony and respected, effective leadership.[45]

How to work towards resolution of conflicts:

- Use perspective-taking: try to see the other party's point of view.
- Think about how they are likely to respond to any action you take.
- Look for aspects of the situation that you may have missed or that may have changed.
- Do not be tempted into demonizing your opponent.

- Be prepared to listen to and fully appreciate your opponent's arguments, even though they may not be convincing or justify their attitude or behaviour.
- Use silence or active listening to get your opponent to express his or her emotions; never throw fuel on the flames.
- Treat the repair process as a shared problem to be worked on together.
- To succeed in these actions you will need to handle your own emotional responses to the conflict. Discussing the problem with a constructive friend can help in this.[46]

Conflict handling and cmc

In conflict situations the effect of cmc appears to be largely negative. For instance, the tendency for people to write and send an email quickly 'was found to create a multitude of problems in relation to conflict', particularly in the areas of 'email brevity and a failure on the part of the sender to explain the topic sufficiently'. Furthermore, unlike in ftfc, 'emails could be reread, creating excessive "reading into", and message misinterpretation'.[47]

Friedman and Currall (2003) listed four ways in which email may stimulate conflict escalation:

- By encouraging the use of aggressive tactics or the perception that aggressive tactics are being used;
- By lessening empathy towards the other person (making him or her seem different or amoral);
- By weakening social bonds or encouraging deindividuation;
- By the limitations of email (obstacles to understanding and asynchrony costs) making it harder to resolve problems.

Friedman and Currall (2003) argued that the structural features of email – the fact that it is asynchronous, textual and electronic, and lacks features of ftfc that support mutual understanding – make it more likely that disputes escalate when using that medium in comparison with ftf or telephone-based communication: being asynchronous, textual and electronic, email provides diminished feedback: because email is asynchronous it doesn't allow turn taking; because it is textual, individuals cannot see or hear the reactions of the people they are interacting with. It thereby reduces the amount of feedback each party receives from the other party, which can result in receivers interpreting messages as 'more aggressive than intended'; there are 'more likely to be face-damaging interactions due to the lack of opportunities for self-repair'; 'reduced feedback can lead to lowered self-awareness so that people feel a greater sense of anonymity and detect less individuality in others'. In sum: 'the diminished feedback inherent in email reduces self-awareness and information about the other party. These effects, in turn, increase the probability that the following conflict escalation trigger will occur: weakened interpersonal bonds'.

Conversely, in ftfc, copresence (both parties in the same surroundings), visibility (seeing one another), audibility (hearing the other party's tone and intonation), cotemporality (hearing an utterance just as it is produced), simultaneity (both parties can send and receive messages at once) and sequentiality (where turn-taking rules apply) allow communicators to eliminate or reduce dispute-escalation. There is evidence that interruptions are often made to prevent a speaker saying something offensive to the hearer or to allow the hearer to self-disclose a 'fault' (which is preferred over having it expressed by another). Asynchronicity means that email is more like a series of intermittent, unidirectional comments than a conversation. Email comments, being free from the norms of turn taking in ftf, 'can be very long' and include multiple arguments all in one 'bundle'.[48]

> To learn more of Friedman and Currall's (2003) reasons for asserting that email escalates conflict, visit the companion website... 8.2.2.

> Look back at Box 6.2. How should the bank regulatory reporter respond to her colleague's angry complaint? How should their boss reply to the colleague?

Empirical findings to date are indeed rather gloomy about the effects of cmc on conflict. Although one study found that group conflict appeared to be only slightly affected by whether groups communicated ftf or by cmc (task conflict was unaffected on all three days of the study; on Day 1 there was more process and relationship conflict in cmc than ftf groups, but this difference disappeared on Days 2 and 3),[49] in the longer term, virtual working can be damaging:

- After a period where team members developed teamwork experience, relationship conflict and process conflict damaged team performance more seriously in cmc teams than in ftf teams.[50]
- Again, a field study of 43 teams, 22 co-located and 21 distributed, from a large multinational company, showed that the distributed teams reported more task and interpersonal conflict than the co-located teams did.[51]
- Groups displayed significantly more negative conflict handling, such as avoidance, in cmc than in ftfc; in cmc, positive conflict handling, such as a discussion of differences, decreased over time. In ftfc, where positive conflict handling was higher from the beginning, there were no significant changes over time. Further research found that the type of conflict affected the differences in performance effects among cmc, ftf and video-conference. A laboratory experiment was conducted comparing

ftf video-conference and cmc teams at work for a month. Results showed that video-conference teams were the highest performing teams and cmc teams the lowest. However, when task conflict increased, video-conference team performance diminished at the first stage of the teamwork. Ftf team performance, on the other hand, was improved by conflict, whether over task or process.[52]

Summary

Arguments have been made that conflict is beneficial for organizations in multiple ways; overall, however, findings point to conflict damaging performance and trust as well as leading to increased employee turnover. Some conflicts are conflicts of interest, but many originate in miscommunication. Conflict handling styles include competition, avoidance, accommodation, compromise and collaboration. Culture influences which conflict handling style people prefer. Conflicts easily escalate, especially by email, whose characteristics encourage escalation. Teams using cmc are more likely to use negative than positive conflict handling, in contrast to teams using ftfc.

8.3 NEGOTIATING

When most people think of negotiations, they probably think first of those between governments in the context of international relations, or between organizations in the context of business deals, or between representatives of workers and management in the context of industrial relations: and all these are obviously very important. Negotiation is much more widespread than these contexts, however, and has been described as pervasive in social life: it occurs wherever two or more parties attempt to resolve a perceived divergence of interest, ideas or opinions. Within organizations, people negotiate with colleagues, managers and subordinates; groupwork and teamwork involve negotiation over tasks and relationships.

A core distinction in negotiation is that between distributive and integrative goals and tactics. In distributive bargaining (win–lose) one party benefits only if the opponent makes a concession; in integrative negotiations (win–win) two parties work cooperatively to seek a mutually beneficial solution. Distributive tactics divide resources among the parties and are aimed at maximizing one's own share; integrative tactics, on the other hand, aim to maximize the amount of resources available so that both parties can win. Distributive tactics include threats, positional commitments and persuasive arguments. Integrative tactics include exchanging information and multiple-item offers.[53]

An understanding of negotiation has to consider processes, intrapersonal influences on negotiator behaviour, such as motivations and emotions, and contextual influences such as culture, as well as negotiation techniques. This section examines these and also considers the impact of communication mode on negotiation.

Visit the companion website... 8.3.1 for a link to a video about negotiation. How practical are the suggestions it makes?

Negotiation processes

Negotiators can often improve their performance by regarding negotiations as complex decision-making tasks for which obtaining information is a critical process. People often fail to seek important information during negotiations:

> **❝** Rather than ask their counterparts to explain their interests and priorities, negotiators often assume that their counterpart's positions directly oppose their own, which in turn causes them to miss compatible issues and forgo opportunities to create value by making tradeoffs across issues. Moreover, people often misuse readily available yet flawed information. They allow first offers to anchor their value judgments, and they may alter their information search to justify rather than contest their assumptions.[54]

Delays in pursuing missing information during negotiations can influence negotiators' targets and the final settlements they reach. In fact, the process of obtaining information can itself benefit outcomes: a study showed that negotiators achieved more value on an issue they thought important after seeking missing information about that issue compared to when the same information was readily accessible.[55]

In complex negotiations with large numbers of issues there is greater potential for integrative bargaining and so better outcomes, but the enhanced complexity may also make negotiators more susceptible to bias, making it less likely for them to reach win–win agreements. Van der Schalk et al. (2010) showed that negotiating over larger numbers of issues is only beneficial for negotiators who are motivated to think deeply and thoroughly – that is, who have a high level of epistemic motivation.[56]

You are in a negotiation when the customer says something like 'I can get this same thing cheaper from your competitor' or 'You know, you're pretty good, but you're not really worth the price premium you're bringing up' or 'You're much tougher on your terms and conditions than the rest of the market.'
In each of these situations, what do you need in order to be able to respond effectively?

Effects of motivation and emotions in negotiations

Motivational states and goals can alter perceptions and demands in negotiations and so affect outcomes: negotiators with egoistic motives are more likely to reach an impasse; negotiators with competitive goals achieve lower profits; having extremely demanding goals reduces the likelihood of integrative (win–win) bargaining.

Emotions affect negotiators' goals, attitudes, behaviours and outcomes. Anger increases the perceived importance of competitive goals. High levels of negative emotion prior to engaging in negotiation increase the likelihood of mistrust, suspicion and sinister attribution error (and do so to a greater extent in the online world than in the offline world).[57] Feelings of anxiety, which may themselves be triggered by negotiations, reduce negotiator performance. Anxious negotiators expect lower outcomes, make lower first offers, respond more quickly to offers, exit bargaining situations earlier and ultimately obtain worse outcomes. High self-efficacy, however, mitigates the harmful effects of anxiety.[58]

Uncertainty surrounding a negotiation may lead to a negotiator perceiving that the opposing negotiator is being unfair and thus to flaming and anger directed toward them.[59] There are costs attached to expressing anger in negotiations, because opponents retaliate. While equal-power negotiators often make concessions when their opponents express anger, they sabotage their opponents covertly if they feel mistreated. Low-power negotiators make larger concessions when high-power opponents express anger, but they retaliate covertly against the high-power negotiators even when they do not feel mistreated. High power negotiators also retaliate covertly against low power negotiators who express anger.[60] Anger reduction can effectively decrease flaming, independent of the existence of flaming antecedents such as unfairness.[61]

> For further explanation of how motivational states and goals can alter perceptions and demands in negotiations and so affect outcomes, visit the companion website... 8.3.2.
>
> Visit the companion website... 8.3.3 for a link to a video about negotiation. How practical are the suggestions this video makes?

Contextual influences on negotiations

The context for negotiations significantly affects how they are conducted and their outcomes both in terms of material gains and losses and in terms of satisfaction. For instance, where the parties have existing social ties, in most two-party negotiations they quickly 'co-ordinate a shared logic of exchange' (reach an implicitly agreed basis for how to conduct the negotiation) and improvise in accord with its implied rules throughout their interaction. The improvisations take the form of opening up, working together or haggling. When they have difficulty moving the interaction toward a coherent, mutually agreed upon improvisation, negotiators attempt to test whether their opponents can be trusted, clarify the negotiation process and introduce an emotional call for progress. [62]

Three further contextual factors are considered here: the cultures of the negotiators, their relative power and the advocacy context.

Negotiators from different cultures need to manage simultaneously the task and the culture-related ambiguity that they are confronted with.[63] Culture influences negotiators' goals: respondents from the United States, Turkey and Qatar held different **mental models** about the goals a party has when resolving a work-related dispute. In particular, US respondents had a more variable-sum orientation than the other cultural groups, especially Qataris, whose mental model evidenced a fixed pie assumption regarding both economic and relational goals. For example, Qataris and Turks viewed a goal of maximizing one's own gain as impeding a goal of maximizing the other party's gain. Similarly, Qataris viewed defending honour as incompatible with the goals of relationship building and giving face, whereas Americans and Turks did not hold such a view.[64]

In intercultural negotiations the parties' culturally embedded bargaining patterns lead to culturally determined strategies, and so to differences between the parties in the initial offer, the strategic approach, the valuation of time, the frequency of rejection and the objectives of the negotiation. 'Studies of intracultural simulated buyer–seller negotiations indicate that while cooperative problem-solving strategies are most effective in the United States, competitive behaviour works better in Russia, Taiwan, Germany, Great Britain, Mexico and Francophone Canada.'[65] Similarly, how negotiators from different cultures think about relationships influences their offers, targets and limits, negotiation strategy and, ultimately, economic and relational outcomes. Relationships have more salience in some cultures – for example 'Latin' cultures – than others, such as 'Anglo' cultures.[66] Culture also influences non-verbal behaviour during negotiations, a study found. Male Canadian negotiators engaged in more relaxed postures and displayed more negative emotion, while male Chinese negotiators occupied more space at the negotiation table. In addition, use of space and negative emotion partially mediated the relationship between culture and joint gains, as well as satisfaction with the negotiation process.[67]

Despite differences such as these, building toward consensus is not necessarily more challenging in intercultural than in intracultural negotiations, although movement toward consensus (in the form of mental model convergence) is more likely in intracultural than intercultural negotiations. The degree of difficulty depends on negotiators' epistemic and social motives: need for **closure** (for ambiguity-ending information) inhibited consensus more for intercultural than intracultural dyads, while concern for face fostered consensus more for inter-cultural than intracultural dyads.[68]

Cultural norms can transfer to email negotia-tions: cultural norms lead Hong Kong Chinese negotiators, whether negotiating with other Hong Kong Chinese or with Americans, to engage in more aggressive opening offers when using email; in this way they attain higher distributive outcomes than similar negotiators in the United States.[69]

> *Visit the companion website... 8.3.4 for a link to a video that gives a practical example of how cultural differences affect intercultural negotiations.*

Both the absolute and the relative power of negotiators impacts on how effective it is for them to accommodate to the other party, according to a study by Olekalns and Smith (2013). When both negotiators are high in power they achieve better outcomes (create more value) by accommodat-ing more to one another; conversely, when both negotiators are low in power they achieve better outcomes when they communicate in more contentious ways. Asymmetric power dyads maximize value creation when they adopt a neutral stance, neither over-using nor under-using any one strategy.[70]

Advocacy as bargaining on another person or organization's behalf is a 'particularly important contextual variable' in negotiating. People behave differently according to whether they are acting or speaking on their own behalf or that of someone else. A particular example is that women bargain less assertively on their own behalf than when they are acting as an advo-cate for another person or persons. As a result they often achieve better outcomes from negotiations on others' behalf than on their own. The expla-nation may lie in their using different impression management strategies in what they see as different situations: in contexts where they are negoti-ating on their own behalf, women anticipate that assertiveness will evoke negative evaluations of their behaviour as incongruent with female gender roles, and so provoke a 'backlash': 'hence, women hedge their assertive-ness, using fewer competing tactics and obtaining lower outcomes. However, in other-advocacy contexts, women achieve better outcomes as they do not expect incongruity evaluations or engage in hedging'. Controlled laboratory experiments supplied support for this hypothesis.[71]

Negotiation and cmc

Negotiation outcomes and negotiators' satisfaction with the process have been the main concerns of research into cmc and negotiation. There seems to be some consistency in findings that negotiation may lead to better outcomes in ftf conditions. In one study, negotiation by cmc took fewer rounds to reach an agreement but had lower outcomes with lower firm profit and negotiators reporting lower perceived autonomy.[72] These findings may be explained by the results of other studies which show that interactions that allow for greater social perception – offering the opportunity to detect and understand others' emotions, words and behaviour – produce more cooperative behaviour in multi-party negotiations. The reverse is also true. 'Without the opportunity to truly perceive others, economic efficiency suffers.'[73]

On the other hand, Geiger (2010), who argued that negotiator satisfaction is an important outcome of a negotiation, found higher negotiator satisfaction in cmc (here called electronic medium or EM) negotiations than in ftf negotiations. Geiger (2010) explained this finding in terms of EM negotiators having lower targets. Individual negotiator profits were similar, so EM negotiators were more likely to achieve or get near to their targets than ftf negotiators were. Differences in aspirations and expectations between ftf and EM negotiations may be explained by differences in negotiation preparation and negotiator confidence:

> **❝** If there are restrictions to the number and richness of communicative cues allowed by the medium prior to an important negotiation it is reasonable to believe that a negotiator in such a situation would engage in more thorough negotiation preparation. Also, he or she would exhibit less confidence in his or her ability to come to a very advantageous negotiation result due to perceived medium restrictions. Since he would have more realistic outcome expectancies and fall less prey to an eventual overconfidence bias, we argue that his profit expectancies would also be lower.

Levels of contentious behaviour were similar in the two modes, Geiger (2010) found, though fewer positive and more negative relational messages were sent ftf versus EM. Positive relational messages and contentious behaviour also affected negotiator satisfaction in EM negotiations, but less in ftf negotiations. This may be because what is 'said' in EM negotiations is more important for the formation of negotiator satisfaction than what is said ftf.[74] Another study similarly found that individuals negotiating via IM were more satisfied with the negotiation process than individuals negotiating ftf, although they were more likely to use 'forcing' negotiating, experience more tension and have lower deception detection accuracy.[75]

> **❝** I find email a useful tool for negotiating. It allows you to take a considered position and removes the pressure to bluff; I am aware I'm not good at that. Face-to-face or on the phone I can end up giving away too much. I don't like the pressure to respond instantly to an offer. Email also helps reduce misunderstanding about exactly what you are offering; this is especially useful in complex negotiations.
>
> (Author's interview with an executive from a
> media organization)

These findings that negotiator satisfaction is greater in cmc are somewhat surprising, because when cmc involves a lack of feedback immediacy it can be frustrating for negotiators for two reasons: first, decreased immediacy reduces negotiators' abilities to understand what is being communicated because more rapid exchanges enable people to identify communication patterns; second, not being able to interject brief clarifying questions, which are more effective when rapid exchanges are possible, makes it harder for people to understand one another. Moreover, negotiators tend to behave as if they are in synchronous (ftf) negotiations, independent of the actual communication mode. When cmc is used and the expected conversational turn taking does not occur, negotiators can become frustrated with the process.

Another cmc characteristic that impedes negotiation is being unable to transfer verbal, pictorial and non-verbal cues; this 'can lead to frustration due to the attendant reduction in understanding that can be conveyed'. Being able to hear and speak to an interaction partner (i.e. having an audio channel available) during multi-party negotiations increases user satisfaction with the communication process and reduces the time it takes to find a solution, without affecting the quality of the negotiated result. Conversely, adding text chat to an audio channel does not help solve problems with negotiation. Audio-based communication seems to meet the requirements of negotiating better than text chat in terms of a more satisfying and faster communication process.[76]

According to Thompson and Nadler (2002), however, the main problem with email negotiation is the implicit assumptions people make regarding time delays in hearing back from the other party and about the other party's motivations. For example, people tend to assume that the other party to the negotiation reads and is aware of the content of an email message as soon as that message is sent; thus any delays in hearing back are attributed to stalling or intentional disrespect by the other party.[77]

In highly emotional circumstances, lack of social cues may create greater distance and mistrust, but lack of non-verbal cues may be an advantage in low-level conflict situations, as it allows negotiating parties to focus on the message content and reduces the influence of exogenous distractions. Thus integrative solutions to a low-level conflict were more common in synchronous computer conferencing (IM) and least common in ftf; email led to an intermediate level of integrative solutions.[78]

> *For suggestions on how to be a skilled negotiator ftf or by cmc, visit the companion website... 8.3.5.*

Summary

Negotiation at various levels of significance and complexity is pervasive within and between organizations. Negotiators need to understand intrapersonal influences on negotiator behaviour, such as motivations and emotions, and contextual influences such as culture and power, as well as negotiation techniques.

Negotiating by cmc usually leads to worse joint outcomes and less effective processes; a significant cause is the assumptions people make regarding time delays; others include lack of feedback immediacy and being unable to interject brief clarifying questions or transfer verbal, pictorial and non-verbal cues. Despite these drawbacks, negotiators' satisfaction can be greater in cmc than ftfc, possibly because their prior aspirations are lower and therefore more likely to be met. Cmc is less disadvantageous for performance in situations of low as opposed to high-level conflict.

The student companion website gives a number of suggestions for negotiating effectively; these differ between integrative and distributive negotiations.

Part III

The Impact of the Communication Revolution on Work and Organization

The third and final part of this book relates interpersonal communication both ftf and by cmc directly to major concerns of modern organizations and businesses: cooperation, work relations, knowledge sharing and coordination (Chapter 9), groupwork and teamwork (Chapter 10), management and leadership (Chapter 11), organizational structures and processes (Chapter 12) and inter-organizational relations (Chapter 13).

9 COOPERATION, WORK RELATIONS, KNOWLEDGE SHARING AND COORDINATION

Although cooperative behaviour among colleagues has always been desirable, and in some countries, such as Norway, was always 'a norm of appropriateness',[1] during what is now known as the industrial age, coordination was often achieved without the need for cooperation between co-workers. On an assembly line, providing each individual performed his or her task satisfactorily and on time, production was accomplished and productivity was guaranteed by the system: it was not essential for workers to behave cooperatively towards their fellows. In the post-industrial age, however, with automation of much manufacturing, the increasing emphasis on services and the essential role of information in all aspects of work, adequate levels of coordination can no longer be achieved in most organizations without cooperation from and among their employees. Critical here is the role of cooperation in knowledge sharing. Cooperation in turn is a function of interpersonal communication. In fact, knowledge transfer and coordination of work have been described as the two organizational processes perhaps most dependent on communication.[2]

This chapter therefore discusses these inter-related issues, starting with cooperation and its underpinning of good work relations, then the two functions that depend on it: knowledge sharing and coordination. There is feedback in the relationship among these processes: work relationships

On completing your study of this chapter, you will be able to explain and apply the implications of:

- Influences on whether people cooperate or compete at work.
- Influences on whether work relationships are harmonious or conflictual.
- Influences on interpersonal knowledge-sharing.
- Influences on task coordination.
- How different communication modes affect cooperation, work relationships, knowledge-sharing and coordination.

develop out of the need to cooperate and coordinate over tasks and in turn affect how well people cooperate and how well work is coordinated.

9.1 COOPERATION, COMPETITION AND WORK RELATIONS

A central issue facing every organization is how employees and business partners can be motivated to invest in cooperation; the need to cooperate and coordinate over tasks creates work relations. These topics are the focus of this section.

Cooperation and competition

As in most social situations, at work individuals may at times benefit more personally from competitive rather than cooperative behaviour. Cooperation is working together to maximize joint outcomes; competition is an attempt to maximize a person's own outcomes relative to that of others. Competitive behaviour is appropriate for an individual when there is only a limited amount of reward available, such that if one person wins another must lose, as is commonly the case, for example, for promotions in hierarchical organizations. Cooperative behaviour is most appropriate for an individual when it is possible for all participants to achieve their goals, and especially when if one person achieves his or her goal, the others may also gain; this situation arises more often in team-based organizations when rewards are allocated to whole teams. Newer ways of organizing, such as using virtual teams, depend on and should therefore reward cooperative behaviour.

Competition can be beneficial, leading people to try harder and be more creative. Misplaced competitiveness, however, leads to behaving secretively, springing surprises, using threats and bluffs, defending all positions (if 'necessary' by non-rational arguments) and derogating rivals.[3] When people do engage in misplaced competitive behaviour, both the organization and individuals suffer. The opposing members are seen as inferior, judgement is distorted, so that 'own' contributions are automatically seen as better than others', and there is a tendency to think that others' points of view are understood, when in fact they are not. They are distorted in a polarized way and areas of common ground can go unrecognized.[4] From the perspective of the individual, competitive behaviour is often defensive rather than aggressive, as the following example suggests:

> **"**You were forced to wage psychological warfare. For example, not getting a reply to a draft sent by email counted as clearance, but to make sure I would send an email saying I took it that my draft was accepted. If I didn't get a reply to that I would send a similar email but copy in the Minister's office.
>
> (Author's interview with a former UK civil servant)

In contrast to behaving competitively, behaving cooperatively implies acting with openness, flexibly but without springing surprises, not defending weak positions, considering new ideas on their merits, not on the basis of who originated them, and trying to improve working relationships. People are more likely to behave cooperatively if they believe they have been treated fairly. For instance, the decision whether to cooperate in negotiations (such as over working late) is affected by information about the fairness of the procedure, including memories of past treatment.[5] Norms, as Chapter 7 explained, are implicit rules governing how to behave. Many of the norms adopted by co-workers are designed to support cooperative behaviour, though not always to the advantage of the organization; for example, field workers whose wages depend on their output relative to their co-workers', cooperate by restricting their output and, in the case of workers joining an existing group, restrict their output more as they become more familiar with the norm.[6]

Many work situations are mixed, however, and the people involved have mixed motives. They want the organization to succeed but they also want to get their own way: 'selfish' motives can lead people to compete against their colleagues. Furthermore, the motivation to compete is often amplified in organizations, for instance where the hierarchy leads to competition for promotion. According to Lawler (1983), in some long-term relationships there is a continuous struggle for power, which leads to constant competition or conflict.[7] Moreover, difficulty in anticipating how others will behave leads to competitiveness. If others are about to behave in a competitive way, this may make the situation one where cooperative behaviour will lead to losses for the individual. Again, cooperating requires people to trust one another; trust takes time to build up and is easily destroyed.

Work roles and norms can either constrain or encourage competitive behaviour. Role ambiguity (a lack of clarity about what is expected in a job), role conflict (where a job places conflicting demands on its holder) and role overload (unreasonable job requirements) can make working life stressful and impair the interactive behaviour of those affected. Again, work can be stressful for those who for some reason do not conform to the organization's norms, as they can suffer sanctions for breaches and may experience social exclusion. Experiencing stress can lead people to behave uncooperatively.

Cmc and cooperation/competition

A major concern for organizations regarding the impact of cmc is how it affects cooperation among co-workers and whether it leads to increased levels of competition of a damaging kind.

Physical distance and time differences are impediments to collaboration and relationship development. This is linked to the fact that physically or temporally distant events or objects are more psychologically distant and are more likely to be thought of in terms of their more general character-istics, while views of more proximal events or objects will be more detailed and nuanced. A study of global software development showed the follow-ing:

> ❝ Disruption to a second, vital communication channel (the face-to-face channel not available when relying on mediated communication) can be surprisingly crippling; developers not located together have very little informal, spontaneous conversation across sites. One result is that the issues, big and small, that crop up on a nearly daily basis in any soft-ware project can go unrecognized or lie dormant and unresolved for extended periods.[8]

Against the problems caused by cmc, however, there is evidence that because email makes it easy for people to contact others outside their department and to gain an appreciation of the bigger picture, it can increase their organizational and departmental awareness and lead them to become more engaged with others in relationships that may not otherwise have occurred.[9] Again, some consequences of using cmc by geographically dispersed partners have a positive effect on the underlying conditions for cooperation. As SIDE theory argues, people who communicate by cmc are more inclined to think in group rather than individual terms. Together with long-term interaction this increases intimacy and affection toward a communication partner and increases their social attractiveness, while never having seen the partner increases their perceived physical attractive-ness. Overall, in cmc the effects of long-term duration of communication and group identification are 'greater than those achieved in FtF interac-tion'.[10] As this finding suggests, the duration of work relationships through mediated communication is a strong influence on how cooperative they are: one study found that while initially non-co-located groups who communi-cated by video were significantly worse at cooperating on tasks than ftf groups, these differences disappeared over time.

> ❝ The organization I work for has 140,000 employees – 40,000 in India, 40,000 in the USA, the rest split across Europe and Asia. On the profes-sional social networking site I use, most of my regular contacts are fellow employees, whom I probably would not have met in any other way. In fact I am in two or three groups of fellow employees. If one of us has a problem we might put it to the group and ask their advice.
> (Interview with a knowledge worker from a major information technology and business processing outsourcing organization)

Overall, there is consistent evidence that while cooperation is more difficult to establish and maintain in cmc, this form of communication too has a positive influence on cooperation: that is, any communication is better than none.[12] The effect of communication by any mode on cooperation seems to be particularly robust, even when the communication is irrelevant to any material payoff (labelled 'cheap talk'). People in situations that allow them to hope that the partner will respond in a cooperative manner show a higher degree of cooperation when engaging in cheap-talk cmc. Furthermore, low social distance, collective orientation and experience with a medium are favourable for demonstrating trust, trustworthiness and cooperation.[13]

Importantly, the impact of communication channels is shaped by whether communicators have favourable orientations (attitudes towards and intentions regarding) cooperation. For 'communicators with a cooperative orientation' the communication mode does not significantly affect the outcomes of their interactions. For communicators with a neutral orientation toward cooperation, the presence of visual channels, vocal channels or communication synchronicity increases the achievement of high-quality outcomes. For communicators with a non-cooperative orientation the outcomes are worse when the communication mode lacks vocal and visual channels or synchronicity. These findings tend to be stronger for the presence or absence of visual and vocal channels than for synchronicity, suggesting that 'the opportunity to give direct feedback is not as important for achieving high-quality ... outcomes as seeing and hearing fellow group members'.[14]

Once again it may be that a mixture of modes is optimal. Findings show that introductory ftf interaction plays an important role in the development of trust and collaboration in a cmc environment, especially when the context is competitive. Trust and collaboration for dyad members whose introductory meeting took place in competitive/electronic conditions lagged significantly behind those who first met electronically but not for those who met in a cooperative climate or those who first met ftf even if the climate was competitive.[15]

> **❝** Any time I really needed someone senior to read my email, I would phone them first to tell them I was sending them an email.
> (Author's interview with a former UK civil servant)

Work relationships

As the start of this section pointed out, work relationships develop out of the need to cooperate and coordinate over tasks. Over time, however, they come to acquire social and psychological meanings for colleagues. Whether employees consider the interactions they have in the workplace to be positive (e.g. pleasant) or negative (e.g. conflictual) affects their moods and job satisfaction.[16] Having high-quality relationships with co-workers is also important for avoiding burnout: where workers lack self-determined work motivation, high-quality relationships compensate to some degree in preventing burnout.[17] Being socially embedded with colleagues also increases the level of organizational support that employees perceive themselves to receive, regardless of the support given by supervisors and upper management.[18]

People often experience relations with co-workers as complex: they must relate to one another simultaneously as sources of power and influence, of resources that need to be shared, and of personal satisfaction. To handle this complexity they develop solutions to the interpersonal communication problems that important work relationships present and apply these solutions in other work relationships, so that their way of interacting at work becomes largely habitual. However, according to one study, more than 88 per cent of employees engage in co-worker relational maintenance strategies: that is, they pay attention to and make efforts to maintain their relations with their co-workers – with conflict management, sharing tasks and positivity reported most often. These efforts provide psychological rewards: 'coworker relational maintenance behaviors were positively related to organizational commitment, job satisfaction, and communication satisfaction, and negatively related to work alienation'.[19]

> Look at the Glossary for the meaning of **social embeddedness**.

> Look back at the situation described in Box 7.1. How is the situation and the probable behaviour of the sales staff likely to affect their work relations with the credit control staff?

People at work value each other partly for their competence, which is less of a concern between friends and relations. Shared goals, shared knowledge and mutual respect are the core elements of high quality relationships at work and foster 'psychological safety'. In turn, psychological safety enables organizational members to engage in learning from failures.[20] Although there are exceptions, the more closely people work together the more likely they are to be friendly. At work – for instance among supermarket employees – as well as in private life, people succeed in winning friendship and trust by their attempts to improve how others are feeling.[21]

Employees often want to maintain workplace relationships at what they consider an appropriate level, not allowing them to either escalate or deteriorate. To maintain peer relationships at a desired state where the other person seems to want to increase intimacy, they use communication tactics such as refocusing the conversation away from topics that could lead to it becoming intimate; where the relationship seems to be deteriorating below the level they consider appropriate, they use communication tactics such as open disclosure. The strongest influence on which of these tactics will be used in a given situation is perceived politeness.[22]

Demographic differences have been linked to people being less focused on establishing a positive social bond with their co-workers. However, when thinking in advance about an interaction with someone with whom they expect to disagree, people from different backgrounds give the other person's perspective more thought than people from similar backgrounds do. This

> To learn more about how people maintain the level of workplace relationships, visit the companion website... 9.1.1.

occurs in part precisely because they focus on their relationship. This more elaborate pre-meeting consideration can lead to diverse pairs performing better on a decision-making task than homogeneous pairs do.[23]

Effects of communication mode on work relations

How does the mode of communication affect the factors and processes underlying work relations? Positive behavioural effects of using cmc include the benefits that arise from making new contacts, greater control of information flow, more information sharing, impression management and social influence. Email allows people to find other people with common interests at a low cost to either party. This new communication creates links between people who would otherwise not be in direct contact.

There are, however, offsetting disadvantages for work relationships from the use of cmc. The 'key unintended negative outcome of increasing email contact in the workplace is an increase in information overload'. The fear of missing important information creates 'a need in people to access emails that on first glance they may have deemed irrelevant'. Additionally, 'the speed of email tends to create the impression that it is a verbal channel and therefore many employees both think and act in a different manner from written communication'.[24] 'Email "talk", as social interaction, may both create and affect overload.' 'Unstable requests, pressures to respond, and delegation of tasks and shifting interactants' lead to information overload, which reduces people's job satisfaction, and that in turn has a negative impact on perceived work relationships.[25] Information overload may contribute to an overall decrease in communication. As email use increases, the overall volume of all forms of communication decreases, mostly because of fewer greetings and other informal interactions between co-workers. In addition, and perhaps as a result, employees report feeling less connected to their co-workers as their email use increases.[26]

Work relationships are often negatively affected when people telework (use cmc to work from home or at a local telework centre). The relationship between a telecommuter and his or her manager often deteriorates after an initial 'honeymoon' phase has passed.[27] Among professional employees, the more teleworkers there are in a group or unit, the lower the work satisfaction of their co-workers, especially when the teleworking

---

BOX 9.1

'I don't think information overload through emails is a big problem for me. If I have 25 emails in my inbox in the morning, I can easily recognize the four or five I need to read and I just don't read the others. Where they are a problem is the way they intrude into the structure of your day. Like other people I find knowing that a new email has arrived hard to resist: it offers immediate gratification and is a spectacular distraction. I aspire to limit the amount of checking I do, but it's not easy.'

(Author's interview with an executive from a media organization)

---

colleagues are mainly absent, the amount of face-to-face (ftf) interaction is low, and job interdependence is high. Moreover, a non-teleworker's dissatisfaction with co-workers is positively associated with an intention to leave the organization.[28] Similarly, in comparison to subordinates with managers who work in a traditional mode, work experiences and outcomes are generally less positive for subordinates with teleworking managers who spend a portion of the week away from the office, as well as for subordinates with virtual managers who are away from the office full time.[29] Finally, the physical separation of virtual employees leads to them thinking themselves less respected by their colleagues – that is, how included and valued they feel. This lowered perception of their status leads virtual employees to identify less with their organization.[30]

Despite these negative consequences of working by cmc, physical proximity is becoming less important for forming friendships with co-workers: although ftf interaction is still primary for workplace friendship initiation and communication, email, phone and texting are also central. Younger people make more use of mediated communication than older workers in the context of workplace friendship.[31]

Two particular concerns at work are misuse of the email system through excessive irrelevant communication, inappropriate use and the avoidance of ftf contact and 'back-covering'. Back-covering is 'the misuse of email in order to blame-shift, imply to others that they [the senders] are working harder, involve inappropriate people in the communication, or to force another person to react (by placing your or their manager on the circulation list)'. Dealing with the repercussions of these misuses is time-consuming for the individual employee, negates some of the benefits associated with email, and damages work relationships.[32]

❝I was once accused of making a serious error that I had not made. The woman who had made it sent out an email to all and sundry saying I had made this error. When the IT record was checked, it proved that she had made it, not me. Our boss acknowledged that I had been right, but I never received an apology.

> (Author's interview with a bank regulatory reporting specialist who has worked on a series of contracts)

Other negative effects on work relationships and so on cooperation flow from employees having concerns about workplace email monitoring – particularly about the organization's ability to infringe on email privacy. Perceptions of workplace email monitoring are related to the perceived quality of employees' workplace relationships, especially with top management.[33] Privacy concerns are also found with IM; privacy preferences vary from individual to individual: inadequate support for managing privacy can lead to suboptimal use of IM.[34]

> **"** There's an app called 'Office Communicator' which people use for internal instant messaging but I've avoided having it installed because it records when you start and stop using the keyboard; is it used to monitor whether we are working?
>
> (Author's interview with a former UK civil servant)

Summary

While both competition and cooperation can be beneficial, modern organizations tend to have a higher need for their employees to cooperate. Employee motives, however, can be mixed, particularly in hierarchical organizations. Nevertheless, most employees consider that they put significant efforts into maintaining workplace relationships at an appropriate level by their communicative practices.

Cmc increases the range of colleagues with whom people are in contact, but information overload and teleworking can actually reduce the overall amount of communication in an organization and damage work relationships. There is evidence that cooperation and work relationships benefit from ftfc, but the impact of cmc is contested, with some findings showing benefits and others damage. A mixture of modes, especially with ftfc early on, may be optimal.

9.2 SHARING KNOWLEDGE

Given the importance of information and knowledge in what has been termed the 'information age', it is not surprising that the interpersonal processes involved in sharing knowledge have attracted attention. Knowledge sharing (also labelled knowledge transfer, flows or acquisition) refers to the process through which organizational actors – individuals, teams, units or entire organizations – transmit, receive and exchange knowledge, especially undocumented knowledge. Although some case study evidence suggests the reverse, in general it is agreed that the successful transfer of knowledge between organizational units is critical for a number of organizational processes, performance outcomes and innovation.[35] Garicano and Wu (2012) argued that organizations actually emerge to achieve the intensive use of the knowledge that is required to perform specific tasks and to achieve the integration of dispersed knowledge that is embodied in different human minds. Depending on the codifiability of knowledge (how well it can be turned into symbols), different communication modes arise as a coordination mechanism to deepen the division of labour, leverage managerial talent and exploit increasing returns to knowledge.[36]

The importance of information flows and knowledge sharing is illustrated by a number of findings: for example, Keller (2001) showed that R&D groups that depend on knowledge transfer by cross-functional communication do significantly better on technical quality, time and budget performance than groups that only communicate within their own function.[37]

> *For more findings that show the importance of information flows and knowledge sharing, visit the companion website... 9.2.1.*

Before further examining the communication of information and knowledge, it is worth understanding the characteristics of these resources. Data can be defined as a set of objective facts. Since, however, these facts are unrelated either to one another or to any information about how to use them, data are of little use in themselves except as the raw material from which information can be constructed. For example, if a company's management information system generates a large amount of sales data for an area of a country, before that data becomes useful information it must be related to something else: perhaps to other comparable areas, perhaps to past series, perhaps to competitors' sales, perhaps to market size. By itself it is of little use. Information can be defined as 'data with significance'. When data is given meaning within a given context or system, it becomes information. Knowledge is created by combining and interpreting information; it has a quality of 'justified belief'.

A useful distinction can be drawn between explicit and tacit knowledge. Tacit knowledge is non-verbalized, intuitive and unarticulated, depends on the experience of the individual, and includes beliefs and emotions, acquired knowledge and personal skills that someone can exercise without being able to articulate fully their knowledge: an example would be recognizing a face in a crowd. Explicit knowledge uses a systematic language and is

> *To learn more about data, information and knowledge and their link to communication, visit the companion website... 9.2.2.*

codified through words, numbers and symbols. This codification makes explicit knowledge amenable to transfer, whereas tacit knowledge is hard to transfer. In practice, most items of knowledge contain elements of both explicit and tacit knowledge. In the view of the originator of this distinction (Polanyi 1968), however, a wholly explicit knowledge is impossible:

> ❛❛ 'Tacitness' is always present and of especial significance in situations of high uncertainly and complexity, where participants are actively integrating innumerable clues to generate and sustain meaning ... Thus, in recognizing a friend in a crowd, one would attend from the colour of hair, shape of face, nose and mouth, to the recognition of the person. People can rarely specify what it is about the numerous facial particulars that enable them to recognize a face in a crowd; they make a tacit act of integration. Awareness of something at the centre of one's attention is dependent upon clues on which one is not directly attending.[38]

Thus how well what people know can be shared depends in part on how they acquired it. It is relatively easy for them to integrate knowledge acquired by working together, whereas individuals' accumulated practical skill or expertise, such as industry and firm experience and work-related training – skill or expertise that allows them personally to do something smoothly and efficiently – is much harder for them to integrate.[39]

Tacit knowledge that can serve as a critical resource for an organization is of four kinds: discrete, linked, productive and administrative tacit knowledge. There is also knowledge held by senior managers and organizational knowledge which is available to organizational decision-makers.

> *To learn more about discrete, linked, productive and administrative tacit knowledge, visit the companion website... 9.2.3.*

The economic importance of tacit knowledge depends in part on the ability to articulate it and thus transform it into explicit knowledge, and in part on being able to transfer it between individuals, business units and from individuals and business units to the organization as a whole.

Knowledge is sticky: it flows between possessors and locations only with difficulty. Although tacit knowledge is particularly sticky, there are factors that impede the transfer of even the explicit knowledge needed for executing processes from one set of personnel to another. The more ambiguous and complex explicit knowledge is, the less easily it transfers. Equally important, though, are the social and psychological factors that affect knowledge sharing. The rest of this section will analyse these factors, then examine different knowledge-sharing processes – search, distribution, using explanatory objects and knowledge sharing within groups and teams.

Finally it will explore how different communication modes are related to knowledge sharing.

Social and psychological factors that influence knowledge sharing

Psychological and social factors, including culture, are as important for knowledge sharing as the characteristics of the knowledge; these factors often make it problematic:

- Findings from employees in three organizations (an entrepreneurial computer technology company, staff personnel at an academic institution, and employees in a large information technology corporation), suggest that people will avoid working with someone they dislike, even though they recognize the other person's competence in the task. Across organizational contexts and types of task, people appear to need active liking to seek out the knowledge resources of potential work partners.[40]
- Furthermore, employees may resist learning new knowledge: organizations experience problems in keeping relatively unskilled, low-paid knowledge workers current with the latest information on those products they support. For example, customer call centre support technicians are often reluctant to adopt knowledge management tools because these have features that they find hard to learn and they find it easier to ask someone they know.[41]

> "Some of the technology-based attempts I have seen to get people to communicate across departments are too badly set up or maintained to be usable. For instance, there are knowledge sharing tools called things like 'Briefing at ...' or 'Our Network' where teams from separate policy areas are supposed to post up material that could be useful to others. But if I wanted to find something – for instance what 'We' were saying about the US economy – I could never find it. For one thing, however basic, it might not have been there: people didn't know how to upload to it. And almost no resources were put into maintaining it, so that those few resources were all used up in helping people upload their material.
>
> (Author's interview with a former UK civil servant)

Over and above knowledge characteristics, then, psychological, social and cultural factors can either assist or impede interpersonal knowledge transfer:

- A positive finding is that social interaction between managers from different units of a **multinational enterprise (MNE)** has been shown to be an important factor stimulating intra-MNE knowledge-sharing.

'Face-to-face social interactions form a communication channel particularly conducive to the transfer of tacit, non-codified knowledge.' Intensive social interaction also provides opportunities for social construction of knowledge in a learning dialogue. In fact, while tacit knowledge transfer does occur, the social learning effects appear stronger, affecting all intra-MNE knowledge flows.[42]

- Findings from a contract R&D (research and development) firm showed that both social cohesion and network range ease knowledge transfer. Social cohesion around a relationship affects the willingness and motivation of individuals to invest time, energy and effort in sharing knowledge with others, while ties to different knowledge pools increase a person's ability to convey complex ideas to heterogeneous audiences.[43] Strong ties, network cohesion and wide network range are contextual factors that contribute to the flow of knowledge between organizational units.[44] Unfortunately, however, social cohesion and network range may conflict. Although large, open networks foster network positions that provide access to non-redundant knowledge, such networks may impair knowledge sharing, because trust and reciprocity do not thrive in them.[45]

- Employees are sometimes unwilling to share their knowledge even when organizational practices are designed to facilitate transfer. In fact, there are several circumstances in which employees actively hide their knowledge: they may engage in evasive hiding (agreeing to help but instead intentionally giving information different from what was requested), playing dumb (pretending not to know what the requester was talking about) or rationalized hiding (for example, because the person who has the information considers it confidential). Unlike evasive hiding and playing dumb, rationalized hiding 'does not necessarily involve deception'. Each of these hiding behaviours is predicted by distrust of the person requesting the information, but whereas evasive hiding is more common when the knowledge requested is complex or task-related and when the organizational climate does not strongly support information sharing, these factors are unrelated to playing dumb and rationalized hiding.[46] In computer-supported information exchange, people frequently withhold their own information and free-ride on the others' contributions.[47]

There are, however, conditions that motivate people to share their knowledge. For instance, individuals are more motivated to contribute discretionary information to other database users when they are highly committed to their organization, consider the information very useful to the wider organization, believe that information contributed to the database will reach other members of the collective and believe that their contribution is of value to other database users.[48]

Other psycho-social factors that impact on knowledge sharing include:

- Greater self-interest on the part of individuals reduces their support for information and knowledge sharing, but a belief in organizational ownership of work encourages attitudes favouring sharing. Work experience and business schooling contribute to these attitudes.
- Expertise belongs to a special category of information that is part of a person's identity and is self-expressive. While sharing tangible work information may depend on prosocial attitudes and norms of organizational ownership, sharing expertise may depend on people's own self-expressive needs.[49]

Intercultural knowledge sharing

Cultural differences in the approach to knowledge can create difficulties in knowledge transfer and help make knowledge sticky. For instance, national cultural differences strongly affected knowledge transfer in international acquisitions made by Finnish corporations, a study found.[50] Such difficulties are more marked between individualists and collectivists than between people who differ in terms of power distance.[51] On the other hand, people with a collectivist cultural orientation respond more positively when instructors, group members and close classmates communicate social norms about attitudes toward sharing knowledge by email. This increase may result from the focus on social obligations in collectivist culture being beneficial to a positive attitude toward knowledge sharing.[52]

Organizational cultures also influence knowledge sharing; hierarchical cultures are positively related to explicit knowledge sharing, but less compatible with sharing of tacit knowledge, whereas group cultures, which emphasize flexibility and maintain a primary focus on the internal organization, and rational cultures, which focus on internal stability and the external environment, are both positively related to implicit knowledge sharing.[53]

Knowledge sharing processes

The characteristics of knowledge sharing vary according to whether it originates in a search by an individual or unit, or in an individual's or unit's wish to spread the information, according to whether explanatory objects can be and are used and according to whether it takes place between individuals or within groups or teams.

> *Visit the companion website... 9.2.4 for a link to videos about knowledge sharing. What are their main learning points? How good are their presentations?*

Knowledge search

Knowledge transfer very often begins with an individual or a unit seeking it. When looking for help with tasks, knowledge workers may contact individuals in rival firms across the globe as easily as a co-worker sitting at the next desk. Findings from Europe's largest information technology services and management consulting company show that communication outside the unit or organization leads to higher creativity and general performance, and that relying on co-located co-workers as knowledge sources lowers creativity.[54]

How efficiently people search for information is affected in part by their mood: a positive mood leads to less efficient searching when risk is low but not when it is high; negative mood makes for more efficient searching when risk is high, but not when it is low.[55] A factor that reduces stickiness is how relevant the people seeking the information perceive it to be, presumably because if they think it highly relevant they are more persistent about obtaining it.[56]

Success for knowledge seekers also depends, of course, on those who hold the knowledge being willing to impart it. Altruistic traits, social rewards and reciprocity all positively influence willingness to provide information, a Korean study found, though how long someone has been working for the organization also affects these relationships.[57]

Knowledge distribution

Not all knowledge transfer begins with the seeker. Individuals or organizations may instigate the process because they believe that colleagues, associates or the public need the information. Holders of knowledge may also be motivated to initiate knowledge transfer by self-presentation or organizational citizenship behaviour motives.[58] The highest level of effectiveness in distributing information is achieved when the appropriate media and message format are adjusted for the initial involvement and need for the information of the intended recipients. For example, simple informational messages about health are more persuasive than testimonials when the recipients are highly involved and have a high need for the information, while testimonials are more persuasive when presented orally rather than in writing.[59]

Using explanatory objects to facilitate knowledge sharing

When individuals with different types of knowledge communicate with each other, they often employ explanatory or 'boundary' objects, such as sketches, photographs, tables of data, graphs, research reports, computer-aided drafting models and project management tools, to help them convey ideas. **Boundary objects** are physical objects that enable people to understand other perspectives. An 'effective boundary object facilitates a process where individuals can jointly transform their knowledge' or jointly translate ideas and information. Many things can serve as boundary objects, though such an object must provide a common focus for different ways of knowing.[60] Some of these objects will be ambiguous (with 'the potential to support multiple concurrent interpretations') while others will be clear (likely to 'promote a shared unified meaning').

Creating ambiguous explanatory objects may be a deliberate strategy. For example, in one instance, when creating explanatory objects, engineers favoured a strategy of ambiguity, which they believed would foster healthy long-term group interactions, over a strategy of clarity, which they tended to employ only when they expected resistance to their ideas. As a result the engineers' product design drawings of an industrial product were ambiguous; assemblers saw them as installation guidelines, while the inventory control staff viewed the same drawings as indices of part numbers.[61]

Knowledge sharing within groups and teams

Groups are sometimes inefficient at sharing information and tend to focus on only a portion of the available information, thus partially obviating their advantage over individuals of having access to a larger pool of expertise and knowledge. Remote (i.e. computer-mediated) communication, high information load, the majority of the information being known to all group members and low information-carrying capacity of the communication medium all increase this tendency towards inefficient information sharing.[62] If information relevant to a decision being made by a team is distributed among its members, the group tends to focus on common information and to neglect information held by only one person. However, this may not always be illogical: information search and discussion highlights information that is perceived as relevant in the population from which groups are composed.[63]

The strength of members' communication ties and the level of task interdependence, but also the individual member's level of expertise (or knowledge) of directory development, decide how the exchange of expertise in teams is channelled. These expertise (or knowledge) directories (the terms are used interchangeably) are 'directories of who knows what'; at an individual level, they are defined as 'individual mental maps of knowledge distribution'; when shared, they are referred to as 'compositional' or 'collective' **knowledge directories**. Individual expertise exchange takes place more frequently in teams with well-developed team-level expertise directories, as well as with higher team communication tie strength and shared task interdependence.[64] The following is an example of how power influences what knowledge becomes embedded in a group:

A case study that examined the processes of knowledge generation and translation in multidisciplinary medical teams showed how meaning was developed and manifest in team decisions and how tacit knowledge shapes clinical practice. It suggested that the knowledge of the more powerful team members got reconstituted as multidisciplinary group practice, and embedded in the practices of the group, so that the creation of a multidisciplinary structure may support rather than challenge existing power hierarchies.[65]

Differences in the specialist knowledge of members of cross-functional teams impede their work by making knowledge integration difficult. One approach for overcoming these difficulties is for team members to identify, elaborate and then explicitly confront the differences and dependencies across the knowledge boundaries. This approach emphasizes deep dialogue and requires significant resources and time. The following illustrates how teams can overcome problems caused by specialism differences:

> An exploratory in-depth longitudinal study of three quite different cross-functional teams found that the teams were able to cogenerate a solution without needing to identify, elaborate, and confront differences and dependencies between the specialty areas. The practices that minimized members' differences during the problem-solving process were avoiding interpersonal conflict, fostering the rapid cocreation of intermediate scaffolds, encouraging continued creative engagement and flexibility to repeatedly modify solution ideas, and fostering personal responsibility for translating personal knowledge to collective knowledge.[66]

Knowledge sharing and different communication modes

Empirical research on knowledge transfer has tended to focus on communication between geographically and culturally distant locations and so is predominantly concerned with cmc. Sillince and Saeedi (1999) described information sharing as 'the bane of current computer-mediated communication'. They pointed to recent findings that there had been a lack of impact on collaborative rather than merely communicative behaviour in organizations, that 'although communication has increased, organization-wide information systems are often sabotaged by departmental conflict and the unwillingness to share information' and that 'managers prefer to gather soft information (anecdotes, rumours, opinions) for their greater timeliness and relevance over computerised information or formal reports'.[67]

Other findings on knowledge sharing by cmc are mainly positive: 'when compared to FTF communication, information transferred via email was found to be both more accurate and current. For example, unlike F2F, email enabled employees to spend time both writing and rephrasing their communication, without interruption or pressure to come up with a reply immediately.' 'Using email as a communication tool results in employees receiving information that previously would have remained unknown to them.'[68] Other studies have found no differences in how information is distributed among group members or between groups of people working in a fully identified, synchronous cmc environment similar to instant messaging and those working ftf.[69]

As Chapter 4 noted, while organizational members have some control over information flow even in a co-located setting, through social constraints, cmc increases individuals' control over the release of information.[70] This may help explain findings that, under time constraints, cmc teams were less successful in exchanging and processing information than ftf teams and were thus less successful at solving a 'hidden profile' problem, in which information critical to its solution was dispersed among team members who had to share it to solve the problem.[71] Similarly, an experiment in which groups worked on a mixed-motive task and in which participants had different information, so that they had to pool it, showed that both decision processes and outcomes varied between co-located and distributed groups:

- Frustration with the process 'was found to be higher for members in FTF groups than for those in CMC groups', possibly because ftf is better at conveying negative cues such as facial or verbal expressions that indicate animosity or hostility.
- The truthfulness of information exchange was also affected by the difference in communication modes, though here there was an interaction effect with whether the group had a leader or not. Members in ftf groups were more truthful when they had a leader; members in cmc groups, however, revealed their information to others more truthfully when they did not have a leader.

'These results seem to indicate that in the CMC mode members perceive that the leader is more likely to make decisions that may be detrimental to them, hence they tend to provide him/her with information that is to their advantage.'[72]

The social context – that is, pre-existing social networks, groups and intergroup boundaries – significantly constrains the flow of information across cmc groups. However, other factors, such as national culture and individuals' expectations about the outcomes of internet use, moderate the influence of the social context on cmc collaboration. Together, these findings suggest that all three of social networks, the nature of the communication (mediated or non-mediated) and culture interact to influence information flows in intercultural groups.[73] Among teleworkers, trust, interpersonal bonds and commitment predict knowledge sharing.[74]

Lin (2011) argued that in virtual teams members' level of commitment to their teams influences knowledge sharing and job effectiveness. In turn, 'structural links or connections between online individuals', 'individuals' cognitive capability that helps [them] understand the feelings of others who are online' and 'social relationships that reflect strong, positive character-istics and values among online individuals' influence team commitment and so indirectly influence knowledge sharing.[75]

Summary

A number of findings strongly suggest the importance of sharing knowl-edge for both individuals at work and for their organizations. Knowledge is created by combining and interpreting information. Tacit knowledge, which is non-verbalized, intuitive and unarticulated and depends on the experi-ence of the individual, may be particularly important but is also particularly difficult to share.

There are significant barriers to interpersonal knowledge sharing. Psychological, social and cultural factors can either assist or impede inter-personal knowledge transfer. Groups are sometimes inefficient at sharing information and tend to focus on only a portion of the available information, thus partially obviating their advantage over individuals of having access to a larger pool of expertise and knowledge. Although there are negative find-ings, on balance cmc has been found to be as productive for interpersonal information sharing as ftfc, but it is not clear that this applies to sharing tacit knowledge.

9.3 COORDINATION

With the increase of teamworking and outsourcing, many organizations are experiencing a major impact from coordination issues. For instance, a change in the membership of a team causes coordination problems when there is low information transfer during the change.[76] Again, intergroup coordination becomes a major challenge when groups have high levels of autonomy, according to a case study which investigated two alternatives to traditional hierarchical control. Neither rotating group spokespersons nor shared leadership proved satisfactory solutions to the problem.[77] Offshore outsourcing helps firms to produce more, may reduce their costs and enhance their flexibility and may also provide them with new resources and market knowledge. These benefits, however, depend on the firms being able to manage a network of foreign suppliers and to absorb foreign knowl-edge.[78] Problems of ensuring cooperation and coordination issues in verti-cal and horizontal relations have caused outsourcing failures. Both the number of relations across organizational boundaries and the extent of cooperation and coordination problems that arise in any one relationship give rise to costs that sometimes outweigh the benefits.[79]

At the root of coordination issues is interdependence – where units performing work, whether internally or externally to the organization, depend on one another to receive outputs, or be supplied with inputs such as components or raw materials, or, very significantly, information. Whenever actions are interdependent, for them to be coordinated both or all interdependent units must be able to predict what the others will do. Ultimately, coordination depends on knowledge that is shared and known to be shared.

Research has shown that there are further coordination problems caused by geographical distance and time lags and so for distributed settings such as virtual teams, offshoring or MNEs. Cultural differences potentially increase the coordination 'problem' further, because the ability to predict another's behaviour is fundamental to coordination, and cultural differences increase the difficulties of accurate prediction of what others will do. Costly communication and information processing requirements are generated by interdependence.

> " The simplest set of factors that increase the *information* costs of communication and the exchange of ideas and knowledge is the *spatial separation* of individuals who hold complementary knowledge and who could gain from coordinating their actions. Spatially-separated individuals are also likely to have different first languages, notwithstanding the adoption of English as the world's business language. Furthermore, there may be more fundamental differences between national outlooks and routines, which fundamentally influence communication and coordination.[80]

Horizontal communication and informal social networks are important for resolving coordination problems within organizations. However, there are two ways to coordinate that do not rely on ongoing communication. One is to use tacit rather than explicit methods to coordinate efforts; the other is to use common ground. As an example of tacit coordination, consider two people walking towards one another along a pavement: without speaking or even necessarily making eye contact, one moves to the right, the other to the left (or vice versa) and they do not collide. Tacit coordination can also work well in more complex situations providing the people who need to coordinate have relevant social information about one another.

When people have tacitly to match their decisions they focus on the characteristics they share with one another. For instance if two people need to meet but have no pre-arranged venue or way of communicating, they maximize their chances by going to where they met before, using the social information that the other knows the place and is likely to choose it. When success requires them to differ in their decisions, however, they focus on interpersonal differences as a basis for coordination. For instance, to avoid another person on a given occasion, someone might arrange to be somewhere they know that other person does not know about.

Tacit coordination requires that there is a clear association between the social information held about the other and the available choice options: for instance, in the examples given here, knowing that the other person is verbose or good at their job may be of little help. This factor – the need for the social information to relate clearly to the possible option – can significantly limit the usefulness of this kind of tacit coordination.[81]

There is also a second path to coordination with little or no ongoing communication: this is to rely on common ground, which is 'the sum of... [parties'] mutual, common or joint knowledge, beliefs and suppositions'.[82] Coordinating through common ground is useful when the people whose work needs to be coordinated are not co-located and when rich media are not available.[83] Other terms for this concept of common ground are convergent expectations, shared knowledge and mutual knowledge. Common ground is usually generated by socialization, shared location and prior interactions. However, research into 60 software services companies found that common ground can be generated across locations: organizations 'may achieve coordination by generating common ground regarding decision making procedures, work contexts and among individuals ... [The] common ground referred to here is usefully stated as "pre-existing stock of common ground" to distinguish it from flows of common ground generated by ongoing communication.' Three kinds of common ground are of value: procedural, contextual and interpersonal common ground:

- Procedural common ground is knowledge that interdependent individuals share about how they make decisions regarding the joint task.
- Contextual common ground is knowledge that interdependent individuals have about each others' locations and working environments.
- Interpersonal common ground is knowledge individuals have about the preferences/strengths/weaknesses, etc. of each other.

Given a pre-existing common ground, what appears to an observer as thin and structured communication using poor media, such as passing standardized documentation via email, may actually be very rich from the perspective of the individuals involved in the communication. 'This occurs not only because the "template" that is emailed is common ground, but also the process that the individual used to fill out the template is part of the common ground. The reader is able to put himself in the shoes of the writer and therefore interpret what the documents most likely mean.'

> To learn more about procedural, contextual and interpersonal common ground, visit the companion website... 9.3.1.

Attempts to achieve coordination with limited ongoing communication notwithstanding, information sharing and knowledge of group and individual activity are central to successful coordination and ongoing communication is often essential. In these circumstances combinations of modes can provide for more effective communication. Furthermore, as the following quotation shows, introducing a new mode can have indirect as well as direct benefits:

> **"** When voice mail was introduced into the relationship between a manufacturing firm and its network of dealerships it enhanced interorganizational effectiveness as measured by dealership sales performance in two primary ways: directly, due to the 'store and forward' nature of voice mail; but also indirectly, due to improved interorganizational relationships between the manufacturer's field representatives and the dealerships' sales managers enabled by the more effective use of written communication media.[84]

For shared knowledge to be used effectively for coordination, it needs to be organized, retained, maintained and retrieved. Although teams often rely on human capabilities for this purpose, computer-based mechanisms are available; these range from simple keyword organizing principles to complex intelligent agents and neural networks that grow with the growth of the knowledge repositories. They are various forms of collaborative tools (CTs) or virtual workplaces, which were described in Chapter 1. For comparatively routine tasks, it has been shown, teams often move from a relatively high level of interpersonal channel use in the early stages of a project to using the CT for nearly all their coordination in the later stages.

How CTs are used to coordinate among team members with routine tasks may not apply for tasks involving high levels of ambiguity, such as managing external relationships and conflicts (including obtaining resources or information outside the team, resolving design conflicts with others outside the team, clarifying project objectives and priorities with those outside the team, and getting appropriate team members to participate), brainstorming (e.g. quickly generating new ideas, transforming a concept sketch into a fully articulated drawing), or strategic direction-setting (e.g. moving the project forward when stalled or clarifying project objectives). However, a study in a natural setting compared the use of a CT with interpersonal modes (ftf and telephone) for a creative engineering design task with high levels of these kinds of ambiguity and concluded that 'sharing knowledge virtually using a CT is not determined solely by the ambiguity of the task but rather by the identification of a common language and artifacts through face-to-face communication. Once the commonality is created, even ambiguous tasks such as

For a description of CTs and virtual workplaces, look at Section 1.3.

creative brainstorming can be performed using CTs'.[85]

Summary

Two important developments in how organizations function give rise to coordination issues: these are team working, especially when teams enjoy a high level of autonomy, and outsourcing. Interdependence of separate individuals and units is the source of coordination issues. Geographical distance, time lags and cultural differences increase coordination problems.

Informal networks and horizontal communication are important for resolving coordination problems within organizations. When people are geographically distant and located in different time zones, however, tacit coordination based on social knowledge about another person or pre-existing common ground created through earlier interactions or documentation offers an alternative path to achieving coordination.

Virtual workplaces, or CTs coordination. When used for relatively routine tasks, they typically come to replace high levels of interpersonal channel use only in the later stages of projects. When used for non-routine tasks, however, studies show that they are used at a roughly consistent level, with peaks and troughs throughout, and although mainly used for the more routine aspects of the project, can be used for aspects involving high ambiguity.

> For more on this study of CT use, visit the companion website... 9.3.2.

> You are a member of a virtual team working on a statistics-based report. The Indian team supplies the data and statistical analysis; the UK team supplies the client-need knowledge and the version of English demanded by the (mainly European) clients. What issues might arise? How might they be overcome?

10 WORKING IN GROUPS AND TEAMS

When more than two people meet together face-to-face (ftf), on the telephone or by computer-mediated communication (cmc), the collective term for them is a group. (This term is also frequently and confusingly used for societal subdivisions such as genders or social classes.) At work, such groups may meet in order to make a decision, reach an agreement, solve a problem or perform a task. Performance groups, if they meet regularly and coordinate their work, are called teams.

In Sections 10.1, 10.2 and 10.3 respectively this chapter examines the factors and processes that make for effective and ineffective groupwork in general, then group decision-making and teamwork. These factors and processes are mainly concerned with communication. Two further sections, 10.4 and 10.5, analyse the effects of diversity and of working by cmc on groupwork, group decision-making and teamwork. Section 10.6 considers the issues that arise when teams, especially global teams, communicate exclusively or primarily by cmc.

> On completing your study of this chapter you will be able to explain in outline and apply the implications of:
>
> - Group dynamics, development and performance.
> - Decision-making by groups and influences on its effectiveness.
> - Teamwork and team-meeting processes and influences on team effectiveness.
> - Effects of diversity in groups and teams.
> - Effects of working by different communication modes on groups and teams; virtual teams.

10.1 GROUPWORK

Initially, working in a group can be less efficient and effective than working alone; a degree of conflict among the individuals' differing attitudes and expectations can absorb energy and time. Only after a process of development, which often involves 'storming' as well as forming and norming, does the collection of individuals become a cohesive body whose members are each performing functional roles and where interactions are governed by a set of norms.

For effective group development, members' individual, group and task needs must be met. The relative importance of these needs changes as group development proceeds. Other processes suggested as influences on group development include identity negotiation and the

To learn more about group development, visit the companion website... 10.1.1.

cognitive development of individual members to the point where they can continually adjust their cognitive frames and learn afresh. All these developments depend on interaction within the group.

Effective work groups have collective psychological capital, which is:

> ❝ The group's shared psychological state of development that is characterized by having confidence (collective efficacy) to take on and put in the necessary effort to succeed at challenging tasks; making a positive expectation (optimism) about succeeding now and in the future; persevering toward goals and, when necessary, redirecting paths to goals (hope) in order to succeed; and when beset by problems and adversity, sustaining and bouncing back and even beyond (resilience) to attain success.[1]

Together with trust, psychological capital influences group-level performance and citizenship behaviour.

Groups also have social capital, which is a combination of their internal cohesiveness and external networks. Internal cohesiveness is greater when group members are demographically similar, as the mutual support and coordination in cohesive ethnic communities suggests. However, demographic dissimilarity of group members increases the external ties of team members; such external ties generate 'information benefits' because they represent points of contact into different network clusters, each of which tends to represent a relatively non-redundant concentration of information and resources.[2] Such **boundary-spanning** ties (relationships with external individuals or groups) provide access to a broader array of ideas and opportunities than do ties that are restricted to a single cluster.[3]

While the research on small group performance shows that groups tend to outperform individuals in some task domains (especially idea generation and estimation tasks), there is also clear evidence that groups often perform worse than individuals, occasionally with severe negative consequences. Theoretical attempts to explain such negative performance events have tended to point to characteristics of the group or the group process that were different from those found for better performing groups, though the same typical group processes can often result in good or bad outcomes.[4]

Unfortunately, people are not naturally good at working in groups. The ubiquitous finding across many decades of research is that groups usually fall short of reasonable potential productivity base lines – i.e. they exhibit process losses. A very few studies have reported a process gain – group perform- ance that is better than the performance of any individual member efforts, but there are issues with these about estimates of the potential of the group.[5]

> Visit the companion website... 10.1.2 for links to two videos about groupwork.

Process losses occur in both decision-making groups and teams: 'process losses represent that portion of potential productivity that is not employed by the group and reflect the relative weaknesses of the group's decision process'.[6] Four particular examples of process losses are domi- nance (the tendency of some individuals or small subgroup of individuals to contribute a disproportionate share of group deliberations), evaluation apprehension (people not contributing out of fear of being judged by the others), information overload (being unable to take in information because too many people are giving out too much information too quickly) and production blocking (the fact that a group member may be prevented from expressing an idea because someone else is speaking and so may lose his or her train of thought). Of these, only production blocking is a problem particular to ftf groups; the others can also occur in cmc groups.

Group process gains occur when the dynamics of group interaction increase or enhance the total performance of that group and move the group toward better choices or decisions. Process gains represent the portion of actual productivity that would be greater than the sum of individ- ual productivity from a particular group. Process gains derive from learn- ing and synergy.[7] Although a very few studies have reported process gains, these are usually small and do not change the overall picture. Thus the burden of coordinating efforts can mean that the process gains in terms of delivering projects on time and on budget from enlarging teams are offset or outweighed by the process losses, though organizations often underes- timate these losses.[8]

Part of the explanation for relatively low performances by groups is that members often have lower motivation than when they work alone. In fact, they may indulge in **social loafing** (working less hard in the group than they would alone). Figure 10.1 shows the factors that affect the level of social loafing in a group. It is worth noting, however, that some degree of non- participation, or 'lurking' as it is known in the context of cmc, is usual and necessary: 'in most face-to-face group discussion environments, most

Figure 10.1 Factors that affect the level of an individual's social loafing in a group

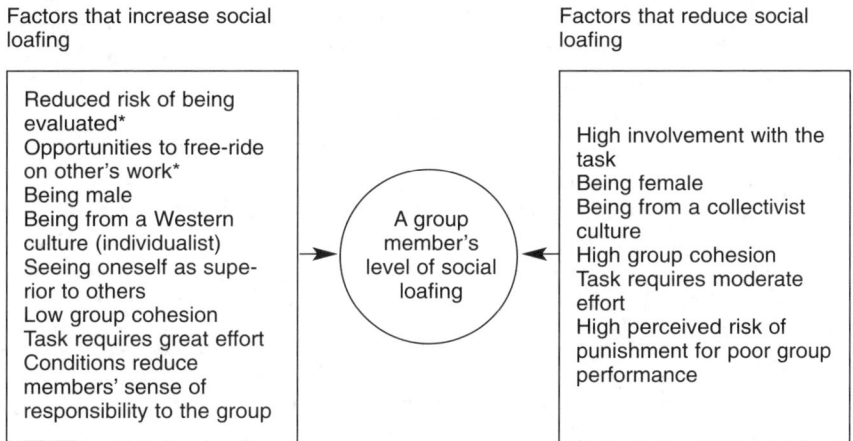

Factors that increase social loafing

Reduced risk of being evaluated*
Opportunities to free-ride on other's work*
Being male
Being from a Western culture (individualist)
Seeing oneself as superior to others
Low group cohesion
Task requires great effort
Conditions reduce members' sense of responsibility to the group

A group member's level of social loafing

Factors that reduce social loafing

High involvement with the task
Being female
Being from a collectivist culture
High group cohesion
Task requires moderate effort
High perceived risk of punishment for poor group performance

* Factors inherent in groupwork

Based on Kerr, N.L. and Tindale, R.S. (2004) 'Group performance and decision making', *Annual Review of Psychology*, **55**: 623–55.

participants lurk most of the time, and make occasional contributions. Indeed, most discussion forums, whether online or offline, would be impossible if all participants tried to actively contribute more frequently than they do'.[9]

There is a view of groups as information processors. It assumes that group members search and process information and that, through communication, individual-level information processing becomes integrated at the group level, where it affects other individuals in the group, who may distort or ignore it or analyse it deliberately. However, information processing at the group as well as at the individual level can be shallow and heuristic, or it can be deliberate and systematic. Under systematic information processing, more attention is given to both already available and new information, additional information is searched for, and information is communicated and integrated in a deliberate manner. The extent to which information is processed systematically depends on group members' epistemic motivation. There is evidence that group decision-making improves when group members are given task-relevant information that simplifies or reframes their task.[10]

Unfortunately, however, as we have known since 1985, group discussion is a poor means of exchanging new information. Stasser and Titus (1985) predicted that group members should be

To learn more about the evidence in support of the information-processing view of groups, visit the companion website... 10.1.3.

more interested in hearing novel information contributed by the other members, should be more persuaded by that information, and therefore should readily discover the 'hidden profile' as the members seek to hear previously unknown information from each other. Instead,

> *Look at the Glossary for a definition of a* **hidden profile problem.**

however, hidden profile groups mostly failed to discover the optimal decision, and the uniquely held information was hardly mentioned.[11]

Subsequent studies have consistently found that group members tend to discuss already shared information in preference to information that is unique or new. Designating some members as experts has some effect and so do team leaders' efforts to increase the amount of novel information shared, but teams still discuss more common than unique information. The reason is that people judge the importance and accuracy of information from others' evaluations; information that is also familiar to other group members will tend to be socially validated, and this mutual endorsement will lead group members to be more likely to mention and repeat shared information. Thus ftf discussions often fail to disseminate unshared information.[12]

> *Visit the companion website... 10.1.4 to learn about how group members' beliefs concerning whether they have enough information to solve a problem, affect information sharing.*

A further problem is that group members tend to spend more time discussing information that agrees with their initial preferences. In sum, groups evaluate information more favourably that agrees with their preferences, judge information that they think others possess as more accurate and relevant than information that cannot be corroborated in this way, and favour information that group members knew before the discussion.[13]

Factors that can lead to better groupwork

Recently, **transactive memory systems** have been shown to improve groupwork. They can be defined as:

> ❝a group information-processing system made up of the memory systems possessed by individuals as well as the communication processes linking these individual memory systems together ... The development of shared transactive memory systems relies on individual-level processes involving individuals' actions to update their directories of who knows what, allocate information to other team members, and retrieve information from other team members.[14]

Transactive memory has both benefits and costs. The benefits of collaborative remembering are that people remember more with less effort – in effect they divide a memory task among themselves so as to make it easy for them to fill in gaps in each other's recall. In this way, they distribute the burden of remembering, using one another as external memory aids. Experimenters have repeatedly shown that the group, as a unit, recalls more than at least some of the individual members of the group would recall alone. Costs of transactive memory include collaborative inhibition (similarly to production blocking, this may prevent some memories being shared), information sampling biases in favour of shared rather than uniquely held information, and speakers tuning their recollections to what they believe the audience expects to hear. This last cost, known as audience tuning, is shown by the fact that people will recount more details, such as everything involved in a trip to the doctors, when talking to a hypothetical Martian, who they presume knows little about how things work on Earth, than when talking to a peer, who they presume knows a lot more.[15]

There are other factors that improve group performance. It is better in more cohesive groups; these tend generally to be more productive so long as group norms favour high productivity, group members are committed to performance goals and task requirements allow higher productivity. Good performance in turn may enhance the group's productivity. Recognizing which of their members has the greatest expertise also improves group performance, and, at least for some tasks, groups can recognize member expertise using cues such as loquacity, use of reason to influence, member

Figure 10.2 Factors that help improve group performance

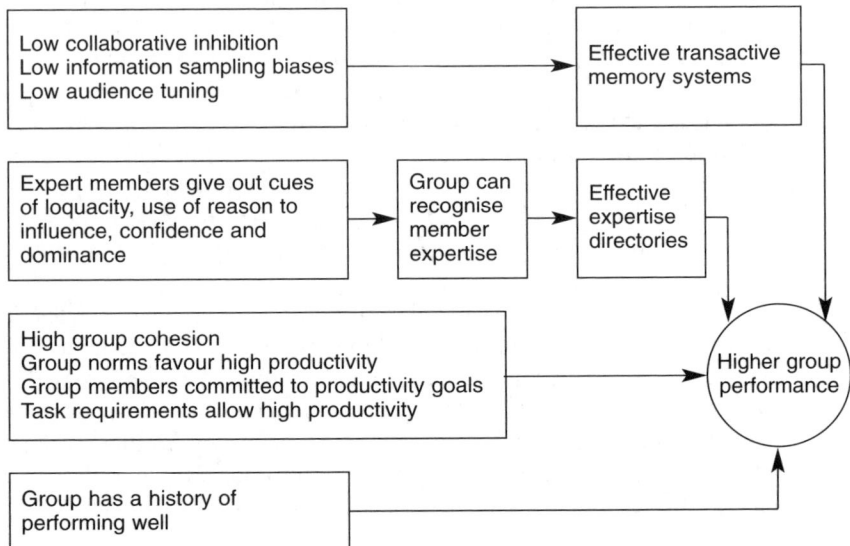

confidence and dominance. Larger groups are better at recognizing which members have most expertise.[16] Figure 10.2 shows these factors that improve group performance.

Culture and gender in groupwork

Cultures may differ significantly in the degree to which certain process losses affect their group behaviour, or at least the degree to which process losses are reported. A study showed that not only were there differences in process losses across cultures, but these differences existed both for group support system (GSS) groups working by cmc and for ftf groups. For example, Hong Kong groups reported greater production blocking than US groups across both modes. However, production blocking in both countries was lower by GSS than ftf.[17]

Group composition in terms of gender is related to many group process variables in significant ways; however, in general, task differences are less strong. Female-only groups, regardless of task, send more words per message, are more satisfied with the group process, and report higher levels of group development than either mixed or male only groups.[18]

Summary

Before they perform well, most groups go through a process of development, which can be conflictual. For groups to develop effectiveness, individual members' needs must be met; if they are then the group can develop psychological capital in the form of efficacy. They may also develop social capital, though this is a function of two conflicting forces: cohesiveness, which is fostered by similarity among the members, and network information benefits that come from group members having different external contacts, which is fostered by heterogeneity.

Groups exhibit process losses caused by dominance, evaluation apprehension, information overload or production blocking. Bigger groups have more process losses and these are not offset by their greater process gains. Individual motivation is lower in groups, leading to social loafing.

Factors that improve knowledge transfer, such as transactive memory systems, may improve group performance, but they are subject to problems such as collaborative inhibition, information sampling biases and audience tuning. Furthermore, group discussion tends to focus around preference-consistent information. More cohesive groups, groups that have performed well in the past, and groups with identified experts, perform better. Gender and culture both affect how groups work.

10.2 DECISION-MAKING BY GROUPS

Decision-making is a central activity for organizations: 'it is difficult to specify the attributes of organisations without asking who makes what kind of decisions, and what procedures are used to make them'.[19] With the possible exception of small organizations headed by an autocrat, all such decision-making must involve interpersonal communication; in general, at least a board or top management group makes the top-level strategic decisions, and in large organizations several or many lower-level groups make subordinate but still important decisions. Increasingly, decision-making in organizations is participative; this makes interpersonal communication increasingly significant. Other important issues in group decision-making covered in this section are performance, brainstorming, how groups reach agreements, the effects of leadership, the impact of minority versus majority views, and cultural difference.

Participative decision-making

A number of rationales have led to an increase over time in participative decision-making (PDM) in organizations: these rationales include an assumption that individuals should have the right and the ability to participate in decisions that affect their lives, and an assumption that PDM is a means to achieve higher productivity, efficiency and profits[20] because it increases satisfaction, motivation, commitment, group cohesion and identification.[21] A further reason is that the increasing environmental complexity that organizations face forces them to adopt forms of participation; where organizational tasks are primarily complex, PDM is needed to bring all the relevant knowledge held by different individuals or units to bear. Finally, there is an argument in favour of PDM in terms of decision quality: as it has been recognized increasingly that decision implementation is vital, there has been an increase in the understanding that participation in making the decision is likely to increase commitment to it and so to lead employees to be motivated to implement it effectively. For example, PDM can reduce resistance to change.

There are arguments against PDM: firstly, in large organizations, an increase in the number of participants leads to an exponential increase of the number of interactions: this slows down the decision process and increases the problems of reaching agreement. Secondly, PDM is a time-consuming process, so that it is not appropriate when a decision is needed urgently. Despite these issues, in most organizations PDM has increased, in part because technology facilitates it. Since participation and communication are correlated, the more two-way communication occurs, the greater the increase in the amount, social range, double directionality and supervisor's openness: that is the more elements of a participative organizational climate are present.

Decision-making performance of groups

While decisions made by groups under time constraints are no better than those made by their best individual member, given enough time they do tend to outperform individuals in many domains. Over time, errors get corrected as the group sifts through suggestions, the group's social support helps members think clearly and competition for respect mobilizes members' energies.[22] Watson et al. (1992), who showed that given enough time groups can outperform individuals at problem-solving and decision-making, suggested that groups' advantages take time to show benefits because newly formed groups are not likely to be efficient enough at processing information to take full advantage of the knowledge that members bring to the pool.

However, although groups can perform better than individuals at problem-solving and decision-making, they are subject to the same biases as individual decision-makers. Whether groups will be more, less or equally as biased as individuals depends on the type of bias, the way the group makes its decisions, how strong the bias is and who in the group introduces that bias.[23] Groups also have a greater tendency than individuals to lead to people believing that erroneous conclusions are correct (to suffer from **groupthink**). While more people working on a problem increases the number of accurate answers, the better the people concerned know one another the greater their confidence that what are actually errors are not wrong. This tendency is all the greater when the group is working on a professionally salient task, because the members compete to be the one to produce the group's solution.[24]

> *Would a group considering an investment proposal be likely to take the same or a different view of the prospective return or to be similarly likely to discount uncertainties and unknowns than its members would be on average if they were considering the proposal on their own? Why or why not?*

Brainstorming

As Section 10.1 has shown, groups are poor at sharing information, tending to discuss what they all already know rather than seek out information that one member may have that is not already shared. Once groups have enough information (or often before – they tend to be easily satisfied) they turn to generating ideas about how to solve the problem or which alternative of those they have identified to adopt. Group brainstorming is a method of collective idea generation; it was once believed to enable groups routinely to outperform equal-sized sets of non-interacting individuals (nominal groups). However, research has shown the reverse to be true:

process losses in interacting groups mean that nominal groups generally outperform brainstorming groups.

> **"** All senior managers, at some point, experience the pain of pursuing new ideas by way of traditional brainstorming sessions – still the most common method of using groups to generate ideas at companies around the world. The scene is familiar: a group of people, often chosen largely for political reasons, begins by listening passively as a moderator (often an outsider who knows little about your business) urges you to 'Get creative!' and 'Think outside the box!' and cheerfully reminds you that 'There are no bad ideas!'
>
> The result? Some attendees remain stone-faced throughout the day, others contribute sporadically, and a few loudly dominate the session with their pet ideas. Ideas pop up randomly – some intriguing, many preposterous – but because the session has no structure, little momentum builds around any of them. At session's end, the group trundles off with a hazy idea of what, if anything, will happen next. 'Now we can get back to real work,' some whisper.[25]

Some of the problems with ftf brainstorming can be overcome: a trained facilitator can reduce evaluation apprehension; using a facilitator, splitting a problem into subtasks and taking the subtasks in a logical sequence can minimize production blocking. Other suggestions include the following:

1. Know your organization's decision-making criteria.
2. Ask the right questions.
3. Choose the right people.
4. Divide and conquer – have them conduct multiple, discrete, highly focused idea generation sessions among subgroups of three to five people.
5. After your participants arrive, but before the division into subgroups, orient them so that your expectations about what they will – and won't – accomplish are clear.
6. Wrap it up – describe to them exactly what steps will be taken to choose the winning ideas and how they will learn about the final decisions.
7. Follow up quickly.[26]

How groups reach agreements on decisions

One issue on decision-making by groups is how members who may have different initial solutions or preferences reach an agreement. This is related to the operation of social influence, which was described in Chapter 7. Social influence in group decision-making includes normative influence – the pressure to conform to others' expectations – and informational influence, which is based on logical arguments or factual material. In general, for groups working under time pressure, normative influence is more likely to emerge and be stronger. On the other hand, for groups working under low time pressure and for groups working on 'intellective' tasks – problems that 'have factually correct solutions', which are contrasted with 'judgmental tasks', problems 'whose solutions are determined by group consensus' – informational influence is more likely to emerge and to be stronger than normative influence. The more informational influence is used, the more accurate the solution is likely to be.[27] Unfortunately, many work-related decision tasks do not have 'factually correct' solutions.

In ftf decision-making groups, high-status individuals often dominate discussions and are first to advocate a particular solution. Both dominating discussions and **first advocacy** lead to an individual having more influence than other members. However, these status inequalities are only pronounced when the high-status member's standing is based on expertise and that expertise is relevant to the decision task. When the same groups make comparable decisions using electronic mail, however, status and expertise inequalities in participation are reduced, and both high and low-status members are equally likely to be first to advocate the solution.[28]

The degree to which a group's leader regulates the process by which the group reaches a decision has a powerful, and generally positive, effect on the quality of group process and outcomes. However, this does not mean that high-process-directive leaders will always be effective. For example, such a leader who systematically excludes certain group members or particular ideas from emerging could be particularly ineffective.[29]

Majority versus minority views

Another issue in groups' decision-making is the question of majority versus minority views. While it might be expected that the majority would prevail, in fact the outcome is not so clear. For instance, moderate, as opposed to extreme, deviation by a minority often does influence the majority as it prompts the majority to search for an explanation for the behaviour. One factor that affects the degree of **minority influence** is whether the holders of the minority view are geographically distant – a situation that arises through mediated communication. For instance, while 'a consistent position by a geographically *collocated* minority opinion holder has a negative influence on the majority's individual and group decisions [i.e. leads the majority to differ further from the minority opinion], because ingroup members react strongly against fellow group members who are deviant', a minority opinion that is presented by a geographically isolated group member can positively influence majority members' decisions. This is because the majority expect those who are similar to themselves to hold similar information and ideas but also expect those who are different from themselves – even if only in their location – to hold different information and ideas. Ultimately, the group is liable to be influenced by the minority opinion because arguing leads members to think about and sometimes be convinced by the reason for the disagreement.[30] There is some evidence that minority views are more influential on how the majority think about the issue than on their eventual decision.

To learn more about the influence of minority views, visit the companion website... 10.2.1.

Cultural differences in group decision-making

Culture influences decision-making by groups. As Olson and Olson (2003) argued, 'in Western societies, decisions are made on the basis of input from those involved. Or, they gather individual preferences and democratically vote on the solution. In cultures with greater hierarchies, group members assume an authority will decide and they are only to enact the decision, not to have input or take responsibility. [Moreover] ... not only do the processes differ, the basis for evaluation of alternatives and the outcome also differ'.[31] Yates et al. (1997) found that Chinese and several other East Asian groups (but not Japanese) were more confident than Americans that their decisions were correct. They attributed this to a greater propensity to select the first adequate problem solution that is identified rather than to survey a range of alternatives before deciding.[32]

Summary

Most decision-making in organizations depends on interpersonal communication. PDM has costs as well as benefits but is increasingly used, partly owing to technological facilitation; PDM in turn leads to more interpersonal communication.

Given enough time, groups can outperform individuals at decision-making, but they suffer from the same biases as individual decision-makers and in addition they may be subject to groupthink. One explanation of the better decision making of groups relieved of time pressure is that in such groups informational influence is likely to outweigh normative influence.

Process losses can significantly impede ftf brainstorming by groups, although there are ways of lessening their impact. Individuals who have high status due to relevant expertise often lead group decisions; leaders who actively direct the decision-making process produce better outcomes, although when they determine the decision they can do harm.

Minority views are more likely to be 'heard' by the majority when the minority is not co-located, but minority views in general affect how groups approach issues rather than strongly influencing their decision. Culture may influence both the process and the goal of decision-making by groups.

10.3 TEAMWORK

Visit the companion website... 10.3.1 for a link to a video on the power of teamwork.

As the start of this chapter explained, teams are performance groups that interact regularly and coordinate their work. Teams can also be understood as complex, multilevel systems that function over time, tasks and contexts.[33] Team performance and the effects on it of interaction patterns, pressure to perform and size are discussed in this section as are suggested ways of improving team performance such as sharing of team member mental models and developing external networks.

Team performance

Factors that impact on team performance include the team's pattern of interaction, whether members identify with the team, whether they are under pressure to perform and team size:

- Teams take time to perform effectively but stable patterns of interaction in teams emerge very quickly. More effective swift-starting teams, such as emergency or rescue teams, with highly trained members who have not previously worked together, interact in ways that are stable in complexity and duration and more reciprocal compared to those of less effective swift-starting teams.[34]
- In less effective teams generally, patterns of interaction can often be negative. Sequences or cycles of interactions with a particular character, such as complaining, can be identified in work-related meetings, studies of group discussion in two German industrial enterprises found.[35] Complaining cycles are linked to a passive group mood: 'complaining begets further complaining statements, while simultaneously inhibiting the expression of solution-oriented statements'. However, more effective teams exhibit positive patterns of interaction: 'when solutions are proposed they are followed by further discussion of solutions. If support is expressed for either complaint or solution statements, circles of these two types of interaction arise'.[36]
- Teams that show more functional interaction in their meetings, such as problem-solving interaction and action planning, are significantly more satisfied with their meetings. Better meetings are also associated with higher team productivity. Moreover, constructive meeting interaction processes were related to organizational success more than two years after the meeting, a study found. Dysfunctional communication, such as criticizing others or complaining, showed significant negative relationships with organizational success. Thus processes in team meetings shape outcomes for both the team and their organization.[37]

- The more employees identify with their team, the more their effort and the higher, usually, their performance. Additionally, when the team leader provides inspirational motivation and is 'prototypical' of the team (a model of what the team believes its members are or should be), the relationship between employees' identification with their team and their performance is strengthened.[38]
- Pressure to 'perform' acts as a 'double-edged sword' for teams, providing positive effects by enhancing the team's motivation to achieve good results while simultaneously triggering process losses, a study of 78 audit and consulting teams from two global professional firms found. Even though motivated to perform well on a high-stakes project, pressured teams are more likely to engage in behaviours that actually detract from their performance. As performance pressure increases, team members begin to rely excessively on general expertise while discounting domain-specific expertise, leading to suboptimal performance. A drive toward consensus, a focus on common knowledge, a shift from learning to project completion, and increased conformity to the status hierarchy also undermine team performance when teams are under pressure.[39]
- Individuals in smaller teams perform better than individuals in larger teams; part of the reason is that people in smaller teams feel they have more support and these feelings of support buffer stressful experiences and promote performance.[40] Again, a dynamic process can occur in smaller teams in which the sense of having shared feelings and being drawn to one another through similarity reinforce the quality of their members' interpersonal relationships. Contextual factors may diminish or strengthen these relationships. Figure 10.3 shows these contextual factors that affect group members' feelings towards their group.

> *Your five-person team is in competition for a prize that is awarded annually. There were originally ten teams in the competition but six have been eliminated. How is this situation likely to affect the team's behaviour? If it wins, how is its behaviour likely to change? If it loses, how is its behaviour likely to change?*

Ways of improving team performance

A growing stream of theory and research suggests that teams have better processes and outcomes when team members have closely similar mental models of their task, situation and environment, providing the models are accurate. Shared team-member models improve coordination by enabling members to anticipate one anothers' actions and needs.

A literature review suggests that mental models that 'emphasize ownership, learning and heedful interrelating' give rise to more effective

Figure 10.3   Factors that affect group members' feelings towards the group

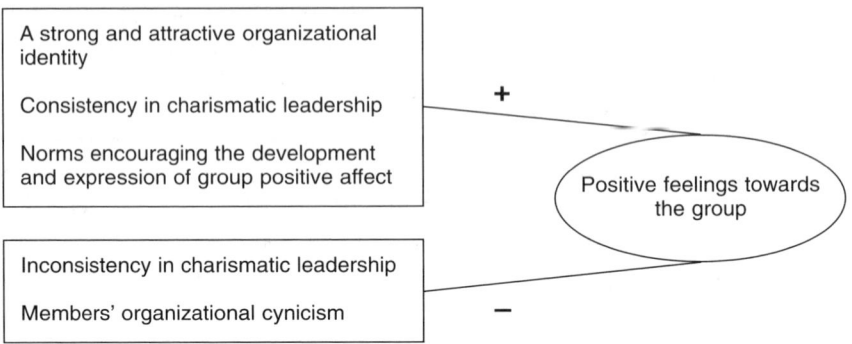

Based on Walter, F. and Bruch, H. (2008) 'The positive group affect spiral: A dynamic model of the emergence of positive affective similarity in work groups', *Journal of Organizational Behavior*, **29**(2): 239–261.

teamwork; such team mental models 'flourish when the organization supports these values'. However, since mental models are fluid and adapt to explicit and implicit messages, they weaken if shifting organizational priorities cause support to wane.[41] Thus, for instance, an organization that at one time supported 'learning' might withdraw support for it during a period of economic downturn when it was downsizing; this would undermine the 'learning' element of team mental models in that organization and could lead to less effective teamwork.

Groups and teams and their work must, necessarily, be part of a larger whole and so must be integrated with other units both within and often beyond the organization. The denser and more heterogeneous a team's external networks, the greater is its productivity. How well teams perform overall is related to the extent of their 'outward bound' activities, such as informing, probing and 'parading' (making themselves known). The more the external communication, the higher the managerial ratings of innovation, while more functionally diverse groups are more inclined to communicate outside the group. Effective external team lead-

To learn more about team mental models, visit the companion website... 10.3.2.

Factors that help groups perform better include cohesiveness, having members who are socially rewarding and socially skilled, having powerful members who help others, ensuring that goal structure is cooperative, not competitive or individualistic, and arguing constructively.

To learn more about these factors that help groups perform better visit the companion website... 10.3.3.

ers actively engage in four outward-bound strategies (relating, scouting, persuading and empowering) to facilitate team effectiveness.[42]

Summary

Teams are groups that undertake work together. Team meeting processes shape both team and organizational outcomes. Pressure to perform, though motivational, leads teams to dysfunctional behaviours. In smaller teams, members' sense of their interpersonal relationships can impact positively on performance, though contextual factors such as leadership style, norms and the organization's identity can affect this. Convergence of team members' mental models through communication boosts team performance, especially if these mental models emphasize the team's psychological ownership of its work, learning or heedful interrelating. Teams' external networks and communication strongly influence their effectiveness; functional diversity of team membership and having an effective team leader promote teams' external networks.

10.4 EFFECTS OF DIVERSITY IN GROUPS AND TEAMS

Diversity in groups has been shown to have both negative effects such as division through social categorization and positive effects such as providing non-redundant value-adding information resources. The negative effects and some positive effects are evident in newly formed groups, but the main positive effects can only be seen in mature groups. Demographic diversity and psychological dissimilarity lead to differences in the nature of socially integrated teams and ultimately to differences in member turnover and task performance.[43]

In groups, diversity of gender, age, ethnicity and job tenure all affect how much task and relationship conflict take place within them. Both these kinds of conflict have a negative effect on group performance, but task conflict increases group-level organizational citizenship behaviour whereas relationship conflict decreases it. Again, demographic and job tenure differences between subgroups within an organizational unit can create communication barriers between the subgroups, especially when there is high similarity among the subgroups' members and when two 'dimensions of demographic diversity' are well aligned, for example, when a unit consists of old males and young females. When the two dimensions originate from social categories (gender–age and age–race 'faultlines') relationship conflict but not task conflict is greater, though task

> To learn more about how diversity affects how socially integrated teams are, visit the companion website... 10.4.1.

conflict is increased when tenure-based subgroups are differentiated by gender (e.g. female senior members vs male junior members); tenure–age 'faultlines' increase relationship conflict.[44]

Diversity of opinions as well as demographic and tenure diversity can affect group and team functioning. When a team has 'cognitive diversity', that is when its individual members differ in thinking styles, knowledge, skills, values and beliefs, the creativity of individual team members is higher, but only when these individuals have confidence in their own creativity and when the team's leaders practise transformational leadership (inspire, intellectually stimulate and are individually considerate of team members).[45] However, 'deviants' – people who take a contrarian view – can sometimes foster innovation in groups and improve decision quality. When the group's task is difficult, deviants do improve decision quality even though their presence is associated with lowered group confidence, group cohesion and task satisfaction. When the group's task is not difficult, the same negative consequences of the presence of a deviant occur but without any improvement in decision quality. When their view is seen as justified, however, deviants can reduce prejudice in groups and produce fairer decision outcomes.[46]

Highly considerate team leaders can mitigate the tendency of diverse team members to socially categorize and be prejudiced about their fellow members and so can improve team functioning. It is the ability of the leader to see members as unique individuals that explains this positive effect. Suggesting that they recognize this effect, people faced with the prospect of working in a diverse team have a higher preference for considerate leadership than people expecting to work in a homogeneous team have.[47]

Summary

Demographically diverse teams exhibit lower levels of social integration and performance than homogeneous teams when they are engaged in tasks that do not make them highly interdependent, but not when the task makes them interdependent. Psychological diversity, in contrast, has a stronger negative impact when the teams' task involves high interdependence.

Differences based on combinations of gender, age and ethnicity increase relationship conflict but not task conflict; differences based on tenure increase task conflict while the combination of tenure and age differences also increases relationship conflict. Diversity of opinion is generally positive for group creativity. People working in diverse teams tend to categorize their fellow-team members, with negative results such as prejudice, but considerate leadership can mitigate this.

10.5 HOW COMMUNICATION MODES AFFECT WORKING IN GROUPS AND TEAMS

Many issues arise when groups and teams work by cmc; they include performance issues, effects on decision-making, what kinds of task are most affected, the impact of culture and diversity, and the effects on satisfaction, participation and social influence.

Performance issues in cmc groups and teams

There is evidence that how well members understand each other, the group task and the group's decision, is lower in cmc groups than ftf groups. Researchers have also reported on how the group member who finally records the group's choice or decision makes more errors in the cmc condition than in the ftf condition. Although some scholars have attributed this result to intentional misrepresentation on the part of the subjects, and others blamed the tediousness of error checking in cmc, the errors could very well be due to poorer comprehension in cmc. Being unable to observe the body language, facial expressions and tone of voice of the other communicator may assist people in focusing on the issue at hand, but the reduced social cues can also lead to misinterpretation, frustration and mistrust.[48]

Text-based cmc groups take longer to complete an allotted task, at least partly because typing takes longer than speaking. However, although in a given time period cmc groups produce fewer remarks than ftf groups, when there are no time constraints, although cmc groups take longer, the number of total remarks is about the same, and groups in cmc perform about as well as the ftf groups. The reason is that cmc groups have as many or more task-oriented remarks and decision proposals. Weisband (1992) reported more implicit decision preferences, explicit decision proposals, social pressure remarks, process remarks and task irrelevant remarks in the cmc condition. The difference seems to be in the socio-emotional exchange. Ftf groups have more tension release and agreement statements, while cmc groups have a tendency to give more suggestions, orientations, opinions and formal expressions, and fewer spontaneous questions.[49]

In another study, nominal groups working with computers did as well as interacting groups. (That is, the average of the opinions of groups of non-interacting individuals were as accurate as the group verdict of interacting individuals.) However, the interacting groups found the task easier, were much less apprehensive and felt they had participated more than the nominal groups.

As group size increases, productivity per person decreases in ftf groups but stays the same in cmc groups. The major advantage of cmc groups lies in reduced production blocking and evaluation apprehension.[50] (When, instead of allowing all participants to produce ideas simultaneously, production blocking is introduced in the cmc condition by freezing the keyboard or introducing 'turn taking' and 'first in' procedures, performance decreases dramatically.)

On performance more generally, although the quality of work completed is similar in cmc and ftf groups, productivity is greater in ftf groups, especially when the group members are more interdependent: that is, the advantage in productivity of ftf groups over cmc groups increases as the level of coordination needed to complete the task increases. The probable explanation is that communication modes that transmit more social context cues foster group performance and satisfaction more as the requirements for member interdependence that the group task poses increases.[51]

Group decision making and cmc

A 2002 meta-analysis of research comparing decision making in ftf versus cmc groups found that cmc led to decreases in group effectiveness, increases in the time required to complete tasks and decreases in member satisfaction, compared to ftf groups. However, a number of other variables affected these measures, not all of which apply to all cmc: limited versus unlimited time to reach decisions, group size and task type were significant for at least one of the dependent variables.[52] Furthermore, nearly all the studies in the meta-analysis dealt with groups with a short history and no expectation of future interaction; it may be that changing these variables would change the results.

Other findings on the impact of cmc on group decision-making include the following:

- A finding that contradicts the meta-analysis is that for decision-making tasks, groups using text-based GSS took more time to arrive at their decisions but made decisions of higher quality than non-GSS-supported groups.[53]
- Influence is more evenly distributed and takes different forms in cmc versus ftf decision-making groups.[54]
- Managers' prior attitudes to and preferences for risk changed less when they discussed issues by real-time cmc than when they discussed them ftf. Part of the explanation of the difference may lie in there having been less argumentation – a lower level of attempts to persuade in cmc than ftf. Norms also had less effect in cmc-based group decision-making, but first advocacy, which was explained in Section 10.2, applied to both modes.[55]
- Cmc has usually been found to be productive at the 'ideas generation' stage of decision-making and one study found that asynchronous cmc

groups working on decision-making tasks improved by nearly 50 per cent over ftf groups.[56] However, choosing among the available alternatives may be negatively affected by cmc. When six groups consisting of four experts cooperated in planning a marketing campaign for solar energy systems, no differences were found between

To learn more about the effects on group decision-making of working by cmc visit the companion website... 10.5.1.

ftf, synchronous and asynchronous text-based communication in terms of group member satisfaction. Group performance, however, was judged to be better in ftf than in either kind of computer-mediated groups, while there were also differences in how well concepts were related to one another when the different communication modes were employed.[57]

Task type

The comparative performance of groups working by ftf or cmc depends on the task. When the goal of communication in a group is to convey information, cmc teams and ftf teams perform equally well. However, when the communication process requires convergence towards an agreement, ftfc results in better performance than cmc.[58] In terms of idea generation, the two mediated communication technologies of email and a GSS differed: the GSS led to groups generating more in total and a higher number of basic ideas; the email to their generating more inferential ideas. These differences may be linked to the fact that GSS communication is synchronous and email is asynchronous.[59]

Cmc groups perform better than ftf groups on tasks involving less, and worse on tasks requiring more, socio-emotional interaction when time is limited. Given enough time, cmc groups perform as well as ftf groups on both types of task. Strong evidence supports the idea that, when a task involves less socio-emotional interaction (such as idea generation), cmc groups perform better than ftf groups. For example, studies of group brainstorming reveal that cmc groups produce more non-redundant ideas than ftf groups. However, because of less socio-emotional interaction in cmc, these groups do not perform as well as ftf groups in tasks that require more socio-emotional conversation or increased interdependence.[60]

Effects on member satisfaction and behaviour

Whatever the performance effects, participants often report dissatisfaction with meetings held by cmc, even though it has been shown to enhance productivity, increase participation equality and improve decision quality. Mejias (2007) argued for distinguishing between satisfaction with outcome and satisfaction with process and showed that dissatisfaction arises mainly from the experience of process losses. These are 'interactions created by individuals working in teams which generate negative influences'. When people knew the other participants in a meeting, cmc generated negative feelings about process; however, this did not occur where they did not know the others. Mejias (2007) suggested that process losses do not affect anonymous cmc environments because anonymity 'leads to a reduction in social context cues and evaluation tendencies that generate positive effects upon satisfaction... Group members may feel less inhibited and less likely to feel evaluation from other group members resulting in more open and honest participation'. Process gains, on the other hand, affect both anonymous and identified cmc environments because of the 'robust effects of group process gains upon meeting satisfaction'.[61]

Communication mode effects on participation

There may be greater equality of participation in cmc groups. In ftf groups, status differences among group members often determine participation, with higher status members participating more. In cmc groups, on the other hand, participation tends to be more balanced or equitable. Status inequalities are attenuated in cmc, probably as a result of reduced evaluation apprehension or less attention to social factors. Equality of participation in the cmc condition is a fairly consistent finding. In addition, in cmc groups, the difference between high and low status member participation is less and they are less likely to have one individual dominating the discussion. Common sense and some case studies suggest the so-called 'democratization argument': since email allows both direct (non-filtered) communication between people and identity/status concealment, it enhances more free and easy participation in decision-making. This view is especially argued by technological imperative approaches to organizational communication and media studies, which more or less explicitly assume that, given certain technological potentialities, sooner or later users will fully explore and exploit them. Whether this is true or not, the technical trait of keeping trace induced some authors to point out the risk of increasing control and surveillance over workers' behaviour.[62] Straus (1996) found that although cmc led to more equal participation in groups, some individuals – particularly extraverts – still dominated and that cmc had few effects on information sharing or performance. Cmc groups were less satisfied with the process.[63]

Other behavioural variations have been noted in cmc compared to ftf: in computer-mediated three-member groups, members made fewer remarks but participated more equally, took longer to reach a decision, which tended to shift further away from members' initial individual choices, and exhibited more uninhibited behaviour, such as using strong and inflammatory expressions.[64] There may also be reduced normative social pressure in cmc groups; more 'social pressure remarks' are made in cmc groups, which is interpreted as arising because cmc groups need more social pressure remarks as there is reduced inherent social pressure in the cmc environment'.[65]

Communication mode effects on status and power in groups

Status seems to influence information exchange and decision quality in groups, whether communication is ftf or by cmc. When only a low-status member of a mixed-status group possesses critical information, decisions are poorer and the critical information is less discussed regardless of the communication mode, compared with what occurs in equal-status groups. However, the relation between status and communication media is complex. Computer mediation can suppress information exchange and the perceived influence on group decision quality of group members, no matter what their status: 'computer-mediated communication produced attenuated status effects for information and perceived influence by suppressing the information and the perceived influence of the equal-status, information-rich individual rather than increasing the participation and the discussion of information by the low-status group member'.[66]

In fact, the anonymity of virtual groups can accentuate the power differentials associated with salient social identities.[67] Weisband et al. (1995), after three different experiments, found that high-status members participated more in the decision process than low-status members in every situation (cmc or ftf, majority or minority). The explanation is that even in computer-mediated settings, people are able to categorize others as members of different status groups (high or low). This categorization creates a bias in favour of ingroup members and against outgroup members. The relative de-individuation of the members of the outgroup (e.g. low-status members) facilitates the development of negative evaluations by high status members: 'if group status differences are strong and salient, as they are in some organizations, status differences will persist or even be magnified, and unique personal information about people will be made less salient, when communication is computer-mediated'.[68] In fact, members of distributed groups (that do not share a geographic location and communicate by cmc) tend to more extreme perceptions of dominance than co-located groups and disagree more with an interaction partner about whether one person is dominating, and who that is. This lack of agreement can make the group less attractive to belong to and less cohesive.[69]

Communication mode effects on social influence in groups

Working by cmc 'can actually reinforce group salience and conformity to group norms, and thereby strengthen the impact of a variety of social boundaries'.[70] The explanation is found in the relative anonymity provided by text-based cmc which can actually 'increase attention to the salient social identity and norms'. When experimental subjects made a choice, and exchanged their decisions and supporting arguments via computer with three ostensible partners who unanimously endorsed the opposite choice, the subjects took a more extreme perception of the group norm, expressed better recall of the interactants' arguments, and made more positive evaluations of these arguments through group identification, albeit only for women; women and subjects with a higher need for public individuation were also more likely to conform to group norms. The researchers attributed these behaviours to the depersonalization (lack of individuating information) effects of cmc.[71]

Benefits of mixed-modes, learning and diversity

Mixed-mode groups are less subject to negative effects on task cohesion and performance than those working by cmc alone. Mixed-mode teams, which first meet ftf then by cmc, have higher levels of PDM than purely cmc teams, report team satisfaction similar to pure ftf teams and deliver a task performance between that of pure cmc and ftf teams. However, they experience increased conflict over time, unlike the pure cmc teams.[72] In mixed-mode groups that communicated both by cmc and ftf, time spent in ftf communication significantly predicted group social cohesion, though time spent in cmc did not. On the other hand, both group task cohesion and group task performance were greater the more time the group spent in cmc. It may be that mixed-mode groups use ftf communication for building social cohesion and cmc communication for getting ahead with a task.[73] Again, in partially distributed work groups – where one individual was separated from the 'core' group but linked via communication and computer support – perceptions of mediated communication by both remote and co-located members improved over time and groups using richer media felt their medium was more effective. Performance, however, did not depend on type of mode.[74]

Learning by users, as in other aspects of mediated communication, overcomes some problems of groupwork by cmc. In computer-mediated team meetings using quasi-synchronous chat, the temporal flow of conversation can be disrupted and make the process of beginning and ending informally structured meetings difficult. However, teams evolve a process for both opening and closing the meetings in two stages, which allows them to 'make consistent use of certain linguistic and conversational devices to mark possible transition points for openings and closings', showing both the need to and the ability of people to adapt to the constraints of this technology.[75]

The additive features of cmc (in particular parallel processing or the ability to carry out multiple operations or tasks simultaneously) and reductive features (absence of visual and verbal cues) of cmc interact with diversity to impact on creative group performance. Ethnic diversity has 'a positive and significant effect on creative group performance'. The authors of a study of diversity and communication modes concluded that communication technology 'serves not just as a performance enhancer for diverse groups, but as a performance equalizer that generally mitigates group process losses attributable to either diversity or homogeneity'.[76]

Summary

Members of cmc groups understand the group task, the decision to be made and each other less well than ftf groups, though their comparative performance varies between tasks: conveying information and generating ideas is achieved as well by cmc but reaching an agreement is not.

Text-based cmc groups may tend to communicate more about the task but have fewer socio-emotional exchanges than ftf groups. The higher the level of socio-emotional input required, the worse cmc groups perform relative to ftf.

The evidence is that cmc-based group decision-making is inferior to ftf decision-making, though the studies which supplied this evidence may have limitations. Process losses affect cmc groups where members are identified but not anonymous cmc groups. Process losses are greater in some cultures than others, but GSS systems reduce them in both cmc and ftf groups.

The extent to which cmc broadens and democratizes participation in groups is contested, as is the extent to which there is reduced normative social pressure in cmc groups. Working by cmc 'can actually reinforce group salience and conformity to group norms, and thereby strengthen the impact of a variety of social boundaries'. Status differences are reflected in cmc groups as well as ftf groups. Mixed-mode groups are less subject to negative effects on task cohesion and performance than those working by cmc alone.

10.6 VIRTUAL TEAMS AND GLOBAL VIRTUAL TEAMS

The points made in the previous section do apply to virtual teams, but in addition particular issues arise in the case of virtual teams and, especially, global virtual teams. Though their problems are many, research has identified ways to improve virtual groupwork and teamwork.

Virtual teams are groups of people who are performing a shared task and who interact solely or primarily by cmc. Although they have certain performance advantages, such as readier access to outgroup resources, they do not perform better than ftf groups, especially with tasks that require close coordination of member efforts. Even boosting transactive memory by giving cmc groups relevant electronic databases does not significantly improve their performance.[77]

> **"** Our team is based in India, the UK and the Midwest of America. Once a week we hold a video meeting of the senior staff from the three parts of the team; because of the time difference it is held at the end of the working day in India, midday in the UK and early in the USA. We have to be constantly in touch to keep everyone updated as trials progress. Most of our communication is by email, but for urgent things that is too slow, again because of the time difference. For instance, the Indian office is closed from 11 p.m. to 6 a.m. Indian time. If the US office sends us an email at 12.30 in the afternoon their time, our office is closed and they won't get a reply until after their office closes. If they phone, they will catch us. So they will phone.
>
> (Interview with a clinical trials analysis team leader in India who at the time had 20 staff and responsibility for 16 ongoing drug trials)

While there seems to be great potential for virtual teams, there are several fundamental sociotechnical difficulties in execution, such as the kind described in the quotation above. Again, communication technologies are often designed with the intention of improving work organization by reducing communication delays (which can mean that a worker is unable to move forward with a task due to insufficient information), but the use of these technologies may, in practice, inadvertently contribute to an increase in work interruptions (which can derail the flow of activities). That is, it might not increase overall efficiency, only shift the locus of control over the workflow.[78]

Again, such teams often use argumentation support systems, which were described in Chapter 1; these allow individuals to explain themselves and to gain recognition and reward for the extra effort involved. They also facilitate an increase in information sharing for organizations, since users must present relevant and convincing evidence for their assertions. On the other hand, they make the work take longer and individuals run the risk that their statements will be taken out of context.[79]

> **"** Some conferencing systems have a built-in way of announcing who is present, in others the meeting will start with everyone present announcing themselves, but in some if a person doesn't speak you don't actually know who is there. This has the odd effect that people will make a lower-value contribution, just to signal that they are present.
>
> (Author's interview with a fund manager)

In lean asynchronous communication environments, the conveyance of cues is hindered, feedback is delayed and there are often interruptions or long pauses in communication. In an asynchronous discussion, it is usual for many topics to be active at the same time and team members make contributions at different times and possibly on different topics. This can increase information overload and may reduce the synergy of the team if there is no linkage among the responses. In addition, long time lapses between communication events can lead to discontinuous and seemingly disjointed discussions. This suggests that a significant challenge facing virtual teams is coordinating the temporal patterns of group behaviour. Virtual teams must find workable substitutes for temporally coordinating their interactions and flows of information.[80]

A factor that may exacerbate the problems of team-working by cmc is the effect of using cmc on team member outcomes. Team members who work with their team through cmc may experience lower levels of positive feelings while working with their teams and feel less commitment to their teams, research has shown. The use of cmc was particularly detrimental to team outcomes when 90 per cent or more of their communication was done in that way.[81] Communication modes have 'important' effects on team interaction styles and cohesion. People's interaction was more constructive ftf than by videoconference or chat, and both ftf and videoconference teams were more cohesive than chat teams, though working in richer communication media (ftf or by videoconference) did not lead teams to achieve higher task performance than those using less rich media.[82] Teams using cmc use less positive socio-emotional communication, attempt fewer answers, ask fewer questions, but also use less frequent negative socio-emotional communication.[83]

Global virtual teams

A global virtual team is an example of a boundaryless network organization form where a (usually) temporary team is assembled on an as-needed basis for the duration of a task and is staffed by members from different countries. By definition, global teams are characterized (though in varying degrees) by certain 'decoupling characteristics' – geographical dispersion, electronic dependence, cultural diversity and dynamic structure – which act as centrifugal forces that pull teams apart through breakdown of coordination, loss of communication 'richness', cultural misunderstandings and loss of 'teamness'.[84] Geographical dispersion and cultural diversity are negatively related to team members' identification with their team.[85]

Global teams are not only widely dispersed both geographically and by time zone, they can form, change and dissolve rapidly and many are composed of members spread among several projects with competing priorities. In the words of Gibbs (2009):

" Global teams face greater complexity than traditional teams in terms of task, context, people, time, and technology. Team members encounter unique communication challenges that traditional teams have not had to contend with, as they coordinate tasks and processes across boundaries of time, space, and multiple layers of cultural complexity. Global teams are thus fraught with contradictions: how to create synergy among members spread around the globe, how to achieve cohesion amidst cultural rifts and competing allegiances, and how to form consistent policies across units embedded in diverse organizational structures ... Composed of members from far-flung locations and crossing multiple contexts, global teams exemplify an organizational form involving ... opposing forces.[86]

A study published in 2009 examined tensions in global virtual teams and the ways in which team members handle those tensions. Data from a global software team revealed three main tensions in global team interaction:

1. The need for flexibility to allow for diverse perspectives and autonomy at local sites is in tension with connectedness, the need for cohesion and interdependence.
2. People assigned to a team may be integrated into the team or treated as temporary; integration may facilitate utilizing the assignees' expertise, and so support collaboration and achieve better performance, but since the assignees would eventually have to leave, there are costs attached to integration.
3. Perceived equity and inequity and privilege versus marginalization within the team are potentially a third source of tension: for instance if an Indian assignee to an American team is rewarded comparably to the Americans it 'can nullify the value and effectiveness of all the awards available in India', while to reward the Indian assignee less well than the Americans creates perceptions of unfairness.

To work round these tensions team members might choose to ignore one alternative – for instance, ignore autonomy and select connectedness; or they might 'walk the line between detachment and involvement'; or they might withdraw, which produced paralysis. Managers were more likely to treat tensions productively, whereas lower-level foreign assignees were less able to cope with the tensions, experiencing them as simple contradictions or paradoxes which constrained and disempowered them.[87]

Teamwork, whether co-located or distributed, requires intense collaboration between team members. (Think, for instance, of the need for members of football teams to collaborate.) The need for intense collaboration originates in four factors: work processes that have to be carried out simultaneously, tight coupling (high interdependence) of tasks, stickiness of information needed for tasks, and uncertainty about aspects of tasks. Collaboration normally translates into processes requiring intense communication and information processing, mostly through direct ftf contact, meetings and feedback. Moreover, to coordinate their work team-members need to maintain a high level of continuous awareness of each other, the activities being carried out, the current state of the work and the context. This awareness is maintained through explicit or subconscious communication, observation and anticipation based on previous experience. These requirements of intense collaboration are 'fundamentally at odds with the defining characteristic of globally distributed teams: that is, work distribution'.[88]

The nature of these teams means that their success relies to a large extent on communication. Communication breakdown can severely limit their performance. Unfortunately, however, the very fact of their dispersion together with their commonly being composed of people from different social and business cultures, specialities and work backgrounds increases the risk of communication breakdown. The main factors that bring about communication breakdown in global virtual teams are lack of trust, poor interpersonal relations, weak leadership and technological problems. Without trust people will not 'engage in risk-associated activities that they cannot control or monitor'; poor interpersonal relations 'can lead to anxiety, confusion, and miscommunication'; without a strong team leader 'different team members work towards different goals and in different directions losing the sense of the team mission'; and virtual teams will fail unless they have access to technology which is adequate for their communication needs.[89] As Section 8.2 described, even without a complete breakdown in communication, virtual teams are liable to conflict; how they manage it is critical for their success or failure.

Feedback delays, the lack of social cues and team heterogeneity (diversity) may have negative effects on communication in virtual teams:

> **"** Because of delays in remote communication, feedback about others' behaviors is difficult to obtain. With delayed feedback or inaccurate feedback, messages may require several iterations for clarification. Some messages are long, making a response effortful and time consuming. To reduce this uncertainty, group members need information about the remote work and what other group members are doing ... All interdependent work entails uncertainty about others' behaviors. Will other group members complete their part of the work in time? Will they do the work they said they would do? Will they pay attention to quality? Will they be available to work this weekend?[90]

In ftf groups, information about what others are doing is readily available and can be acquired passively. In contrast, in virtual teams, there are long periods of silence during which team members may not obtain any information about their team-mates' activities. Virtual team members often have to rely entirely on the messages that appear on the computer screen to work out what other members of the work group are doing.[91]

The lack of social cues may lead team members to misunderstand their own and others' performance. When rating one's own and others' contributions to team performance on either electronically or ftf communicated tasks, participants' self-ratings were inflated and less accurate on tasks performed via computer. Observing the input of others via a computer results in members focusing on only the content of the delivered task; sensitivity to the 'behind the scenes' work needed for successful task completion is lacking.[92]

Diversity in transnational teams can exacerbate conflict. Differences in cultural values, tensions between local and global perspectives, and differences in power and status can mean that such teams need to develop an internal process that is able to deal with these differences. They also need to supply externally oriented 'ambassadorial' and task coordinating activities directed vertically to corporate management and laterally to other local units. Such an outward focus, however, confronts the team with complexity and potential conflicts.[93] Fortunately, however, there is some evidence that working by cmc helps groups to reduce the negative consequences of dissimilarity. Age dissimilarity is negatively related to trust in ftf groups but not in cmc groups, while birthplace dissimilarity is positively related to trust in cmc groups.[94]

Benefits for teams of working by cmc

There are mitigating conditions which ameliorate the effect of cmc on virtual teamwork:

- There is some evidence that virtual team performance is linked not to which communication mode is used but to members having compatible views on which mode to use and, when cmc is used, by the confidence of the team members. When people meet successively over a period, whether by cmc or ftf, the success of their meetings is strongly related to how similar the mode preferences of the members of the group are.
- Goal setting effects – the greater effectiveness of challenging goals versus 'do your best' instructions and of participative against directive goal setting – are robust; for example they are found when communication is based on a videoconference.[95]
- The anonymity furnished by some cmc systems may counteract groupthink, which can greatly reduce the effectiveness of teams. Successful groups are quite likely to develop a conviction that the group is superior in knowledge and ability to almost everybody else and to mount

conformity pressures so strong that any deviation from the group consensus is censored. The anonymity provided by some cmc systems increases how often people in groups put forward arguments that run counter to the group position.

How well cmc teams perform is significantly predicted by how well they expect to perform and how good their decisions are by how good they think their team's problem-solving ability is; neither is true for ftf teams. The difference may be that working by computer leads team members to evaluate the message content and not be distracted by peripheral cues. In contrast, peripheral cues such as the source's personality, gender, attractiveness and speaking style can influence members of ftf groups. This is likely to have made it relatively easy for cmc groups both to 'predict their group's decision success' and to 'make realistic judgments of the combined problem-solving skill in the group' compared with ftf groups.[96]

Factors that improve team working by cmc

- On the basis of a review of ten years' research into working at a distance, Olson and Olson (2000) concluded that four factors are critical to success: common ground, loose coupling of work (low task interdependence), collaboration readiness and collaboration technology readiness. Groups with high common ground and loosely coupled work, with readiness both for collaboration and for using collaboration technology, have a chance of succeeding with remote work.[97]
- Conflict is lower when global virtual team members communicate spontaneously. First, spontaneous communication is associated with a stronger shared identity and more shared context: these moderate the effect of dispersal on interpersonal and task conflict respectively; second, it helps team members to recognize and deal with any conflicts that do arise.[98]
- Research on global software teams has identified forces that can bind teams together; these include a good telecommunications infrastructure, team building efforts, appropriate managerial techniques, use of collaborative technology, identification with the team or other targets,

> *Peter had been appointed facilitator of a group given the task of designing the packaging of a new breakfast cereal product. They were to work by cmc. Peter knew that these people would tend to quickly establish an agreed view and then be locked in to it. He wanted the discussion to remain more open and creative. He therefore decided that the group would work anonymously as that would lead them to provide more counter-arguments as a consensus became apparent.*
>
> *What further information might change Peter's logic and his decision, and how?*

cultural liaisons and documentation of knowledge, and processes to preserve them even when members leave.[99]

- The negative effects of cmc openness and lowering of observable status barriers and social context cues (effects such as flaming) may not apply where subjects are members of intact work groups (i.e. 'permanent' teams). For instance, Walther (1996) found that team members working together internationally via cmc can, over the longer term, develop affection, group identity and a social orientation.[100]

> *For more findings that show that in the long run cmc teams can avoid serious conflict, visit the companion website....*
> *10.5.2.*

Trust and virtual team effectiveness

Trust is vital for cmc team effectiveness. Trust in one another, in their direct manager and in top management affect how well teams perform. The relationship among these different focuses for trust is dynamic, and trust among team-mates affects whether or not trust in the direct manager and team cohesion influence how well teams perform.

In the early phases of teamwork, how well team members trust one another depends strongly on their perceptions of other team members' integrity, and weakly on their perceptions of the others' benevolence. How competent one member thinks his or her co-members are affects trust decreasingly as time goes on. Members' own propensity to trust has a significant, though unchanging, effect on trust.[101]

An analysis of six teams' email messages suggested the presence of **'swift trust'**. This is a kind of trust that can develop in temporary teams – they act as if they trust one another from the start, although the feelings and thoughts that usually accompany trust may be absent.[102] A longitudinal study of architecture, engineering and construction management students engaged in designing and planning a $5 million construction project in distributed teams suggested that cross-functional, geographically distributed workers may rely on early impressions of perceived trustworthiness when evaluating how their distant partners are delivering on commitments, because reliable information about actual follow-through is lacking or difficult to interpret. Consistent with this, perceived trustworthiness, perceived follow-through and trust were relatively stable over time.[103] Finally, initial trust correlates to both later communication and later cohesiveness. Initial perceptions of trustworthiness are thus particularly important in cross-functional, geographically distributed work.

In global virtual teams, trust is critical for coordination. Members of work-oriented virtual teams formed on a temporary basis swiftly develop calculus-based trust in order to assess the outcomes and costs of maintaining team relationships. Members also rely on prior knowledge to determine other members' competence so that they can make predictions about one another's behaviours. Thus, both calculus-based and knowledge-based trust are important in the initial development of work-oriented virtual teams. This initial trust may correlate to both the level of later communication and to later cohesiveness.[104]

Research has shown that the following 'rules' increase trust and so performance in cmc groups:

- Get started right away (to compensate for slow development of trust and liking in cmc).
- Communicate frequently.
- Multitask – get organized and do substantive work simultaneously.
- Overtly acknowledge that you have read one another's messages.
- Be explicit about what you are thinking and doing.
- Set deadlines and stick to them.
- If possible use media that increase copresence. Virtual copresence is significantly correlated with intragroup trust and the performance quality that decision-making groups achieve.[105]

Organizational communities of practice

A community of practice is a collection of people who engage on an ongoing basis in some common endeavour.[106] Organizational communities of practice bring together people with common work-related interests and knowledge from across distributed units and locations of organizations. Ethnographic studies of workplace practices have shown that how people actually work usually differs fundamentally from organizational descriptions in manuals, training programmes, organizational charts and job descriptions. It has recently begun to be understood that significant learning and innovation are generated in informal communities of practice at work;[107] and more recently still organizations have begun to support these communities. According to an article in the *Harvard Business Review*, by the year 2000 the World Bank had over 100 communities of practice and funded most of them, because they were central to its strategy of providing development expertise to supplement its loan support to countries. Again, a group of airline consultants met regularly to develop new business opportunities for the business's clients; after four years the community had created a new line of marketing approaches for financial services companies.[108]

Participants in communities of practice interact to provide specific knowledge to each other that is not available in their local environment and that enables them to perform common functions, to learn from each other and to build on their collective knowledge.[109] They therefore rely on cmc.

Intranets can contribute to the mutual reinforcement of local communities and to growing complementarities among colleagues at different levels.[110]

Organizational communities of practice have become increasingly global in their reach in order to draw on the expertise of a global workforce. They tend, as a result, to be diverse in terms of nationality. A study found that the relationship between national diversity and community performance was U-shaped, declining initially as the amount of national diversity rose then increasing as it rose further. The arc relating nationality diversity and performance became more positive at the higher end and less negative at the lower end, to the extent that communities reported higher psychological safety (a shared belief that it is safe to trust the other members of the community) and use of richer communication media.[111]

Summary

Virtual teams have great potential but face sociotechnical difficulties that can increase information overload and reduce the synergy of the team. Team member outcomes such as satisfaction can be negative. Geographical dispersion, electronic dependence, cultural diversity and dynamic structure also impact on virtual teams in a negative way.

Teamwork requires intense collaboration, but work distribution conflicts with this need. Communication breakdown occurs more readily and impacts even more on performance when teams work by cmc. Crucial information about what others are doing is not readily available. Lack of social cues may lead team members to misunderstand their own and others' performance. In global virtual teams time differences and diversity may exacerbate problems.

Compatible views on communication modes, appropriate goals, common ground, loose coupling of work, collaboration readiness and collaboration technology readiness all enable and support global teamwork. Spontaneous communication and building trust on the basis of swift trust are also of value. In communities of practice, being global and diverse can bring benefits.

11 MANAGEMENT AND LEADERSHIP

Managers in modern organizations confront many new, wide-ranging and demanding challenges linked to interpersonal communication: a whole range of coordination problems; knowledge management; governance issues; counteracting the depersonalizing effect of mediated communication on employees' identification with the organization and the organization's climate; meshing social media with existing communications processes; deciding and implementing the optimal configuration of communication methodologies; making operations faster, more agile and more efficient with minimal additional cost; IT and computer-mediated communication (cmc) security; enabling the organization as a whole to become more responsible for customer engagement. The last four of these challenges are beyond the scope of this book; coordination has been covered in Chapter 9; this chapter considers communication and knowledge management and governance issues in Section 11.1; Section 11.2 is concerned with the interpersonal communication of managers themselves in terms of their relations with subordinates and managerial functions such as delegation, performance feedback, communicating issues and policies and communicating change; Section 11.3 examines the relationship between leadership and interpersonal communication. Sections 11.2 and 11.3 also explore the implications of different communication modes for management and leadership respectively.

On completing your study of this chapter you will be able to explain and apply the implications of:

- Communication management, knowledge management and governance.
- Managers' interpersonal communication as managers of people.
- Leadership and interpersonal communication.
- How different communication modes are related to managerial communication and leadership.

11.1 COMMUNICATION MANAGEMENT, KNOWLEDGE MANAGEMENT AND GOVERNANCE

This chapter starts with a necessarily introductory consideration of what two major themes of this book, communication and knowledge transfer, imply for management: communication and knowledge management. Implications for governance are also considered.

Communication management

Wilson et al. (2011) gave an example of the kind of challenges that new communication technology presents for management:

> A global bank executive recently described to us a challenge for our times. It turns out that a customer who normally would qualify for the lowest level of service has an impressive 100,000 followers on Twitter. The bank isn't doing much yet with social media and has no formula for adapting it to particular customers, but the executive still wondered whether the customer's 'influence' might merit special treatment.
>
> It's the kind of perplexing question many companies face as they formulate their thinking about social media.[1]

A survey of CEOs in 2013 found that they 'most often attribute the success of digital programs to managerial factors – senior management's interest and attention, internal leadership, good program management, and alignment between organizational structure and goals – and are less likely to cite any technical considerations. Interestingly, the absence of senior-management interest is the factor respondents most often identify as contributing to an initiative's failure'.[2] Unfortunately, according to Tapscott (Kirkland 2012), managers sometimes fail to act as project champions for digital programmes:

> We're in the very early stages of these collaborative suites transforming the nature of work ... You need to understand the application requirements. Typically, there's some customization that's involved. And you need to develop a strategy where senior management is clearly endorsing this, encouraging this, and using the technology themselves so that others will. These are big cultural changes. They're often received with coolness or worse, mockery and hostility. And typically, vested interests fight against change. People that have an interest in the old ways of working, people that dominate face-to-face meetings and like that a lot, for example – they don't want to move toward some other kind of platform where it's more of a meritocracy, rather than a personality thing.[3]

By 2013, however, change was occurring:

" across most of the C-suite, larger shares of respondents report that their companies' senior executives are now supporting and getting involved in digital initiatives. This year, 31 percent say their CEOs personally sponsor these initiatives, up from 23 percent who said so in 2012. This growth illustrates the importance of these new digital programs to corporate performance, as well as the conundrum that many organizations face: often, the CEO is the only executive who has the mandate and ability to drive such a cross-cutting program.[4]

The following is an example of how companies are using social media:

" GE's commitment to social media is perhaps most visible through its digital platform GE Colab, designed by GE employees for GE employees to facilitate global teamwork and collaboration. GE Colab combines the capabilities of Facebook, Twitter and other social applications, allowing easy networking, information sharing, instant communication, advanced search, blogging, videoblogs and more.[5]

The following is an example of the problems companies are experiencing with communication management:

" At Atos, the IT and business services company where I work, we've come to understand the volume of email we send and receive internally is unsustainable for our business. Incredibly, we estimate that the company as a whole, some 74,000 employees worldwide, send or receive as much as one billion emails a year. All of which have to be read, replied to, stored and actioned. Surveys suggest that more than half our employees spend over two hours a day managing email and the interruption it causes really disrupts productivity and efficiency. Furthermore, only around 10% of it is actually necessary to do our job. Surely there's a better way to communicate?[6]

> *You are a middle manager in a medium-sized company where senior management pay no attention to communication issues (as opposed to IT issues). You see them as important and there are a good many problems, especially with time wasting. What do you do and how do you do it?*

> *To learn what Atos is trying to do about this problem, visit the companion website....*
> *11.1.1.*

Business's concerns about privacy have generated interest in virtual social networks tailor-made for the corporate world. These work in much the same way as public social websites, but keep information out of the public domain and behind a corporate firewall. Benefits to organizations from virtual social networking may include the following:

- Staff can find data faster.
- Duplication of knowledge-finding work is reduced.
- Knowledge-sharing is increased.
- Good ideas can emerge from anywhere in the organization.
- A more open/democratic workplace is created.
- The effect of existing IT systems, which are geared towards reinforcing separate silos rather than building bridges between them, is counteracted.
- Knowledge can be captured and experts within an organization identified.
- 'Social business intelligence' can be supplied. For instance, identifying people for a project team based on their expertise and their links to others may be facilitated.
- A big improvement over early knowledge-management systems is supported, as virtual social networking combines content with commentary from people with know-how.

Problems that organizations fear from virtual social networking include the following:

- What happens to personal data? Could it be used to spy on colleagues?
- Will informal networks spring up outside managerial control?
- There is fear of staff broadcasting politically incorrect comments. All comments can be traced to their originators, however, so people are careful.

Social media are tools that can be a powerful driver of knowledge and relations management,

> **❝** but many leaders fear the risks of uncontrolled information and see difficulties in meshing the open dynamics of social media with existing communications processes. When leaders shy away from social media, they inhibit collaboration, knowledge sharing, and the tapping of employee capabilities that collectively can create a competitive advantage. On the other hand, social media give employees active relationships and communications with others outside as well as within the company. This can lead to undesired situations such as employees reacting directly to customer complaints or employees developing new product ideas with people outside the company.

Therefore:

> **❝** Managers need to develop new social-media skills and help their organizations do the same: at the personal level, managers must be able to produce compelling authentic content; master the new distribution

dynamics; and navigate information overload. At the organizational level, managers should encourage usage through thoughtful orchestration and role modelling, become architects of a social-media friendly infrastructure and stay ahead of technology shifts.[7]

Knowledge management

Chapter 9 discussed knowledge sharing – the interpersonal communication of knowledge among co-workers. Here we are concerned rather with the managerial implications of the need for knowledge sharing in modern organizations. Managing this stock of knowledge, adding to it and deploying it are critical for organizational success:

" Knowledge Management (KM) is based on the premise that, just as human beings are unable to draw on the full potential of their brains, organizations are generally not able to fully utilize the knowledge that they possess. Through KM, organizations seek to acquire or create potentially useful knowledge and to make it available to those who can use it at a time and place that is appropriate for them to achieve maximum effective usage in order to positively influence organizational performance. It is generally believed that if an organization can increase its effective knowledge utilization by only a small percentage, great benefits will result.[8]

KM requires identification of the source (recognition that there is knowledge and where it is), evaluation (for its usefulness, which is a function in part of its generalizability), customized storage, distribution (also referred to as transformation, dissemination, transfer or sharing) and application.[9]

Chapter 9 showed that in principle organizations can generate the shared knowledge or common ground needed for work coordination by using technological tools, standardized coding and documentation. These methods can be inadequate, however, for creating common ground and, when they are, personnel may need to be rotated to generate it; this, of course, may be more costly than the ongoing communication it is designed to replace. Furthermore, to coordinate simple tasks inter-organizationally firms frequently opt for expensive co-location even

'Knowledge management has failed', said University of Toronto professor Don Tapscott in a video interview. The problem, he said, is that executives think corporate knowledge is a finite asset that can be confined within a 'container'. 'They are wrong: The most important knowledge is not inside the boundaries of a company. You don't achieve it through containerisation, you achieve it through collaboration.'[10]

Do you agree with the assertions made by this professor? Why or why not?

though within their own boundaries they coordinate more complex tasks across geographic distance with limited or no need for rich communication. In fact, projects that cross firm boundaries rely much more on ongoing communication, mainly because standardized coding processes are inefficient when applied to projects performed by multiple firms: the different firms have their own processes, and this lack of standardization prevents procedural common ground, which is needed for being able to anticipate others' expected action, from emerging.[11]

Managerial support is important for setting up organizational communities of practice (which were explained in Chapter 10) and for sustaining them over time. Participation levels often fall rapidly in the online communities of organizations unless managers are core members of the community, frequent and complementary promotional activities are undertaken, entry barriers to would-be participants are very low, and the discussion is focused both in terms of content and time, a study found.[12] Managers should identify potential communities of practice that will enhance the company's strategic capabilities, provide the infrastructure that will support such communities and enable them to apply their expertise effectively. Managerial support takes the form of: investing time and money; intervening when communities run up against obstacles to their progress, such as IT systems that overlook community contributions; changing reward structures that discourage collaboration; and using non-traditional methods to assess the value of the company's communities of practice.[13]

It is generally agreed that KM should be strategically driven.[14] One view is that firms need different kinds of structure, culture and organizational capabilities for each strategy. However, other researchers believe that this is not a one-or-the-other choice, but rather a case of sequencing. For example, during the early stages of a new product development process, a firm may be prospecting for new wealth-creating opportunities. During this discovery period, the exploratory search involves basic research, invention, risk-taking and building new capabilities with the goal of developing new knowledge or capabilities that it can subsequently exploit to create value. Once potentially valuable knowledge and skills have been acquired through exploration, the firm then turns to exploitation activities. In reality, most firms engage in both activities simultaneously because they manage concurrent projects that are at different stages in the product development process. The processes that lead to direct innovation can be attributable to the coordinated sequencing of knowl-

Visit the companion website... 11.1.2 for a link to a video by McKinsey about KM. Could the McKinsey approach to KM be implemented by a small firm? Or by a start-up? Why and how, or why not?

edge exploration and exploitation processes, as opposed to the selection of one or the other.[15]

There are cultural differences in the way that knowledge is managed. Hedlund and Nonaka (1993) examined how information and knowledge are constructed in different cultures. They summarized common perceptions about the differences between Japanese and Western firms in terms of differences in the extent to which the firm's knowledge is 'tacit' or 'articulated' and the degree to which knowledge is held by individuals or groups. Western firms are characterized by individually held, articulated knowledge and Japanese firms by tacit knowledge held at the level of the group.[16]

Governance

Governance is composed of a set of formal or informal processes and decision rights that together support accountability, which is the ability of an entity to satisfy stakeholders about its conduct; they include the mechanisms that a company employs to achieve business results and safeguard information. IT-based networking trends pose a significant challenge to the traditional approaches of companies towards governance. Standard practices developed with a hierarchical model of the company in mind are inadequate for providing governance in the era of the internet.[17] Figure 11.1 shows how workplace use of IM, for example, creates substantial dangers for organizational governance, which somewhat offset its benefits.

Other widespread governance problems stem from employees' internet use: cyberloafing, cyberslacking and cyberdeviancy do undoubtedly have serious negative consequences for organizations.[18] Cyberloafing is the practice of time-wasting on the internet, cyberslacking is typically defined as the use of internet and mobile technology during work hours for personal purposes, and cyberdeviancy involves behaviour such as breaking security protocols and so compromising sensitive customer and organizational data. Both the range and the frequency of cyberslacking are greater among people who are young, male and members of a racial minority.[19] Other influencing factors are routinized internet use at work, higher perceived internet utility, perceived cyberloafing by co-workers, and managerial support for internet usage. Being involved with the job, however, reduces cyberloafing; this finding gives some encouragement for positive ways to counteract the practice.[20]

All three misuses are growing concerns for organizations due to the potential in lost revenue. Weatherbee (2010) wrote: 'the misuse of information and communications technology (ICTs) in the workplace is a growing problem that is expected to continue to trend upward. The consequences of this form of behaviour range from minor outcomes with little impact, to more serious outcomes with significant negative impacts to individuals, groups, and even for entire organizations'.[21]

Figure 11.1 Benefits and governance dangers from workplace instant messaging

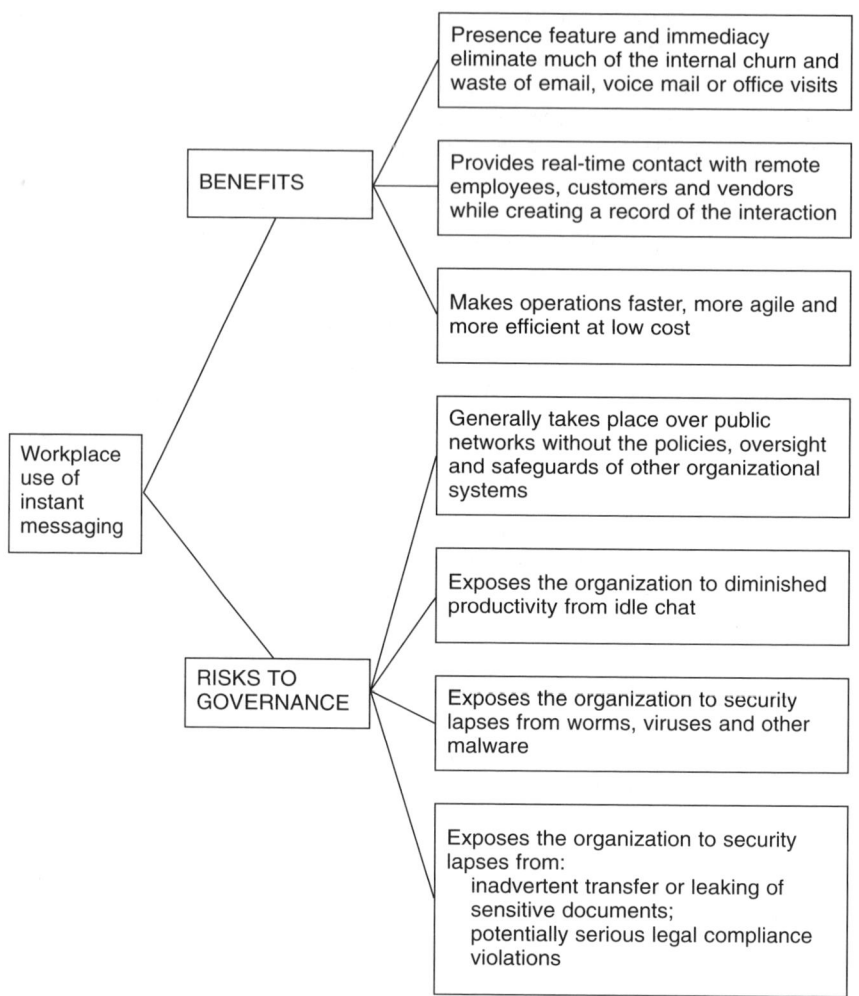

Based on Quest Software, Inc. 'Best practices in instant messaging management: Enabling productive, secure and compliant instant messaging policies and usage in the business environment', www.majorcities.eu/...pdf/best_practices_in_instant_messaging.pdf.

Many organizations are concerned about the problem of excessive internet use at work. Employees may spend large amounts of time 'surfing, online shopping, gaming, chatting', which 'may result in a misallocation of online resources and clog bandwidth, leading to productivity losses'; or they may 'engage in inappropriate (e.g. viewing pornographic sites) or even illegal activities (e.g. distributing copyrighted materials) at work, so placing organizations at legal risk'; for the individuals there can be 'negative consequences for working life and even the loss of the job'.[22]

Many inter-organizational relations that now depend on cmc, such as franchise operations, joint ventures and onshore and offshore outsourcing, also give rise to **network governance** issues. Although some inter-organizational relations can be governed by contracts, many governance issues escape contractual control. Governance must deal with networks of companies and other agents, high product demand uncertainty, customized exchanges of human resources which are high in asset specificity, complex tasks that are under intense time

> *Look at the Glossary for the meaning of* **trust***; look at Section 7.4 for how trust affects work relations; look at Section 13.1 for how trust substitutes for formal control in inter-organizational relations.*

pressure and difficult to assess by non-specialists, and fuzzy firm boundaries. In these circumstances, many organizations are dependent for governance on trust.

Ibrahim and Ribbens (2009) distinguished **competence trust** from **openness trust**.[23] Competence trust is the level of confidence a user has, for instance in a supplier; openness trust is the level of confidence that a counterpart will handle information relevant to the relationship with transparency and equity. Governance calls for high competence trust when human assets are specific and task uncertainty is high, and for high openness trust when it is difficult to find the best solution or it is unclear what the best solution is – open innovation and crowd sourcing are needed. When tasks are easy to perform and the knowledge needed is clearly described, traditional methods of governance are appropriate.

Summary

Managing communication so that it supports rather than impedes organizational strategies, competitiveness and effectiveness is a challenge for managers that has dramatically increased with the advent of new technologies such as social media. Vested interests within organizations may resist changes that reduce their power, while the capacity of some customers and clients to harm or benefit the organization have hugely expanded with their contact networks.

Knowledge is a critical resource for competing in the modern world. Firms therefore need effective KM strategies to ensure that finding new knowledge and exploiting existing knowledge are optimized and coordinated.

Governance issues – issues of accountability and safeguarding the information needed for business results – differ between traditional hierarchical organizations and networked operations. IM carries risks to governance as well as benefits to organizations. Cyberloafing, cyberslacking and cyberdeviancy are examples of serious governance problems that organizations confront.

The benefits of modern communications can sometimes be outweighed by the risks to governance. Managers should differentiate those tasks that necessitate trust and openness from those where traditional methods of governance can be used.

11.2 MANAGERS' INTERPERSONAL COMMUNICATION AS MANAGERS OF PEOPLE

Management interactions are, of course, a matter of vital importance in work organizations. In the words of Clarke et al. (2012), 'the naturally occurring talk of senior managers in meetings ... is arguably the most important ... venue for strategizing'.[24] Again, managers' interactions with subordinates are central to how they carry out functions such as coordinating, controlling, delegating, giving feedback and many other essential functions:

- Middle managers and employees collaborate to interpret tasks in relation to the organizational context; managers articulate the process, explicitly defining what counts as reality and framing issues; employees show that they expect to have their experiences interpreted by managers but may sometimes challenge managers with competing interpretations.[25]
- Management interactions are also critical for exerting authority: 'the complex distribution and negotiation of authority in real time is a key issue for today's organizations'. Employees can ignore procedures, policies and statuses; people who are interacting, 'whether they are in authority on the basis of their position in an organization or not, must establish their authority and bring it to bear on work relations'. According to this view, exerting authority is achieved by making sources of authority 'present' during interactions, for instance by speaking in the name of something, as in 'at Company X we believe in...', or by such practices as using the company letterhead when putting up notices that give directives.[26]

Manager–subordinate relations

The quality of relations between managers and supervisors and their subordinates is critical for organizations. For instance, high attrition among employees who 'survive' layoffs is common and costly, but employees who survive downsizing and perceive that they receive supervisor

---

BOX 11.1

'Communication is not always a good thing. My suspicion is that too much of it releases you from the discipline of having to structure, allocate tasks. With less communication someone with responsibility is forced to think out how they are actually going to resolve issues and allocate tasks.'

(Author's interview with an executive from a media organization)

---

support can be highly committed to their organization.[27] Again, when subordinates trust their supervisor, the negative effect on their work behaviour of conflict with peers is lessened.[28] Furthermore, managers are aware that 'their behaviors have a direct impact on their employees', and say that one-on-one interactions help managers to 'be available to their employees, have an open door policy, be open to recommendations for workplace improvements, listen, reward, be honest, fair and loyal to employees as well as partner with the employees in workplace challenges'.[29]

Communication from managers to subordinates is important for employee trust, but the relationship between communication and trust is complex: while quality of information predicts trust of co-workers and supervisors, it is adequacy of information that predicts trust of top management. Trust influences employees' perceptions of organizational openness, which in turn influence their level of involvement in the organization's goals.[30]

Fair treatment during interactions with supervisors has a significant effect on a supportive climate for employee creativity. Because 'specific types of justice are important in creating a supportive relational environment that in turn supports creative behaviours', two kinds of justice have been investigated: interpersonal justice, or 'the fairness of treatment, including such factors as respectful and dignified treatment', and informational justice, or 'the fairness of information conveyed during the encounter, including such factors as honest and complete explanations'. At the supervisor level, a study found, 'both interpersonal and informational justice perceptions played a role in creating a supportive relational context'; at the organizational level, only informational justice created this supportive context. The researchers suggested that 'the significance of informational justice is understandable given that the free exchange of ideas and information (such as may occur in an informationally fair setting, in which communication is open, honest, and timely) seems to enhance creativity'.[31]

Unfortunately, important though good manager–subordinate relations are, research has found several forces that undermine them: for example there is evidence that when they experience conflict with their peers, managers sometimes displace their aggression onto their subordinates; this abusive supervision results in reduced work effort and fewer organizational citizenship behaviours on the part of the subordinates.[32]

Managers also have to contend with a negativity bias in how subordinates regard them in their role of supervisors. While mentoring-style behaviour by supervisors does increase their subordinates' communication satisfaction, organizational commitment and job satisfaction, this relationship is a weak one. Any verbal aggression from supervisors decreases their subordinates' communication satisfaction, organizational commitment and job satisfaction, however, and this relationship is a much stronger one.[33] Again, subordinates who face an incompetent leader perceive the leader's incompetence as a lack of power and compensate for it by taking on a more powerful position themselves (i.e. more dominance behaviour and more resistance to the leader's influencing attempts). In sum, having a task-incompetent leader affects not only the subordinates' perception of the leader but also how the subordinate interacts with the leader. This applies whether their interaction is via email or face-to-face (ftf).[34]

Delegation

Delegating tasks and responsibilities to subordinates is of the essence of management. It allows managers to carry out the range of work for which they have responsibility, concentrate on key aspects of their job, develop subordinates and widen their experience, and train successors. Delegation is primarily about entrusting authority to others. This means that those others can act and initiate independently; and that they assume responsibility for certain tasks. With delegation, subordinates have the authority to react to situations without referring back to their manager, but the manager remains responsible.

You are head of a major department. You have just attended a meeting with your CEO where you were told that your department needs to save 20 percent in the following year. This will mean forced redundancies. What do you do and how do you do it?

For more findings on forces that can undermine manager–subordinate relations, visit the companion website... 11.2.1.

Can abusive supervision be carried out by email? The following, overheard by the author in the lift of an international hotel in India, suggests that it can: 'I've got to get in by 8.30 to talk to the team. Stanley is killing them. I've spent an hour this morning already on emails. There were 20 from Stanley. How can anybody cope?'

Delegating requires careful planning, to decide what work is to be done, what can and should be delegated and to identify and match abilities, development needs and the potential of subordinates with the delegatable tasks. In a delegation interview, the manager should communicate clearly what the task or project is and involves, what outcomes are looked for, what standards expected, what resources available, and what benefits to the subordinate flow from successfully undertaking this additional or new responsibility. In that interview the manager should also: receive from the subordinate what their reactions to the proposal are and how they see themselves developing within this role; agree with the subordinate that they have accepted the work, agree on the method of work, its nature, the means and timing of reporting, standards of performance and the degree of delegated authority, accountability and responsibility; and discuss the subordinate's hopes and fears and establish communication channels through openness.

Follow-through of the delegation is essential, in case the subordinate has misunderstood any part of the new role he or she is expected to play or is having difficulty with it. The manager needs to ensure that the subordinate has the resources and authority required for the job. This means, for instance, that others are informed of the delegated responsibility he or she has undertaken and are alerted to the need to supply information, equipment, staff or other necessaries. The manager needs to be readily available to the subordinate, especially in the early days after the delegation comes into effect, to supply needed information, help resolve problems, provide support for initiatives, and to encourage and show interest in the subordinate's progress. Gradually, the delegatee should be weaned towards greater independence. Results must be assessed. Mistakes should not be made too much of unless they persist. Initially they should be treated as inevitable and simply corrected.

The scene is a noisy meeting room with about ten people seated round an oval table which has papers strewn all over it. A manager comes in, takes up a position at the head of the table, but remains standing and says:'All right, people. Settle down, settle down. We have to cut this company's budget by 20 percent and we are not leaving this room until we do it. Is that clear?' He gets no response.

'Is that clear?''Yes, sir' unenthusiastically from one or two people round the table.'Good. Now, I want you all to dig deep. I need your best ideas and I need them now. Danny?'Danny does not reply but a woman speaks up:'Sir, I looked at the budget and frankly I think we are spending way too much on transportation.''Too much on transportation, Huh? Seb, what do you think?'

What do you think of this manager's communication style? How is it likely to affect his staff?

The precise plan of the delegation may need to be modified with experience. The subordinate may need to take on more to make sense of the role, or less to have a tolerable workload, or some other modification may be needed.

Culture has a strong influence on whether and how delegation can be effective. According to Hui et al. (2004), in high-power distance countries employees are accustomed to taking orders from their supervisors and may neither expect nor desire delegation.[36] In India, a high-power distance cultural setting, Robert et al. (2000) found that empowerment was negatively associated with job satisfaction. They also found no significant association between empowerment and job satisfaction in Mexico and Poland, which also represent high-power distance cultures.[37] Pellegrini and Scandura (2006) showed that delegation is negatively related to employee job satisfaction in the Turkish context, but also that Turkish leaders who have high-quality relationships with their subordinates do delegate authority. Pellegrini and Scandura (2006) therefore suggested that leaders who have good quality relationships with their subordinates delegate regardless of the cultural context in which the relationship is embedded.[38]

Delegation by cmc

As yet, there seems to have been rather little research into how cmc affects delegation effectiveness and processes, although there are some findings from a limited number of studies in which delegation is not the direct focus. In the main, these imply that skilful delegation is more, not less, necessary and important for working by cmc:

The following are the points to cover in a delegation briefing as recommended in a teaching video:[35]

1. *Background and history of the task.*
2. *Why they are being chosen to complete it (positive spin).*
3. *How this task fits into the overall work of the team or organization.*
4. *How long this task will last.*
5. *When they are expected to start.*
6. *What the outcome will look like (show the end results).*
7. *How the task will be measured: time, budget restrictions.*
8. *Special procedures.*
9. *Constraints: which computer?*
10. *Level of authority.*
11. *How often do you want to be updated on progress?*
12. *Who to ask if they need help.*
13. *Do I need to monitor them?*
14. *What is the best method for monitoring?*
15. *How will I offer positive feedback?*
16. *Is a reward appropriate?*

Using these points as a guide, brief someone to prepare a list of potential customers for the sales team of a consumer market research organization. Invent as necessary.

- One study found that an effective leader of a virtual team needs to be more flexible to accommodate the complexities and volatility of the virtual team environment, and to be willing to let others take the lead when necessary. Furthermore, the study suggested that virtual team leadership should focus on facilitating and empowering team members to take action on their own.[39]
- Kirkman et al. (2004) found that empowerment, which includes a belief in having freedom to make decisions, is positively related to two independent assessments of virtual team performance – process improvement and customer satisfaction. Further, team empowerment is a stronger predictor for teams that meet ftf less, rather than more, frequently.[40]
- A 2009 pilot study using students found that virtual team leaders delegate more to competent virtual teams and that such delegation is positively correlated with team member satisfaction with their leader and with team member motivation.[41]

In contrast to these positive findings, Paré and Dubé (1999) argued that, due to the distributed nature of virtual teams, management by observation is simply not possible, and that much more discipline and control is required in a virtual setting.[42] Additionally, Paré and Dubé (1999) suggested, team effectiveness in virtual environments may be hindered by excessive autonomy coupled with exclusive reliance on electronic communication and lack of ftf interaction.

Performance appraisal/feedback

Giving feedback is one of the most important of a manager's responsibilities. Positive feedback increases the receiver's self-reported motivation and actual performance on tasks requiring creativity. On tasks requiring vigilance and attention to detail, however, it is negative feedback that increases motivation and performance.[43] A meta-analytic review suggests that feedback intervention in general results in improved performance but it depends on how complex the task is and the underlying aims of giving the feedback.

Even when the relationship with the manager is good, frequent negative feedback increases job anxiety, whether or not the feedback is perceived as fair.[44] Receiving contemptuous feedback at work has effects on people's task performances but not always in obvious ways. People who receive contemptuous feedback perform significantly better afterwards but are also more aggressive towards the person who gave the feedback. Status modifies these outcomes, with low-status receivers of contemptuous feedback both performing better and showing less aggression than equal-status receivers, while high-status receivers perform worse.[45] Overall, research suggests, feedback, especially positive feedback, should be given often, though not constantly. Giving feedback too frequently can overwhelm an individual's ability to absorb it, thus reducing task effort and producing an inverted-U relationship with learning and performance over time.[46]

> For guidance on giving feedback visit the companion website... 11.2.2.

Supervisors often find the process of carrying out performance appraisal interviews that give critical feedback socially problematic. Ironically, this orientation of the supervisor to the social problematic in negative assessments only increases the difficulty for employees of dealing with them.[47] Because appraisal interviews can be occasions of fear or nervousness for appraisees and appraisers alike, both parties collaborate to establish an ethos of 'no fault' so that they maintain a good working relationship. For example, as a way of not threatening the receiver's face, managers ensure that they give explanations (accounts) before they announce actions that will be unwelcome; or join in with laughter, which constitutes an invitation to intimacy; or leave vagueness unrepaired and 'delicate' topics not developed; or use the 'we' and 'us' pronouns to build identification and jointly construct 'them and us' dichotomies.[48]

> For some guidance about what to do in an appraisal interview, visit the companion website... 11.2.3 for links to some videos

Communication mode and feedback

When managers or colleagues give their performance appraisals ftf they are more often positive than those given by cmc. Targets' ability to discern accurately the evaluations is at least equal, and for task-relevant information greater, when done ftf than by cmc. This is related to the fact that clearer feedback on task-relevant issues is given in ftf interactions, though this might be either because appraisal information is also communicated via non-verbal behaviour and/or because the motivation to provide a high-quality evaluation is greater ftf than by cmc.[49]

When ftf is not possible or not desirable, feedback must be mediated in some way. Differences in the media used for sending feedback over a distance (voicemail versus email) do not affect feedback effectiveness, but they do affect perceptions. Receivers of feedback by email regard the feedback as significantly less negative than the senders do, whereas receivers of feedback by voicemail do not perceive feedback significantly differently from senders. On the other hand, senders of negative feedback by voicemail feel significantly less comfortable about it than their receivers; this does not apply to senders and receivers of feedback by email.[50]

Providing employees with praise or comparative information on others' performance improves intrinsic motivation even when it is automatically computer-generated and communicated. When praised by a computer, participants persisted in the task longer and those whose performances were comparatively low persisted longer than those whose performances were comparatively high. Additionally, the mere presence of an embodied agent on the screen increased participants' motivation.[51] Again, employees are more likely to seek feedback when it is computer-generated, so that they believe that their performance feedback is confidential and unscrutinized by another person; they are least likely to seek feedback when it involves ftf exchange. This is because the removal of social cues and therefore lowered 'face-loss' costs in computer-generated feedback leads to more active self-evaluation seeking behaviours. Employees find the experience of facing criticism from another person more threatening, leading to face-loss and lowered confidence. When feedback is provided through a computer system, the emotions that employees may still experience when being given feedback are private and do not pose the threat of public face-loss.[52]

Communicating issues and policies

The link between managerial communication with employees and corporate success is quite clear. It has been shown that strong organizational identification on the part of employees positively contributes to a company's success. It leads the staff to make decisions that are consistent with organizational objectives and to behave in accordance with the company's identity, reputation and strategy – behaviours which are particularly important in service organizations, where employees play a vital role in delivering quality and in achieving customer satisfaction.

Effective communication strategies to strengthen members' identification differ among successful and unsuccessful organizations. Less successful organizations, whose members cannot easily 'bask in reflected glory', can increase members' involvement with the company mission and/or invest in strengthening the emotional bonds between members, whereas successful companies can emphasize their victories. Managers should thus choose whether to communicate their companies' successes (often attained by means of external communication) or to emphasize the intrinsic qualities of the organization for its members (by means of internal communication).[53]

The communication climate (or *how* information is communicated in the organization) is important to identification. A positive climate will increase the attractiveness of the organization. The management of communication openness is one of the easiest and most effective ways to foster employee involvement within organizations, and thus the perceived value of membership.

Employee communication adds to the explanation of organizational identification, over and above the effect of perceived external prestige. Furthermore, both the content and the climate of employee communication affect identification. The adequacy of the information the employee receives about his or her personal role and about the organization substantially affects identification through the communication climate, which 'is the most important communication antecedent of OI [organizational identification]'.

There is evidence, however, that managers often undermine the communication climate when discussing issues and policies. For example, when employees express objections to a company policy, their attitude, their attributed motives and their communication style all affect managers' reactions. Based on a sample of 185 middle managers working in various organizations in South Korea, a study showed that when the employee's overall attitude is not trusting, managers are more likely to engage in social undermining and less likely to provide social support. The motives the managers attribute to the employee also influence their responses to employee-voiced objections: if they attribute the objection to personal attack, their response to the expression of discontent is negative. Finally, if the employee's communication style is aggressive, the managers are likely to attribute their objection to self-interest.[54]

> **"** As a line manager, face-to-face discussions give you more authority when you win the argument, where if you just tell people what to do you don't gain in authority. It can be frustrating, but if you are the line manager you do in the end have the whip hand. You get your way, though you couldn't operate like that on a daily basis.
>
> (Author's interview with an executive from a media organization)

Improving the communication climate demands continuous and long-term management commitment.[55]

Communicating change

There is clear evidence that many people dislike and resist change, especially when it impacts on their vested interests, but also when it disturbs existing relationships and habits, affects loyalties, when they are not given enough information to be able to see the reason for the change, and when it is associated with high levels of uncertainty. Employees are, however, normatively committed to change when organizations provide appropriate inducements to them to accept it and emotionally committed to it when they are themselves resilient individuals. Both these kinds of commitment to change are positively related to behavioural and creative support for change and negatively related to leaving the organization. Importantly, both are influenced by communication with co-workers (social exchange).[56]

Findings from a longitudinal study of 37 medical clinics suggested that instead of seeking consensus on a singular vision of a strategic change initiative, managers are more likely to improve organization performance by focusing their interventions on creating integrative methods for encouraging and learning from diverse and opposing views of an organizational change initiative. Integrative methods are 'the extent to which a clinic fosters and utilizes the diverse perspectives of its members to make decisions'. In the study integrative methods were measured using a 'scale of openness to ideas and change involvement', which measures 'the extent to which employees are encouraged to critique plans, voice their opinions, and influence change'. The findings were that the interaction of integrative methods and diversity of models for organizing among employees had a significant positive effect on clinic revenue, productivity and patient satisfaction.[57]

> Visit the companion website... 11.2.4 for links to videos about how managers should communicate change.
>
> What are the main learning points in them? Do they cover all a manager needs to know and do? Would they work equally well in all cultures? Do they have implications for media choice?

A major consequence of organizational change for employees is uncertainty, which they try to alleviate by seeking information. Direct supervisors are the preferred sources of implementation-related and job-relevant information during change, while senior management typically provide more strategic information; however, trust influences which sources employees seek information from and how they appraise the information they receive. Employees who perceive that they receive quality change communication are more open toward the

> Look back at Box 11.1. Do you agree that communication is not always a good thing? Do you agree with the argument supporting that point of view? Why or why not?

change.[58] Perceived available support also plays an important role when employees are coping with change. Support from colleagues and supervisors mediates the relationship between change-related stress and job satisfaction.[59]

How to present change to the people affected:

- Frame the event as a discussion, not a one-to-many presentation. This will use more resources, but is more likely to get those affected committed to the change.

- Ask questions to find out if those affected have objections and if so what they are. Do not assume that you know.
- Wait until you have understood the attitudes and possible objections to the proposal before developing your arguments advocating it.
- Show positive regard for the people you are asking to change.
- Be open to the possibility that a better idea than yours might be forthcoming in the discussion.
- If you meet with resistance, avoid pushing harder, using more facts and figures, appeals to fair play or loyalty, and above all anything that can be taken as a threat. All of these are likely to increase reactance.
- Take into account cultural variations in how people respond to change presentations.

> *Visit the companion website... 11.2.5 for links to a video that advocates outsourcing change management to specialists.*
>
> *What are the advantages and disadvantages of this approach, do you think?*

Communication modes and management

Issues that arise regarding managers' choice of mode for communication with subordinates relate to power, violation of expectations (giving bad news), the challenges of managing virtual teams and the overall impact of cmc on manager-subordinate relations.

Power effects

Managers often engage in redundant communication; that is, they send the same message to the same recipient sequentially. Findings indicate that they use different types of 'technologies' (modes) for these sequential pairings, and that power influences their choice. The important distinction between technologies in this case is between delayed media that 'allow senders to rehearse messages before they are sent and to provide receivers the opportunity to respond at their leisure' – that is, email, text messaging and electronic documents –and instant media that 'allow senders to receive immediate feedback on their message, to reduce ambiguity on the spot, and to change message content on the fly'– that is, telephone, IM and GDSS. This technology choice may be based on whether managers' motivation is 'simply to transmit a communication of threat or to persuade people that a threat' exists.

The study found that managers who had positional power were more likely to engage in redundant communications that led with a delayed communication followed by an instant communication. Conversely, managers who were not in direct authority were significantly more likely to make redundant communications that led with an instant communication and followed with a delayed communication.[60]

To learn more about why managers sequence communication modes visit the companion website... 11.2.6.

Violating expectations (giving bad news)

When a manager refuses a subordinate's request, thereby violating the subordinate's expectations, it is usual for him or her to provide an explanation ('account') in order to lessen anger or complaints. To be effective, however, the explanation must provide adequate reasons for the refusal; it must also seem sincere.[61] Managers sometimes use electronic media to distance themselves from the people to whom they are giving bad news, such as the refusal of a request, but doing so can lead to more negative employee reactions than is necessary. Employees are more likely to accept an undesired outcome if the way the manager communicates it balances sensitivity with efficiency. The more severe the outcome from the employee's perspective, the 'greater the need to promote interactional justice by using a richer communication medium'; when the explanation required is complex, there is a need for clarity and also a need for media richness allowing two-way exchanges and sensitivity to the employee's responses. This points to giving an initial explanation ftf, followed by a written confirmation. There are four types of explanation that managers can use for giving bad news:

- Shift the blame away from the person giving it (as in, 'It's the fault of the economic downturn').
- Reframe a negative outcome by providing a different comparison standard for evaluating the outcome; so the manager could 'compare [the employee] favorably to others who received worse outcomes', 'suggest better outcomes in the future', or 'signify that the employee's expectations were unrealistic'.
- Justify the bad news by 'appealing to superordinate goals such as "for the good of the organization" or that the action was intended to be "character building" for the employee'.
- Acknowledge the harm, take responsibility for causing it, and offer a sincere apology.

The first type, where managers blame factors beyond their control, is the easiest for receivers of bad news to accept; therefore, 'when an electronic medium is used, a sensitive and thorough causal account will achieve more positive effects than the other types of explanations'. If any of the other kinds of explanation are used, they require delivery via greater media richness.[62]

Managing virtual teams

Among the main challenges for managers of virtual teams is the mainte-nance of high work motivation due to reduced ftf interaction. Management practices such as operationalizing outcome interdependence with team-based rewards help support motivation, especially during the initial year, and make teams more effective.[63] Another challenge is to persuade teams to discontinue failing projects. Continued investment in failing projects is costly for firms, but teams display a tendency to escalate commitment. Priming team members with thinking about sunk costs (cognitive priming) has been shown to mitigate this tendency in all decision-making settings, but to an even greater extent in computer-mediated teams than in other settings.[64]

Against these problems caused by virtuality in managing teams, however, Berry (2011) argued that while managing virtual teams is differ-ent and more complex than managing ftf teams, virtual teams are still groups of individuals that share most of the characteristics and dynamics found on traditional teams.[65]

Overall impact of cmc on management–subordinate relations

Changed employee expectations and lower trust resulting from the replacement of ftfc by cmc can disrupt manager–subordinate relations. More and more, workers' contact with their managers is by cmc, and such workers have changed expectations of their managers. In many cases these new expectations have yet to be agreed upon within the manager–employee relationship, according to Mackenzie (2010). Furthermore, cmc leads to a decrease in ftfc, which influences the devel-opment of trusting at-work relationships. Although managers seem to understand the importance of offsetting this effect on their employees – 88 per cent of a sample of managers selected ftf as their top choice for communication with their staff – according to the employees, managers are not doing enough.[66]

Contrary to the received view, however, Van Dyne et al. (2007) suggested that less visible physical time at the workplace, as a result, for instance, of flexible work arrangements or teleworking, can result in enhanced group-level organizational citizenship behaviour under certain conditions. There are work practices that enhance group processes and effectiveness, including collaborative time management, redefinition of work contribu-tions, proactive availability, and strategic self-presentation; these can both reduce the process losses usually associated in the literature with reduced face time, and enhance overall awareness of others' needs in the group and overall caring about group goals, they argued.[67]

❛❛I don't think the new technologies have made the workplace more formal or less personal, or undermined morale. I haven't noticed that.
(Author's interview with an executive from
a media organization)

Summary

To carry out their functions managers interact intensively; these interactions also allow them to make their authority known. Good relations with subordinates are vital for managers to work effectively; subordinate perceptions of fairness influence these. Too close surveillance undermines supervisor–subordinate relations; so does abusive supervision. Subordinates are more affected by supervisors' negative than their positive behaviours.

Delegation helps train subordinates as well as reducing the manager's workload. There are well-established guidelines for effective delegation. However, culture can make delegation inappropriate, except where the manager and the subordinate have very strong interpersonal relations. There are some findings that managers working by cmc will delegate when they are sure the subordinates are competent, and that the subordinates' work satisfaction is thereby increased. Overall, though, we still know very little about how cmc affects delegation.

Positive feedback is valuable within limits; negative feedback improves performance but leads to negative attitudes to the person giving the feedback. Both givers and receivers of performance appraisals ftf find them difficult and collaborate to reduce the discomfort. Mediation affects both the performance appraisal given and how it is perceived. Evaluations by cmc are less positive but less accurately discerned than those given ftf. Face concerns mean that employees are more likely to seek feedback when it is computer-generated.

Employee identification with their organization is causally linked to corporate success. Openness – the adequacy of the information employees receive – and perceived external prestige influence how fully employees identify with their organization. Improving the communication climate demands a continuous and long-term management commitment.

Encouragement to express concerns over proposed changes increases employees' commitment to them. Being given relevant information from trusted managers increases employees' openness to change and perceiving that they will have support during the change reduces their change-related stress.

In manager–employee e-relationships, employees have changed expectations of their managers. Managers do make efforts to communicate – for example, sending messages to employees by more than one medium. How they sequence the media depends on their perception of their own power. To refuse employees' requests, or give other kinds of bad news, managers sometimes use cmc to distance themselves, but this can increase negative employee reactions. When text-based cmc is used for giving bad news, managers should give sensitive and thorough explanations that blame factors outside their control; other kinds of explanations require richer media.

Managers of virtual teams face challenges in maintaining team work motivation and in persuading teams to discontinue failing projects. Research has found possible solutions. Virtual teams are, after all, groups of people. Reduced ftfc lowers trust; managers understand this but do too little to compensate for it, though there are work practices available that do so compensate.

11.3 LEADERSHIP AND INTERPERSONAL COMMUNICATION

The study of leadership has spawned an array of perspectives attempting to identify the characteristics or behaviours that distinguish successful leaders: transformational, charismatic, authentic and relational perspectives are among those currently pursued:

- Transformational leadership is seen as a way in which organizations can encourage employees to perform beyond expectations.[68] In contrast to transactional leaders who merely practise contingent reinforcement of followers (that is, reward or punish according to behaviour or performance), transformational leaders inspire, intellectually stimulate and are individually considerate. Transformational leadership is more effective than transactional leadership in a wide variety of business, military, industrial, hospital and educational circumstances, although the reasons for this are not fully understood.[69]
- Charismatic leaders 'arouse followers emotionally, evoking positive affective reactions by communicating an emotionally captivating vision'. They 'instil pride, faith, and respect in followers by acting as optimistic and confident role models and by emphasizing the relevance of collective goals'.[70]
- Authentic leaders are self-aware, process self-relevant information in an unbiased way, act on their values and strive for truthful relationships. Self-awareness refers to the leader's 'awareness of and trust in his/her personal characteristics, values, motives, feelings, and cognitions'. Authentic leaders strive for open and truthful relationships. Relational authenticity is most likely to influence their followers, especially those who are critical.[71]
- Relational leaders engage with the world by holding themselves as always in relation with, and therefore morally accountable to, others

and engage in relational dialogue. Features of conversations and everyday mundane occurrences can reveal new possibilities for morally responsible leadership.[72]

> *To learn more about transformational, charismatic, authentic and relational leadership visit the companion website...* 11.3.1.

All these models of leadership present it as a set of traits, qualities and behaviours possessed by the leader that encourage the participation, development and commitment of others. The leader is thus seen to act as an energizer, catalyst and visionary equipped with a range of abilities (communication, problem-solving, people management, self-awareness, etc.) that can be applied across a diverse range of situations and contexts. While situational factors may be considered, they are not generally viewed as barriers to an individual's ability to lead under different circumstances; rather it is assumed that the person simply needs to apply a different combination of skills.

However, research has started to expose limits to the applicability of these models. For instance, when interactors could be identified, transactional leadership was associated with greater group efficacy and solution originality than transformational leadership, a study found. Social loafing, too, in the form of lower participation and cooperation was lower when leadership was transactional rather than transformational.[73] Furthermore, the way in which good leadership is conceived differs as between, for instance, the UK and the USA.[74] In the USA (from where much traditional leadership theory has originated) the image of the leader is primarily that of someone 'distant' – removed from the day-to-day experience of others within the organization, whereas in the UK, leaders tend to be conceived of as someone more 'nearby' – in daily contact with his or her followers. The style of leadership desired of nearby leaders tends to be far more inclusive than that of distant leaders and thus points to a significant cultural dimension to the recognition of what it means to be a leader; this challenges the conception currently embodied by most of the models.[75] More broadly, differences in leadership styles, practices and preferences are associated with cultural differences.[76]

Dissatisfaction with the leadership models that largely ignore differences in situations and cultures has led to new approaches. Some contemporary theorizing about leadership emphasizes the perceptions of followers. 'Leader categorization theory, for instance, suggests that subordinates use their cognitive representation of an ideal leader (ideal leader prototype) as an implicit "benchmark" to determine their openness towards the target's leadership, i.e. influence.' Such benchmarking processes are subject to individual differences among followers.[77]

Other new approaches recognize that effective leadership requires skills such as problem solving, conflict management, motivation, communication and listening. Communicating intent is particularly important.[78] Most significant of these new approaches is leader-member exchange (LMX) theory, which places strong emphasis on leader–follower communication. It is, after all, clear that, since it is not what the leaders themselves do that is important so much as what they influence their followers to do, effective communication with those followers is central. In LMX theory, the quality of the exchange relationship between a leader and a particular member of a work unit, team or organization is considered a strong influence on a range of variables such as subordinates', groups' and teams' performances, job satisfaction, turnover intentions and so on. Empirical LMX-based research has shown that high quality LMX positively influences follower job satisfaction, affective commitment and job performance.[79] It also influences employees' satisfaction with communication in interpersonal contexts, including personal feedback and supervisory communication, group contexts such as co-worker communication and integration in a workgroup, and organizational contexts including corporate communication, communication climate and organizational media quality.[80]

Findings on the importance of LMX show that: economic-based LMX is negative and social LMX is positive for performance; poor quality LMX with supervisors undermines employees' feelings towards the organization; high quality LMX fosters creativity; LMX affects the integration of new staff; and LMX is related to employee altruism and performance.

For more detail on these findings on the importance of LMX visit the companion website... 11.3.2.

In addition to these direct consequences of LMX, it affects the relationship among other work variables. Perceived fairness of feedback is positively related to job satisfaction and feelings of control at work, and negatively related to job-related depression and turnover intentions, especially when the quality of LMX is high. Subordinates' job performance in general is affected by the fit between the job and their self-identity (how they define themselves relative to others), but this relationship is mediated by the quality of their communication with their leaders.[81]

LMX quality itself is influenced by how congruent the personalities of the leader and followers are in terms of being proactive at work,[82] and from the fit between their identities. When both leaders and followers define themselves similarly, their communication quality is high, and viceversa.[83] The more subordinates feel that they are being treated disrespectfully by their leaders, and thus are explicitly undermined in their efforts toward self-enhancement, the less they identify with their leaders and the lower their openness towards them.[84] Leaders of multinational teams are more likely to profit from the local knowledge of team members from minority (under-represented) nationalities – i.e. to listen to an employee's 'voice' – when they are from the same nationality as themselves but also when the leader has high affective commitment and psychological safety.[85]

Communication mode and leadership

The effects of communication mode on leadership are unclear. Studies have found that transformational leadership has a stronger effect in teams that use only cmc; increased use of cmc by transformational leaders results in higher levels of team performance[86] and increases creativity of teams under both identified and anonymous brainstorming conditions.[87] Against this, another study found that leadership style (transformational or transactional) had no effect on team interaction styles or outcomes, in contrast to communication mode, which had 'important' effects (described in Chapter 10).[88] A third study found that in virtual teams transactional leadership behaviours improved the task cohesion of the team, whereas transformational leadership behaviours improved the cooperative climate within the team which, in turn, improved task cohesion. However, these effects of leadership depended on media richness. Specifically, they occurred only when media richness was low. The results also suggested that task cohesion leads to group consensus and members' satisfaction with the discussion, whereas a cooperative climate improves discussion satisfaction and reduces time spent on the task.[89]

Ftf, extraversion and emotional stability predict who becomes a transformational leader, a study found. However, they were largely unrelated to such leadership in the virtual team context, where linguistic quality in a person's written communication was found to predict the emergence of transformational leadership.[90]

Another study found that responses to leadership are different in virtual environments. As Chapter 7 showed, when followers and leaders work in the same location, followers' level of engagement with their work is positively associated with receiving personal recognition. However, personal recognition has less effect in virtual environments: when leaders and followers work at separate sites, personal recognition 'is likely to be conveyed as an abstract, rather than concrete, message ... As a result, these followers might feel the leader is extolling one of their unobservable traits and not offering feedback about a specific activity. The praise could momentarily boost the self-esteem of followers but concomitant variability in self-esteem can also provoke fragility'.[91]

When social software systems are used for knowledge-sharing practices in project work contexts, leaders emerge to organize participants' interactions for effective outcomes. The patterning of interactions, i.e. the structure of a social network, is a significant predictor of a person being perceived as a leader by other virtual collaborators. The most effective emergent leaders are those who primarily assume mediating rather than directing or monitoring roles during virtual collaborations; this finding is consistent across different social software systems such as a virtual world system and a text-based chatroom discussion system.[92]

Summary

Different forms of effective leadership have been identified; all of them depend on the quality of the interpersonal communication of leaders and followers. Transformational leaders encourage, envision, support, inspire and recognize their followers. Charismatic leaders arouse followers emotionally; charisma is a personal power base. Authentic leaders are self-aware, process self-relevant information in an unbiased way, act on their values and strive for truthful relationships. Relational leaders engage in dialogues with others and hold themselves as always in relation with, and therefore morally accountable to, others.

Dissatisfaction with the leadership models that largely ignore differences in situations and cultures has led to new approaches that emphasize leader-follower communication. Most significant of these is LMX theory. Empirical research has found numerous direct and indirect links between the quality of LMX and important aspects of subordinate work behaviour. The fit between leader-follower identities, respectful treatment of subordinates and listening to employees' 'voice' affect LMX.

We have few findings as yet on the effects of communication mode on different leadership styles; findings on the effects of transformational leadership are unclear. We do know that personal recognition from leaders has less impact in virtual environments.

12 ORGANIZATIONAL STRUCTURES AND CULTURES

Although sole traders and tiny partnerships are a surprisingly large part of any economy, most work undoubtedly takes place in an organizational context. In traditional organizations, activities are grouped into jobs, responsibilities are allocated and relationships are specified. These activities, responsibilities and relationships constitute organizational structures (or models). Organizations also have shared values, beliefs about what works well and ways of doing things that are their cultures and climates, which are the degree to which they focus on such attributes as being innovative, flexible, concerned for employee well-being and empowerment, supportive of learning, citizenship, ethics and quality. Organizational structures, cultures and climates both reflect and are reflected by the patterns of interpersonal communication that take place within them. Multinational enterprises (MNEs) exemplify some particular structural and cultural features and challenges for interpersonal work communication.

On completing your study of this chapter you will be able to explain and apply the implications of:

- How interpersonal communication and organizational structures are related.
- How interpersonal communication and organizational cultures and climates are related.
- How computer-mediated communication (cmc) affects and is affected by organizational structures and cultures.
- Interpersonal communication in multinational enterprises.

12.1 ORGANIZATIONAL STRUCTURES AND INTERPERSONAL COMMUNICATION

An organization's structure is driven by its goals and serves as the context in which processes operate and, in the case of enterprises, in which business is done. One typology of organizations (there are many) identifies four separate models: the system bureaucratic model, the market-oriented model, the profession/occupation model, and the community model. Historically, most organizational structures have been hierarchical, designed to permit a few members to direct, coordinate and control the activities of the majority. Over recent decades, however, dissatisfaction grew with some aspects of the way hierarchies function, and in particular with how well they are adapted to their changing environments. This led to greater experimentation in organizational forms in some Western countries: matrixes, federations, networks and adhocracies became common. Technological change accelerated these developments.

> To learn more about models of organizational structure, visit the companion website... 12.1.1.

In the traditional view organizational structures influence work communication rather than vice versa. For instance, in hierarchical organizations, which focus on the logic of the internal organization and emphasize stability, uniformity, security, order, rules, control, coordination, regulations and efficiency, much communication flows vertically – information from bottom to top, instructions and questions from top to bottom. Command structures within such organizations produce relational contexts that create consequences for communication behaviours between subordinates and their supervisors. These may be damaging: for instance, when interacting with subordinates, supervisors are motivated by the context of the command structure to protect their own public self-image but not those of their subordinates. In addition, subordinates' reluctance to disagree with supervisors results in silence or equivocation, and this organizational suppression of dissent produces a barrier to organizational learning and adaptation:

> " Subordinates are sensitive barometers of the changes needed for organizational learning, adaptation, and survival. All subordinates, whether frontline workers or vice presidents, have tacit and explicit knowledge about what does and does not accomplish work-related goals and objectives. [Thus] subordinates' ability to scan for internal deficiencies and external threats and then communicate that information to supervisors, who likely have more authority to enact and coordinate functionally adaptive changes, is a lynchpin of organizational sustainability and innovation... The hierarchical mum effect often hinders the relaying of crucial dissent and disagreement from subordinates and, in turn, results in forms of organizational ignorance.[1]

In contrast, decentralized organizations benefit from broader communication channels. This is because decentralization increases units' dependence on mutual adjustment to coordinate activities, and consequently improves the quality and quantity of ideas and knowledge that are shared. In addition, in principle decentralization augments the perception of freedom among units and increases their motivation and willingness to share organizational knowledge. (It must be noted, however, that a meta-analytic review in 2008 found no link between organizational decentralization and actual knowledge sharing.[2]) Informal lateral relations, in the form of social interaction, are more effective than centralization for coordinating sub-units.[3] Interacting with each other socially helps organizational units to share knowledge and to coordinate: social interaction at work promotes trust and reduces perceived uncertainty about providing new knowledge to other units or acquiring new knowledge from other units. The following is an example of contrasting structural effects on communication:

> A comparison of the actual communication of managers and subordinates in two plants, one organized by an organic, self-managing team philosophy and one by a mechanistic, authority-based philosophy, found that the use of a variety of question-and-answer combinations and conversational elaboration, and a lack of managerial orders and commands, characterised communication at the self-managed plant. Conversely, competitive interchanges, interruptions and statements of non-support typified interaction at the authority-based plant.[4]

A recent departure in organizational theorizing conflicts with not only the analyses of organizational structures listed at the start of this section but with the very idea that organizations are structures. Unlike in the traditional view where organizational structures influence work communication, in this view communication is what constitutes organization:

" Organization emerges in the interactive exchanges of its members... The general claim is that if communication is indeed constitutive of organization, it cannot be simply one of the many factors involved in organizing, and cannot be merely the vehicle for the expression of pre-existing 'realities'; rather, it is the means by which organizations are established, composed, designed, and sustained. Consequently, organizations can no longer be seen as objects, entities, or 'social facts' inside of which communication occurs. Organizations are portrayed, instead, as ongoing and precarious accomplishments realized, experienced, and identified primarily – if not exclusively – in communication processes.[5]

Although organizational communication, in the traditional sense of top-down or centre-out transmissions, is part of the story, it is clear that inter-personal communication is far more important. 'Although its textualized and institutionalized forms may persist beyond any given conversation, it is only in and from the ongoing flow of interaction that organization emerges.' Communication is not limited to words: 'organizational values, knowledge, or ideologies can be conveyed, incarnated and constituted not only through what people say and write, but also through what they wear, how they look, and how they gesture or behave'.[6] Taylor et al. (1996) asked *how* communication supplies the basis for organization. Their answer pointed to aspects including management of information load and related stress, ability to adapt to processing asynchronous rather than simultaneous exchanges, performing multiple tasks through multiple media, constraints on reflective thinking due to rapid turn-around and development of computer literacy.[7]

This communication-based perspective has considerable implications and ramifications for the study of organizations; these are beyond the scope of this book, but it is important to note the central role that interpersonal communication is now believed to play in our work arrangements.

Summary

Until recently, organizational structures, such as bureaucracies, markets, professions and communities, were considered to influence – almost to determine – the communication within them: who communicated with whom about what, whether communication was almost exclusively vertical or somewhat horizontal, and so on. The effects of structure were often viewed as damaging to communication and so to organizational performance. A more recent view is that communication is the means by which organizations are established, composed, designed and sustained; this view prioritizes interpersonal two-way communication.

12.2 INTERPERSONAL COMMUNICATION AND ORGANIZATIONAL CULTURES AND CLIMATES

Understandings of organizational cultures and climates are so varied that, unsurprisingly, they largely overlap. In this section I will therefore discuss the inter-relationships of both with interpersonal communication.

Organizational culture has been defined as a 'system of shared values (what is important) and beliefs (how things work) that interact with a company's people, organizational structures and control systems to produce behavioural norms (the way things are done around here)'.[8] Again, 'organizational culture is the basic assumptions about the world and the values that guide life in organizations. Leadership and national culture are influences on organizational culture'. Organizational cultures can also be understood as a combination of 'visible organizational structures and processes, espoused beliefs, values, strategies and goals' and 'unconscious, taken-for-granted beliefs and perceptions'. Consistently with revised views on organizational structure, another perspective on organizational culture treats it as created by communication: 'communication

Table 12.1 Four kinds of organizational culture, their foci and values

Type of organizational culture	Focus	Values
Hierarchical culture	The logic of the internal organization; emphasis on stability	Uniformity, security, order, rules, control, coordination, regulations, efficiency
Group culture	Flexibility and the internal organization	Belonging, **attachment**, cohesiveness, trust, participation
Rational culture	Internal stability, external environment	Planning, productivity, efficiency, the successful achievement of predetermined goals
Development culture	Flexibility and change, the external environment	Growth, stimulation, creativity, resource acquisition

Based on Quinn, R.E. and Spreitzer, G.M. (1991) 'The psychometrics of the competing values culture instrument and an analysis of the impact of organizational culture on quality of life', *Research in Organizational Change and Development*, **5**: 115–42.

creates and constitutes the taken-for-granted reality of the world that is culture; culture is not something an organization has but something an organization is'.[9]

Quinn and Spreitzer (1991) distinguished four kinds of organizational culture: hierarchical, group, rational and development cultures;[10] Table 12.1 sets out the values and foci of these kinds of organizational culture.

Quinn and Spreitzer (1991) asserted that organizational culture 'is communicated through organizational narratives of three kinds: corporate stories that reinforce management ideology and policies, personal stories that define how individuals would like to be seen within an organization, and collegial stories – usually unsanctioned by management – that are positive or negative anecdotes about others within the organization that pass on how the organization "really works"'.[11]

Another analysis of organizational cultures into 'innovation culture', 'bureaucratic culture' and 'supportive culture' showed varying associations with different aspects of business and organization, according to a 2008 index of organizational efficiency, sales growth and employee satisfaction assessments. Table 12.2 shows the relationships.

Some organizational cultures, such as bureaucratic cultures, can impede effective decision-making by their senior executives, because they lead them to avoid innovative, risk-taking or flexible solutions to issues. The greatest damage is done to important decisions, not to minor ones.[12]

Table 12.2 Relationships among three types of organizational culture, subsequent sales growth/organizational efficiency and employee satisfaction

Type of organizational culture	Description of culture	Subsequent sales growth/ organizational efficiency	Employee satisfaction assessments
Innovative culture	An enterprising and opportunity-seeking environment	Positive for sales growth	Weakly but significantly positive
Bureaucratic culture	Performance is enhanced through rules, procedures and defined structures	Positive for organizational efficiency	Negative
Supportive culture	Characterized by trust, safety and collaborative atmosphere	Negative	Positive

Based on Berson, Y., Oreg, S. and Dvir, T. (2008) 'CEO values, organizational culture and firm outcomes', *Journal of Organizational Behavior*, **29**(5): 615–33.

Organizational climate is 'the meanings people attach to interrelated bundles of experiences they have at work'.[13] Various kinds of organizational climate have been studied, including socio-moral climate and communication climate. A firm's socio-moral climate ('its organizational leadership principles and mechanisms of communication, co-operation, and conflict resolution') affects whether employees participate in democratic forms of organizational decision-making and their commitment to the organization. Furthermore, 'socio-moral climate is assumed to have an impact on the (further) development of moral standards and moral competencies among employees'.[14]

An organization's communication climate is distinguished from its overall organizational climate in that it includes only communicative elements; these are elements such as judgements on how receptive management is to communications from employees and the trustworthiness of information being disseminated in the organization. Relevant dimensions are openness and trust (candour) in communication, perceived participation in decision-making (or the feeling of having a voice in the organization) and supportiveness (or the feeling of being taken seriously).[15]

Attitudes to communication and information can have their roots in a dominant organizational culture; in a published case this contributed to the demise of the company. The firm was family-run, with a culture that was a 'product of tradition' whose features included a strong personnel orientation, a high level of reciprocal loyalty upwards from the employees, a democratic organization, a co-operative work environment, a slow-moving pace of work and limited professionalism. Communication was 'ad hoc', there was a strong preference for 'face-to-face meeting and oral information exchange', and 'informal grapevine communications were dominant'. Additionally most employees, including senior executives, 'lacked a sophisticated understanding of the concepts of "information as a resource" and "information management"'. The company was soon taken over by a competitor; in the view of the researchers the lack of a management information system contributed substantially to this outcome.[16]

The interaction of organizational culture with technology also affects the work experiences of individuals. For professionals working in traditional, physically based and hierarchically structured organizations, using mobile phones makes them 'more vulnerable to organizational claims and ... as a result "the office" is always present as professionals, because of the use of mobile phones, become available "anytime"'.[17]

> ❝ It has become part of the organizational culture – both in the civil service and in banks – not seeing an email is not an excuse. In the bank where I work now, there is an expectation that you are looking at your emails almost continuously. In fact, soon after I joined, I was told by someone senior, 'Things can happen at very short notice, and not knowing about them is not an excuse'.
>
> (Author's interview with a former UK civil servant)

Summary

Organizational culture has been defined in a variety of ways connecting it to values, beliefs, structures, processes and, importantly, communication. Organizations are considered to have different types of culture such as a hierarchical culture, group culture, rational culture, development culture, innovation culture, bureaucratic culture or supportive culture, all with different impacts on aspects of work.

One view of organizational climate is that it is the meanings that people attach to the interrelated bundles of experiences they have at work. Various kinds of organizational climate have been distinguished, including socio-moral and communication climate. Organizational cultures and climates can strongly influence how their staff communicate and so affect both performance and individuals' work experiences.

12.3 COMMUNICATION MODES AND ORGANIZATIONAL STRUCTURES AND CULTURES

A very large range of organizational consequences flows from the choice of communication mode, ranging from effects on organizational participation to the handling of inter-organizational disputes. These consequences follow in some cases from a centralized decision about the pattern of work communication within the organization: for instance, a decision that the most effective interactions for the job are face-to-face (ftf) determines high levels of co-location of personnel and so affects work-related travel patterns. Other consequences flow from the combined effect of large numbers of individual choices: for instance, in many organizations individuals have a choice of communicating at a distance mainly by email or mainly over the telephone, and overall these choices affect a wide range of work behaviours and outcomes. In the words of a 2007 review, 'as computer-mediated communication (cmc) in organizations intensifies, communication is increasingly characterized by a complex interplay between cmc and ftf... affecting communication in positive and negative ways, and also with intended and unintended outcomes'.[18]

> Discuss the assertion that cmc has politicized organizational life. Refer to the material in Box 12.1.

Cmc and organizational participation

It is often asserted that cmc allows for greater democracy of communication. Field studies published in 1992 showed that the effects of technological change on organizational group decision-making included redistributions of work time, relative advantages in participation for peripheral workers and increases in complexity of group organization.[19] However, as Chapter 10 noted, a later study found that although participation was more equal in cmc, some individuals dominated, just as they did face-to-face. Patterns of interaction and performance did not differ substantially between cmc and ftf groups.[20] Again, assertions that members of minority groups would participate more fully in cmc discussions were contradicted by research: while a direct comparison of messages from men and from women in two professional listservs found little difference in male and female communication styles, it also found that male users were more likely to dominate discussions by posting longer messages and posting more frequently. Thus the democracy claim was not supported.[21] A third study (described in Section 8.1) found that although it is seen as a lean medium, email signals hierarchical differences instead of alleviating them.[22]

BOX 12.1

'There's a lot of office politics done by email. Who you copy in, for instance. Sometimes I get copied in on an email about something I've had no part in, and I don't know why I've been copied in, but I know something's going on. The sender is trying to self-promote, or they are trying to put someone else down, or they have copied me in to retaliate for who the recipient copied in on the email they are responding to.'

(Author's interview with an executive of a media and information firm)

Email is used strategically when employees wish to express organizational dissent: as a means of promoting strategic self-presentation, as a means of inviting dissent, and as a means of documenting/archiving potentially problematic interactions.[23]

'Emails can be used to make trouble for people. In one bank, my team leader, who sat in the same room, gave me my work face-to-face for several months; then he started giving me some of it, but not all of it, by email. I realized afterwards that he had heard that there were to be redundancies and wanted to create a picture that I was under-employed. I was known to be better at the work than he was, and he was afraid that I might be kept on and he would be made redundant himself.'

(Author's interview with a bank regulatory reporting specialist who has worked on a series of contracts)

The greater positive effect of cmc on organizational participation is indirect: by making possible, and leading, to the widespread use of newer forms of organization that make extensive use of teams and project groups to perform tasks, cmc has increased the relative importance of communication among co-equals. This communication is concerned with knowledge exchange rather than with commands and reporting back. As a result cultures and climates have also changed in many cases, with power more widely diffused and more often based on expertise or knowledge, so that learning becomes a major objective of interpersonal work communication and political skills are legitimated. Moreover, with the growth of outsourcing, the boundaries of the organization's work often extend well beyond its employees and structure; this means that more emphasis is necessarily placed on inculcating at least central features of culture and climate in the supplying or customer organization, or at a minimum finding a match between the cultures of the two organizations. Since these advances can only be achieved through interpersonal communication, the overall dependence of the organization on the interpersonal skills of its employees increases.

" Sometimes the hierarchy is not so important when you are emailing. In a meeting, you always know everyone's status but that is not so obvious when you email. What you are dealing with at the time you email is a computer screen, not your boss. Some people are shy or are too low in the hierarchy to speak up much in meetings and email gives them a voice.

(Author's interview with an executive from a media and information company)

Formal and informal organization(s) and cmc

The overall effects of cmc on organizations have been analysed using three perspectives: the technological imperative perspective, the organizational imperative perspective and the emergent perspective:

1. *The technological imperative*: technology is an exogenous variable that forces or strongly constrains the behaviours of individuals and organizations. While providing insight into the sometimes determining aspects of technology, the technological imperative largely ignores the ways in which people develop, appropriate and change technology. A study conducted in the USA and France found that, when pursuing the same sales strategy, American and French sales representatives behaved differently and used different media: while the Americans' behaviour corresponded to the technological imperative model, the French salespeople's behaviour did not.[24]

2. *The organizational imperative*: the information processing and communication needs of organizations, and managers' choices to satisfy them, determine information technology adoption and use (that is, actors rationally choose technologies that fit with their needs). This perspective has been criticized as relying too heavily on the capability of human agents.

3. *The emergent perspective*: the consequences of information technology emerge from complex social interactions (technology and behaviours are mutually affected). The introduction of IT into an organizational setting acts as a catalyst, initiating a series of reciprocal causes and effects from which the use of the technology and the organizational outcomes arise.[25] This perspective, which has most credibility, means that the results of introducing new technologies are unpredictable a priori and must be established piecemeal by research.

Historically, organizational communication scholars made important theoretical and empirical distinctions between formal or 'mandated' networks which represented the legitimate authority of the organization and were typically reflected by the organizational chart, and emergent networks that were informal, naturally occurring networks. The formal networks were presumed to represent the channels of communication through which orders were transmitted downward and information was transmitted upward. Early organizational theorists were aware that the formal organizational structure failed to capture many of the important aspects of communication in organizations and so discussed the importance of informal communication and the grapevine. Fukuyama (1999) argued that social and organizational structures span a continuum that ranges from formal to informal: 'no one would deny that social order is often created hierarchically. But it is useful to see that order can emerge from a spectrum of sources that extends from hierarchical and centralized types of authority, to the completely decentralized and spontaneous interactions of individuals'.[26]

There is considerable evidence for the importance of informal networks. For example, Stevenson and Gilly (1991) found that managers tended to discuss problems with personal contacts rather than with formally designated problem solvers, thus bypassing the formal network.[27] Similarly, Albrecht and Ropp (1984) discovered that 'workers were more likely to report talking about new ideas with those colleagues with whom they also discussed work and personal matters, rather than necessarily following prescribed channels based upon hierarchical role relationships'.[28]

The distinction between formal and informal structures in organizations has diminished significantly in recent years and may become increasingly irrelevant in coming decades. The reasons for this convergence centre on shifts in organizational structure and management philosophy, as well as the pervasive use of cmc. Increased use of team-based forms of organizing and shifts to network forms of organizing has eroded the difference between the formal and the informal organization. 'At the core of these changes has been the explosion of lateral forms of communication made possible by new information technologies that facilitate considerable point-to-point and broadcast communication without regard for traditional hierarchy.'[29]

Despite some contrary findings, most empirical research has supported the idea that, with the advent of cmc, many organizations have been fundamentally changed. In a two-year study of over 800 members of a Research & Development (R&D) organization, Eveland and Bikson (1987) found that electronic mail served to augment, and in some cases complement, formal structures.[30] On the other hand, Bizot et al. (1991) found that electronic communication patterns corresponded closely to the formal organizational structures in a traditionally hierarchical R&D organization.[31] However, Rice (1994) found that the electronic communication structures initially mirrored formal organizational structures, but these similarities diminished over time.[32] Hinds and Kiesler (1995) explored the relationship between formal and informal networks in a telecommunications company.

They found that communication technologies were increasingly used as a tool for informal lateral communication across formal organizational boundaries; this finding was most pronounced for technical workers.[33]

Increasing numbers of contemporary 'organizations' are constructed out of emergent communication linkages, linkages that are ephemeral in that they are formed, maintained, broken and reformed with considerable ease. The networks that emerge by these processes are usually referred to as network organizational forms, although they are organizations only in the sense that they allow the organization of work, not that they are a legal entity. One example of these new forms of organizing is the development of 'e-lancers', that is, electronically connected freelancers, people who work together on a temporary basis to produce goods and services. These new kinds of workers broker their services on the open market, see themselves as transients, and have little if any loyalty or commitment to the organizations for which they work. Instead, their loyalty is invested in their craft. Indeed, internet websites like guru.com thrive by connecting e-lancers with each other and with contract projects.[34]

Summary

Patterns of interaction do not differ greatly between cmc and ftf groups; cmc groups are not more democratic, nor has email made organizations more participative. However, knowledge sharing among co-equals has increased, power based on expertise has become more important and the boundaries of organizations now extend beyond the legal entity. These indirect effects of cmc in organizations are greater than its direct consequences.

Empirical work has not supported either the technological imperative or the organizational imperative; rather it seems technology and behaviour mutually affect each other. The 'explosion' of lateral forms of communication has led to increased use of team-based forms of organizing and shifts to network forms that have eroded the difference between the formal and the informal organization.

12.4 INTERPERSONAL COMMUNICATION IN MULTINATIONAL ENTERPRISES

MNEs have a particular need for effective coordination and so for knowledge sharing and interpersonal communication. The significance of knowledge transfer in MNEs is so great that Gupta and Govindarajan (2000) conceptualized multinational corporations (MNCs) as networks of transactions that are engaged in knowledge flows,[35] while Peng (2001) argued that MNCs exist because they can transfer and exploit knowledge more effectively than markets.[36] Monge and Fulk (1999) argued that the network flows of capital, material, labour, messages and symbols that circulate through suppliers, producers, customers, strategic partners, governing agencies and affiliates constitute the bulk of organizational activity, and so global organizations should be understood as processes.[37] On a practical level, in MNCs subsidiaries can potentially find local or global solutions and help renew MNC competences, provided two-way knowledge flows support the transfer of these solutions.[38]

External market imperfections mean that the exploitation of firms' assets across national boundaries is often most efficiently undertaken internally within its structure. There is thus an incentive to bring its activities under common ownership. If these activities are located in different countries, then an MNE will result. These imperfections are particularly significant in the markets for knowledge-based assets and capabilities. However, based on a sample of 88 organizations in the computer products industries, Andersen and Foss (2005) showed that MNEs are exposed to high levels of complexity and uncertainty due to their presence in multiple locations; and they incur costs due to the need to acquire and transmit information from different units, to integrate units and to coordinate activities. Multinationality *in itself* does not guarantee a higher level of strategic opportunity: it depends on communication among managers across functional and geographical boundaries.[39]

> *To learn more about external market imperfections for knowledge-based assets, visit the companion website...12.3.1.*

Knowledge sharing and the role of expatriates in MNEs

As Chapter 1 noted, network theory asserts that weak ties are better for knowledge sharing than strong ties. A 1999 study found, however, that neither weak nor strong relationships between operating units of MNEs were necessarily better for efficient sharing of knowledge among them. Weak and strong inter-unit ties had their respective strengths and weaknesses in facilitating the search for and transfer of useful knowledge across organization sub-units. The net effect on project completion time of having either weak or strong inter-unit ties depended on how complex was the knowledge to be transferred across sub-units. Strong inter-unit ties provided the strongest positive net effect on completion time when the knowledge was highly complex, whereas weak inter-unit ties had the strongest positive effect on completion time when the knowledge was not complex.[40]

Expatriate relationships can provide ties that function as channels of knowledge sharing across borders. Providing that subsidiaries have sufficient absorptive capacity, expatriates' knowledge transfer competencies —

their ability, motivation and opportunity seeking – have a positive effect on a subsidiary's performance through the knowledge received by the subsidiary.[41] When compared with other more arm's-length cross-border relationships, expatriate relationships have several typical characteristics that have positive consequences for knowledge sharing:

- First, they are characterized by a higher level of trust and multiplexity (range of kinds of ties), driven by shared experience, physical proximity and prolonged ftf interaction.
- Second, expatriate relationships are, on average, richer and longer term than arm's-length cross-border relationships, creating more opportunities for knowledge sharing. (An exploratory case study of 79 expatriates in the field found that interpersonal relationships may be the key enablers of cross-boundary resource and information exchanges.[42]) They also have a higher multiplying effect, spreading ties more effectively across new units.
- Third, a lengthened participation in the assignment unit typically leads to a higher level of shared cognitive ground, effectively facilitating knowledge sharing. Expatriation may therefore have a sustained effect on knowledge sharing within MNCs.[43]

Expatriate managers experience high failure rates, however, due to frustration related to perceiving themselves as vulnerable in unfavourable environments and disidentification related to remoteness and isolation. Costs of these expatriate management failures are very high for the managers – who report personal relationship problems and a fear of career derailment – and for their companies – in terms of opportunity and hard costs. However, cmc makes possible a far higher level of support for expatriates than was ever available previously. E-support during the foreign assignment is 'a critical step' that includes e-learning, e-mentoring, e-counselling and ongoing e-support. A comprehensive expatriate support system should include the manager, spouse, dependents and host-country sponsor, with e-support provided for all four stakeholders.[44]

Summary

MNEs have particular needs for coordination and knowledge sharing and so for interpersonal communication; indeed their existence at all may be based on those needs being met better within than across organizations. However, MNEs confront high levels of complexity and uncertainty due to their presence in multiple locations; and they incur costs due to the need to acquire and transmit information from different units, to integrate units and to coordinate activities. The value of strong versus weak inter-unit ties depends on how complex is the knowledge that units need to share.

Expatriate relationships can improve subsidiary performance through providing strong ties that function as channels of knowledge sharing across borders. However, expatriate managers experience high failure rates; they need continuous support. Cmc makes possible a higher level of support for expatriates than was ever available previously.

13 INTER-ORGANIZATIONAL RELATIONS

Inter-organizational and international relationships – such as trading relationships between suppliers and customers, subcontracting relationships between manufacturers and component makers, and advisory relationships between consultants or advisers and clients – have always been important. In addition, now, because electronic networks reduce transaction costs, new relationships have proliferated. These include offshore outsourcing, joint ventures and **collaborative network organizations**.[1] These relationships give rise to communication, control and knowledge sharing issues. Cultural differences may be prominent in these and they are affected by the necessarily predominant use of mediated communication.

On completing your study of this chapter you will be able to explain and apply the implications of:

- Communication, coordination and control issues and solutions in inter-organizational relations.
- Knowledge sharing issues and the impact on them of cultural differences.
- How computer-mediated communication (cmc) affects aspects of inter-organizational relations such as trust.

13.1 CONTROL IN INTER-ORGANIZATIONAL RELATIONS

Inter-organizational relations give rise to communication and control issues, for which formal contracts are of limited use and social controls are needed, and which create a need for boundary spanners. Communication problems occur when organizations with different cultures find it difficult to negotiate the terms of their future interactions with one another, and so to mould their inter-organizational relations. The difficulties arise in part because the organizations at times fail to share the symbolic meaning of the common terms they use, as a study of a waste disposal business, a grass-roots community organization, and a state regulatory agency found. Control issues arise from the need for coordination of work and processes with 'outside' organizations:

> **"** To create ... value, inter-organizational relationship partners pool resources, determine tasks to be performed and decide on a division of labour ... [This results in] interdependence between the subtasks the partners agree to perform ... [The performance of these tasks] needs to be coordinated across organizational boundaries to ensure a fit between their points of contact ... As the inter-organizational relationship's tasks become more interdependent, the need for coordination and joint decision making increases.[2]

Ultimately it can be necessary to coordinate across organizational boundaries as effectively and efficiently as within them and to integrate the inter-organizational coordination methods and systems with the internal ones.

Control issues can also arise because of partner organizations' opportunistic behaviour. For example, there is often a lack of symmetry within inter-organizational relationships. Switching costs bind customers to vendors if products are incompatible – for instance, changing to a different supplier's payroll program can be very costly because it would be incompatible with other systems. The result is to lock customers in to early choices. Lock-in hinders customers from changing suppliers when a supplier's efficiency changes, and gives vendors power over buyers.[3] This asymmetry can lead to opportunistic behaviour on the part of suppliers. Contracts and formal controls are of limited use in this situation.[4]

Formal versus social control

Whereas formal control 'consists of contractual obligations and formal organizational mechanisms for co-operation', 'informal control, also referred to as social control and relational governance, relates to informal cultures and systems influencing members'. Fryxell et al. (2002) found from a study of 129 US-based international joint ventures (IJVs) that social control mechanisms, provided affect-based trust obtained between the parent companies, outlasted formal control mechanisms over the life of the IJVs in their positive influence on general managers' perceptions of the IJVs' performance.[5]

Informal control complements or sometimes substitutes for formal control. Social control depends on communication and, indeed, may require a sharing of goals and values, implying a higher degree of integration than formal control. Informal control is based on trust. Trust in inter-organizational relationships involves the expectation that another organization will perform in the interests of the relationship and be capable of performing a task satisfactorily, and that it has a commitment to and interest in the outcomes of the relationship.

Formal controls in the shape of binding contracts can actually reduce inter-organizational trust because they lead the parties to attribute the other's cooperation to the constraints imposed by the contract rather than to the individuals themselves, thus reducing the likelihood of trust developing. Non-binding contracts, in contrast, generate personal rather than situational attributions for any cooperation that results and therefore do not interfere with trust development.[6] Another way of deliberately generating trust 'and thereby mitigating control problems before a governance structure is designed and implemented' is 'selecting an appropriate partner, based on good predictors of desirable cooperative behaviors'. Selecting a good partner 'increases confidence in another's goodwill and capabilities'.[7]

Both calculus-based and relational trust have been identified in inter-organizational relations. In a context of global sourcing, research has found that governance based on relational trust is key in the collaboration between IT service providers and clients. A field survey of 293 employees from 20 outsourcing enterprises showed that relational norms are linked to mutual dependence and that communication frequency is linked to relational norms and indirectly but significantly affects how well IT outsourcing projects perform.[8] Again, survey data on R&D projects developed by European biotechnology companies show that contracts, norms about how to behave in the relationship and trust act as complementary mechanisms; although contracts are more effective in exploitation projects, relational norms and trust are more effective in exploration projects.[9] However, in US franchise operations, a study found, neither trust based in a belief in the franchisor's competence, nor trust based in a belief in the franchisor's honesty, increased franchisees' compliance with franchisor directives, suggesting that there are limits to trust-based social control. On the other hand, they did enhance satisfaction with the franchisor, increase perceived relationship quality and reduce active non-compliance with franchisor directives. Mutual commitment was more important than length of time as a franchisee in influencing the two kinds of trusting beliefs.[10]

Embedding economic exchanges in ongoing social relationships can promote stronger commitments and greater cooperation, as participants' interests shift from the short-term gains of exploiting structural advantage to the longer-term benefits of nurturing and maintaining a relationship of loyalty and trust. In arm's-length ties, exchanges are negotiated and typically bound by contract; in embedded relationships, negotiated exchanges are situated in a larger context of reciprocal exchange. In negotiated exchange, participants jointly bargain over the terms of exchange to reach mutually beneficial (and typically binding) agreements. Because the task of negotiation requires communication and joint decision-making, participants know the terms of exchange – what each is getting for what each is giving – before making an agreement. In reciprocal exchange, however, participants initiate exchange by performing a beneficial act for another (such as giving assistance or advice), without knowing whether, when or to what extent the other will reciprocate. The equality or inequality of exchange is established only over time. Reciprocal exchanges are most common among family and friends, but they are also an important component of business relations and international trade.[11]

Conflict is perhaps inevitable in inter-organizational relationships and certainly there is plenty of evidence that it occurs. There is also evidence of a link between communication mode and inter-organizational conflict: use of cmc affects how inter-organizational disputes are handled, but also conflict can lead to a change of communication mode. Myers (2007), in the context of an exploratory case study of an inter-organizational dispute between the BBC and the UK Government found that, because communicators can review and replicate their email messages, 'discourse is explicit, irrevocable and potentially public'. 'When, particularly across the lines of a dispute, communications are contentious, this can lead to sensemaking through behavioural commitment and the evocation of justifying beliefs; or it can lead to emotional dynamics justifying communication as passion or obviating the need to attend to others' responses.'[12] In a case study of a collaboration between businesses, it was found, the use of media shifted substantially from face-to-face (ftf) meetings to email as the relationship turned conflictual. The researchers concluded that due to the competitive nature of the inter-organizational collaboration involved, business strategic conflict significantly influences media selection and, in turn, is influenced by the selected media.

Boundary spanning

Interactions that are aimed at establishing or maintaining relationships with external individuals or organizations in support of organizational or team goals are termed boundary-spanning interactions. The role of individual actors in the management of inter-organizational relationships is 'pivotal' and the 'skills, competencies and behaviour of boundary spanners' are critical to the performance and endurance of inter-organizational relationships, Williams (2002) found.[13] Organizational structure, culture and processes can influence the extent and nature of boundary spanning. As a proactive response to the environment, active boundary spanning is usually considered beneficial.[14]

> *You are the owner of a start-up in the field of business information, specializing in medical appliances. A selling agent for Korea has been recommended to you. Email the agent, setting out a proposal, including the compensation scheme you are offering.*

Boundary spanning may be undertaken by designated or self-appointed individuals or by whole teams. While boundary spanning is intrinsic to some roles, such as personal selling, consultancy or service roles, it can originate in the experiences, perceptions, attitudes, values, cognitions or behaviours of individuals or team members who are not designated boundary spanners.

Thus a boundary spanner does not necessarily occupy a formal position traditionally viewed as a link between organization boundaries. An effective boundary spanner can be anyone who possesses the necessary explicit and tacit knowledge of how to do things, what to do, who to build and maintain a network with, and why something is important.[15] Expatriates and team leaders often serve as boundary spanners, seeing it as part of their role. An exploratory case study of 79 expatriates found that interpersonal relationships may be the cornerstones of the role and the enablers of other cross-boundary resource exchanges.[16] Expatriates have been shown to relay local information and identify opportunities that meet internal needs of MNCs. Local experience and the diversity of the expatriate's social networks are conducive to boundary spanning activities by expatriates.[17] Team leaders communicate more with teams in other organizations than other team members do.[18]

Boundary spanning functions include information processing, representing the organization externally, the acquisition and disposition of resources, and acquiring and acting as an agent of influence for the organization. Particularly important is the function of processing information, which is 'a complex enterprise, as the role occupant does not simply transmit factual information': effective boundary spanners filter, summarize, interpret, draw inferences from, store and selectively act on information. They have 'expertise in determining who gets what information, depending upon the uncertainty in the information processed'; through their actions they absorb uncertainty on behalf of their organization.[19]

To fulfil their role, boundary spanners must have a deep understanding of the business environment in which their organization operates, as well as the socio-cultural, economic and political influences on that environment. Thus the role of boundary spanning is very taxing because the person must handle a variety of work processes that require multiple competence sets. In compensation, boundary spanning correlates with influence, regardless of hierarchical level.[20]

An ethnographic study of Japanese boundary spanners in the Japanese subsidiary of a US business found that they conceived their role as:

- Serving as a conduit between two endpoints (i.e. boundaries) signified by the terms 'Japan' and the 'US'.
- Involving diffuse action unconstrained by position title.
- Serving as a means of resolving problems, or asymmetries, between

Japan and the US that hinder effective communication or task accomplishment.

- Acting as a cultural insider within both Japanese and US cultural frames, switching between frames (and languages) according to the situational demands.

Obviously, not all boundary spanning involves reconciling problems. Normal, non-problematic information constantly flows through these conduits. But the Japanese boundary spanners clearly saw the problem-solving aspect of their role as highly important.[21]

Companies deploy a linking pin strategy in the case of large-scale projects that need boundary spanners for maintaining an overview of inter-site communications. Many offshore outsourcing vendors offer boundary spanners as a service to Western customers. These multi-skilled people promote shared understanding between customer staff used to European, North American, Japanese and Singaporean culture on the one hand, and vendor staff in China, India, Eastern Europe or the Philippines on the other hand.[22] Specialist consultants, too, act as 'bridges' in these intercultural situations.

Effective intercultural boundary spanners deeply internalize identification with the relevant national, as well as with work unit and/or professional, cultures. For example, Japanese boundary spanners from the Japanese subsidiary of a US company responded to both Japanese and US cultural cues, 'appropriately utilizing either one or the other cultural frame in their cross-cultural interactions'.[23]

Boundary spanners' relationships with external parties are generally found to have positive consequences such as increasing their organization's access to knowledge, increasing the level of trust placed in them by members of other organizations, extending the reach of their organization to diverse stakeholders and improving intergroup relations and intergroup productivity. However, the individual boundary spanners themselves sometimes have negative experiences, such as role overload, which in turn leads to teams that are more active in communication networks actually performing worse than less active teams. Other problems experienced by boundaryspanners are work-specific or result from the different organizational cultures.

Examples of work-specific problems include the following: 'Non-government organizations don't follow up on agreement'; 'I found a lack of willingness to cooperate within and between NGOs'; 'the attitude of local authorities with whom we had to cooperate [were not helpful]. They promise a lot but do little and protract the case until you leave.'

Examples of culturally problematic experiences include the following: 'Racial hatred between African colleagues from different countries was the most difficult problem to resolve. Other problems include tribal hatred between Africans from the same countries and irritations between

Pakistani and Indians and colleagues from Bangladesh and Pakistan'; 'Working with Chinese always results in dangerous surprises.'

These negative boundary-spanning experiences and judgements, whether justified or not, can also have a spillover effect, reducing the attractiveness of boundary spanners' jobs and their confidence in their own organization.[24]

13.2 INTER-ORGANIZATIONAL KNOWLEDGE SHARING

Transferring knowledge across different firms is riskier and more compli-cated than transferring knowledge between units within the same organi-zation. Some accounts of strategic alliances between firms suggest that there is a degree of automaticity about the technological and knowledge transfer involved. There is evidence, however, that while in some alliances knowledge transfer does happen, in a substantial number of alliances the capabilities of partner firms become more divergent, suggesting that effort and skill are needed to bring about knowledge sharing.[25]

The transfer of technological know-how in international acquisitions is facilitated by communication, visits and meetings, a study has shown; these effects increase over time. The immediate post-acquisition period is characterized by imposed one-way transfers of knowledge from the acquirer to the acquired, but over time this gives way to high-quality recip-rocal knowledge transfer.[26] This two-way knowledge-sharing between the acquirer and acquired companies can be described as creating a 'social community'.[27]

Zander and Zander (2010) argued on the basis of these findings that in international acquisitions heavy socialization is a rational learning strategy, even if the acquirer aims at appropriating the target's technology or wishes to impose its own logic.[28]

Absorptive capacity, which refers to the ability of the knowledge-receiv-ing organization to recognize, assimilate and apply new knowledge, plays a crucial role in inter-organizational knowledge transfer; it, in turn, depends on communication.[29] Social interaction is a prerequisite as it enables employees to participate in the transformation of new knowledge to the local context and to develop local applications. Organizational conditions that enable or constrain local interaction patterns promote or inhibit knowledge transfer.[30]

Cultural differences impact on inter-organizational and intercultural knowledge flows but, according to Moller and Svahn (2004), the precise impact depends on the nature of the inter-organizational net:

- In stable, well-specified demand/supply nets, such as Toyota's supplier net and Benetton's franchised distribution net, few knowledge-sharing problems arise except among horizontal collectivists and vertical individualists, whose communication orientations are furthest apart.

- In nets that are established but where modifications are made through intentional incremental and local change processes, such as those in multi-party research and development, knowledge sharing takes place most readily among horizontal collectivists because they value knowledge that is historically and contextually grounded.
- In nets concerned mainly with the creation of new knowledge and radical innovations, collectivists are likely to gain a more overall system view, whereas individualists are more likely to penetrate deeply into the core of technical innovations: since significant problems obtain in knowledge sharing between such different cultures, major attention needs to be paid to the issue.[31]

The following is an example of cultural influence on inter-organizational relations:

> Data from 13 companies in Xi'an Software Park in China indicated that in their global sourcing of IT services cultural understanding greatly influenced the level of trust in the relationship, as well as the extent of knowledge sharing and the level of performance.[32]

13.3 COMMUNICATION MODE AND INTER-ORGANIZATIONAL, INTERNATIONAL AND INTERCULTURAL RELATIONS

Studies have found a positive impact on the governance of international exchange relationships from the use of electronic networks. Data from 240 Taiwanese electronics suppliers showed that suppliers' IT resources enable them to work effectively with their key international customers. Importantly, of three governance mechanisms, cooperativeness had a stronger impact on supplier performance than either output monitoring or behaviour monitoring, because it enabled electronic integration.[33]

However, studies that have found positive effects from exclusive use of electronic networks usually focused on large firms that dealt with high volumes of highly routinized transactions; impacts found in these contexts may not generalize to a wider sample. Kraut et al. (1999) found that in a heterogeneous sample the use of electronic networks actually degraded the overall quality of the order process when firms failed to supplement network use with personal relationships. They suggested three reasons for their findings:

- First, some firms may have limited knowledge, skills or technology for proper use of electronic networks (an issue that might be 'transient').

- Second, 'the instantaneous communications networks may encourage firms to wait until the latest possible moment before shipping, increasing the chances of late delivery and last minute errors... This just-in-time effect may increase the likelihood of missed deadlines and mistakes'.
- Third, 'electronic mail worked only because it was supplemented by periodic face-to-face meetings': if network use increased to the extent that ftfc decreased significantly, this seemed to have a negative effect on inter-organizational relationships (and therefore on outsourcing). Thus their data showed that personal relationships and electronic networks complement rather than substitute for each other.[34]

Because organizations involved in inter-organizational business collaborations often operate with different processes, goals and norms, conflict is common in their relations. Where email is the preferred communication medium, the slow and decreasing feedback that is a commonly observed feature in email exchanges signal escalating conflict, though it does not in itself contribute to it.[35]

In inter-organizational virtual organizations, such as joint ventures in which all communication is by cmc, effectiveness depends on trust between the parties. Building trust depends on communicating trustworthiness and is facilitated by reliable information and communication technology (ICT), establishing a common business understanding expressed as common product specifications, cooperative agreements and a sense of shared identity, and strong and accepted policies on business ethics, which 'must exist as a set of formal or informal norms, and also as a demonstrated propensity to behave ethically (i.e. an ethical reputation)'. Specifically, lack of ICT standardization, bandwidth and reliability are associated with less effective communication of trustworthiness in inter-organizational virtual organizations. 'Effective communication of trustworthiness in inter-organizational virtual organizations depends in part on the capacity of the cmc to permit members to transmit emotional and non-verbal messages, preferably involving transmission of facial expression, supported by, for example, use of emoticons in email communication.'[37]

> *Lee and Panteli (2010) gave a useful example, taken from the email communication between a Taiwanese business and a Korean business that shows the confusions that can arise from an inter-organizational email discussion.[36]*
>
> *To see an extract from this example, visit the companion website... 13.3.1.*

In addition to bandwidth issues, which may apply most to international inter-organizational relations, the potential obstacles to the development of trust in the inter-organizational virtual context include a lack of familiarity with the participating organizations, an inability to communicate across organizational boundaries, competition for resources and territoriality.

In these circumstances created by the virtual inter-organizational context, there are key factors that support trust development. They include:

- Having a 'felt need' to collaborate.
- Establishing a common goal.
- Developing social capital.
- Building mechanisms for effective communication and information exchange.
- Creating strong leadership support and commitment.[38]

A number of findings help clarify what is involved in creating and maintaining effective inter-organizational intercultural linkages by cmc: for example, for Chinese global suppliers of IT services, four key factors are positively associated with performance: the supplier team's IT-based skills, communication with the client's team, cultural understanding of the client's culture and collaboration with the client's team.[39]

Trust as a condition underlying cooperation and risk-taking clearly can and does exist between and among organizations over time. Inter-organizational relationships frequently bring new individuals into contact with each other; those individual relationships do not start afresh but rather on a foundation of past fulfilment of expectations upon which new experiences are built, all channelled through institutionalized processes.[40]

> *For more findings on what is involved in creating and maintaining effective inter-organizational intercultural linkages by cmc, visit the companion website...*
> *13.3.2.*

Summary

Inter-organizational relations, which have increased as a result of technological change, raise issues of coordination and control. Contracts are of limited use, especially when the 'locked-in' effect applies. Governance based on relational trust is then more effective than calculus-based trust.

Boundary spanners fulfil a range of functions including information processing, representing the organization externally, the acquisition and disposition of resources, and acquiring and acting as an agent of influence for the organization; the role is demanding and can be stressful. Expatriates and team leaders often act as boundary spanners.

Inter-organizational knowledge sharing is riskier and more complex than intra-organizational knowledge sharing. Interpersonal communication is critical for knowledge transfer in international acquisitions. Absorptive capacity also depends on social interaction.

Cultural differences impact on international knowledge sharing, though in different ways depending on the inter-organizational net. Cultural understanding greatly influences the level of trust in the relationship.

Although some circumstances allow effective governance of inter-organizational relations exclusively by cmc, in general personal relationships and electronic networks complement rather than substitute for each other. In inter-organizational virtual organizations, effectiveness depends on trust between the parties. ICT bandwidth is significant here, so that emotional and non-verbal messages can be conveyed. Interpersonal communication processes are 'critical' in software and services outsourcing industries.

CASES AND EXERCISES

1. You are a senior manager in a pharmaceuticals business. You came from a business in a different industry – retail. There, organizational position counted for a lot. In your new organization you find that relatively junior scientists and technologists sometimes have as much or more influence than senior managers in departmental meetings and that they send emails to senior managers 'putting them right' with no sign of recognizing their seniority. Why the difference? How do you react? How will you handle the situation?

2. Act as a distributed team of four HR staff (Benson, Carla, Etienne and Jennifer) that has the goal of ensuring that equal-opportunities practices are introduced in staff-selection procedures throughout the organization, which has 15,000 staff.
   Work remotely to execute this initiative.

3. A member of your team has obtained another post and handed in his resignation. In accordance with the policy of your organization he is serving out his two-month notice period. Halfway through this time, the team gets a contract that is a 'breakthrough' that could be very profitable and take the team's reputation both within and outside the organization to a new level but will require members of the team to work long hours, sometimes through the night. The contribution of every member will be vital. How will you influence the man who has resigned to contribute equally to this effort?

4. You represent a business that is the customer of a supplier of industrial lubricants. An order that was placed, recorded and invoiced has not been delivered, with consequences of losses of production for your business. However, your company did not notify the non-receipt of the goods within 14 days of the due date as the contract required.
   Before you meet up with/email the supplier's representative, you consider your alternative strategies to obtain a replacement and compensation:

    a. Raising the possibility of claiming on their insurance for the loss.

    b. Referring to the value of your custom to them.

    c. Mentioning contacts with other potential suppliers.

    d. Querying whether the goods were dispatched and referring to their obligation to supply the goods invoiced.

    e. Committing to investigate/revise your goods receipt procedures subject to a no-questions-asked replacement and compensation.

    f. Committing to insure against similar future instances subject to no-questions-asked replacement and compensation.

    g. Committing to placing further business with them subject to no-questions-asked replacement and compensation.

    h. Threatening to place no further business without immediate replacement and compensation.

    i. Threatening as above plus spreading word of unsatisfactory service to potential customers.

    j. Threatening to sue.

In what circumstances, if any, would each of these alternatives be an effective strategy? Once you have decided, write the email setting out your proposal and/or role play the meeting.

5. Role play persuading a passer-by to give to charity or take part in a market research interview.

6. You are a newly appointed manager of a 1,000 employee web design and software production facility. How should you introduce yourself? By what mode and in what words?

7. You are a fashion department buyer for a department store. You are preparing to go to a planning meeting with other buyers from related departments. Unfortunately you have not been at the latest designer shows. What is at stake for you in this situation and what, if anything, can you do about it?

8. Andrew Cooper is leader of a team doing research into energy companies. He believes that his team would be both more efficient and would produce results that would please clients more if his team subscribed to one or two of the data analytic services available on subscription. These services are not cheap – the annual bill for any one service could equal the salary costs of a member of staff – but Andrew considers that would be a better way of spending the same amount. Data analytic specialists at the present time are not only expensive but hard to recruit, as there has been a huge recent growth in companies quarrying their data. He knows, however, that his manager, and indeed the

top management team of the organization, think differently: they would prefer to keep the entire process in-house for reasons of avoiding copyright issues. Andrew, who, with his team, is located in Malaysia, speaks to his manager once a week in a conference call; otherwise they communicate by email. How should Andrew proceed? How should he put his case?

9. Spalding Interiors, an interior design business, has been charging its clients a flat fee based on the amount of work their project required; it submits an estimate and if it gains the work only charges more if the client makes alterations to their initial specification. Their main competitors, however, charge as a percentage of the 'spend' for the project. The newly appointed CEO of Spalding believes that the industry standard way of charging is more profitable, because clients can often be persuaded to upgrade their specification. The senior management, however, is resisting this change, arguing that they attract more business because clients trust them as they have no incentive to push them to upgrade or do more than they intended. Conduct the meeting at which this proposal of the new CEO is to be discussed and decided on.

10. Ulrich is the founder of a start-up business in the business intelligence field. He has been invited by a client, TEchmart, to join them in a consulting project aimed at chief marketing officers. Ulrich's firm would provide the research capability, TEchmart the expertise. Following a meeting to discuss the project, in which TEchmart showed him, but would not let him take away, a 'needs and gap' survey questionnaire designed for the project, Ulrich has been asked to submit his firm's ideas on other areas that they should cover. Although there has been talk of a retainer for Ulrich's firm, there is no contractual arrangement in place and he recently did a piece of work for TEchmart for which he has not yet been paid. TEchmart is an established firm and Ulrich hopes for a fruitful partnership with them but is suspicious that they want to pick his brains and then not give him any business.

   How should Ulrich proceed and why? According to your opinion, either write the email to which he will attach any suggestions or the one which will explain his withdrawal from the project.

11. Selma, a team leader of eight analysts in a business intelligence start-up, had been receiving complaints from the leaders of other teams about slow responses from her team members to emails. She therefore raised the matter at the weekly team meeting. At once a torrent of explanations and complaints burst forth from every member of the team. They said they were deluged with emails. 'I had 40 new mails in my inbox this morning, though I cleared it last night,' one said. Other

teams were worse in terms of delays in responding: 'It isn't just delays – they don't respond at all unless you chase and chase them,' said another.

What should Selma do?

12. An oil company had a large number of small commercial customers such as builders' merchants, builders, small-scale furniture or garment manufacturers and so on, to which it made 'small-drop' deliveries into their own tanks. Analysis had shown that overall these deliveries were unprofitable, and also that in many cases the contractual conditions were not being adhered to. For example, deliveries were being made in quantities of half the minimum contractual gallonage. An exercise was launched to improve the profitability of this business by enforcing the contractual conditions and by persuading as many customers as possible to accept changes such as taking deliveries at night, widening gates for the entry of larger vehicles and giving longer notice of their orders. The managerial problem here was to motivate the sales force to persuade their customers to make these changes. The sales representatives feared that their customers would resist making costly changes from which they could expect no direct benefit.

How should management approach this issue with the sales force?

13. The founder of a successful start-up operation, who was a forceful personality and had big aspirations, decided the time had come to expand aggressively. He told his sales team that they needed to win more business. In turn, the team started accepting all types of requests from new and existing customers and ultimately overburdened the operation with a volume and type of requests they could not fulfil. Some team members were starting to get frustrated because sometimes a customer they had personally said 'Yes' to didn't get their request fulfilled. When this happened, other team members did not understand the issue – they had been told to win more business and they were delivering on what was asked of them.

What might have gone wrong?

14. You are working as a part-time consultant for your former employer while setting up your own business. It is early days and you need the income from this consultancy. Now they have asked you to make recommendations on the percentage increase in the salary budget for a major part of their business, which employs 500 staff offshore. The problem is that the person you deal with has a preconceived idea that the percentage should be applied to the current salary total. In the country in question, nearly half the staff were promoted in the last year

as replacements for leavers, but they have not yet been paid the rises concomitant with their promotions. These will have to be paid as part of the settlement for the coming year. Most of these promotions were from the lowest grade to the second grade, where a 100 per cent increase in pay is standard. Thus if you follow the formula that your client wants you to, and recommend any likely market-related percentage increase, which would be in the region of 10 percent, the whole of this increase and more will be used up in compensating those who have been promoted, leaving none for market-related increases for those who have not been promoted.

You have both ethical and business objections to doing exactly as you have been asked, though you do want to retain the client. The client's representative tends to be wedded to his ideas.

What method of communication would you use to express your objections?

Assume that for extraneous reasons you have to express them by email and write the email.

Now assume that you decide that you cannot and will not carry out this assignment, though you do want to retain the client's business. Extricate yourself from the situation either by email or by an interactive method (face-to-face, Voice over internet provider, telephone or instant messaging).

15. Wyatt joined his organization, an advertising agency in a provincial town, straight from school and worked in the same office for the next five years. When he changed jobs to an office in a different town within the same organization, he quickly noticed big differences in the ways things were done and how people behaved. In his first office, the atmosphere was relaxed, nearly everyone, women and men, supported the same soccer team and discussed its performance as they greeted one another in the morning or over lunch, most also belonged to a syndicate to buy lottery tickets, there was lots of laughter and yet the job got done; if people had to work late to get it done, they would, out of a sense of loyalty to one another. In his new office, none of this applied, the atmosphere was competitive, everyone seemed to be trying to catch the eye of the boss, and that was why they would stay late if needed to get the job done. Wyatt couldn't see any difference in how efficient or effective the two offices were; it was just that the atmosphere was so different.

How would you describe the culture of the two different offices and what might explain the differences?

16. A charity which counsels young people has only one full-time employee, a counselling supervisor, but on its fourth attempt has won

a Lottery grant to employ a fund-raiser/development worker. The recruitment advertising for this post has stretched its budget to the limit. The post has been advertised in one national daily and four ethnic minority local weeklies. When the advertisement in the national daily appears, it is clear that significant errors have been made which means that the ad reads nonsensically, so making the organization look incompetent and probably discouraging competent applicants; it also omits the key skill/experience requirements for the post and the Lottery logo.

When alerted to the problem, the advertising department of the newspaper points to their disclaimer, which says that their compensation will be limited to a free further insertion of the (corrected) advertisement.

The trustees of the charity are not satisfied with this offer; they think that most of the target readership of that newspaper will have already seen the erroneous advertisement and will reject the idea of applying. They want a refund so that they can use the money to advertise elsewhere or use an agency.

How should the trustees proceed? Assume that they decide to try to negotiate a better deal from the publication; decide their negotiation strategy, opening offer, target, BATNA (Best Alternative To A Negotiated Agreement) and the powerbases of the two parties. Role play the negotiation.

17. You are a management consultant. Some years ago, you were consulted by a company on the subject of reducing complexity; you have now been called in to speak to a group of the company's senior managers on the same topic although they had since developed a reputation for being good at simplification. In discussions with senior management, it emerged that the organizational knowledge about simplification had been lost as people took on new jobs, relocated or retired, or when a new CEO introduced a different agenda or following a merger.

What will you recommend the company to do to prevent a repeat?

18. Susan worked for a business that published trade magazines. One day she met up with an old friend and they started talking about their jobs. 'Everyone in the office always seems to be on a knife edge,' Susan told her friend. 'If anything goes wrong – the magazine they are working on loses an advertiser, or it gets a couple of critical letters, they all feel threatened and are looking round for someone to blame, even though it's well known that in this industry that sort of thing happens and it is often no-one's fault.'

What explanation does your understanding of organizational culture and climate provide for this situation?

19. You are to represent your company on a trade visit to an emerging country. Your group will be headed up by a leading politician.Your brief is to develop contacts that might lead to business for your company. How will you prepare for the visit?

20. Compare the different attitudes to information overload described in Boxes 1.2 and 9.1. What might give rise to such differences? Should the bank at issue in Box 1.2 take action? If so, what action? If not, why not?

21. The leaders of three product teams of a medium-sized business intelligence organization have been asked to submit their bids and make their case to the head of department for their team's allocation of training resources for the following year. The organization's training plan for that year is a focus on basic and intermediate training in using spreadsheets. For this reason the team leaders' arguments need to focus on their section's need for staff with skills in using spreadsheets and what the implications are of sparing staff for training.

    Team Leader 1. You are particularly concerned to obtain a share of the allocation at least proportional to the number of staff in your team, which would mean more than the other teams as yours is the biggest. Last year your team got less than their 'share' and this was resented by staff who felt you had let them down. Unfortunately, it is not obvious why your team's need for spreadsheet skills is as great as that of Team 3.

    Team Leader 2. You don't care how large your allocation is, so long as it is the largest of the three shares. Unfortunately, it is not obvious why your team's need for spreadsheet skills is as great as that of Team 3.

    Team Leader 3. Your team's need for spreadsheet skills is genuine and greater than that of Teams 1 and 2. However, your team is the smallest and least revenue-generating of the three. You also received a larger than proportional share of the training budget for the previous year, which was focused on Business English.

    Adopt the role of Team Leader of Team 1, 2 or 3.

    - Prepare your argument for getting a larger/the largest share of the training budget.
    - What would be your preferred method of presenting your case and why?
    - Make your case in a 200 word document to attach to an email.
    - Assume you have to make a presentation and prepare your slides.
    - Argue your case in an instant messaging interaction with the team leaders of the rival teams.
    - Argue your case in a face-to-face meeting with a fellow student who will role play the head of department.

22. In a major bank, 150 people were called to a departmental meeting. Top executives of the bank gave well-prepared, informative presentations; after 90 minutes the departmental manager asked if there were any questions but nobody raised their hand. A week later, when people were asked to give feedback about the meeting, most recalled that it was 'useful' but very few could remember any particular points.

    What might explain this?

23. You are an executive of a retail company which has experienced poor trading conditions and so taken the decision to close a number of branches over the next few months. You are to visit the branches and give the staff the news that they will be made redundant. One such branch, in an area of the country with high unemployment, has the following staff complement: the manageress is within five years of the usual retirement age, one full-time permanent member of staff is mid-career, the other is a graduate trainee and there are two part-time temporary workers.

    Prepare your presentation.

    What reactions would you anticipate to your news?

    How would you respond?

24. At work, you receive an email with the words 'What are your thoughts?' followed by a chain of forwarded emails. What are your thoughts about the person who wrote the email?

    Write your responses for the following cases. The person who sent the email is (a) your boss; (b) a lateral colleague; (c) your subordinate; (d) the representative of an important customer or client; (e) the representative of a business with which your business has a joint venture; and (f) the representative of a supplier.

    Explain the reasons for the tone you adopt in each case.

25. You are a mid-level executive in a large electrical manufacturer. The business has developed a new battery with great potential. Your team has been instructed to engage in customer discovery – to explore new markets and applications. As part of that process you are to telephone senior managers from potential customers.

    Prepare your approach to one such (initial) call. Role play the call.

26. You are travelling in Europe on business. You have left your staff to work on a data collection and presentation project for an important potential client; the presentation is to be given in ten days' time. When you get an update from your staff, you learn that they have been working on the presentation; you need to tell them to leave the presentation and focus on the research, especially the interviews; the presentation can be prepared on the last day. The message is partly rebuke, partly

instruction; as you will not be returning to the office until just before the presentation you need to make sure that they understand, accept and are motivated to do what they need to.

How will you communicate with them? By email, video link or phone? Why?

Assume that circumstances mean that you have to communicate by email and write the email.

27. You have been given the task of suggesting the topics for a one-week course in professional communication for graduate recruits. What topics will you suggest and why? Justify omitting any topics that you might have included but have not.

28. An agent has used an e-lancer to research and write a report for a client. Up to now, he has not told the e-lancer the name of the client, out of concern that the e-lancer might approach the client directly, depriving him of the benefits of the work he has put in to negotiate with the client, specify the research requirement, organize payment, liaise, etc. However the project has now reached a stage where the report has to be entered on the template provided by the client. To get the e-lancer to supply the information in a word processing format and enter it from there would be time-consuming and costly.

After giving the matter some thought, the agent decided to trust the e-lancer with the client's name but speak to her to say that he was trusting her in this way.

What do you think of this solution? If you are unable to reach a conclusion, what further information would you need in order to do so?

29. Rafi is a 29-year-old salesperson. He has applied for a selling job with your company. You were very (un)impressed by his presentation and his professionalism. It seems to you that his sales experience is (not) exactly that required for the job. Personally, you felt very (un)comfortable with him.

What would expectancy violation theory predict to be your response to an expectancy violation by Rafi?

How would you in fact respond in the two different situations described?

30. At a selection interview for your first job, you are asked how you would add value to a team. How do you reply?

31. At a selection interview, a woman who is an expert in bank regulation reporting procedures is asked how she would add value to the bank regulation reporting team. How should she reply?

32. At a selection interview, you are asked how you would deal with a difficult colleague. How would you reply?

33. Your job involves negotiating for a major utility (electricity) based in one region of the country (one country) with big customers in another region (another country). Sometimes the people you deal with are quite upset at the idea of getting their power from a company based outside their region (country) – it offends their regional (national) sympathies. They never mention it, but it affects their overall attitudes. Introduce yourself by email to a prospective customer.

34. You are the CEO of a long-established publicly owned business that offers hygiene and energy technologies and services for food retailers and caterers of all kinds. This market is close to saturation and recent sales growth has been slow. Now, you and the board want to acquire a water and engineering services business, whose share price has fluctuated substantially but generally declined over recent years and which has high levels of debt. You reason that the volatility of the share price has been due to the business's debt burden, which your purchase will alleviate and that buying it would give your company a global presence in products that your biggest clients increasingly ask for. These clients are starting to realize that water will no longer be abundant and free; you will help them adjust to a world of scarcity and price. This will involve developing anti-microbials that clean with much less water, more efficient systems for processing waste and new ways to use non-potable 'grey' water, for example in factories.

    Your biggest investor doubts your reasoning, believing instead that it is a 'diversification too far'; he thinks that there is little synergy between the two businesses and that the past share price movements show that the business you want to acquire is unsound. His personal shareholding is large enough to hammer your share price if he decides to sell, thus making your acquisition impossible.

    How would you persuade him? What arguments would you use? How would you proceed (for example, in writing or face-to-face)?

35. You are the owner of a small business that employs five people. You have recently offered a post as a salesperson to someone with absolutely the right experience and, to judge from the interview, attitudes. He or she accepted and is due to start in a week's time. Now he or she has left a voicemail message out of hours to say that his or her wife or husband has to have surgery and he or she will not be able to start until two weeks after the planned date. This upsets all your plans for training the new salesperson alongside the existing staff; you have a 'reserve' whom you identified from the selection process as good,

though not equally good, as this person. An added difficulty is that you do not know whether to believe him or her: it might be true or it might be that he or she is keeping your offer open while he or she looks for other opportunities.

How will you proceed?

36. You work for a small business intelligence organization as a researcher. Your company has obtained a contract to research a Chinese manufacturer of automotive parts. The contracting company is a competitor of the Chinese manufacturer. Much of the information is available from secondary sources such as their website and their report and accounts, but there is some essential information that can only be obtained by interviews with staff of the Chinese manufacturer or distributors of their product. This contract is very important because if the contracting business, which is a global one, is pleased with the result, a much larger one is likely to follow.

How do you obtain the interviews you need? That is, how do you approach the individuals who have the information, and what do you say or write?

37. The working language of your organization is English. You are mentoring a young Chinese employee who is a very effective and efficient worker and clearly highly intelligent; her written English is excellent, but although she has worked for the company for some years, people find her spoken English hard to understand because of her pronunciation. You are sure that this is both harming her career progress and meaning that others avoid her – she has noticed the second of these herself but has put it down to prejudice. How do you mentor her?

38. Selection interviews often ask 'competency' questions such as the following. How would you answer them?

   a. Tell us about a situation where you failed to communicate appropriately. In hindsight, what would you have done differently?
   b. Describe a time when you had to explain something complex to a colleague. What problems did you come across and how did you deal with them?
   c. Describe a time in which you had to improve a team's performance. What challenges did you meet and how did you address them?
   d. Describe a time in which members of your team did not get along. How did you handle the situation?
   e. Describe a time in which you were a member of a team. How did you positively contribute to the team?
   f. Describe a time in which you received negative feedback from an

employer, colleague or client. How did you manage this feedback? What was the outcome?

g. Describe a situation where you had to use tact in handling a difficult situation.

39. You work for an electronics and appliances retail chain which is confronted by a threat of being sued by an angry customer. She claims that your company lost her laptop when she left it for repairs and that it tried to cover up the loss for six months. It also failed to react when she reported that the laptop carried confidential information about her own business; in fact, her suspicion is that an employee is somehow using or selling the information. The company's greatest concern is not the amount of damages she is likely to gain, but the bad publicity that her legal action would attract.

    You have been given the task of dissuading her from taking legal action. How do you proceed?

40. You are the newly hired CEO of a publisher of trade magazines. While familiarizing yourself with the business, you notice some readership figures for one of the five divisions – the one that publishes banking magazines – that seem strange. In fact you think that the figures have been not only inflated (by applying unrealistic figures for readers per copy) but that their trend has been reversed from downward to upward. (You know from your previous job that the circulations of print editions of such magazines have steadily declined over the period to which the figures relate, but these numbers suggest the opposite.) As these figures are the basis on which you charge advertisers, the implications, if you are right, are very serious. Clearly you need to have this fully investigated and for that you need the cooperation of the head of the division, who has been in post throughout the period when the figures seem wrong. How do you proceed?

41. You are the newly appointed CEO of a global bank, which has recently been the subject of a major regulatory enquiry, has had to pay out large settlements to avoid court cases and is under notice by the regulator that it will have to hive off its investment bank from its retail bank unless its internal controls are substantially improved. You propose to introduce a 'Five Point Plan' in an attempt to change the ethics, culture and operations of the company; the plan includes expanded training, enhanced focus on talent, balanced performance appraisals, improved communications and strengthened compliance controls. You now need to 'sell' this plan to your board as a preliminary to 'selling' it to the regulator. You know that the board includes two powerful outside directors who are distinguished retired bankers and rather conservative in their views. How do you proceed?

42. You are the owner of a start-up search business; you want to attend a conference that is the leading global event for delegates in search and social marketing. Unfortunately, the tickets are more expensive than you feel able to justify at this early stage for your business. However, you had a friend at university who is now, ten years on, quite senior in the organization that runs the conferences. You haven't been in touch recently – everyone's busy, it happens. Despite this you decide to see if he or she can get you a free or reduced-price ticket. How do you approach him or her – by phone, email or text? And what do you say or write in order to renew contact and ask for his or her help with the ticket?

43. Assume that your former university friend has been able and willing to get you a ticket for the search and social marketing conference at issue in Question 42. Although you expect to learn something useful, your main purpose in attending is to network – to make useful contacts, especially of potential customers, for your business. You are aware that most of the other delegates will have a similar objective.

    (a) How will you make the most of the opportunity? There can be no question of distributing leaflets or any other scatter-gun approach, but it is, you know, accepted and usual to give your business card to someone with whom you have talked. Delegates all wear badges stating their name and company.
    (b) Visualize the scene at the coffee and lunch breaks and describe how you would introduce yourself into a group who seem already engaged in a lively conversation.
    (c) How will you follow up on any useful contacts after the conference?
    (d) Suppose one contact, who represents a company in which you are particularly interested as a potential customer, said as you parted, 'Drop me an email.' Write the email.

FURTHER READING

For links to useful websites, visit the companion website: *Learning Resources.*

For more in-depth coverage of face-to-face work communication: Guirdham, M. (2002) *Interactive Behaviour at Work*, 3rd edn, Hemel Hempstead, UK: Pearson FT.

For more in-depth coverage of cultural and subcultural differences in work communication and intercultural work communication: Guirdham, M. (2012) *Communicating Across Cultures at Work*, 3rd edn, Basingstoke, UK: Palgrave Macmillan.

For a good practical how-to-do-it book, though it does not link strongly to either organizational behaviour or communication theory: Ober, S. (2009) *Business Communication*, 7th edn, Boston, MA: Houghton Mifflin.

For more on managerial communication: Hargie, O., Dickson, D. and Tourish, D. (2004) *Communication Skills for Effective Management*, Basingstoke: Palgrave Macmillan.

For more in-depth coverage of online communication, although it does not cover face-to-face communication and is not work-oriented: Wood, A.F. and Smith, M.J. (2005) *Online Communication: Linking Technology, Identity, and Culture*, Englewood Cliffs, NJ: Laurence Erlbaum.

For more in-depth coverage of gender influences on communication, an edited series of contributions: Barrett, M. and Davidson, M.J (2006) *Gender and Communication at Work*, Aldershot, UK: Ashgate Publishing.

For more coverage of industrial psychology, an American text: Landy, F.J. and Conte, J.M. (2010) *Work in the 21st Century: An Introduction to Industrial and Organizational Psychology*, 3rd edn, New York: McGraw Hill.

For more on organizational communication, an American text: Miller, K. (2012) *Organisational Communication: Approaches and Processes*, 6th edn, London: Cengage Learning.

For an overview of major psychological concepts and techniques: DuBrin, A.J. (2003) *Applying Psychology*, Englewood Cliffs, NJ: Prentice -Hall.

For more on how and why ICTs are used in business or organizational contexts under different circumstances: Browning, L.D., Steinar Saetre, A., Stephens, K. and Sornes, J.-A. (2008) *Information and Communication Technologies in Action*, New York: Routledge.

For more on organizational communication with a concentration on face-to-face communication, though the final chapter focuses on new communication technology: Harris, T. and Nelson, M.D. (2007) *Applied Organizational Communication: Theory and Practice in a Global Environment*, 3rd edn, London: Routledge.

REFERENCES

PREFACE

1 Williams, E. (1998) 'Predicting email effects in organisations', *First Monday*, at http://firstmonday.org/htbin/cgiwrap/bin/ojs/index.php/fm/article/viewArticle/617/538.

CHAPTER 1 INTRODUCTION

1 Mintzberg, H. (1973) *The Nature of Managerial Work*, New York: Harper & Row.
2 Webster, J. and Trevino, L.K. (1995) 'Rational and social theories as complementary explanations of communication media choices: two policy-capturing studies', *Academy of Management Journal*, **38**(6): 1544–72.
3 Culnan, M.J. and Markus, M.L. (1987) 'Information technologies', in F.M. Jablin, L.L. Putnam, K.H. Roberts and L.W. Porter (eds) *Handbook of Organizational Communications*, London: Sage, pp. 420–43.
4 Kettinger, W. and Grover, V. (1997) 'The use of computer-mediated communication in an interorganizational context', *Decision Sciences*, **28**(3): 513–55.
5 Summerhill, C.A. (2001) 'Computer-mediated communication as publication: considering the World Wide Web in the broader sociological context of communication', at www.cni.org/°craig/castalks/cmc.html (accessed 13 March 2013).
6 Williams, E. (1998) 'Predicting email effects in organisations', *First Monday*, at http://firstmonday.org/htbin/cgiwrap/bin/ojs/index.php/fm/article/viewArticle/617/538.
7 Ibid.
8 December, J. (1996) 'What is computer-mediated communication?', at www.december.com/john/study/cmc/what.html (accessed 23 November2013).
9 Romiszowski, A.J. and Mason, R. (1996) 'Computer-mediated communication', *Handbook of Research for Educational Communications and Technology*, New York: Simon & Schuster, pp. 438–56.
10 Culnan and Markus, op. cit.
11 Spitzberg, B.H. (2006) 'Preliminary development of a model and measure of computer-mediated communication (CMC) competence', *Journal of Computer Mediated Communication*, **11**(2): 629–66.
12 Rettie, R. (2009) 'Mobile phone communication: extending Goffman to mediated interaction', *Sociology*, **43**(3): 421–38.

13 Romiszowski and Mason, op. cit.

14 Feenberg, A. (1989) 'The written world: on the theory and practice of computer conferencing', in R. Mason and A. Kaye (eds), *Mindweave: Communication, Computers and Distance Education*, Oxford: Pergamon Press, pp. 22–39.

15 Andersen, T.U. (2005) 'The performance effect of computer-mediated communication and decentralized strategic decision making', *Journal of Business Research*, **58**(8): 1059–67.

16 Licoppe, C. and Smoreda, Z. (2005) 'Are social networks technologically embedded? How networks are changing today with changes in communication technology', *Social Networks*, **27**(4): 317–35.

17 Markus, M.L. and Robey, D. (1988) 'Information technology and organizational change: causal structure in theory and research', *Management Science*, **34**(5): 583–98.

18 Monge, P.R., and Contractor, N.S (2003) *Theories of Communication Networks*, New York: Oxford University Press, ch. 1.

19 Granovetter, M. (1983) 'The strength of weak ties: a network theory revisited', *Sociological Theory*, **1**(1): 201–33.

20 Ellis, P.D. (2011) 'Social ties and international entrepreneurship: opportunities and constraints affecting firm internationalization', *Journal of International Business Studies*, **42:** 99–127.

21 Eveland, J.D. and Bikson, T.K. (1989) 'Work group structures and computer support: a field experiment', *ACM Transactions on Information Systems*, **6**(4): 354–79.

22 Ibid.

23 Burt, R.S., Kilduff, M. and Tasselli, S. (2013) 'Social network analysis: foundations and frontiers on advantage', *Annual Review of Psychology*, **64**: 527–47.

24 Keyton, J., Ford, E.A., Fu, R., Leibowitz, S. A., Liu, T., et al. (2013) 'Investigating verbal workplace communication behaviors', *Journal of Business Communication*, **50**(2): 152–69.

25 White, R. D. (2001) 'Month off doesn't work for CEOs', *Los Angeles Times*, 10 August.

26 Teasley, S.D., Covi, L.A., Krishnan, M.S. and Olson, J.S. (2002) 'Rapid software development through team collocation', *IEEE Transactions on Software Engineering*, **28**(7): 671–83.

27 Ibid.

28 Berry, G.R. (2006) 'Can computer-mediated asynchronous communication improve team processes and decision making? Learning from the management literature', *Journal of Business Communication*, **43**(4): 344–66.

29 Norman, D.A. (1988) *The Psychology of Everyday Things*, New York: Basic Books.

30 Ibid.

31 Rice, R.E., Grant, A.E., Schmitz, J. and Torobin, J. (1990) 'Individual and network influences on the adoption and perceived outcomes of electronic messaging', *Social Networks*, **12**(1): 27–55.

32 Kettinger and Grover, op. cit.

33 Sallis, P. and Kassabova, D. (2000) 'Computer-mediated communication: experiments with email readability', *Information Sciences*, **123**(1): 43–53.

34 Rice, R.E. (1989) 'Issues and concepts in research on computer-mediated communication systems', *Communication Yearbook*, **12**: 436–76.

35 Okazaki, S. and Mendez, F. (2013) 'Perceived ubiquity in mobile services', *Journal of Interactive Marketing*, **27**: 98–111.

36 Lee, C.S. (2010) 'Managing perceived communication failure with affordances of ICTs', *Computers in Human Behavior*, **26**(4): 572–80.

37 Lee, J.Y.-H. and Panteli, N. (2010) 'Conflict escalation in inter-organizational virtual communication', at http://dx.doi.org/10.2139/ssrn.1612545 (accessed 30 November 2013).

38 Quest Software, Inc. 'Best practices in instant messaging management: enabling productive, secure and compliant instant messaging policies and usage in the business environment', at http://media.govtech.net/Digital_Communities/Quest%20Software/Best_Practices_in_Instant_Messaging_Management.pdf (accessed 23 November 2013).

39 Fels, D.I. and Weiss, P.L. (2000) 'Toward determining an attention-getting device for improving video-mediated communication', *Computers in Human Behavior*, **16**(2): 189–98.

40 Lowden, R.J. and Hostetter, C. (2012) 'Access, utility, imperfection: the impact of video conferencing on perceptions of social presence', *Computers in Human Behavior*, **28**(2): 377–83.

41 Kumar, K., van Fenema, P.C. and Von Glinow, M. (2005) 'Intense collaboration in globally distributed work teams: evolving patterns of dependencies and coordination', *Advances in International Management*, **18**: 127–53.

42 Walther, J.B. and Jang, J.-W. (2012) 'Communication processes in participatory websites', *Journal of Computer-Mediated Communication*, **18**: 2–15.

43 McEwan, B. and Sobre-Denton, M. (2011) 'Virtual cosmopolitanism: constructing third cultures and transmitting social and cultural capital through social media', *Journal of International and Intercultural Communication*, **4**(4): 252–8.

44 Walther and Jang, op. cit.

45 McKinlay, A., Procter, R., Masting, O., Woodburn, R. and Arnott, J. (1994) 'Studies of turn-taking in computer-mediated communications', *Interacting with Computers*, **6**(2): 151–71.

46 Ibid.

47 Sillince, J.A.A. and Saeedi, M.H. (1999) 'Computer-mediated communication: problems and potentials of argumentation support systems', *Decision Support Systems*, **26**(4): 287–306.

48 Goel, L., Junglas, I., Ives, B. and Johnson, N. (2012) 'Decision making in-socio and in-situ: facilitation in virtual worlds', *Decision Support Systems*, **52**(2): 342–52.

49 'Making internal collaboration work: an interview with Don Tapscott', at www.mckinsey.com/insights/organization/making_internal_collaboration_work_an_interview_with_don_tapscott (accessed 29 May 2014).

50 De Graaf, F.J. and Velthuijsen, H. (2011) 'Network governance for dealing with IT-enabled interorganizational co-operation networks: when should network IT – such as social media – be used and how to govern it', at http://papers.ssrn.com/sol3/papers.cfm?abstract_id=1749367 (accessed 23 November 2013).

51 Dutton, W., David, P. and Richter, W. (2008) 'The performance of distributed problem solving networks: a final report on the OII-MTI project', at http://ssrn.com/abstract=1302923 (accessed 29 May 2014).

52 Loubser, M. (2008) 'Governance structures in distributed problem-solving networks', working paper in the OII/MTI 'Performance of DPSNs' project.

53 Sun, Y., Wang, N. and Peng, Z. (2011) 'Working for one penny: understanding why people would like to participate in online tasks with low payment', *Computers in Human Behavior*, **27**(2): 1033–41.

54 Kleinnijenhuis, J., van den Hooff, B., Utz, S., Vermeulen, I. and Huysman, M. (2011) 'Social influence in networks of practice: an analysis of organizational communication content', *Communication Research*, **38**: 587–612.

55 Wasko, M.M., Teigland, R. and Faraj, S. (2009) 'The provision of online public goods: examining social structure in an electronic network of practice', *Decision Support Systems*, **47**(3): 254–65.

56 De Graaf and Velthuijsen, op. cit.

57 At www.nationalstemcentre.org.uk/dl/ec5c52a63af25ed8fe1ea51d67e19540 be73485/3058-Employability_skills_guide.pdf.

58 Givens, G. (1978) 'The non-verbal basis of attraction: flirtation, courtship and seduction', *Psychiatry*, **41**: 346–51.

59 Skelton, J.R., Kai, J. and Loudon, R.F. (2001) 'Cross-cultural communication in medicine: questions for educators', *Medical Education*, **35**(3): 257–61.

60 Thomas, G.F. (2007) 'How can we make our research more relevant? Bridging the gap between workplace changes and business communication research', *Journal of Business Communication*, **44**: 283–96.

61 Zorn, M.T. and Violanti, M.T. (1996) 'Communication abilities and individual achievement in organizations', *Management Communication Quarterly*, **10**(2): 139–67.

62 Xia, L., Yuan, Y.C. and Gay, G. (2009) 'Exploring negative group dynamics: adversarial network, personality, and performance in project groups' *Management Communication Quarterly*, **23**: 32–62.

CHAPTER 2 WORK COMMUNICATION MODES

1 Fels, D.I. and Weiss, P.L. (2000) 'Toward determining an attention-getting device for improving video-mediated communication', *Computers in Human Behavior*, 16(2): 189–98.

2 Hsieh, Y.P. (2012) 'Online social networking skills: the social affordances approach to digital inequality', *First Monday*, 17(4), at http://firstmonday.org/ojs/index.php/fm/article/view/3893.

3 Scardamalia, M. and Bereiter, C. (2003) 'Knowledge building', In J.W. Guthrie (ed.), *Encyclopedia of Education*, New York: Macmillan, pp. 1370–3.

4 Buder, J. (2007) 'Net-based knowledge communication in groups: searching for added value', *Zeitschrift für Psychologie*, **215**(4): 209–17.

5 Ibid.

6 Clark, H.H. and Brennan, S. A. (1991) 'Grounding in communication', in L.B. Resnick, J.M. Levine and S.D. Teasley (eds),*Perspectives on Socially Shared Cognition*, Washington: APA Books.

7 Fels and Weiss, op. cit.

8 Scott, C.R. and Rains, S. (2005) 'Anonymous communication in organizations:

assessing use and appropriateness', *Management Communication Quarterly*, **19**(2): 157–97.

9 McLeod, P.L. (2011) 'Effects of anonymity and social comparison of rewards on computer-mediated group brainstorming', *Small Group Research*, **42**(4): 475–503.

10 Cho, V. and Hung, H. (2011) 'The effectiveness of short message service for communication with concerns of privacy protection and conflict avoidance', *Journal of Computer-Mediated Communication*, **16**(2): 250–70.

11 Kupritz, V.W. and Cowell, E. (2011) 'Productive management communication: online and face-to-face', *Journal of Business Communication*, **48**: 54–82.

12 Markman, K.M. (2009) '"So what shall we talk about": openings and closings in chat-based virtual meetings', *Journal of Business Communication*, **46**(1): 150–70.

13 Montero-Fleta, B., Montesinos-López, A., Pérez-Sabater, C. and Turney, E. (2009) 'Computer-mediated communication and informalization of discourse: the influence of culture and subject matter', *Journal of Pragmatics*, **41**(4): 770–9.

14 Shirani, A.I., Tafti, M.H.A. and Affisco, J.F. (1999) 'Task and technology fit: a comparison of two technologies for synchronous and asynchronous group communication', *Information & Management*, **36**(3): 139–50.

15 Barile, A.L. and Durso, F.T. (2002) 'Computer-mediated communication in collaborative writing', *Computers in Human Behavior*, **18**(2): 173–90.

16 Bucy, E.P. and Tao, C.-C. (2007) 'The mediated moderation model of interactivity', *Media Psychology*, **9**(3): 647–72.

17 Chang, H.H. and Wang, I.C. (2008) 'An investigation of user communication behavior in computer-mediated environments', *Computers in Human Behavior*, 24(5): 2336–56.

18 Klein, L.R. (2002) 'Creating virtual experiences in computer-mediated environments', *Review of Marketing Science Working Papers*, **1**(4): 2.

19 Korzenny, F. (1978) 'A theory of electronic propinquity mediated communication in organizations', *Communication Research*, **5**(1):3–24.

20 Klein, L.R. (2003) 'Creating virtual product experiences: the role of telepresence', *Journal of Interactive Marketing*, **17**(1): 41–55.

21 Altschuller, S.and Benbunan-Fich, R.(2010) 'Trust, performance, and the communication process in ad hoc decision making virtual teams', *Journal of Computer-Mediated Communication*, **16**(1): 27–47.

22 Villani, D., Repetto, C., Cipresso, P. and Riva, G. (2012) 'May I experience more presence in doing the same thing in virtual reality than in reality? An answer from a simulated job interview', *Interacting with Computers*, **24**(4): 265–72.

23 Short J., Williams E. and Christie B. (1976) *The Social Psychology of Telecommunication*, London: Wiley.

24 Anderson, A.H., Smallwood, L., Macdonald, R., Mullin, J. Fleming, A.-M. and O'Malley, C. (2000) 'Video data and video links in mediated communication: what do users value?' *International Journal of Human-Computer Studies*, **52**(1): 165–87.

25 Feaster, J.C. (2010) 'Expanding the impression management model of communication channels: an information control scale', *Journal of Computer-Mediated Communication*, **16**: 115–38.

26 Ibid.

27 Dandi, R. (2002) 'Email and direct participation in decision making: a literature review', at http//ssrn.com/abstract+1371604.

28 De Sanctis, G. and Monge, P. (1998) 'Communication processes for virtual organizations', *Journal of Computer-Mediated Communication*, 3: 0. doi: 10.1111/j.1083-6101.1998.tb00083.x internal references omitted.

29 Finholt, T. and Sproull, L. (1990) 'Electronic groups at work', *Organization Science*, **1**: 41–64.

30 Mangrum, F.G., Fairley, M.S. and Wieder, D.L. (2001) 'Informal problem solving in the technology-mediated work place', *Journal of Business Communication*, **38**: 315–36.

31 Clark and Brennan, op. cit.

32 Trevino, L.K., Lengel, R.H. and Daft, R.L. (1987) 'Media symbolism, media richness, and media choice in organizations a symbolic interactionist perspective', *Communication Research*, **14**(5): 553–74.

33 Webster, J. and Trevino, L.K. (1995) 'Rational and social theories as complementary explanations of communication media choices: two policy-capturing studies', *Academy of Management Journal*, **38**(6): 1544–72 .

34 Trevino, L.K., Webster, J. and Stein, E.W. (2000) 'Making connections: complementary influences on communication media choices, attitudes, and use', *Organization Science*, **11**(2): 163–82.

35 van den Hooff, B., Groot, J., and de Jonge, S. (2005) 'Situational influences on the use of communication technologies: a meta-analysis and exploratory study, *Journal of Business Communication*, **42**(1), 4–27.

36 Tillema, T., Dijst, M. and Schwanen, T. (2010) 'Face-to-face and electronic communications in maintaining social networks: the influence of geographical and relational distance and of information content', *New Media & Society*, **12** (6): 965–83.

37 Hee, L., Lee, A. and Law, R. (2012) 'Technology-mediated management learning in hospitality organisations', *International Journal of Hospitality Management*, **31**(2): 451–7.

38 Mason, K. and Leek, S. (2012) 'Communication practices in a business relationship: creating, relating and adapting communication artifacts through time', *Industrial Marketing Management*, **41**(2): 319–32.

39 Rizzuto, T.E. (2011) 'Age and technology innovation in the workplace: does work context matter?' *Computers in Human Behavior*, **27**(6): 1612–20.

40 Fenwick, T. (2012) 'Older professional workers and continuous learning in new capitalism', *Human Relations*, **65**: 1001–20.

41 Cruz, F. and Jamias, S.B. (2013) 'Scientists' use of social media: the case of researchers at the University of the Philippines Los Baños', *First Monday*,18(4), at http://firstmonday.org/ojs/index.php/fm/article/view/4296.

42 Baron, N.S. (2004) 'See you online: gender issues in college student use of instant messaging', *Journal of Language and Social Psychology*, **23**(4): 397–423.

43 Ramirez, A., Jr and Broneck, K. (2009) '"IM me": instant messaging as relational maintenance and everyday communication', *Journal of Social and Personal Relationships*, **26**: 291–314.

44 Ess, C. and Sudweeks, F. (2005) 'Culture and computer-mediated communication:

toward new understandings', *Journal of Computer-Mediated Communication*, **11**(1): 179–91.

45 Ibid.

46 Allwood, J. and Schroeder, R. (2000) 'Intercultural communication in a virtual environment', *Intercultural Communication*, **4**, at http://www.immi.se/inter cultural/ nr4/allwood.htm.

47 Kim, H. et al. (2007) 'Configurations of relationships in different media: FtF, email, instant messenger, mobile phone, and SMS', *Journal of Computer-Mediated Communication*, **12**(4): 1183–207.

48 Ramirez and Broneck, op. cit.

49 Cho and Hung, op. cit.

50 Ibid.

51 Straus, S.G. (1996) 'Getting a clue: the effects of communication media and information distribution on participation and performance in computer-mediated and face-to-face groups', *Small Group Research*, **27**(1): 115–42.

52 Mackenzie, L. (2010) 'Manager communication and workplace trust: understanding manager and employee perceptions in the e-world', *International Journal of Information Management*, **30**(6): 529–41.

53 Nowak, K.L., Watt, J. and Walther, J.B. (2009) 'Computer-mediated teamwork and the efficiency framework: exploring the influence of synchrony and cues on media satisfaction and outcome success', *Computers in Human Behavior*, **25**(5): 1108–19.

54 Räsänen, M., Moberg, A., Picha, M. and Borggren, C. (2010) 'Meeting at a distance: experiences of media companies in Sweden', *Technology in Society*, **32**(4): 264–73.

55 Zorn, T. E., Flanagin, A. J. and Shoham, M. D. (2011) 'Institutional and noninstitutional influences on information and communication technology adoption and use among nonprofit organizations,' *Human Communication Research*, **37**: 1–33.

56 Evolution of the networked enterprise: McKinsey Global Survey results March 2013, at www.mckinseyquarterly.com/High_Tech/Strategy_Analysis/ Evolution _of_the_networked_enterprise_McKinsey_Global_Survey_results_3073?page num=6.

57 Mitchell, J.I., Gagné, M., Beaudry, A. and Dyer, L. (2012) 'The role of perceived organizational support, distributive justice and motivation in reactions to new information technology', *Computers in Human Behavior*, **28**(2): 729–38.

58 Bruque, S., Moyano, J. and Eisenberg, J. (2009) 'Individual adaptation to IT induced change: the role of social networks', *Journal of Management Information Systems*, **25**(3): 177–206.

59 Abdul-Gader, A.H. (1996) 'Usage pattern and productivity impact of computer-mediated communication in a developing country: an exploratory study', *International Journal of Information Management*, **16**(1): 39–49.

60 Cameron, A.F. and Webster, J. (2005) 'Unintended consequences of emerging technologies: instant messaging in the workplace,' *Computers in Human Behavior*, **21**(1): 85–103.

61 Zhang, P., Li, T., Ge, R. and Yen, D.C. (2012) 'A theoretical acceptance model for computer-based communication media: nine field studies', *Computers in Human Behavior*, **28**(5): 1805–15.

62 Turner, J.W., Grube, J.A., Tinsley, C.H., Lee, C. and O'Pell, C. (2006) 'Exploring the dominant media: how does media use reflect organizational norms and affect performance?' *Journal of Business Communication*, **43**(3): 220–50.

63 Zhang et al., op. cit.

64 Fulk, J. (1993) 'Social construction of communication technology', *The Academy of Management Journal*, **36**(5): 921–50.

65 Markus, M.L. (1994) 'Electronic mail as the medium of managerial choice', *Organization Science*, **5**(4): 502–27.

66 Guo, Z., Tan, F.B., Turner, T. and Xu, H. (2010) 'Group norms, media preferences, and group meeting success: a longitudinal study', *Computers in Human Behavior*, **26**(4): 645–55.

67 Bok, H.S., Kankanhalli, A., Raman, K.S. and Sambamurthy, V. (2012) 'Revisiting media choice: a behavioral decision-making perspective', *International Journal of e-Collaboration*, **8**(3): 19–35.

68 Pazos, P., Chung, J.M. and Micari, M. (2013) 'Instant messaging as a task-support tool in information technology organizations', *Journal of Business Communication*, **50**(1): 68–86.

CHAPTER 3 SOCIAL COGNITION AND IMPRESSION FORMATION

1 Malle, B.F. and Holbrook, J. (2012) 'Is there a hierarchy of social inferences? The likelihood and speed of inferring intentionality, mind, and personality', *Journal of Personality and Social Psychology*, **102**(4): 661–84.

2 Allard-Poesi, F. (1998) 'Representations and influence processes in groups: towards a socio-cognitive perspective on cognition in organization', *Scandinavian Journal of Management*, **14**(4): 395–420.

3 Li, Qiong and Hong, Ying-Yi (2001) 'Intergroup perceptual accuracy predicts real-life intergroup interactions', *Group Processes & Intergroup Relations*, **4**: 341–54.

4 Marshall, C. and Novick, D. (1995) 'Conversational effectiveness and multi-media communications', *Information Technology and People*, **8**(1), 54–79.

5 Vignovic, J.A. and Thompson, L.F. (2010) 'Computer-mediated cross-cultural collaboration: attributing communication errors to the person versus the situation', *Journal of Applied Psychology*, **95**(2): 265–76.

6 Clark, H.H. and Krych, M. (2004) 'Speaking while monitoring addressees for understanding', *Journal of Memory and Language*, 50(1): 62–81.

7 He, Y., Ebner, N.C. and Johnson, M.K. (2011) 'What predicts the own-age bias in face recognition memory?', *Social Cognition*, 29(1): 97–109.

8 DeWall, C. N., Maner, J.K. and Rouby, D. A. (2009) 'Social exclusion and early-stage interpersonal perception: selective attention to signs of acceptance', *Journal of Personality and Social Psychology*, **96**(4): 729–74.

9 Mojzisch, A. and Schulz-Hardt, S. (2010) 'Knowing others' preferences degrades the quality of group decisions', *Journal of Personality and Social Psychology*, **98**(5): 794–808.

10 Bente, G., Rüggenberg, S. Krämer, N.C. and Eschenburg, F. (2008) 'Avatar-mediated networking: increasing social presence and interpersonal trust in net-based collaborations', *Human Communication Research*, **34**(2): 287–318.

11 Weisband, S.P. (1992) 'Group discussion and first advocacy effects in computer-mediated and face-to-face decision making groups', *Organizational Behavior and Human Decision Processes*, **53**(3): 352–80.

12 Snyder, M. and Klein, O. (2005) 'Construing and constructing others: on the reality and the generality of the behavioural confirmation scenario', *Interaction Studies*, **6**(1): 53–67.

13 Reinhard, M.-A., Sporer, S.L., Scharmach, M. and Marksteiner, T. (2011) 'Listening, not watching: situational familiarity and the ability to detect deception', *Journal of Personality and Social Psychology*, **101**(3): 467–84.

14 Elfenbein, H.A. and Eisenkraft, N. (2010) 'The relationship between displaying and perceiving non-verbal cues of affect: a meta-analysis to solve an old mystery', *Journal of Personality and Social Psychology*, **98**(2): 301–18.

15 Young, S.G. and Hugenberg, K. (2010) 'Mere social categorization modulates identification of facial expressions of emotion', *Journal of Personality and Social Psychology*, **99**(6): 964–77.

16 Cheshin, A., Rafaeli, A. and Bos, N. (2011) 'Anger and happiness in virtual teams: emotional influences of text and behavior on others' affect in the absence of non-verbal cues', *Organizational Behavior and Human Decision Processes*, **116**(1): 2–16.

17 Tesser, A. and Leone, C. (1977) 'Cognitive schemas and thought as determinants of attitude change', *Journal of Experimental Social Psychology*, **13**(4): 340–56.

18 Martinko, M.J., Harvey, P. and Dasborough, M.T. (2011) 'Attribution theory in the organizational sciences: a case of unrealized potential', *Journal of Organizational Behavior*, **32**: 144–9.

19 Bäck, E., Esaiasson, P., Gilljam, M. and Lindholm, T. (2010) 'Biased attributions regarding the origins of preferences in a group decision situation', *European Journal of Social Psychology*, **40**(2): 270–81.

20 Schaubroeck, J.M. and Shao, P. (2012) 'The role of attribution in how followers respond to the emotional expression of male and female leaders', *Leadership Quarterly*, **23**(1): 27–42.

21 Kim, H.-K. and Davis, K.E. (2009) 'What makes a difference in on-line impressions? Avatars, attribution, and cognitive processes', *Journal of Psychology and Counseling*, **1**(8): 123–33.

22 Cramton, C.D., Orvis, K.L. and Wilson, J.M. (2007) 'Situation invisibility and attribution in distributed collaborations', *Journal of Management*, **33**(4): 525–46.

23 Boucher, E.M., Hancock, J.T. and Dunham, P.J. (2008) 'Interpersonal sensitivity in computer-mediated and face-to-face conversations', *Media Psychology*, **11**(2): 235–58.

24 Johri, A. (2012) 'From a distance: impression formation and impression accuracy among geographically distributed coworkers', *Computers in Human Behavior*, **28**(6): 1997–2444.

25 Sanford, N. (1970) *Issues in Personality Theory*, San Francisco: Jossey-Bass.

26 Orehek, E., Dechesnel, M., Fishbach, A., Kruglanski, A.W. and Chun, W.Y. (2010) 'On the inferential epistemics of trait centrality in impression formation', *European Journal of Social Psychology*, **40**(7): 1120–35.

27 Tsai, W.-T., Huang, T.C. and Yu, H.H. (2012) 'Investigating the unique

predictability and boundary conditions of applicant physical attractiveness and non-verbal behaviours on interviewer evaluations in job interviews', *Journal of Occupational and Organizational Psychology*, **85**(1): 60–79.

28 Sansom-Daly, U. and Forgas, J.P. (2010) 'Do blurred faces magnify priming effects? The interactive effects of perceptual fluency and priming on impression formation', *Social Cognition*, **28**(5): 630–40.

29 Douglas, K.M. and Sutton, R.M. (2010) 'By their words ye shall know them: language abstraction and the likeability of describers', *European Journal of Social Psychology*, **40**(2): 366–74.

30 Bolino, M.C., Varela, J.A., Bande, B. and Turnley, W.H. (2006) 'The impact of impression-management tactics on supervisor ratings of organizational citizenship behavior', *Journal of Organizational Behavior*, **27**(3): 281–97.

31 Rule, N. O., Ambady, N., Adams, R. B. Jr, Ozono, H., Nakashima, S., Yoshikawa, S., and Watabe, M. (2010) 'Polling the face: prediction and consensus across cultures', *Journal of Personality and Social Psychology*, **98**(1): 1.

32 Byron, K. and Baldridge, D.C. (2007) 'Email recipients' impressions of senders' likability: the interactive effect of non-verbal cues and recipients' personality, *Journal of Business Communication*, **44**: 137–60.

33 Liu, Y., Ginther, D. and Zelhart, P. (2002) 'An exploratory study of the effects of frequency and duration of messaging on impression development in computer-mediated communication', *Social Science Computer Review*, **20**(1): 73–80.

34 Kalman, Y.M., Scissors, L.E., Gill, A.J. and Gergle, D. (2013) 'Online chronemics convey social information', *Computers in Human Behavior*, **29**(3):1260–9.

35 Hancock, J.T. and Dunham, P.J. (2013) 'Impression formation in computer-mediated communication', *Communication Research*, **28**(3): 325–47.

36 Okdie, B.M., Guadagno, R.E., Bernieri, F.J., Geers, A.L. and Mclarney-Vesotski, A.M. (2011) 'Getting to know you: face-to-face vs online interactions', *Computers in Human Behavior*, **27**(1): 153–9.

37 Tanis, M. and Postmes, T. (2007) 'Two faces of anonymity: paradoxical effects of cues to identity in CMC', *Computers in Human Behavior*, **23**(2): 955–70.

38 DeAndrea, D.C. and Walther, J.B. (2011) 'Attributions for inconsistencies between online and offline self-presentations', *Communication Research*, 38: 805–25.

39 Sproull, L. and Kiesler S. (1986) 'Reducing social context cues: electronic mail in organizational communication', *Management Science*, **32**(11): 1492–512.

40 Walther, J.B. Anderson, J.F., and Park, D.W. (1994) 'Interpersonal effects in computer-mediated interaction: a meta-analysis of social and anti-social communication', *Communication Research*, **21**: 460–87.

41 Rouse, S.V. and Haas, H.A. (2003) 'Exploring the accuracies and inaccuracies of personality perception following internet-mediated communication', *Journal of Research in Personality*, **37**(5): 446–67.

42 Johri, op. cit.

43 Hewstone, M. and H. Giles (1986) 'Social groups and social stereotypes in intergroup communication: review and model of intergroup communication breakdown', in W.B. Gudykunst (ed.) *Intergroup Communication*, London: Edward Arnold; Giles, H. (1977) *Language, Ethnicity and Intergroup Relations*, London: Academic Press.

44 Crump, S.A., Hamilton, D.L., Sherman, S.J., Lickel, B. and Thakkar, V. (2012)

'Group entitativity and similarity: their differing patterns in perceptions of groups', *European Journal of Social Psychology*, **40**(7): 1212–30.

45 Sherman, J. W. (1996) 'Development of mental representations of stereotypes', *Journal of Personality and Social Psychology*, 70: 1126–41.

46 Bandura, A. (1986) 'The explanatory and predictive scope of self-efficacy theory', *Journal of Social and Clinical Psychology*, **4**(3): 359–73.

47 Woodcock, A., Hernandez, P.R., Estrada, M. and Schultz, P. W. (2012) 'The consequences of chronic stereotype threat: domain disidentification and abandonment', *Journal of Personality and Social Psychology*, **103**(4): 635–46.

48 Krings, F., Sczesny, S. and Kluge, A. (2011) 'Stereotypical inferences as mediators of age discrimination: the role of competence and warmth', *British Journal of Management*, **22**: 187–201.

49 Dotsch, R., Wigboldus, D.H.J. and van Knippenberg, A. (2011) 'Biased allocation of faces to social categories', *Journal of Personality and Social Psychology*, **100**(6): 999–1014.

50 Best, D.L. and Williams, J.E. (1994) 'Masculinity/femininity in the self and ideal self-descriptions of university students in fourteen countries', in A.M. Bouvy, F.J.R. van de Vijver, P. Boski and P. Schmitz (eds) *Journeys into Cross-Cultural Psychology*, Amsterdam: Swets & Zeitlinger.

51 Chiu, W.C.K., Chan, A.W., Snape, E. and Redman, T. (2001) 'Age stereotypes and discriminatory attitudes towards older workers: an East–West comparison', *Human Relations*, **54**(5): 629–61.

52 Epley, N. and Kruger, J. (2005) 'When what you type isn't what they read: the perseverance of stereotypes and expectancies over email', *Journal of Experimental Social Psychology*, **41**(4): 414–22

53 Walther, J., DeAndrea, D., Tong, S., Kim, J. and Spottswood, E.L. (2009) 'Computer-mediated communication versus vocal communication in the amelioration of stereotypes: a replication with three theoretical models', Paper presented at the annual meeting of the NCA 95th Annual Convention, Chicago Hilton & Towers, Chicago, IL, at http://citation.allacademic.com/meta/p365148_index.html.

54 Tavakoli, M., Hatami, J. and Thorngate, W. (2010) 'Changing stereotypes in Iran and Canada using computer mediated communication', at www.immi.se/intercultural/nr23/tavakoli.htm (accessed14 December 2013).

55 Guéguen, N. (2008) 'Helping on the web: ethnic stereotypes and computer-mediated communication', *Research Journal of Social Sciences*, **3**: 1–3.

56 Leach, C.W., Ellemers, N. and Barreto, M. (2007) 'Group virtue: the importance of morality (vs. competence and sociability) in the positive evaluation of in-groups', *Journal of Personality and Social Psychology*, **93**: 234–49; Brambilla, M., Sacchi, S., Rusconi, P., Cherubini, P. and Yzerbyt, V.Y. (2011) 'You want to give a good impression? Be honest! Moral traits dominate group impression formation', *British Journal of Social Psychology*, **50**:149–66.

57 Wojciske, B., Bazinska, R. and Jaworski, M. (1998) 'On the dominance of moral categories in impression formation', *Personality and Social Psychology Bulletin*, **24**: 1251–63.

58 See, K.E. (2009) 'Reactions to decisions with uncertain consequences: reliance on perceived fairness versus predicted outcomes depends on knowledge', *Journal of Personality and Social Psychology*, **96**(1): 104–18.

59 Delton, A.W., Cosmides, L., Guemo, M., Robertson, T.E. and Tooby, J. (2012) 'The psychosemantics of free riding: dissecting the architecture of a moral concept', *Journal of Personality and Social Psychology*, **102**(6): 1252–70.

60 Straus, S.G. and Miles, J.A. (1998) 'The effects of videoconference, telephone, and face-to-face media on interviewer and applicant judgments in employment interviews', Unpublished paper, Carnegie Mellon University, cited in DeSanctis, G. and Monge, P. (1998) 'Communication processes for virtual organizations', *Journal of Computer Mediated Communication*, **3**(4), at http://onlinelibrary. wiley.com/doi/10.1111/j.1083-6101.1998.tb00083.x/abstract.

61 Goffman, E. (1972) *Interaction Ritual: Essays on Face-to-Face Behaviour*, Harmondsworth, Middlesex: Penguin Books.

62 Blair, J.P., Levine, T.R. and Shaw, A.S. (2010) 'Content in context improves deception detection accuracy', *Human Communication Research*, **36**: 423–42.

63 Van Swol, L. (2009) 'The effects of confidence and advisor motives on advice utilization', *Communication Research*, **36**(6): 857–73.

64 Levine, T.R., Serota, K. B., Shulman, H., Clare, D. D., Park, H. S., Shaw, A. S., Shim, J. C. and Lee, J. H. (2011) 'Sender demeanor: individual differences in sender believability have a powerful impact on deception detection judgments', *Human Communication Research*, **37**: 377–403.

65 Green, M.C. and Donahue, J.K. (2011) 'Persistence of belief change in the face of deception: the effect of factual stories revealed to be false', *Media Psychology*, **14**(3): 312–31.

66 Levine, T.R., Shaw, A. and Shulman, H.C. (2010) 'Increasing deception detection accuracy with strategic questioning,' *Human Communication Research*, **36**: 216–31.

67 Blair et al., op. cit.

68 Giordano, G.A., Stoner, J.S., Brouer, R.L. and George, J.F. (2007) 'The influences of deception and computer-mediation on dyadic negotiations' *Journal of Computer-mediated Communication*, **12**(2): 362–83.

69 Zhou, L., Twitchell, D.P., Qin, T., Burgoon, J.K. and Nunamaker, J.F. Jr (2003) 'An exploratory study into deception detection in text-based computer-mediated communication', System Sciences, Proceedings of the 36th Annual Hawaii International Conference on IEEE.

70 Hancock, J.T., Curry, L. E., Goorha, S. and Woodworth, M. (2007) 'On lying and being lied to: a linguistic analysis of deception in computer-mediated communication', *Discourse Processes*, **45**(1): 1–23.

71 Zhou et al., op. cit.

72 Van Swol, L.M., Braun, M.T. and Kolb, M.R. (2012) 'Deception, detection, demeanor, and truth bias in face-to-face and computer-mediated communication', *Communication Research*, **39**(2): 217–38.

73 Donath, J.S. (1999) 'Identity and deception in the virtual community', *Communities in Cyberspace*, **1996**: 29–59.

74 Walther, J.B, Ven der Heide, B., Hamel, L.M. and Shulman, H.C. (2009) 'Self-generated versus other-generated statements and impressions in computer-mediated communication: a test of warranting theory using Facebook', *Communication Research*, **36**(2): 229–53.

75 Rouse and Haas, op. cit.

76 Zitek, E.M. and Tiedens, L.Z. (2012) 'The fluency of social hierarchy: the ease

with which hierarchical relationships are seen, remembered, learned, and liked', *Journal of Personality and Social Psychology*, **102**(1): 98–115.

77 Moshinsky, A. and Bar-Hillel, M. (2010) 'Loss aversion and status quo label bias', *Social Cognition*, **28**(2): 191–204.

78 Jones, D.A. (2009) 'Getting even with one's supervisor and one's organization: relationships among types of injustice, desires for revenge, and counterproductive work behaviors', *Journal of Organizational Behavior*, **30**(4): 525–42.

79 Jones, D.A. and Martens, M.L. (2009) 'The mediating role of overall fairness and the moderating role of trust certainty in justice–criteria relationships: the formation and use of fairness heuristics in the workplace', *Journal of Organizational Behavior*, **30**(8): 1025–51.

80 Ham, J., van den Bos, K. and van Doorn, E.A. (2009) 'Lady Justice thinks unconsciously: unconscious thought can lead to more accurate justice judgments', *Social Cognition*, **27**(4): 509–21.

81 Subrahmaniam T. and Alge, B.J. (2006) 'Reactions to unfair events in computer-mediated groups: a test of uncertainty management theory', *Organizational Behavior and Human Decision Processes*, **100**(1): 1–20.

82 Greenberg, J., Ashton-James, C.E. and Ashkanasy, N.M. (2007) 'Social comparison processes in organizations', *Organizational Behavior and Human Decision Processes*, **102**(1): 22–41.

83 Tyler, J.M. and Feldman, R.S. (2005) 'Deflecting threat to one's image: dissembling personal information as a self-presentation strategy', *Basic and Applied Social Psychology*, 27(4): 371–8.

84 Brown, D.G., Ferris, D.L., Heller, D. and Keeping, L.M. (2007) 'Antecedents and consequences of the frequency of upward and downward social comparisons at work', *Organizational Behavior and Human Decision Processes*, **102**(1): 59–75.

85 Dunn, J., Ruedy, N.E. and Schweitzer, M.E. (2012) 'It hurts both ways: how social comparisons harm affective and cognitive trust', *Organizational Behavior and Human Decision Processes*, 117(1): 2–14.

86 Greenberg et al., op. cit.

CHAPTER 4 CONTRIBUTING TO COMMUNICATION, SELF-PRESENTATION AND IMPRESSION MANAGEMENT

1 Mallon, R. and Oppenheim, C. (2002) 'Style used in electronic mail', *Aslib Proceedings*, **54**(1): 8–22.

2 Attrill, A. and Jalil, R. (2011) 'Revealing only the superficial me: exploring categorical self-disclosure online', *Computers in Human Behavior*, **27**(6): 1634–42.

3 Nguyen, M., Yu S.B. and Campbell, A. (2012) 'Comparing online and offline self-disclosure: a systematic review', *Cyberpsychology, Behavior, and Social Networking*, **15**(2): 103–11.

4 Kock, N. (2007) 'Media naturalness and compensatory encoding: the burden of electronic media obstacles is on senders', *Decision Support Systems*, **44**(1): 175–87.

5 Tu, C.H. (2000) 'On-line learning migration: from social learning theory to social presence theory in a CMC environment', *Journal of Network and Computer Applications*, **23**(1): 27–37.

6 Clark, H.H., and Krych, M.A. (2004) 'Speaking while monitoring addressees for understanding', *Journal of Memory and Language*, **50**(1): 62–81.

7 Kruger, J., Epley, N., Parker, J. and Ng, Z.W. (2005) 'Egocentrism over email: can we communicate as well as we think?' *Journal of Personality and Social Psychology*, **89**(6): 925.

8 Morand, D.A. and Ocker, R.J. (2003) 'Politeness theory and computer-mediated communication: a sociolinguistic approach to analyzing relational messages', Proceedings of the 36th Hawaii International Conference on System Sciences, at www.hicss.hawaii.edu/HICSS36/HICSSpapers/CLDGS02.pdf.

9 Siegel, J., Dubrovsky, V., Kiesler, S. and McGuire, T.W. (1986) 'Group processes in computer-mediated communication', *Organizational Behavior and Human Decision Processes*, **37**(2): 157–87.

10 Hiltz, S.R., Turoff, M. and Johnson, K. (1989) 'Experiments in group decision making, 3: disinhibition, deindividuation, and group process in pen name and real name computer conferences', *Decision Support Systems*, **2**: 217–32.

11 Hastings, S.O. and Payne, H.J. (2013) 'Expressions of dissent in email: qualitative insights into uses and meanings of organizational dissent', *Journal of Business Communication*, **50**(3): 309–31.

12 Riordan, M.A. and Kreuz, R.J. (2010) 'Cues in computer-mediated communication: a corpus analysis', *Computers in Human Behavior*, **26**(6): 1806–17.

13 Ibid.

14 Balvin, N. and Tyler, C. (2006) 'Emotions in cyberspace: the advantages and disadvantages of online communication', *Organisational Psychology*, at http://ssrn.com/abstract=1027510.

15 Searle J. (1969) *Speech Acts: An Essay in the Philosophy of Language*, Cambridge, UK: Cambridge University Press.

16 Cohen, W.W., Carvalho, V.R. and Mitchell, T.M. (2004) 'Learning to classify email into Speech Acts', EMNLP working paper of the Center for Automated Learning & Discovery, Carnegie Mellon University, at www.aclweb.org/anthology/W/W04/W04-3240.pdf.

17 Clark and Krych, op. cit.

18 Atifi, H., Mandelcwajg, S. and Marcoccia, M. (2011) 'The co-operative principle and computer-mediated communication: the maxim of quantity in newsgroup discussions', *Language Sciences*, **33**(2): 330–40.

19 Gouldner, A.M. (1960) 'The norm of reciprocity', *American Sociological Review*, **25**(2): 161–78.

20 Jiang, L.C., Bazarova, N.N. and Hancock, J.T. (2013) 'From perception to behavior disclosure reciprocity and the intensification of intimacy in computer-mediated communication', *Communication Research*, **40**(1): 125–43.

21 Molm, L.D. (2010) 'The structure of reciprocity', *Social Psychology Quarterly*, **73**: 119–31.

22 Pelaprat, E. and Brown, B. (2012) 'Reciprocity: understanding online social relations', *First Monday*, **17**(10), at www.firstmonday.dk/ojs/index.php/fm/article/view/3324.

23 Zuckerman, M., DePaulo, B.M. and Rosenthal, R. (1981) 'Verbal and non-verbal communication of deception', *Advances in Experimental Social Psychology*, **14**(1): 59.

24 Buller, D.B., Burgoon, J.K., Buslig, A. and Roiger, J. (1996) 'Testing interpersonal deception theory: the language of interpersonal deception', *Communication Theory*, **6**(3): 268–89.

25 Van Swol, L. (2009) 'The effects of confidence and advisor motives on advice utilization', *Communication Research*, **36**(6): 857–73.

26 Lewis, C.C. and George, J.F. (2008) 'Cross-cultural deception in social networking sites and face-to-face communication', *Computers in Human Behavior*, **24**(6): 2945–64.

27 Hooi, R. and Cho, H. (2013) 'Deception in avatar-mediated virtual environments', *Computers in Human Behavior*, **29**(1): 276

28 Naquin, C.E., Kurtzberg, T.R. and Belkin, L.Y. (2010) 'The finer points of lying online: email versus pen and paper', *Journal of Applied Psychology*, **95**(2): 387–94.

29 Based on Silverman, D. (2009) 'Four tips for writing better email', *Harvard Business Review* blog.

30 Leary, M.R. (1995) *Self-presentation: Impression Management and Interpersonal Behavior*, social psychology series, Madison, WI: Brown & Benchmark Publishers.

31 Paulhus, D.L., Graf, P. and Van Selst, M. (1989) 'Attentional load increases the positivity of self-presentation', *Social Cognition*, **7**(4): 389–400.

32 de Vries, R.E., Bakker-Pieper, A., Siberg, R.A., van Gameren, K. and Vlug, M. (2009) 'The content and dimensionality of communication styles', *Communication Research*, **36**(2): 178–206.

33 Ibid.

34 McCroskey, J.C., Daly, J.A., Martin, M.M. and Beatty, M.J. (eds), *Communication and Personality: Trait Perspectives*, Cresskill, NJ: Hampton.

35 Postmes, T., Spears, R. and Lea, M. (1998) 'Breaching or building social boundaries? SIDE effects of computer-mediated communication', *Communication Research*, **25**(6): 689–715.

36 de Vries et al., op. cit.

37 Gains, J. (1999) 'Electronic mail: a new style of communication or just a new medium? An investigation into the text features of email', *English for Specific Purposes*, **18**(1): 81–101.

38 Goffman, E. (1959) *The Presentation of Self in Everyday Life*, Garden City, NY: Doubleday.

39 Tracy, K. (1990) 'The many faces of facework', in H. Giles and W.P. Robinson (eds), *Handbook of Language and Social Psychology*, New York: Chichester, pp. 209–26.

40 O'Sullivan, B. (2000) 'What you don't know won't hurt *me*', *Human Communication Research*, **26**: 403–31.

41 Ibid.

42 Feaster, J.C. (2010) 'Expanding the impression management model of communication channels: an information control scale', *Journal of Computer-Mediated Communication*, **16**: 115–38.

43 Sliter, M., Sliter, K. and Jex, S. (2012) 'The employee as a punching bag: the effect of multiple sources of incivility on employee withdrawal behavior and sales performance', *Journal of Organizational Behavior*, **33**: 121–39.

44 Park, H.S. (2008) 'The effects of shared cognition on group satisfaction and performance: politeness and efficiency in group interaction', *Communication Research*, **351**: 88–108.

45 Liberman, S.N. and Trope, Y. (2010) 'Politeness and psychological distance: a construal level perspective', *Journal of Personality and Social Psychology*, **98**(2): 268–80.

46 Locher, M.A. and Watts, R. (2005) 'Politeness theory and relational work', *Journal of Politeness Research, Language, Behaviour, Culture*, **1**(1): 9–33.

47 Morand and Ocker, op. cit.

48 Ibid.

49 Graham, S.L. (2007) 'Disagreeing to agree: conflict, (im)politeness and identity in a computer-mediated community', *Journal of Pragmatics*, **39**(4): 742–59.

50 Morand and Ocker, op. cit.

51 Fragale, A.R., Sumanth, J.J., Tiedens, L.Z. and Northcraft, G.B. (2013) 'Appeasing equals: lateral deference in organizational communication', *Administrative Science Quarterly*, **57**(3): 373–406.

52 Abel, M. (1990) 'Experiences in an exploratory distributed organization', in J. Galegher, R.E. Kraut and C. Egido (eds), *Intellectual Teamwork: Social and Technological Foundations of Cooperative Work*, Hillsdale, NJ: Lawrence Erlbaum Associates.

53 Goffman, op. cit.

54 Leary, M.R. and Kowalski, R.L. (1990) 'Impression management: a literature review and two-component model', *Psychological Bulletin*, **107**(1): 34.

55 Tal-Or, N. and Drukman, D. (2010) 'Third-person perception as an impression management tactic', *Media Psychology*, **13**(3): 301–22.

56 Higgins, C.A. and Judge, T.A. (2004) 'The effect of applicant influence tactics on recruiter perceptions of fit and hiring recommendations: a field study', *Journal of Applied Psychology*, **89**(4): 622.

57 Tyler, J.M. and Rosier, J.G. (2009) 'Examining self-presentation as a motivational explanation for comparative optimism', *Journal of Personality and Social Psychology*, **97**(4): 716–27.

58 Tyler, J.M. and Feldman, R.S. (2005) 'Deflecting threat to one's image: dissembling personal information as a self-presentation strategy', *Basic and Applied Social Psychology*, **27**(4): 371–8.

59 Bergsieker, H.B., Shelton, J.N and Richeson, J.A. (2010) 'To be liked versus respected: divergent goals in interracial interactions', *Journal of Personality and Social Psychology*, **99**(2): 248–64.

60 See www.trystylewriter.com/writing-examples/business-email-example.html.

61 Witt, P.L. (2004) 'An initial examination of observed verbal immediacy and participants' opinions of communication effectiveness in online group interaction', *Journal of Online Behavior*, 2 (1) at www.behavior.net/JOB/v2n1/witt.html.

62 Fairhurst, G.T. (1993) 'Echoes of the vision: when the rest of the organization talks total quality', *Management Communication Quarterly*, **6**(4): 331–71.

63 Birnholtz, J., Dixon, G. and Hancock, J. (2012) 'Distance, ambiguity and appropriation: structures affording impression management in a collocated organization', *Computers in Human Behavior*, **28**(3): 1028–35.

CHAPTER 5 INTERACTION

1 Ellis, D.G. (2011)'Social ties and international entrepreneurship: opportunities and constraints affecting firm internatonalization', *Journal of International Business Studies*, **42**: 99-127..

2 Acton, G.S. and Revelle, W. (1998) 'Interpersonal theory and circumplex structure', manuscript in preparation, Northwestern University, Evanston, IL; Leary, T. (1957) *Interpersonal Diagnosis of Personality*, New York: Ronald; Sullivan, H.S. (1953) *The Interpersonal Theory of Psychiatry*, New York: Norton.

3 Barros, B. and Verdejo, M.F. (2000) 'Analysing student interaction processes in order to improve collaboration: the DEGREE approach', *International Journal of Artificial Intelligence in Education*, **11**(3): 221–41.

4 Eklundh, K.S. (1987) 'Explicit and implicit feedback in computer-mediated communication', *Computer Networks and ISDN Systems*, **14**(2–5): 147–53.

5 Ibid.

6 Sacks, H., Schegloff, E.A. and Jefferson, G. (1974) 'A simplest systematics for the organization of turn-taking for conversation', *Language*, **4**: 696–735

7 Gibson, D.R. (2010) 'Marking the turn: obligation, engagement, and alienation in group discussions', *Social Psychology Quarterly*, **73**: 132–51.

8 Doherty-Sneddon, G., Anderson, A., O'Malley, C., Langton, S., Garrod, S. and Bruce, V. (1997) 'Face-to-face and video-mediated communication: a comparison of dialogue structure and task performance', *Journal of Experimental Psychology: Applied*, **3**(2): 105–25.

9 Halbe, D. (2012) '"Who's there?" Differences in the features of telephone and face-to-face conferences', *Journal of Business Communication*, **49**: 48–73.

10 McKinlay, A., Procter, R., Masting, O., Woodburn, R. and Arnott, J. (1994) 'Studies of turn-taking in computer-mediated communications', *Interacting with Computers*, **6**(2): 151–71.

11 Berry, G.R. (2011) 'Enhancing effectiveness on virtual teams: understanding why traditional team skills are insufficient', *Journal of Business Communication*, **48**: 186–206.

12 Vroman, K. and Kovachich, J. (2002) 'Computer-mediated interdisciplinary teams: theory and reality', *Journal of Interprofessional Care*, **16**: 159–70.

13 Berry, op. cit.

14 Argyle, M., Salter, V., Nicholson, N.C., Williams M. and Burgess P. (1970) 'The communication of inferior and superior attitudes by verbal and non-verbal signals', *British Journal of the Society of Clinical Psychology*, **9**: 222–31.

15 Han, Z.L. (1999) 'Grounding and information communication in intercultural and intracultural dyadic discourse', *Discourse Processes*, **28**(3): 195–221.

16 Wellmon, T.A. (1988) 'Conceptualizing organizational communication competence: a rules-based perspective', *Management Communication Quarterly*, **1**(4): 515–34.

17 Zhong, M. (1997) 'Report on perceived intercultural communication competence of Chinese and Americans', unpublished MA dissertation, Kent State University.

18 Wellmon, op. cit.

19 Madlock, P.E. (2008) 'The link between leadership style, communicator competence, and employee satisfaction', *Journal of Business Communication*, **45**: 61–78.

20 Downing, J.R. (2011) 'Linking communication competence with call center agents' sales effectiveness', *Journal of Business Communication*, **48**: 409–25.
21 Ramsay, S., Gallois, C. and Callan, V.J. (1997) 'Social rules and attributions in the personnel selection interview', *Journal of Occupational and Organizational Psychology*, **70**: 189–203.
22 Lockwood, J. (2012) 'Are we getting the right people for the job? A Study of English language recruitment assessment practices in the business processing outsourcing sector: India and the Philippines', *Journal of Business Communication*, **49**: 107–27.
23 Hwang, Y. (2011) 'Is communication competence still good for interpersonal media?', *Computers in Human Behavior*, **27**(2): 924–34.
24 Waldeck, J., Durante, C. and Helmuth, B. (2012) 'Communication in a changing world: contemporary perspectives on business communication competence', *Education for Business*, **87**(4): 230–40.
25 Ibid.
26 Voakes, P.S. (1997) 'Social influences on journalists' decision making in ethical situations', *Journal of Mass Media Ethics*,**12**(1): 18–35.
27 Lammers, J. and Stapel, D.A. (2009) 'How power influences moral thinking', *Journal of Personality and Social Psychology*, **97**(2): 279–89.
28 Leonard, L.N.K., Cronan, T.P. and Kreie, J. (2004) 'What influences IT ethical behavior intentions: planned behavior, reasoned action, perceived importance, or individual characteristics?', *Information Management*, **42**(1): 143–58.
29 Halbe, op. cit.
30 Jung, I. (2009) 'Ethical judgments and behaviors: applying a multidimensional ethics scale to measuring ICT ethics of college students', *Computers & Education*, **53**(3): 940–9; Leonard, L.N.K. and Haines, R. (2007) 'Computer-mediated group influence on ethical behavior', *Computers in Human Behavior*, **23**(5): 2302–20.
31 Karim, N.S.A., Zamzuri, N.H.A. and Nor, Y.M. (2009) 'Exploring the relationships between internet ethics in university students and the Big Five of Personality', *Computers & Education*, **53**(1): 86–93.
32 Robbins, S. (1990) *Training in Interpersonal Skills*, Englewood Cliffs, NJ: Prentice-Hall.
33 Lee, J. (2002) 'I think therefore IM', *New York Times*, 19 September.
34 Carlo, J.L. and Yoo, Y. (2007) '"How may I help you?" Politeness in computer-mediated and face-to-face library reference transactions', *Information and Organization*, **17**(4): 193–231.
35 Morand, D.A. and Ocker, R.J. (2003) 'Politeness theory and computer-mediated communication: a sociolinguistic approach to analyzing relational messages', *Proceedings of the 36th Hawaii International Conference on System Sciences*. at www.hicss.hawaii.edu/HICSS36/HICSSpapers/CLDGS02.pdf.
36 Clark, H. H., and Brennan, S. A. (1991) 'Grounding in communication', in L.B. Resnick, J.M. Levine and S.D. Teasley (eds), *Perspectives on Socially Shared Cognition*. Washington: APA Books.
37 Ibid.
38 Zack, M.H., and McKenney, J.L. (1995) 'Social context and interaction in ongoing computer-supported management groups', *Organization Science*, **6**(4): 394–422. .
39 Hancock, J.T. and Dunham, P.J. (2001) 'Language use in computer-mediated

communication: the role of coordination devices', *Discourse Processes*, **31**(1): 91–110.

40 Giles, H. (1977) *Language, Ethnicity and Intergroup Relations*, London: Academic Press.

41 Ireland, M.E. and Pennebaker, J.W. (2010) 'Language style matching in writing: synchrony in essays, correspondence, and poetry', *Journal of Personality and Social Psychology*, **99**(3): 549.

42 Taylor, P.J. and Thomas, S. (2008) 'Linguistic style matching and negotiation outcome', *Negotiation and Conflict Management Research*, **1**(3): 263–81.

43 Gasiorek, J. and Giles, H. (2012) 'Effects of inferred motive on evaluations of nonaccommodative communication', *Human Communication Research*, **38**: 309–331.

44 Rogerson-Revell, P. (2010) '"Can you spell that for us nonnative speakers?" Accommodation strategies in international business meetings', *Journal of Business Communication*, **47**(4): 432–54.

45 Sweeney, E. and Hua, Z. (2010) 'Do native speakers of English know how to accommodate their communication strategies toward nonnative speakers of English?', *Journal of Business Communication*, **47**(4): 477–504.

46 Postmes, T., Spears, R. and Lea, M. (2000) 'The formation of group norms in computer-mediated communication', *Human Communication Research*, **26**(3): 341–71.

47 Riordan, M.A., Markman, K.M. and Stewart, C.O. (2013) 'Communication accommodation in instant messaging: an examination of temporal convergence', *Journal of Language and Social Psychology*, **32**(1): 84–95.

48 Campbell, J., Cothren, D. and Burg, A. (2010) 'The perpetuation of entrained behavior during computer-mediated communication', *Social Influence*, **5**(1): 59–73.

49 Berger, C.R. and Calabrese, R.J. (1975) 'Some explorations in initial interaction and beyond: toward a developmental theory of interpersonal communication', *Human Communication Research*, **1**(2): 99–112.

50 Tidwell, L.C. and Walther, J.B. (2002) 'Computer-mediated communication effects on disclosure, impressions and interpersonal evaluations: getting to know one another a bit at a time', *Human Communication Research*, **28**(3): 317–48.

51 O'Malley, C., Langton, S., Anderson, A., Doherty-Sneddon, G. and Bruce, V. (1996) 'Comparison of face-to-face and video-mediated interaction', *Interacting with Computers*, **8**(2): 177–92.

52 Tidwell and Walther, op. cit.

53 Palomares, N.A. (2009) 'Did you see it coming? Effects of the specificity and efficiency of goal pursuit on the accuracy and onset of goal detection in social interaction, *Communication Research*, **36**: 475–509.

54 Krieger, J.L. (2005) 'Shared mindfulness in cockpit crisis situations: an exploratory analysis', *The Journal of Business Communication*, **42**(2):135–67.

55 Ibid.

56 Sherif, M. (1935) 'A study of some social factors in perception', *Archives of Psychology*, **187**(40).

57 Levine, J.M., Higgins, E.T. and Choi, H.-S. (2000) 'Development of strategic

norms in groups', *Organizational Behavior and Human Decision Processes*, **82**(1): 88–101.

58 Hausmann, L.R., Levine, J.M. and Higgins, E.T. (2008) 'Communication and group perception: extending the "saying is believing" effect', *Group Processes & Intergroup Relations*, **11**(4): 539–54.

59 Kopietz, R., Hellmann, J.H., Higgins, E.T. and Echterhoff, G. (2010) 'Shared-reality effects on memory: communicating to fulfill epistemic needs', *Social Cognition*, 28(3): 353–78.

60 Sinclair, S., Huntsinger, J., Skorinko, J. and Hardin, C.D. (2005) 'Social tuning of the self: consequences for the self-evaluations of stereotype targets', *Journal of Personality and Social Psychology*, **89**(2): 160–75.

61 Arasaratnam, L.A. and Doerfel, M.L. (2005) 'Intercultural communication competence: identifying key components from multicultural perspectives', *International Journal of Intercultural Relations*, **29**(2): 137–63.

62 Olaniran, B.A. (1994) 'Group performance in computer-mediated and face-to-face communication media', *Management Communication Quarterly*, **7**(3): 256–81.

63 Bordia, P. (1997) 'Face-to-face versus computer-mediated communication: a synthesis of the experimental literature', *Journal of Business Communication*, **34**(1): 99–118.

64 Newlands, A., Anderson, A.H. and Mullin, J. (2003) 'Adapting communicative strategies to computer-mediated communication: an analysis of task performance and dialogue structure', *Applied Cognitive Psychology*, **17**(30): 325–48.

65 Dixon, K.R. and Panteli, N. (2010) 'From virtual teams to virtuality in teams', *Human Relations*, **63**(8): 1177–97.

66 Rettie, R. (2009) 'Mobile phone communication: extending Goffman to mediated interaction', *Sociology*, **43**(3): 421–38.

67 Smith, B. (2003) 'The use of communication strategies in computer-mediated communication', *System*, **31**(1): 29–53.

68 St. Amant, K. (2002) 'When cultures and computers collide: rethinking computer-mediated communication according to international and intercultural communication expectations', *Journal of Business and Technical Communication*, **16**(2): 196–214.

69 Pflug, J. (2011) 'Contextuality and computer-mediated communication: a cross-cultural comparison', *Computers in Human Behavior*, **27**(1): 131–7.

CHAPTER 6 DEMOGRAPHY, CULTURE, SITUATION AND MODE AS INFLUENCES ON COMMUNICATION

1 Anant, Hardeep Singh, 'Interpersonal communication: a fresh look', 8 December 2009, at http://ssrn.com/abstract=1520394 or http://dx.doi.org/10.2139/ssrn.1520394.

2 Hogg, M.A. and Abrams, D. (1988) *Social Identifications*, London: Routledge.

3 Schienle, A., Schafer, A., Stark, R., Walter, B. and Vaitl, D. (2005) 'Gender differences in the processing of disgust- and fear-inducing pictures: an fMRI study', *Neuroreport*, **16**(3): 277–80.

4 Sasson, N.J., Pinkham, A.E., Richard, J., Hughett, P., Gur, R.E. and Gur, R.C. (2010) 'Controlling for response biases clarifies sex and age differences in facial affect recognition', *Journal of Non-verbal Behavior*, **34**(4): 207–21.

5 Sherman, R.A., Nave, C.S. and Funder, D.C. (2010) 'Situational similarity and personality predict behavioral consistency', *Journal of Personality and Social Psychology*, **99**(2): 330.

6 Eagly, A.H. and Karau, S.J. (2002) 'Role congruity theory of prejudice toward female leaders', *Psychological Review*, **109**: 573–98.

7 Foschi, M. (1996) 'Double standards in the evaluation of men and women', *Social Psychology Quarterly*, **59**: 237–54.

8 Canary, D.J. and, K. (eds) (1998) *Sex Differences and Similarities in Communication: Critical Essays and Empirical Investigations of Sex and Gender in Interaction*, Mahwah, NJ: Lawrence Erlbaum Associates.

9 Vrugt, A. and Van Eechoud, M. (2002) 'Smiling and self-presentation of men and women for job photographs', *European Journal of Social Psychology*, **32**(3): 419–31.

10 Wolfinger, N.H. and Rabow, A. (1997) 'The different voices of gender: social recognition', *Current Research in Social Psychology*, **2**(6): 50–65.

11 Timmerman, L.M. (2002) 'Comparing the production of power in language on the basis of sex', In M. Allen, R.W. Preiss, B.M. Gayle and N.M. Burrell (eds), *Interpersonal Communication Research: Advances Through Meta-analysis*, Mahwah, NJ: Lawrence Erlbaum Associates, pp. 73–88.

12 Leaper, C. and Robnett, R.D. (2011) 'Women are more likely than men to use tentative language, aren't they? A meta-analysis testing for gender differences and moderators', *Psychology of Women Quarterly*, **35**(1): 129–42.

13 Amanatullah, E.T. and Morris, M.W. (2010) 'Negotiating gender roles: gender differences in assertive negotiating are mediated by women's fear of backlash and attenuated when negotiating on behalf of others', *Journal of Personality and Social Psychology*, **98**(2): 256–67.

14 Moss-Racusin, C.A. and Rudman, L.A. (2010) 'Disruptions in women's self-promotion: the backlash avoidance model', *Psychology of Women Quarterly*, **34**(4): 186–202.

15 Tannen, D. (1991) *You Just Don't Understand: Women and Men in Conversation*, London: Virago, p. 113.

16 Mulac, A., Bradac, J.J. and Gibbons, P. (2001) 'Empirical support for the gender-as-culture hypothesis: an intercultural analysis of male/female language differences', *Human Communication Research*, **27**(1): 121–52.

17 Leaper, C. and Ayres, M.M. (2007) 'A meta-analytic review of gender variations in adults' language use: talkativeness, affiliative speech, and assertive speech', *Personality and Social Psychology Review*, **11**: 328–63.

18 Palomares, N.A., Reid, S.A. and Bradac, J.J. (2004) 'A self-categorization perspective on gender and communication: reconciling the gender-as-culture and dominance explanations', in S.H. Ng, C.N. Candlin and C.Y. Chiu (eds), *Language Matters: Communication, Identity, and Culture*, Hong Kong: City University of Hong Kong Press, pp. 85–109.

19 Sun, X., Wiedenbeck, S., Chintakovid, T. and Zhang, Q. (2007) 'The effect of gender on trust perception and performance in computer-mediated virtual environments', *Proceedings of the American Society for Information Science and Technology*, **44**: 1–14.

20 Sutterby, S.R., Bedwell, J.S., Passler, J.S., Deptula, A.E. and Mesa, F. (2012) 'Social anxiety and social cognition: the influence of sex', *Psychiatry Research*, **197**(3): 242–5.

21 Atai, M.R. and Chahkandi, F. (2012) 'Democracy in computer-mediated communication: gender, communicative style, and amount of participation in professional listservs', *Computers in Human Behavior*, **28**(3): 881–8.

22 Herring, S.C. (1993) 'Gender and democracy in computer-mediated communication', *Electronic Journal of Communication*, **3**(2), at http://ella.slis.indiana.edu/~herring/ejc.doc; Savicki, V., Kelley, M. and Lingenfelter, D. (1996) 'Gender and small task group activity using computer mediated communication', *Computers in Human Behavior*, **12**: 209–24; Guiller, J. and Durndell, A. (2007) 'Students' linguistic behaviour in online discussion groups: does gender matter?', *Computers in Human Behaviour*, **23**(5): 2240–55.

23 Flanagin, A.J., Tivaamorncong, V., O'Connor, J. and Seibold, D.R. (2002) 'Computer-mediated group work: the interaction of sex and anonymity', *Communication Research*, **29**(1): 66–93.

24 Sussman, N.M. and Tyson, D.H. (2000) 'Sex and power: gender differences in computer-mediated interactions', *Computers in Human Behavior*, **16**(4): 381–94.

25 Herring, S.C. (2008) 'Gender and power in on-line communication', in J. Holmes and M. Meyerhoff (eds), *The Handbook of Language and Gender*, NJ: John Wiley, p. 202.

26 Michaelson, G. and Pohl M. (2001) 'Gender in email based co-operative problem solving', In E.E. Green and A. Adams (eds), *Virtual Gender*, London: Routledge, pp. 28–44.

27 Herschel, R.T., Cooper, T.R., Smith, L.F. and Arrington, L. (1994) 'Exploring numerical proportions in a unique context: the group support systems meeting environment', *Sex Roles*, **31**: 99–123.

28 Palomares, N.A. (2004) 'Gender schematicity, gender identity salience, and gender-linked language use', *Human Communication Research*, **30**(4): 556–88.

29 Brunet, P.B. and Schmidt, L.A. (2010) 'Sex differences in the expression and use of computer-mediated affective language: does context matter?', *Social Science Computer Review*, **28**(2): 194–205.

30 Thomson, R. (2006) 'The effect of topic of discussion on gendered language in computer-mediated communication discussion', *Journal of Language and Social Psychology*, **25**(2): 167–78.

31 Prosser, J. (1998) *Second Skins: The Body Narratives of Transsexuality*, New York: Columbia University Press.

32 Ess, C., and Sudweeks, F. (2005) 'Culture and computer-mediated communication: toward new understandings', *Journal of Computer-Mediated Communication*, **11**(1): 179–91.

33 Friedman, A. and Waggoner, A.S. (2010) 'Subcultural influences on person perception', *Social Psychology Quarterly*, **73**: 325–7.

34 Shweder, R.A. and Bourne, E.J. (1982) 'Does the concept of the person vary cross-culturally?', *Culture, Illness, and Healing*, **4**: 97–137.

35 Kashima, Y., Yamaguchi, S., Kim, U., Choi, S.C., Gelfand, M.J. and Yuki, M. (1995) 'Culture, gender, and self: a perspective from individualism-collectivism research', *Journal of Personality and Social Psychology*, **69**(5): 925–34.

36 Kim, Y.-H., Cohen, D. and Au, W.-T. (2010) 'The jury and abjury of my peers: the self in face and dignity cultures', *Journal of Personality and Social Psychology*, **98**(6): 904–16.

37 Shteynberg, G. (2010) 'A silent emergence of culture: the social tuning effect', *Journal of Personality and Social Psychology*, **99**(4): 683–9

38 Du-Babcock, B. (2003) 'A comparative analysis of individual communication processes in small group behavior between homogeneous and heterogeneous groups', *Proceedings of the 2003 Association for Business Communication Annual Convention*, at www.businesscommunication.org/conventionsNew/ .../41ABC03.

39 Cai, D. and Donohue, W.A. (1997) 'Determinants of facework in intercultural negotiation', *Asian Journal of Communication*, **7**(1): 85–110.

40 Susa, K.J., Meissner, C.A. and de Heer H. (2010) 'Modeling the role of social-cognitive processes in the recognition of own- and other-race faces', *Social Cognition*, **28**(4): 523–37.

41 Young, S.G. and Hugenberg, K.M. (2010) 'Social categorization modulates identification of facial expressions of emotion', *Journal of Personality and Social Psychology*, **99**(6): 964–77.

42 Pauluzzo, R., Cagnina, M.R. and Poian, M. (2010) 'Values, beliefs, artifacts and avatars: cultural issues mediated by virtual worlds', Networking and Electronic Commerce Research Conference (NAEC), at http://ssrn.com/abstract= 1836385.

43 Nozawa, S. (2012) 'The gross face and virtual fame: semiotic mediation in Japanese virtual communication', *First Monday*, **17**(3), at http://firstmonday. org/htbin/cgiwrap/bin/ojs/index.php/fm/article/view/3535/3168.

44 Kelman, H. (1961) 'Processes of opinion change', *Public Opinion Quarterly*, **35**: 57–78.

45 Tetlock, P.E. (1996) 'Accountability' in A.S.R. Manstead and M. Hewstone (eds), *Blackwell Encyclopaedia of Social Psychology*, Oxford: Blackwell.

46 Brauer, M. and Chaurand, N. (2010) 'Descriptive norms, prescriptive norms, and social control: an intercultural comparison of people's reactions to uncivil behaviors', *European Journal of Social Psychology*, **40**(3): 490–9.

47 Glynn, C.J. and Huge, M.E. (2007) 'Opinions as norms: applying a return potential model to the study of communication behaviors', *Communication Research*, **34**(5): 548–68.

48 Goel, S., Mason, W. and Watts, D.J. (2010) 'Real and perceived attitude agreement in social networks', *Journal of Personality and Social Psychology*, **99**(4): 611–21.

49 Chartrand, T.L. and Lakin, J.L. (2013) 'The antecedents and consequences of human behavioural mimicry', *Annual Review of Psychology*, **64**: 285–308.

50 Danis, W.M., Chiaburu, D.S. and Lyles, M.A. (2010) 'The impact of managerial networking intensity and market-based strategies on firm growth during institutional upheaval: a study of small and medium-sized enterprises in a transition economy', *Journal of International Business Studies*, **41**: 287–307.

51 Osigweh, C., Huo, A.B. and Yg, Y.P. (1993) 'Conceptions of employee responsibilities and rights in the United States and the People's Republic of China', *The International Journal of Human Resource Management*, **4**(1): 113–28.

52 Fulk, J., Schmitz, J. and Ryu, D. (1995) ' Cognitive elements in the social construction of communication technology', *Management Communication Quarterly*, **8**: 259–88.

53 Stephens, K.K. and Davis, J. (2009) 'The social influences on electronic multitasking in organizational meetings', *Management Communication Quarterly*, **23**(1): 63–83.

54 Lee, E.-J. (2005) 'Effects of the influence agent's sex and self-confidence on informational social influence in computer-mediated communication: quantitative versus verbal presentation', *Communication Research*, **32**(1): 29–58.

55 http://blogs.hbr.org/cs/2013/04/xeroxs_cmo_on_leading_by_examp.html.

56 Adams, D.A., Todd, P.A. and Nelson, R.R. (1993) 'A comparative evaluation of the impact of electronic and voice mail on organizational communication', *Information & Management*, **24**(1): 9–21.

57 Cameron, A.F. and Webster, J. (2005) 'Unintended consequences of emerging technologies: instant messaging in the workplace,' *Computers in Human Behavior*, **21**(1): 85–103.

58 Smilowitz, M., Compton, D.C. and Flint, L. (1988) 'The effects of computer-mediated communication on an individual's judgment: a study based on the methods of Asch's social influence experiment', *Computers in Human Behavior*, **4**(4): 311–21.

59 Swan, K. and Shih, L.F. (2005) 'On the nature and development of social presence in online course discussions', *Journal of Asynchronous Learning Networks*, **9**(3): 115–36.

60 Williams, E. (1975) 'Medium or message: communications medium as a determinant of interpersonal evaluation', *Sociometry*, **38**(1): 119–30.

61 Rutter, D.R., Pennington, D.C., Dewey, M.E. and Swain, J. (1984) 'Eye-contact as a chance product of individual looking: implications for the intimacy model of Argyle and Dean', *Journal of Non-verbal Behavior*, **8**(4): 250–8.

62 Sproull, L. and Kiesler S. (1986) 'Reducing social context cues: electronic mail in organizational communication', *Management Science*, **32**(11): 1492–512.

63 Daft, R.L. and Lengel, R.H. (1986) 'Organizational information requirements, media richness and structural design', *Management Science*, **32**(5): 554–71.

64 Schmitz, J. and Fulk, J. (1991) 'Organizational colleagues, media richness, and electronic mail', *Communication Research*, **18**: 487–9.

65 Ibid.

66 Thompson, L. and Nadler, J. (2002) 'Negotiating via information technology: theory and applications', *Journal of Social Issues*, **58**(1): 109–24.

67 Gibbons, L.J., Kennedy, R.M. and Gibbs, J.M. (2002) 'Cyber-mediation: computer-mediated communication – medium massaging the message', *New Mexico Law Review*, **32**: 27–74.

68 Walther, J.B. (1992) 'Interpersonal effects in computer-mediated interaction: a relational perspective', *Communication Research*, **19**(1): 52–90.

69 Walther, J.B. (1996) 'Group and interpersonal effects in international computer-mediated collaboration', *Human Communication Research*, **23**(3): 342–69.

70 Walther, J.B. Anderson, J.F. and Park, D.W. (1994) 'Interpersonal effects in computer-mediated interaction: a meta-analysis of social and anti-social communication', *Communication Research*, **21**: 460–87.

71 Walther, J.B. (1994) 'Anticipated ongoing interaction versus channel effects on relational communication in computer-mediated interaction', *Human Communication Research*, **20**(4): 473–501.

72 Walther, J.B., DeAndrea, D.C. and Tong, T.S. (2010) 'Computer-mediated communication versus vocal communication and the attenuation of pre-interaction impressions', *Media Psychology*, **13**(4). 364–86.

73 Walther (1992) op. cit.

74 Walther J.B. (1995) 'Relational aspects of computer-mediated-communication: experimental observations over time', *Organization Science*, **6**(2): 186–203.

75 Walther, J.B. (2007) 'Selective self-presentation in computer-mediated communication: hyperpersonal dimensions of technology, language and cognition', *Computers in Human Behavior*, **23**(5): 2538–57.

76 Spears, R., Lea, M. and Postmes, T. (2001) 'Social psychological theories of computer-mediated communication: social pain or social gain?', in W.P. Robinson and H. Giles (eds), *The New Handbook of Language and Social Psychology*, NJ: John Wiley.

77 Postmes, T., Spears, R. and Lea, M. (1998) 'Breaching or building social boundaries? SIDE effects of computer-mediated communication', *Communication Research*, **25**(6): 689–715.

78 Ibid.

79 Moral-Toranzo, F., Canto-Ortiz, J. and Gómez-Jacinto, L. (2007) 'Anonymity effects in computer-mediated communication in the case of minority influence', *Computers in Human Behavior*, **23**(3): 1660–74.

80 Thompson and Nadler, op. cit.

CHAPTER 7 INTRAPERSONAL INFLUENCES ON COMMUNICATION

1 Kopietz, R., Hellmann, J.H., Higgins, E.T. and Echterhoff, G. (2010) 'Shared-reality effects on memory: communicating to fulfill epistemic needs', *Social Cognition*, **28**(3): 353–78.

2 Bechtoldt, M.N., De Dreu, C.K.W., Nijstad, B.A. and Choi, H.-S. (2010) 'Motivated information processing, social tuning and group creativity', *Journal of Personality and Social Psychology*, **99**(4): 622–37.

3 Kim, J. (2010) 'Balancing uniqueness and assimilation in computer-mediated groups', *Computers in Human Behavior*, **26**(4): 778–84.

4 Brewer, M.B. (1991) 'The social self: on being the same and different at the same time', *Personality and Social Psychology Bulletin*, **17**: 475–82.

5 Bandura (2001) 'Social cognitive theory: an agentic perspective', *Annual Review of Psychology*, **52**(1): 1-26.

6 Liberman, S.N. and Trope, Y. (1998) 'The role of feasibility and desirability considerations in near and distant future decisions: a test of temporal construal theory', *Journal of Personality and Social Psychology*, **75**: 5–18.

7 Dou, W., Li, H., Zhou, N. and Su. C. (2010) 'Exploring relationship satisfaction between global professional service firms and local clients in emerging markets', *Journal of International Business Studies*, **41**: 1198–217.

8 Hazlett, A., Molden, D.C. and Sackett, A.M. (2011) 'Hoping for the best or

preparing for the worst? Regulatory focus and preferences for optimism and pessimism in predicting personal outcomes', *Social Cognition*, **29**(1): 74–96.

9 Palomares, N.A. (2009) 'Did you see it coming? Effects of the specificity and efficiency of goal pursuit on the accuracy and onset of goal detection in social interaction, *Communication Research*, **36**: 475–509.

10 Walther, J.B., Van Der Heide, B., Tong, S.T., Carr, C.T. and Atkin, C.K. (2010) 'Effects of interpersonal goals on inadvertent intrapersonal influence in computer-mediated communication', *Human Communication Research*, **36**: 323–47.

11 Palomares, N.A. (2008) 'Toward a theory of goal detection in social interaction: effects of contextual ambiguity and tactical functionality on goal inferences and inference certainty', *Communication Research*, **35**(1): 109–48.

12 Palomares (2009), op. cit.

13 Palomares, N.A. (2013) 'When and how goals are contagious in social interaction', *Human Communication Research*, **39**: 74–100.

14 Kim, op. cit.

15 Ajzen, I. (2001) 'Nature and operation of attitudes', *Annual Review of Psychology*, **52**: 27–58.

16 Avramova, Y.R., Stapel, D.A. and Lerouge, D. (2010) 'Mood and context-dependence: positive mood increases and negative mood decreases the effects of context on perception', *Journal of Personality and Social Psychology*, **99**(2): 203–14.

17 Lount, R.B. Jr (2010) 'The impact of positive mood on trust in interpersonal and intergroup interactions', *Journal of Personality and Social Psychology*, **98**(3): 420–33.

18 Forgas, J.P. and Tan, H.B. (2013) 'To give or to keep? Affective influences on selfishness and fairness in computer-mediated interactions in the dictator game and the ultimatum game', *Computers in Human Behavior*, **29**(1): 64–74.

19 Quy N.H. (2002) 'Emotional balancing of organizational continuity and radical change: the contribution of middle managers', *Administrative Science Quarterly*, **47**(1): 31–69.

20 Baumann J. and Desteno D. (2010) 'Emotion guided threat detection: expecting guns where there are none', *Journal of Personal and Social Psychology*, **99**(4): 595–610.

21 Polman, E. (2011) 'When more pain is preferred to less: the effect of anger in decision making', *Social Cognition*, **29**(1): 43–55.

22 Liu, M. and Wang, C. (2010) 'Explaining the influence of anger and compassion on negotiators' interaction goals: an assessment of trust and distrust as two distinct mediators', *Communication Research*, **37**(4): 443–72.

23 Perkins, A.M., Inchley-Mort, S.L., Pickering, A.D., Corr, P.J. and Burgess, A.P. (2012) 'A facial expression for anxiety', *Journal of Personality and Social Psychology*, **102**(5): 910–24.

24 Douglas, W. (1991) 'Expectations about initial interaction: an examination of the effects of global uncertainty', *Human Communication Research*, **17**: 355–84.

25 Harville, D.L. (1993) 'Person/job fit model of communication apprehension in organisations', *Management Communication Quarterly*, **6**: 150–65.

26 Blume, B.D., Dreher,G.F. and Baldwin, T.T. (2010) 'Examining the effects of communication apprehension within assessment centres', *Journal of Occupational and Organizational Psychology*, **83**(3): 663–71.

27 Daly, J.A. (1977) 'The effects of writing apprehension on message encoding', *Journalism Quarterly*, **54**: 566–72.

28 Ibid.

29 Scott, C.R. and Timmerman, C.E. (2005) 'Relating computer, communication and computer-mediated communication apprehensions to new communication technology use', *Communication Research*, **32**(6): 683–725.

30 Mabrito, M. (1992) 'Computer-mediated communication and high-apprehensive writers: rethinking the collaborative process', *Bulletin of the Association for Business Communication*, **55**(4): 26–9.

31 Ellemers, N., Sleebos, E., Stam, D. and de Gilder, D. (2013) 'Feeling included and valued: how perceived respect affects positive team identity and willingness to invest in the team', *British Journal of Management*, **24**: 21–37.

32 Filipowicz, A., Barsade, S. and Melwani, S. (2011) 'Understanding emotional transitions: the interpersonal consequences of changing emotions in negotiations', *Journal of Personality and Social Psychology*, **101**(3): 541–56.

33 Feinberg, M., Willer, R. and Keltner, D. (2012) 'Flustered and faithful: embarrassment as a signal of prosociality', *Journal of Personality and Social Psychology*, **102**(1): 81–97.

34 Chentsova-Dutton, Y.E. and Tsai, J.L. (2010) 'Self-focused attention and emotional reactivity: the role of culture', *Journal of Personality and Social Psychology*, **98**(3): 507–19.

35 Ashforth, B.E. and Humphrey, R.H. (1993) 'Emotional labor in service roles: the influence of identity', *Academy of Management Review*, **18**(1): 88–115.

36 Korczynski, M. (2003) 'Communities of coping: collective emotional labour in service work', *Organization*, **10**(1): 55–79.

37 Yen, J.-U., Yen, C.F., Chen, C.S., Wang, P.W., Chang, Y.H. and Ko, C.H. (2012) 'Social anxiety in online and real-life interaction and their associated factors', *Cyberpsychology, Behavior, and Social Networking*, **15**(1): 7–12.

38 Thomas, M. and Tsai, C.I. (2012) 'Psychological distance and subjective experience: how distancing reduces the feeling of difficulty', *Journal of Consumer Research*, **39**(2): 324–40.

39 Kato, Y., Kato, S. and Akahori, K. (2007) 'Effects of emotional cues transmitted in email communication on the emotions experienced by senders and receivers', *Computers in Human Behavior*, **23**(4): 1894–905.

40 Byron, K. and Baldridge, D.C. (2007) 'Email recipients' impressions of senders' likability: the interactive effect of non-verbal cues and recipients' personality', *Journal of Business Communication*, **44**: 137–60

41 Luor, T., Wu, l.-L., Lu, H.-P. and Tao, Y.-H. (2010) 'The effect of emoticons in simplex and complex task-oriented communication', *Computers in Human Behavior*, **26**(5): 889–95.

42 Laflen, A. and Fiorenza, B. (2012) '"Okay, my rant is over": the language of emotion in computer-mediated communication', *Computers and Composition*, **29**(4): 296–308.

43 Zillmann, D. (1971) 'Excitation transfer in communication-mediated aggressive behavior', *Journal of Experimental Social Psychology*, **7**(4): 419–34.

44 Ho, S.S. and McLeod, D.M. (2008) 'Social-psychological influences on opinion expression in face-to-face and computer-mediated communication', *Communication Research*, **35**(2): 190–207.

45 Rice, L. and Markey, P.M. (2009) 'The role of extraversion and neuroticism in influencing anxiety following computer-mediated interactions', *Personality and Individual Differences*, **46**(1): 35–9.

46 Ku, L. (1996) 'Social and nonsocial uses of electronic messaging systems in organizations', *Journal of Business Communication*, **33**(3): 297–325.

47 Gibson, D.E. and Schroeder, S.J. (2002) 'Grinning, frowning, and emotionless: agent perceptions of power and their effect on felt and displayed emotions in influence attempts', in N.M. Ashkanasy, W.J. Zerbe and C.E. Härtel (eds), *Managing Emotions in the Workplace*, Armonk, NY: M.E. Sharpe.

48 Baumeister, R.F., Masicampo, E.J. and Vohs, K.D. (2011) 'Do conscious thoughts cause behavior?', *Annual Review of Psychology*, **62**: 331–61.

49 Ajzen, op. cit.

50 Fussell, S.R. and Krauss, R.M. (1992) 'Coordination of knowledge in communication: effects of speakers' assumptions about what others know', *Journal of Personality and Social Psychology*, **62**(3): 378–91.

51 McGregor, D.M. (1960) *The Human Side of Enterprise*, New York: McGraw-Hill.

52 Fisher, S. and Groce, S.B. (1985) 'Doctor–patient negotiation of cultural assumptions', *Sociology of Health & Illness*, 7(3): 342–74.

53 At adamjwalker.com/2013/01/assumptions-that-kill-communication/ (accessed 25 September 2013).

54 Bandura, A. (1986) 'The explanatory and predictive scope of self-efficacy theory', *Journal of Social and Clinical Psychology*, **4**(3): 359–73.

55 Zellars, K.L., Perrewe, P.L., Rossi, A.M., Tepper, B.J. and Ferris, G.R. (2008) 'Moderating effects of political skill, perceived control, and job-related self-efficacy on the relationship between negative affectivity and physiological strain', *Journal of Organizational Behavior*, **29**(5): 549–71.

56 Collins, C.G. and Parker, S.K. (2010) 'Team capability beliefs over time: distinguishing between team potency, team outcome efficacy, and team process efficacy', *Journal of Occupational and Organizational Psychology*, **83**(4): 1003–23.

57 Hwang, Y. and Grant, D. (2011) 'Behavioral aspects of enterprise systems adoption: an empirical study on cultural factors', *Computers in Human Behavior*, **27**(2): 988–96.

58 Miltiadou, M. and Yu, C.H. (2000) *Validation of the Online Technologies Self-efficacy Scale (OTSES)*, ERIC Clearinghouse, Institute of Education Sciences of the US Department of Sciences, New Jersey.

59 Tsui, A.S., Porter, L.W. and Egan, T.D. (2002) 'When both similarities and dissimilarities matter: extending the concept of relational demography', *Human Relations*, **55**(8): 899–930.

60 Miller, D.T. and Turnbull, W. (1986) 'Expectancies and interpersonal processes', *Annual Review of Psychology*, **37**: 233–56.

61 Walther, J.B. (1994) 'Anticipated ongoing interaction versus channel effects on relational communication in computer-mediated interaction', *Human Communication Research*, **20**(4): 473–501.

62 Kalkhoff, W., Younts, C.W. and Troyer, L. (2011) 'Do others' views of us transfer to new groups and tasks? An expectation states approach', *Social Psychology Quarterly*, **74**: 267–90.

63 Van Swol, L. (2009) 'The effects of confidence and advisor motives on advice utilization', *Communication Research*, **36**(6): 857–73.

64 Snyder, M. and Klein, O. (2005) 'Construing and constructing others: on the reality and the generality of the behavioural confirmation scenario', *Interaction Studies*, **6**(1): 53–67.

65 Dougherty T.W., Turban D.B. and Callender J.C. (1994) 'Confirming first impressions in the employment interview: a field study of interviewer behavior', *Journal of Applied Psychology*, **79**· 659–65.

66 Brenders, D.A. (1987) 'Perceived control: foundations and directions for communication research', *Communication Yearbook*, **10**: 86–116.

67 Balvin, N. and Tyler, C. (2006) 'Emotions in cyberspace: the advantages and disadvantages of online communication', University of Melbourne Legal studies Research Paper no. 277, at http://ssrn.com/abstract=1027510.

68 Kalman, Y.M. and Rafaeli, S. (2011) 'Online pauses and silence: chronemic expectancy violations in written computer-mediated communication', *Communication Research*, **38**: 54–69.

69 Vásquez, C. (2011) 'Complaints online: the case of *TripAdvisor*', *Journal of Pragmatics*, 43(6): 1707–17.

70 Toegel, G., Kilduff, M. and Anand, N. (2013) 'Emotion helping by managers: an emergent understanding of discrepant role expectations and outcomes', *Academy of Management Journal*, **56**: 334–57.

71 Kalman and Rafaeli, op. cit.

72 Ali, A.J. (1993) 'Decision-making style, individualism and attitudes toward risk of Arab executives', *International Studies of Management and Organization*, **23**(3): 53–74.

73 Epley, N. and Kruger, J. (2005) 'When what you type isn't what they read: the perseverance of stereotypes and expectancies over email', *Journal of Experimental Social Psychology*, **41**(4): 414–22.

74 Walther, J.B., Van Der Heide, B., Tong, S.T., Carr, C.T. and Atkin, C.K. (2010) 'Effects of interpersonal goals on inadvertent intrapersonal influence in computer-mediated communication', *Human Communication Research*, **36**(3): 323–47.

75 Tong, S.T. and Walther, J.B. (2012) 'The confirmation and disconfirmation of expectancies in computer-mediated communication', *Communication Research*.

76 Kalman and Rafaeli, op. cit.

77 David, P.A. (2008) 'Toward an analytical framework for the study of distributed problem-solving networks', OII DPSN working paper No. 1, at http://ssrn.com/abstract=130292.

78 Ota, H., McCann, R.M. and Honeycutt, J.M. (2012) 'Inter-Asian variability in intergenerational communication', *Human Communication Research*, **38**: 172–98.

79 Savani, K., Morris, M.W. and Naidu, N.V.R. (2012) 'Deference in Indians' decision making: introjected goals or injunctive norms?', *Journal of Personality and Social Psychology*, **102**(4): 685–99.

80 Markus, M.L. and Robey, D. (1988) 'Information technology and organizational change: causal structure in theory and research', *Management Science*, **34**(5): 583–98.

81 Postmes, T., Spears, R. and Lea, M. (1998) 'Breaching or building social bound-

aries? SIDE effects of computer-mediated communication', *Communication Research*, **25**(6): 689–715.

82 Kalman, Y.M., Ravid, G., Raban, D.R. and Rafaeli, S. (2006a) 'Speak *now* or forever hold your peace: power law chronemics of turn-taking and response in asynchronous CMC', Paper presented at the 56th Annual Conference of the International Communication Association, Dresden, Germany, June.

83 Kalman, Y.M., Ravid, G., Raban, D.R. and Rafaeli, S. (2006b) 'Pauses and response latencies: a chronemic analysis of asynchronous CMC', *Journal of Computer-Mediated Communication*, **12**(1): 1–23.

84 Postmes, T., Spears, R. and Lea, M. (2000) 'The formation of group norms in computer-mediated communication', *Human Communication Research*, **26**(3): 341–71.

85 Graham, C.R. (2003) 'A model of norm development for computer-mediated teamwork', *Small Group Research*, **34**(3): 322–52.

86 Ajzen, op. cit.

87 Ibid.

88 Ibid.

89 Mayer, R.C., Davis, J.H. and Schoorman, F.D. (1995) 'An integrative model of organizational trust', *Academy of Management Review*, **20**(3): 709–34.

90 Liu and Wang, op. cit.

91 Walumbwa, F.O., Luthans, F., Avey, J.B. and Oke, A. (2011) 'Authentically leading groups: the mediating role of collective psychological capital and trust', *Journal of Organizational Behavior*, **32**: 4–24.

92 Gibson, C.B. and Manuel, J.A. (2003) 'Building trust: effective multi-cultural communication processes in virtual teams', In C.B. Gibson and S.G. Cohen (eds) *Virtual Teams That Work: Creating Conditions for Virtual team Effectiveness*, San Francisco, CA: Jossey-Bass.

93 Bos, N., Olson, J., Gergle, D., Olson, G. and Wright, Z. (2002) 'Effects of four computer-mediated communications channels on trust development', *Proceedings of the SIGCHI Conference on Human Factors in Computing Systems*, pp. 135–40, at http://129.105.146.12/pubs/BosOlsonGergle OlsonWright_RichMediaTrust_CHI02.pdf.

94 Lount R.B. Jr. and Pettit. N.C. (2012) 'The social context of trust: the role of status', *Organizational Behavior and Human Decision Processes*, 117(1): 15–23.

95 Righetti, F. and Finkenauer, C. (2011) 'If you are able to control yourself, I will trust you: the role of perceived self-control in interpersonal trust', *Journal of Personality and Social Psychology*, **100**(5): 874–86.

96 Muthuel, M., Siebdrat, F. and Hoegl, M. (2012) 'When do we really need interpersonal trust in globally dispersed new product development teams?', *R&D Management*, **42**(1): 31–46.

97 Riegelsberger, J., Sasse, M.A. and McCarthy, J.D. (2003) 'The researcher's dilemma: evaluating trust in computer-mediated communication', *International Journal of Human-Computer Studies*, **58**(6): 759–81.

98 Bente, G., Rüggenberg, S., Krämer, N.C. and Eschenburg, F. (2008) 'Avatar-mediated networking: increasing social presence and interpersonal trust in net-based collaborations', *Human Communication Research*, **34**(2): 287–318.

99 Bos et al., op. cit.

100 Iacono, C.S. and Weisband, S. (1997) 'Developing trust in virtual teams', *Proceedings of the Thirtieth Hawaii International Conference on System Sciences*, vol. 2, IEEE.

101 Rockmann, K.R. and Northcraft, G.B. (2008) 'To be or not to be trusted: the influence of media richness on defection and deception', *Organizational Behavior and Human Decision Processes*, **107**(2): 106–22.

102 Rudman, L.A., Greenwald, A.G., Mellott, D.S. and Schwartz, J.L. (1999) 'Measuring the automatic components of prejudice: flexibility and generality of the implicit association test', *Social Cognition*, **17**(4): 437–65.

103 Schmid, K., Hewstone, M., Küpper, B., Zick, A. and Wagner, U. (2012) 'Secondary transfer effects of intergroup contact: a cross-national comparison in Europe', *Social Psychology Quarterly*, **75**: 28–51.

104 McKenna, K.Y. and Bargh, J.A. (2000) 'Plan 9 from cyberspace: the implications of the Internet for personality and social psychology', *Personality and Social Psychology Review*, **4**(1): 57–75.

105 Kahn, K.B. (2004) 'Prejudice, discrimination, and the Internet', at http://ist-socrates.berkeley.edu/~glaserj/intprej_draft_070104.pdf (accessed 28 September 2013).

106 Dotsch, R. and Wigboldus, D.J.H. (2008): 'Virtual prejudice', *Journal of Experimental Social Psychology*, **44**(4): 1194–8.

107 Ajzen, op. cit.

108 Sagiv, L., Sverdlik, N. and Schwarz, N. (2011) 'To compete or to cooperate? Values' impact on perception and action in social dilemma games', *European Journal of Social Psychology*, **41**(1): 64–77.

109 Ravlin, E.C., and Meglino, B.M. (1987) 'Effect of values on perception and decision making: a study of alternative work values measures', *Journal of Applied Psychology*, **72**(4): 666.

110 Chou, L.F., Wang, A.-C., Wang, T.-Y., Huang, M.-P. and Cheng, B.-S. (2008) 'Shared work values and team member effectiveness: the mediation of trustfulness and trustworthiness', *Human Relations*, **61**: 1713–42.

111 Locke, K.D., Craig, T., Baik, K.-D. and Gohil, K. (2012) 'Binds and bounds of communion: effects of interpersonal values on assumed similarity of self and others', *Journal of Personality and Social Psychology*, **103**(5): 879–97.

112 Wolak, A. (2009) 'Australian and Canadian managerial values: a review', *International Journal of Organizational Analysis*, **17**(2): 139–59.

113 Gudykunst, W.B., Matsumoto, Y., Ting-Toomey, S., Nishida, T., Kim, K. and Heyman, S. (1996) 'The influence of cultural individualism?collectivism, self construals, and individual values on communication styles across cultures', *Human Communication Research*, **22**(4): 510–43.

114 Rowe, F. and Struck, D. (1999) 'Cultural values, media richness and telecommunication use in an organization', *Accounting, Management and Information Technologies*, **9**(3): 161–92.

115 Ajzen, op. cit.

116 Cattell, R.B. (1987) *Intelligence: Its Structure, Growth, and Action*, New York: Elsevier Science.

117 Conway, A.R., Cowan, N., Bunting, M.F., Therriault, D.J. and Minkoff, S.R. (2002) 'A latent variable analysis of working memory capacity, short-term memory capacity, processing speed, and general fluid intelligence', *Intelligence*, **30**(2): 163–83.

118 Mayer, J.D., Salovey, P. and Caruso, D.R. (2008) 'Emotional intelligence: new ability or eclectic traits?', *American Psychologist*, **63**(6): 503.

119 Planalp, S. and Fitness, J. (1999) 'Thinking/feeling about social and personal relationships', *Journal of Social and Personal Relationships*, **16**(6): 731–50.

120 O'Boyle, E.H., Humphrey, R.H., Pollack, J.M., Hawver, T.H. and Story, P.A. (2011) 'The relation between emotional intelligence and job performance: a meta-analysis', *Journal of Organizational Behaviour*, **32**: 788–18.

121 Schlaerth, A., Ensari, N. and Christian, J. (2013) 'A meta-analytical review of the relationship between emotional intelligence and leaders' constructive conflict management', *Group Processes and Intergroup Relations*, **16**(1): 126–36.

122 Côté, S. and Miners, C.T.H. (2006) 'Emotional intelligence, cognitive intelligence, and job performance', *Administrative Science Quarterly*, **51**(1): 1–28

123 Lindebaum, D. and Cassell, C. (2012) 'A contradiction in terms? Making sense of emotional intelligence in a construction management environment', *British Journal of Management*, **23**(1): 65–79.

124 Näsi, M. and Koivusilta, L. (2013) 'Internet and everyday life: the perceived implications of internet use on memory and ability to concentrate', *Cyberpsychology, Behavior, and Social Networking*, **16**(2): 88–93.

125 Digman, J.M. (1990) 'Personality structure: emergence of the five-factor model', *Annual Review of Psychology*, **41**: 417–40.

126 Bond, R. and Smith, P.B. (1996) 'Culture and conformity: a meta-analysis of studies using Asch's (1952b, 1956) line judgment task', *Psychological Bulletin*, **119**(1): 111.

127 Fleeson, W. and Gallagher, P. (2009) 'The implications of Big Five standing for the distribution of trait manifestation in behavior: fifteen experience-sampling studies and a meta-analysis', *Journal of Personality and Social Psychology*, **97**(6): 1097.

128 Kalman, Y.M. and Rafaeli, S. (2013) 'Online chronemics convey social information', *Computers in Human Behavior*, **29**(3): 1260–9.

129 Johnson, R.E., Rosen, C.C and Levy, P.E. (2008) 'Getting to the core of core self-evaluation: a review and recommendations', *Journal of Organizational Behavior*, **29**(3): 391–413.

130 Cheung, F.M., Leung, K., Zhang, J.X., Sun, H.F., Gan, Y.Q., Song, W.Z. and Xie, D. (2001) 'Indigenous Chinese personality constructs: is the Five-Factor Model complete?', *Journal of Cross-Cultural Psychology*, **32**(4): 407–33.

131 Orchard, L.J. and Fullwood, C. (2010) 'Current perspectives on personality and internet use', *Social Science Computer Review*, **28**(2): 155–69.

132 Ibid.

133 Caplan, S.E. (2005) 'A social skill account of problematic Internet use', *Journal of Communication*, **55**(4): 721–36.

134 Neo, R.L. and Skoric, M.M. (2009) 'Problematic instant messaging use', *Journal of Computer-Mediated Communication*, **14**(3): 627–57.

135 Lammers, J.C., Atouba, Y.L. and Carlson, E.J. (2013) 'Which identities matter? A mixed-method study of group, organizational, and professional identities and their relationship to burnout', *Management Communication Quarterly*, **27**(4): 503–36.

136 Gonzalez, A.L. and Hancock, J.T. (2008) 'Identity shift in computer-mediated environments', *Media Psychology*, **11**(2): 167–85.

137 Critcher, C.R. and Dunning, D. (2009) 'How chronic self-views influence (and mislead) self-assessments of task performance: self-views shape bottom-up experiences with the task', *Journal of Personality and Social Psychology*, **97**(6): 931.

138 Kim, Y.-H., Chiu, C. and Zou, Z. (2010) 'Know thyself: misperceptions of actual performance undermine achievement motivation, future performance and subjective well-being', *Journal of Personality and Social Psychology*, **99**(3): 395–409.

139 Allik, J., Realo, A., Mõttus, R., Borkenau, P., Kuppens, P. and Hebíková, M. (2010) 'How people see others is different from how people see themselves: a replicable pattern across cultures', *Journal of Personality and Social Psychology*, **99**(5): 870–82.

140 Judge, T.A. and Bono, J.E. (2001) 'Relationship of core self-evaluations traits - self-esteem, generalized self-efficacy, locus of control, and emotional stability – with job satisfaction and job performance: a meta-analysis', *Journal of Applied Psychology*, **86**(1): 80.

141 Bandura, A. (2001) 'Social cognitive theory: an agentic perspective', *Annual Review of Psychology*, **52**(1): 1–26.

142 Matheson, K. and Zanna, M.P. (1988) 'The impact of computer-mediated communication on self-awareness', Computers in *Human Behavior*, **4**(3): 221–33.

CHAPTER 8 INFLUENCING HANDLING CONFLICT AND NEGOTIATING

1 Flynn, F.J., Gruenfeld, D., Molm, L.D., and Polzer, J.T. (2012) 'Social psychological perspectives on power in organizations', *Administrative Science Quarterly*, **56**: 495–500.

2 Subasic, E., Reynolds, K.J., Turner, J.C., Veenstra, K.E. and Haslam, S.A. (2011) 'Leadership power and the use of surveillance: implications of shared social identity for leaders' capacity to influence', *Leadership Quarterly*, **22**(1): 170–81.

3 Student, K.R. (1968) 'Supervisory influence and work-group performance', *Journal of Applied Psychology*, **52**(3): 188.

4 Buckley, W. (1970) 'Society as a complex adaptive system', in Buckely, W. (ed.), *Modern Systems Research for the Behavioral Scientists*, Chicago, IL: Aldine.

5 Blader, S.L. and Chen, Y.-R. (2012) 'Differentiating the effects of status and power: a justice perspective', *Journal of Personality and Social Psychology*, **102**(5): 994–1014.

6 Darley, J.M. (2001) 'The dynamics of authority influence in organizations and the unintended action consequences', in J.M. Darley, D.M. Messick and T.R. Tyler (eds), *Social Influences on Ethical Behavior in Organizations*, Mahwah, NJ: Lawrence Erlbaum Associates Publishers, pp. 37–52.

7 Carli, L.L. (2001) 'Gender and social influence', *Journal of Social Issues*, **57**(4): 725–41.

8 Yukl, G. and Falb, C.M. (1990) 'Influence tactics and objectives in upward, downward, and lateral influence attempts', *Journal of Applied Psychology*, **75**(2): 132.

9 Carli, L.L. (1999) 'Gender, interpersonal power, and social influence', *Journal of Social Issues*, **55**(1): 81–99.

10 Carli (2001), op. cit.

11 Torelli, C.J. and Shavitt, S. (2010) 'Culture and concepts of power', *Journal of Personality and Social Psychology*, **99**(4): 703–23.

12 Panteli, N. (2002) 'Richness, power cues and email text', *Information & Management*, **40**(2): 75–86.

13 Liu, Y. (2011) 'Power perceptions and negotiations in a cross-national email writing activity', *Journal of Second Language Writing*, **20**(4): 257–70.

14 Tan, B.C., Wei, K.K., Watson, R.T. and Walczuch, R.M. (1998) 'Reducing status effects with computer-mediated communication: evidence from two distinct national cultures', *Journal of Management Information Systems*, **15**: 119–42.

15 Douglas, C., Martin, J.S. and Krapels, R.H. (2006) 'Communication in the transition to self-directed work teams', *Journal of Business Communication*, **43**(4): 295–321.

16 Joule. R.-V. and J. -L. Beauvois (1997) 'Cognitive-dissonance theory: a radical view', *European Review of Social Psychology*, **8**: 1–32.

17 Kiesler, S. (1978) *Interpersonal Processes in Groups and Organizations*, Arlington Heights, IL: AHM Publishing Corporation.

18 Heider, F. (1958) *The Psychology of Interpersonal Relations*, New York: Wiley.

19 Hoeke, H. and Hustinx, L. (2009) 'When is statistical evidence superior to anecdotal evidence in supporting probability claims? The role of argument type', *Human Communication Research*, **35**(4): 491–510.

20 Cinnirella, M. and Green, B. (2007) 'Does "cyber-conformity" vary cross-culturally? Exploring the effect of culture and communication medium on social conformity', *Computers in Human Behavior*, **23**(4): 2011–25.

21 Guadagno, R.E. and Cialdini, R.B. (2002) 'Online persuasion: an examination of gender differences in computer-mediated interpersonal influence', *Group Dynamics*, **6**(1): 38–51.

22 Moon, Y. (1999) 'The effects of physical distance and response latency on persuasion in computer-mediated communication and human-computer communication', *Journal of Experimental Psychology: Applied*, **5**(40): 379–92.

23 Di Blasio, P. and Milani, L. (2008) 'Computer-mediated communication and persuasion: peripheral vs. central route to opinion shift', *Computers in Human Behavior*, **24**(3): 798–815.

24 Miller, M.D. and Brunner, C.C. (2008) 'Social impact in technologically-mediated communication: an examination of online influence', *Computers in Human Behavior*, **24**(6): 2972–91.

25 Stasson, M.F. and Davis, J.H. (1989) 'The relative effects of the number of arguments, number of argument sources and number of opinion positions in group-mediated opinion change', *British Journal of Social Psychology*, **28**(3): 251–62.

26 Skalski, P. and Tamborini, R. (2007) 'The role of social presence in interactive agent-based persuasion', *Media Psychology*, **10**(3): 385–413.

27 Stephens, K.R. and Rains, S.A. (2011) 'Information and communication technology sequences and message repetition in interpersonal interaction', *Communication Research*, **38**(1): 101–22.

28 Wilson, E.V. (2003) 'Perceived effectiveness of interpersonal persuasion strategies in computer-mediated communication, *Computers in Human Behavior*, **19**(5): 537–52.

29 Steizel, S. and Rimbau-Gilabert, E. (2013) 'Upward influence tactics through technology-mediated communication tools', *Computers in Human Behavior*, **29**(2): 462–72.

30 Gorley, P.J. (1975) 'In the sales call: a study of the industrial sales interview', unpublished PhD dissertation, London Business School.

31 Webster, D.M. and Kruglanski, A.W. (1997) 'Cognitive and social consequences of the need for cognitive closure', *European Review of Social Psychology*, **8**: 133–74.

32 Tjosvold, D. (2008) 'The conflict-positive organization: it depends upon us', *Journal of Organizational Behavior*, **29**(1): 19–28.

33 De Dreu, C.K.W. (2008) 'The virtue and vice of workplace conflict: food for (pessimistic) thought', *Journal of Organizational Behavior*, **29**(1): 5–18.

34 Lau, R.S. and Cobb, A.T. (2010) 'Understanding the connections between relationship conflict and performance: the intervening roles of trust and exchange', *Journal of Organizational Behavior*, **31**(6): 898–917.

35 DeWall, C. N., Twenge, J.M., Gitter, S.A. and Baumeister, R.F. (2009) 'It's the thought that counts: the role of hostile cognition in shaping aggressive responses to social exclusion', *Journal of Personality and Social Psychology*, **96**(1): 45–59.

36 Bendersky, C. and Hays, N.A. (2012) 'Status conflict in groups', *Organization Science*, **23**(2): 323–40.

37 Houshmand, M., O'Reilly, J., Robinson, S. and Wolff, A. (2012) 'Escaping bullying: the simultaneous impact of individual and unit-level bullying on turnover intentions', *Human Relations*, **65**: 901–18.

38 Baruch, Y. (2005) 'Bullying on the net: adverse behavior on email and its impact', *Information & Management*, **42**(2): 361–71.

39 Friedman, R.A. and Currall, S.C. (2003) 'Conflict escalation: dispute exacerbating elements of email communication', *Human Relations*, **56**: 1325–47.

40 Sullivan, D., Landau, M.J. and Rothschild, Z.K. (2010) 'An existential function of enemyship: evidence that people attribute influence to personal and political enemies to compensate for threats to control', *Journal of Personality and Social Psychology*, **98**(3): 434–49.

41 De Dreu, C.K.W. (2008), op. cit.

42 Somech, A., Desivilya, H.S. and Lidogoster, H. (2009) 'Team conflict management and team effectiveness: the effects of task interdependence and team identification', *Journal of Organizational Behavior*, **30**(3): 359–78.

43 Kim, T.Y., Shapiro, D.L., Aquino, K., Lim, V.K.G. and Bennett, R.J. (2008) 'Workplace offense and victims' reactions: the effects of victim-offender (dis)similarity, offense-type, and cultural differences', *Journal of Organizational Behavior*, **29**(3): 415–33.

44 Volkema, R.J., Farquhar, K. and Bergmann, T.J. (1996) 'Third-party sensemaking in interpersonal conflicts at work: a theoretical framework', *Human Relations*, **49**(11): 1437–54; Weick, K.E. (1995) *Sense-making in Organizations*, Thousand Oaks, CA: Sage; Weick, K.E. (2000) *Making Sense of the Organization*, Malden, MA: Blackwell Publishers.

45 Tjosvold, D. (2008) 'The conflict-positive organization: it depends upon us', *Journal of Organizational Behavior*, **29**(1): 19–28.

46 Schein, E.H. (1983) 'SMR forum: improving face-to-face relationships', *Sloan Management Review*, Winter: 43–52.

47 O'Kane, P. and Hargie, O. (2007) 'Intentional and unintentional consequences of substituting face-to-face interaction with email: an employee-based perspective', *Interacting with Computers*, **19**(1): 20–31.

48 Friedman, R.A. and Currall, S.C. (2003) 'Conflict escalation: dispute exacerbating elements of email communication', *Human Relations*, **56**: 1325–47.

49 Hobman, E.V., Bordia, P., Irmer, B. and Chang, A. (2002) 'The expression of conflict in computer-mediated and face-to-face groups', *Small Group Research*, **33**(4): 439–65.

50 Martínez-Moreno, E., González-Navarro, P., Zornoza, A. and Ripoll, P. (2009) 'Relationship, task and process conflicts on team performance: the moderating role of communication media', *International Journal of Conflict Management*, **20**(3): 251–68.

51 Hinds, P.J. and Mortensen, M. (2005) 'Understanding conflict in geographically distributed teams: the moderating effects of shared identity, shared context, and spontaneous communication', *Organization Science*, **16**(3): 290–307.

52 Zornoza, A., Ripoli, P. and Peiró, J.M. (2002) 'Conflict management in groups that work in two different communication contexts: face-to-face and computer-mediated communication', *Small Group Research*, **33**(5): 481–508.

53 Pruitt, D.G., and Carnevale, P.J. (1993) *Negotiation in Social Conflict*, Belmont, CA: Thomson Brooks/Cole Publishing Co.

54 Thompson, L.L. (2001) *The Mind and Heart of the Negotiator*, 2nd edn., Upper Saddle River, NJ: Prentice-Hall, pp. 18–19.

55 Young, M.J., Bauman, C.W., Chen, N. and Bastardi, A. (2012) 'The pursuit of missing information in negotiation', *Organizational Behavior and Human Decision Processes*, **117**(1): 88–95.

56 Van der Schalk, J., Beersma, B., Van Kleef, G.A. and De Dreu, C.K.W. (2010) 'The more (complex), the better? The influence of epistemic motivation on integrative bargaining in complex negotiation', *European Journal of Social Psychology*, **40**(2): 355–65.

57 Tan, J. (2005) 'Negotiating online', in M. Conley Tyler, E. Katsh and D. Choi (eds), *Proceedings of the Third Annual Forum on Online Dispute Resolution*, at www.odr.info.

58 Brooks, A.W. and Schweitzer, M.E. (2011) 'Can nervous Nelly negotiate? How anxiety causes negotiators to make low first offers, exit early and earn less profit', *Organizational Behavior and Human Decision Processes*, **115**(2): 43–54.

59 Johnson, N.A., Cooper, R.B. and Chin, W.W. (2009) 'Anger and flaming in computer-mediated negotiation among strangers', *Decision Support Systems*, **46**(3): 660–72.

60 Wang, L. Northcraft, G.B. and Van Kleef, G.A. (2012) 'Beyond negotiated outcomes: the hidden costs of anger expression in dyadic negotiation', *Organizational Behavior and Human Decision Processes*, **119**(1): 54–63.

61 Johnson et al., op. cit.

62 McGinn, K.L. and Keros, A.T. (2002) 'Improvisation and the logic of exchange in socially embedded transactions', *Administrative Science Quarterly*, **47**(3): 442–73.

63 Kumar, R. and Patriotta, G. (2011) 'Culture and international alliance negotiations: a sensemaking perspective', *International Negotiation*, **16**(3): 511–33.

64 Tinsley, C.H., Turan, N., Aslani, S. and Weingart, L.R. (2011) 'The interplay between culturally- and situationally-based mental models of intercultural dispute resolution: West meets Middle East', *International Negotiation*, **16**(3): 481–510.

65 Ott, U.F. (2011) 'The influence of cultural activity types on buyer-seller negotiations: a game theoretical framework for intercultural negotiations', *International Negotiation*, **16**(3): 427–50.

66 Ramirez-Marin, J.Y. and Brett, J.M. (2011) 'Relational construal in negotiation: propositions and examples from Latin and Anglo cultures', *International Negotiation*, **16**(3): 383–404.

67 Semnani-Azad, Z. and Adair, W.L (2011) 'The display of dominant nonverbal cues in negotiation: the role of culture and gender', *International Negotiation*, **16**(3): 451–79.

68 Liu, L.A., Friedman, R., Barry, B., Gelfand, M.J. and Zhang, Z.X. (2012) 'The dynamics of consensus building in intracultural and intercultural negotiations', *Administrative Science Quarterly*, **57**(2): 269–304.

69 Rosette, A.S., Brett, J.M., Barsness, Z. and Lytle, A.L. (2012) 'When cultures clash electronically: the impact of email and social norms on negotiation behavior and outcomes', *Journal of Cross-Cultural Psychology*, **43**(4): 628–43.

70 Olekalns, M. and Smith, P.L. (2013) 'Dyadic power profiles: power-contingent strategies for value creation in negotiation', *Human Communication Research*, **39**: 3–20.

71 Amanatullah, E.T. and Morris, M.W. (2010) 'Negotiating gender roles: gender differences in assertive negotiating are mediated by women's fear of backlash and attenuated when negotiating on behalf of others', *Journal of Personality and Social Psychology*, **98**(2): 256–67.

72 Mahenthiran, S., Greenberg, P.S. and Greenberg, R.H. (1993) 'The impact of computer-mediated communication on the processes and outcomes of negotiated transfer pricing', *Accounting, Management and Information Technologies*, **3**(4): 229–48.

73 Swaab, R.I., Kern, M.C., Diermeier, D. and Medvec, V. (2009) 'Who says what to whom? The impact of communication setting and channel on exclusion from multiparty negotiation agreements', *Social Cognition*, **27**(3): 385–401.

74 Geiger, I. (2010) 'Negotiator satisfaction in face-to-face and electronically mediated negotiations', paper presented at the IACM 23rd Annual Conference, at http://dx.doi.org/10.2139/ssrn.1612524.

75 Giordano, G.A., Stoner, J.S., Brouer, R.L. and George, J.F. (2007) 'The influences of deception and computer-mediation on dyadic negotiations', *Journal of Computer-Mediated Communication*', **12**(2): 362–83.

76 Scheck, S. (2008) 'The effect of media richness on multilateral negotiations in a collaborative virtual environment', *Journal of Media Psychology: Theories Methods and Applications*, **20**(2): 57–65.

77 Thompson, L. and Nadler, J. (2002) 'Negotiating via information technology: theory and applications', *Journal of Social Issues*, **58**(1): 109–24.

78 Balvin, N. and Tyler, C. (2006) 'Emotions in cyberspace: the advantages and disadvantages of online communication', University of Melbourne Legal studies Research Paper no. 277, at http://ssrn.com/abstract=1027510.

CHAPTER 9 COOPERATION, WORK RELATIONS, KNOWLEDGE SHARING AND COORDINATION

1 Espedal, B., Kvitastein, O. and Grønhaug, K. (2012) 'When cooperation is the norm of appropriateness: how does CEO cooperative behaviour affect organizational performance?', *British Journal of Management*, **23**: 257–71.

2 Ibid.

3 Rubin, J. and Brown, B. (1975) *The Social Psychology of Bargaining and Negotiation*, New York: Academic Press.

4 Lawler, E. E. III (1983) 'Reward systems in organizations', in J. Lorsch (ed.), *Handbook of Organisational Behaviour*, Englewood Cliffs, NJ: Prentice-Hall.

5 Müller, P.A., Greifeneder, R., Stahlberg, D., Van den Bos, K. and Bless, H. (2010) 'Shaping cooperation behavior: the role of accessibility experiences and uncertainty', *European Journal of Social Psychology*, **40**(1): 178–87.

6 Bandiera, O., Barankay, I. and Rasul, I. (2006) 'The evolution of cooperative norms: evidence from a natural field experiment', *Advances in Economic Analysis & Policy*, 5(2), at www.ucl.ac.uk/~uctpimr/research/evolution_be.pd www.degruyter.com/view/j/bejeap.2006.5.2/bejeap.2006.5.2.1484/bejeap.2006. 5.2.1484.xml (accessed 26 November 2013).

7 Lawler, op. cit.

8 Herbsleb, J.D. and Moitra, D. (2001) 'Global software development', *IEEE Software*, March/April: 16–20.

9 O'Kane, P. and Hargie, O. (2007) 'Intentional and unintentional consequences of substituting face-to-face interaction with email: an employee-based perspective', *Interacting with Computers*, **19**(1): 20–31.

10 Walther, J.B. (1996) 'Computer-mediated communication: impersonal, interpersonal, and hyperpersonal interaction', *Communication Research*, **23**(1): 3–43.

11 van der Kleij, R., Paashuis, R. and Schraagen, J.M. (2005) 'On the passage of time: temporal differences in video-mediated and face-to-face interaction', *International Journal of Human-Computer Studies*, **62**(4): 521–42.

12 Bicchieri, C. and Lev-On, A. (2007) 'Computer-mediated communication and cooperation in social dilemmas: an experimental analysis', *Politics, Philosophy & Economics*, **6**(2): 139–68.

13 Fiedler, M. (2009) 'Cooperation in virtual worlds', *Schmalenbach Business Review*, **61**: 173–94.

14 Swaab, R.I., Galinsky, A.D., Medvec, V. and Diermeier, D.A. (2012) 'The communication orientation model: explaining the diverse effects of sight, sound, and synchronicity on negotiation and group decision making outcomes', *Personality and Social Psychology Review*, **16**(1): 25–53.

15 Hill, N.S., Bartol, K.M., Tesluk, P.E. and Langa, G.A. (2009) 'Organizational context and face-to-face interaction: influences on the development of trust and collaborative behaviors in computer-mediated groups', *Organizational Behavior and Human Decision Processes*, **108**(2): 187–201.

16 Dimotakis, N., Scott, B.A. and Koopman, J. (2011) 'An experience sampling investigation of workplace interactions, affective states, and employee well-being', *Journal of Organizational Behavior*, **32**: 572–88.

17 Fernet, C., Gagné, M. and Austin, S. (2010) 'When does quality of relationships with coworkers predict burnout over time? The moderating role of work motivation', *Journal of Organizational Behavior*, 31: 1163–80.

18 Hayton, J. C., Carnabuci, G. and Eisenberger, R. (2012) 'With a little help from my colleagues: a social embeddedness approach to perceived organizational support', *Journal of Organizational Behavior*, **33**. 235–49.

19 Madlock, P.E. and Booth-Butterfield, M. (2012) 'The Influence of relational maintenance strategies among coworkers', *Journal of Business Communication*, **49**: 21–47.

20 Carmeli, A. and Gittell, J.H. (2009) 'High-quality relationships, psychological safety, and learning from failures in work organizations', *Journal of Organizational Behavior*, **30**(6): 709–29.

21 Niven, K., Holman, D. and Totterdell, P. (2012) 'How to win friendship and trust by influencing people's feelings: an investigation of interpersonal affect regulation and the quality of relationships', *Human Relations*, **65**(6): 777–805.

22 Sias, P.M., Gallagher, E.B., Kopaneva, I. and Pedersen, H. (2012) 'Perceived politeness and predictors of maintenance tactic choice', *Communication Research*, **39**(2): 239–68.

23 Loyd, D.L., Wang, C.S., Phillips, K.W. and Lount, R.B. (2013) 'Social category diversity promotes premeeting elaboration: the role of relationship focus', *Organization Science*, **24**(3): 757–72.

24 O'Kane and Hargie, op. cit.

25 Thomas, G.F. and King, C. (2006) 'Reconceptualizing email overload', *Journal of Business and Technical Communication*, **20**: 252–88.

26 Sarbaugh-Thompson, M. and Feldman, M.S. (1998) 'Electronic mail and organizational communication: does saying "hi" really matter?', *Organization Science*, **9**(6): 685–98.

27 Reinsch, N.L. (1997) 'Relationships between telecommuting workers and their managers: an exploratory study', *Journal of Business Communication*, **34**(4): 343–67.

28 Golden, T.D. (2007) 'Co-workers who telework and the impact on those in the office: understanding the implications of virtual work for co-worker satisfaction and turnover intentions', *Human Relations*, **60**(11): 1641–67.

29 Golden, T.D. and Fromen, A. (2011) 'Does it matter where your manager works? Comparing managerial work mode (traditional, telework, virtual) across subordinate work experiences and outcomes', *Human Relations*, **64**: 1451–75.

30 Bartel, C.A., Wrzesniewski, A. and Wiesenfeld, B.M. (2012) 'Knowing where you stand: physical isolation, perceived respect, and organizational identification among virtual employees', *Organization Science*, **23**(3): 743–57.

31 Sias, P.M., Pedersen, H., Gallagher, E.B. and Kopaneva, I. (2012) 'Workplace friendship in the electronically connected organization', *Human Communication Research*, **38**: 253–79.

32 O'Kane and Hargie, op. cit.

33 Snyder, J.L. (2010) 'Email privacy in the workplace: a boundary regulation perspective', *Journal of Business Communication*, **47**(3): 266–94.

34 Patil, S. and Kobsa, A. (2010) 'Enhancing privacy management support in instant messaging', *Interacting with Computers*, **22**(3): 153–240.

35 Tortoriello, M., Reagans, R. and McEvily, B. (2012) 'Bridging the knowledge gap: the influence of strong ties, network cohesion, and network range on the trans-

fer of knowledge between organizational units', *Organization Science*, **23**(4): 1024–39.

36 Garicano, L. and Wu, Y. (2012) 'Knowledge, communication, and organizational capabilities', *Organization Science*, **23**(5): 1382–97.

37 Keller, W. (2004) 'International technology diffusion', *Journal of Economic Literature*, **42**(3): 752–82.

38 Polanyi, M. (1968) *Knowing and Being*, London: Routledge.

39 Gardner, H.K., Gine, F. and Staats, B.R. (2012) 'Dynamically integrating knowledge in teams: transforming resources into performance', *Academy of Management Journal*, **55**(4): 998–1022.

40 Casciaro, T. and Lobo, M.S. (2008) 'When competence is irrelevant: the role of interpersonal affect in task-related ties', *Administrative Science Quarterly*, **53**(4): 655–84.

41 Downing, J.R. (2004) '"It's easier to ask someone I know": call center technicians' adoption of knowledge management tools', *Journal of Business Communication*, **41**: 166–91.

42 Noorderhaven, N. and Harzing, A.-W. (2009) 'Knowledge-sharing and social interaction within MNEs', *Journal of International Business Studies*, **40**: 719–41.

43 Reagans, R. and McEvily, B. (2003) 'Network structure and knowledge transfer: the effects of cohesion and range', *Administrative Science Quarterly*, **48**(2): 240–67.

44 Tortoriello, M., Reagans, R. and McEvily, B. (2012) 'Bridging the knowledge gap: the influence of strong ties, network cohesion, and network range on the transfer of knowledge between organizational units', *Organization Science*, **23**(4): 1024–39.

45 Reinholt, M., Pederson, T. and Foss, N.J. (2011) 'Why a central network position isn't enough: the role of motivation and ability for knowledge sharing in employee networks', *Academy of Management Journal*, **54**(6): 1277–97.

46 Connelly, C.E., Zweig, D., Webster, J. and Trougakos, J.P. (2012) 'Knowledge hiding in organizations', *Journal of Organizational Behaviour*, **33**: 64–88.

47 Kimmerle, J. and Cress, U. (2013) 'The impact of cognitive anchors on information-sharing behavior', *Cyberpsychology, Behavior, and Social Networking*, **16**(1): 45–9.

48 Kalman, M.E., Monge, P., Fulk, J. and Heino, R. (2002) 'Motivations to resolve communication dilemmas in database-mediated collaboration', *Communication Research*, **29**(2): 125–54.

49 Constant, D., Kiesler, S. and Sproull, L. (1994) 'What's mine is ours, or is it? A study of attitudes about information sharing', *Information Systems Research*, **5**(4): 400–21.

50 Sarala, R.M. and Vaara, E. (2009) 'Cultural differences, convergence, and crossvergence as explanations of knowledge transfer in international acquisitions', *Journal of International Business Studies*, **41**(8): 1365–90.

51 Ibid.

52 Hwang, Y. (2012) 'Understanding moderating effects of collectivist cultural orientation on the knowledge sharing attitude by email', *Computers in Human Behavior*, **28**(6): 2169–74.

53 Shao, C., Feng, Y. and Liu, L. (2012) 'The mediating effect of organizational culture and knowledge sharing on transformational leadership and enterprise

resource planning systems success: an empirical study in China', *Computers in Human Behavior*, **58**(6): 2400–13.

54 Teigland, R. and Wasko, M.M. (2003) 'Integrating knowledge through information trading: examining the relationship between boundary spanning communication and individual performance', *Decision Sciences*, **34**(2): 261–86.

55 Blay, A.D., Kadous, K. and Sawers, K. (2012) 'The impact of risk and affect on information search efficiency', *Organizational Behavior and Human Decision Processes*, **117**(1): 80–7.

56 Stasser, G., Abele, S. and Parsons, S.V. (2012) 'Information flow and influence in collective choice', *Group Processes & Intergroup Relations*, **15**(5): 619–35.

57 Lee, G., Lee, W.J. and Sanford, C. (2011) 'A motivational approach to information providing: a resource exchange perspective', *Computers in Human Behavior*, **27**(1): 440–8.

58 Shin, H.K. and Kim, K.K. (2010) 'Examining identity and organizational citizenship behaviour in computer-mediated communication', *Journal of Information Science*, **36**(1): 114–26.

59 Braverman, J. (2008) 'Testimonials versus informational persuasive messages: the moderating effect of delivery mode and personal involvement', *Communication Research*, **35**(5): 666–94.

60 Feldman, M.S., Khademian, A.M., Ingram, H. and Schneider, A.S. (2006) 'Ways of knowing and inclusive management practices', *Public Administration Review*, **66**(1): 89–99.

61 Barley, W.C., Leonardi, P.M. and Bailey, D.E. (2012) 'Engineering objects for collaboration: strategies of ambiguity and clarity at knowledge boundaries', *Human Communication Research*, **38**: 280–308.

62 Hightower, R. and Sayeed, L. (1995) 'The impact of computer-mediated communication systems on biased group discussion', *Computers in Human Behavior*, **11**(1): 33–44.

63 Stasser et al., op. cit.

64 Yuan, Y.C., Fulk, J., Monge, P.R. and Contractor, N. (2010) 'Expertise directory development, shared task interdependence, and strength of communication network ties as multilevel predictors of expertise exchange in transactive memory work groups', *Communication Research*, **37**(1): 20–47.

65 Oborn, E. and Dawson, S. (2010) 'Knowledge and practice in multidisciplinary teams: struggle, accommodation and privilege', *Human Relations*, **63**: 1835–57.

66 Majchrzak, A., More, P.M. and Faraj, S. (2012) 'Transcending knowledge differences in cross-functional teams', *Organization Science*, **23**(4): 951–70.

67 Sillince, J.A.A. and Saeedi, M.H. (1999) 'Computer-mediated communication: problems and potentials of argumentation support systems', *Decision Support Systems*, **26**(4): 287–306.

68 O'Kane and Hargie, op. cit.

69 Valacich, J.S., Sarker, S., Pratt, J. and Groomer, M. (2009) 'Understanding risk-taking behavior of groups: a "decision analysis" perspective', *Support Systems*, **46**(4): 902–12.

70 Birnholtz, J., Dixon, G. and Hancock, J. (2012) 'Distance, ambiguity and appropriation: structures affording impression management in a collocated organization', *Computers in Human Behavior*, **28**(3): 1028–35.

71 Kerr, D. and Murthy, U.S. (2009) 'The effectiveness of synchronous computer-mediated communication for solving hidden-profile problems: further empirical evidence', *Information & Management*, **46**(2): 86–9.

72 Barkhi, R., Jacob, V.S., Pipino, L. and Pirkul, H. (1998) 'A study of the effect of communication channel and authority on group decision processes and outcomes', *Decision Support Systems*, **23**(3): 205–26.

73 Cho, H. (2008) 'Collaborative information seeking in intercultural computer-mediated communication groups: testing the influence of social context using social network analysis', *Communication Research*, **35**(4): 548–73.

74 Golden, T.D. and Raghuran, S.R. (2010) 'Teleworker knowledge sharing and the role of altered relational and technological interactions', *Journal of Organizational Behavior*, **31**(1): 1061–85.

75 Lin, C.-P. (2011) 'Modeling job effectiveness and its antecedents from a social capital perspective: a survey of virtual teams within business organizations', *Computers in Human Behavior*, **27**(2): 915–23.

76 Summers, J.K., Humphrey, S.E. and Ferris, G.R. (2012) 'Team member change, flux in coordination, and performance: effects of strategic core roles, information transfer, and cognitive ability', *Academy of Management Journal*, **55**(2): 314–38.

77 Ingvaldsen, J.A. and Rolfsen, M. (2012) 'Autonomous work groups and the challenge of inter-group coordination', *Human Relations*, **65**: 861–81.

78 Bertrand, O. (2011) 'What goes around, comes around: effects of offshore outsourcing on the export performance of firms', *Journal of International Business Studies*, **42**: 334–44.

79 Hecker, A. and Kohleick, H. (2006) 'Explaining outsourcing failure', at http://dx.doi.org/10.21 39/ssrn.939411.

80 Buckley, P.B. and Strange, R. (2010) 'The governance of the multinational enterprise: insights from internalization theory', *Journal of Management Studies*, **8**(2): 460–70.

81 De Kwaadsteniet, E.W., Homan, A.C., Van Dijk, E. and Van Beest, I. (2012) 'Social information as a cue for tacit coordination', *Group Processes & Intergroup Relations*, **15**: 257–71.

82 Clark, H.H. (1996) *Using Language*, vol. 4, Cambridge: Cambridge University Press.

83 Puranam, P., Singh, H. and Chaudhuri, S. (2009) 'Integrating acquired capabilities: when structural integration is (un)necessary', *Organization Science*, **20**(2): 313–28.

84 Lind, M.R. and Zmud, R.W. (1995) 'Improving interorganizational effectiveness through voice mail facilitation of peer-to-peer relationships', *Organization Science*, **6**(4): 445–61.

85 Majchrzak, A., Rice, R.E., King, N., Malhotra, A. and Ba, S. (2000) 'Computer-mediated inter-organizational knowledge-sharing: insights from a virtual team innovating using a collaborative tool', *Information Resources Management Journal*, **13**(1): 44–53.

CHAPTER 10 WORKING IN GROUPS AND TEAMS

1 Walumbwa, F.O., Luthans, F., Avey, J.B. and Oke, A. (2011) 'Authentically leading groups: the mediating role of collective psychological capital and trust', *Journal of Organizational Behavior*, **32**: 4–24.

2 Burt, R.S. (1997) 'The contingent value of social capital', *Administrative Science Quarterly*, **42**(2): 339–65.

3 Granovetter, M. (1983) 'The strength of weak ties: a network theory revisited', *Sociological Theory*, **1**(1): 201–33.

4 Tindale, R.S., Smith, C.S., Dykema-Engblade, A. and Kluwe, K. (2012) 'Good and bad group performance: same process – different outcomes', *Group Processes & Intergroup Relations*, **15**: 603–18.

5 Mejias, R.J. (2007) 'The interaction of process losses, process gains, and meeting satisfaction within technology-supported environments', *Small Group Research*, **38**(1): 156–94.

6 Ibid.

7 Ibid.

8 Staats, B.R., Milkman, K.L. and Fox, C.R. (2012) 'The team scaling fallacy: underestimating the declining efficiency of larger teams', *Organizational Behavior and Human Decision Processes*, **118**(2): 132–42.

9 Romiszowski, A.J. and Mason, R. (1996) 'Computer-mediated communication', in J. Michael Spector, M. David Merrill, Jeroen van Merrienboer and Marcy P. Driscoll (eds), *Handbook of Research for Educational Communications and Technology*, 3rd edn, New York: Simon and Schuster, pp. 438–56.

10 Bechtoldt, M.N., De Dreu, C.K.W., Nijstad, B.A. and Choi, H.-S. (2010) 'Motivated information processing, social tuning and group creativity', *Journal of Personality and Social Psychology*, **99**(4): 622–37.

11 Stasser G. and Titus W. (1985) 'Pooling of unshared information in group decision making: biased information sampling during discussion', *Journal of Personality and Social Psychology*, **48**: 1467–78.

12 Stasser, G. and Stewart, D. (1992) 'Discovery of hidden profiles by decision making groups: solving a problem versus making a judgment', *Journal of Personality and Social Psychology*, **63**(3): 426–34.

13 Mojzisch, A., Grouneva, L. and Schulz-Hardt, S. (2010) 'Biased evaluation of information during discussion: disentangling the effects of preference consistency, social validation, and ownership of information', *European Journal of Social Psychology*, **40**(6): 946–56.

14 Krieger, J.L. (2005) 'Shared mindfulness in cockpit crisis situations: an exploratory analysis', *The Journal of Business Communication*, **42**(2): 135–67.

15 Hirst, W. and Echterhoff, G. (2012) 'Remembering in conversations: the social sharing and reshaping of memories', *Psychology*, **63**(1): 55.

16 Staats et al., op. cit.

17 Reinig, B.A. and Mejias, R.J. (2003) 'An investigation of the influence of national culture and group support systems on group processes and outcomes', . *Proceedings of the 36th Annual Hawaii International Conference on System Sciences, 2003*, IEEE, at http://ieeexplore.ieee.org/xpl/login.jsp?tp=&arnumber=1173774&url=http%3A%2F%2Fieeexplore.ieee.org%2Fxpls%2Fabs_all.jsp%3Farnumber%3D1173774 (accessed 20 June 2014).

18 Savicki, V., Kelley, M. and Lingenfelter, D. (1996) 'Gender and small task group activity using computer mediated communication', *Computers in Human Behavior*, **12**: 209–24.

19 Dachler, P.H. and Wilpert, B. (1978) 'Conceptual dimensions and boundaries of participation in organizations: a critical evaluation', *Administrative Science Quarterly*, **23**(1):1–39.

20 Black, S.J. and Gregersen, H.B. (1997) 'Participative decision making: an integration of multiple dimensions,' *Human Relations*, **50**(7): 859–78.

21 Magjuka, R.J. (1989) 'Participative systems: toward a technology of design', *Research in the Sociology of Organizations*, **7**: 79–115.

22 Watson, W., Michaelson, L. and Sharp, W. (1992) 'Member competence, group interaction and group decision making: a longitudinal study', *Journal of Applied Psychology*, **76**(6): 803–9.

23 Kerr, N.L., Niedermeier, K.E. and Kaplan, M.F. (1999) 'Bias in jurors vs bias in juries: new evidence from the SDS perspective', *Organisational Behavior and Human Decision Processes*, **80**(1): 70–86.

24 Clark, N.K. and Stephenson, G.M. (1999) 'Social remembering: individual and collaborative memory for social information', in W. Stroebe and M. Hewstone (eds), *European Review of Social Psychology*, vol. 6, Chichester: John Wiley, pp. 127–60.

25 At www.mckinseyquarterly.com/Strategy/Strategy_in_Practice/Seven_steps_to_better_brainstorming_2767.

26 Ibid.

27 Kelly, J.R., Jackson, J.W. and Hutson-Comeaux, S.L. (1997) 'The effects of time pressure and task differences on influence modes and accuracy in decision making groups', *Personality and Social Psychology Bulletin*, **23**(1): 10–22.

28 Dubrovsky, V.J., Kiesler, S. and Sethna, B.N. (1991) 'The equalisation phenomenon: status effects in computer-mediated and face-to-face decision making groups', *Human-Computer Interaction*, **6**(2): 119–46.

29 Peterson, R.S. (1997) 'A directive leadership style in group decision making can be both virtue and vice: evidence from elite and experimental groups', *Journal of Personality and Social Psychology*, **72**(5): 1107–21.

30 Bazarova, N.N., Walther, J.B. and McLeod, P.L. (2012) 'Minority influence in virtual groups: a comparison of four theories of minority influence', *Communication Research*, **39**(3): 295–316.

31 Olson, J.S. and Olson, G.M. (2003) 'Culture surprises in remote software development teams', *Queue*, **1**(9): 52.

32 Yates, J.F., Lee, J.-W. and Bush, J.G.G. (1997) 'General knowledge overconfidence: cross-national variations, response style, and "reality"', *Organizational Behavior and Human Decision Processes*, **70**(2): 87–94.

33 Ilgen, D.R., Hollenbeck, J.R., Johnson, M. and Jundt, D. (2005) 'Teams in organizations: from input-process-output models to IMOI models', *Annual Review of Psychology*, **56**: 517–43.

34 Zijlstra, F.R.H., Waller, M.J. and Phillips, S.I. (2012) 'Setting the tone: early interaction patterns in swift-starting teams as a predictor of effectiveness', *European Journal of Work and Organizational Psychology*, **21**(5): 749–77.

35 Lehmann-Willenbrock, N., Meyers, R.A., Kauffeld, S., Neininger, A. and Henschel, A. (2011) 'Verbal interaction sequences and group mood: exploring

the role of team planning communication', *Small Group Research*, **42**(6): 639–68.

36 Ibid.

37 Kauffeld, S. and Lehmann-Willenbrock, N. (2012) 'Meetings matter: effects of team meetings on team and organizational success', *Small Group Research*, **43**(2): 130–558.

38 Hirst, G., Van Dick, R. and Van Knippenberg, D. (2009) 'A social identity perspective on leadership and employee creativity', *Journal of Organizational Behavior*, **30**(7): 963–82.

39 Gardner, H.K. (2012) 'Performance pressure as a double-edged sword: enhancing team motivation but undermining the use of team knowledge', *Administrative Science Quarterly*, **57**(1): 1–46.

40 Mueller, J.S. (2012) 'Why individuals in larger teams perform worse', *Organizational Behavior and Human Decision Processes*,**117**(1): 111–24.

41 Druskat, V.U. and Pescosolido, A.T. (2002) 'The content of effective teamwork mental models in self-managing teams: ownership, learning and heedful interrelating', *Human Relations*, **55**(3): 283–314.

42 Hansen, M.T. (1999) 'The search-transfer problem: the role of weak ties in sharing knowledge across organization subunits', *Administrative Science Quarterly*, **44**(1): 82–111.

43 Guillaume, Y.R.F., Brodbeck, F.C. and Riketta, M. (2012) 'Surface- and deep-level dissimilarity effects on social integration and individual effectiveness related outcomes in work groups: a meta-analytic integration', *Journal of Occupational and Organizational Psychology*, **85**(1): 80–115.

44 Choi, J.N. and Sy, T. (2010) 'Group-level organizational citizenship behavior: effects of demographic faultlines and conflict in small work groups', *Journal of Organizational Behavior*, **31**: 1032–54.

45 Shin, S.J., Kim, T.-Y. and Lee, Y. (2012) 'Cognitive team diversity and individual team member creativity: a cross-level interaction', *Academy of Management Journal*, **55**(1): 197–212.

46 Rijnbout, J.S. and McKimmie, B.S. (2012) 'Deviance in organizational group decision making: the role of information processing, confidence, and elaboration', *Group Processes Intergroup Relations*, **15**(6): 813–28.

47 Homan, A.C. and Greer, L.L. (2013) 'Considering diversity: the positive effects of considerate leadership in diverse teams', *Group Processes Intergroup Relations*, **16**(1): 105–25.

48 Balvin, N. and Tyler, C. (2006) 'Emotions in cyberspace: the advantages and disadvantages of online communication', *Organisational Psychologist*, 5–8 (University of Melbourne legal studies research paper no. 277), at SSRN: http://ssrn.com/abstract=1027510.

49 Weisband, S.P. (1992) 'Group discussion and first advocacy effects in computer-mediated and face-to-face decision making groups', *Organizational Behavior and Human Decision Processes*, **53**(3): 352–80.

50 Gallupe, R.B., Dennis, A.R., Cooper, W.H., Valacich, J.S., Bastianutti, L.M. and Nunamker, J.F. (1992) 'Electronic brainstorming and group size', *Academy of Management Journal*, **35**(2): 350–69.

51 Straus, S.G. and McGrath, J.E. (1994) 'Does the medium matter? The interac-

tion of task type and technology on group performance and member reactions', *Journal of Applied Psychology*, **79**(1): 87–97.

52 Baltes, B.B., Dickson, M.W., Sherman, M.P., Bauer, C.C. and LaGanke, J.S. (2002) 'Computer-mediated communication and group decision making: a meta-analysis', *Organizational Behavior and Human Decision Processes*, **87**(1): 156–79.

53 Smith, C.A.P. and Hayne, S.C. (1997) 'Decision making under time pressure: an investigation of decision speed and decision quality of computer-supported groups', *Management Communication Quarterly*, **11**(1): 97–126.

54 Zigurs, I., Poole, M.S. and DeSanctis, G.L. (1988) 'A study of influence in computer-mediated group decision making', *MIS Quarterly*, **12**(7): 625–44.

55 McGuire, T.W., Kiesler, S. and Siegel, J. (1987) 'Group and computer-mediated discussion effects in risk decision making', *Journal of Personality and Social Psychology*, **52**(5): 917.

56 Rhoads, M. (2010) 'Face-to-face and computer-mediated communication: what does theory tell us and what have we learned so far?', *Journal of Planning Literature*, **25**(2): 111–22.

57 Becker-Beck, U., Wintermantel, M. and Borg, A. (2005) 'Principles of regulating interaction in teams practicing face-to-face communication versus teams practicing computer-mediated communication', *Small Group Research*, **36**(4): 499–536.

58 Murthy, U.S. and Kerr, D.S. (2003) 'Decision making performance of interacting groups: an experimental investigation of the effects of task type and communication mode', *Information & Management*, **40**(5): 351–60.

59 Shirani, A.I., Tafti, M.H.A. and Affisco, J.F. (1999) 'Task and technology fit: a comparison of two technologies for synchronous and asynchronous group communication', *Information & Management*, **36**(3): 139–50.

60 Straus and McGrath, op. cit.

61 Mejias, R.J. (2007) 'The interaction of process losses, process gains, and meeting satisfaction within technology-supported environments', *Small Group Research*, **38**(1): 156–94.

62 Biggiero, L. (2008) 'Does email communication increase participation in organizational decision making?', at http://ssrn.com/abstract=1233611 or http://dx.doi.org/10.2139/ssrn.1233611.

63 Straus, S.G. (1996) 'Getting a clue: the effects of communication media and information distribution on participation and performance in computer-mediated and face-to-face groups', *Small Group Research*, **27**(1): 115–42.

64 Siegel, J., Dubrovsky, V., Kiesler, S. and McGuire, T.W. (1986) 'Group processes in computer-mediated communication', *Organizational Behavior and Human Decision Processes*, **37**(2): 157–87.

65 Weisband (1992), op. cit.

66 Hollingshead, A.B. (1996) 'Information suppression and status persistence in group decision making: the effects of communication media', *Human Communication Research*, **23**(2): 193–219.

67 Spears, R., Lea, M., Corneliussen, R.A., Postmes, T. and Ter Haar, W. (2002) 'Computer-mediated communication as a channel for social resistance: the strategic side of SIDE', *Small Group Research*, **33**(5): 555–74.

68 Weisband, S.P., Schneider, S.K. and Connolly, T. (1995) 'Computer mediated-communication and social information: status salience and status differences', *Academy of Management Journal*, **38**(4): 1124–51.

69 Pena, J., Walther, J.B. and Hancock, J.T. (2007) 'Effects of geographic distribution on dominance perceptions in computer-mediated groups', *Communication Research*, **4**(3): 313–31.

70 Postmes, T., Spears, R. and Lea, M. (1998) 'Breaching or building social boundaries? SIDE effects of computer-mediated communication', *Communication Research*, **25**(6): 689–715.

71 Lee, E.-J. (2006) 'When and how does depersonalisation increase conformity to group norms in computer-mediated communication?', *Communication Research*, **33**(6): 423–47.

72 Kennedy, D.M., Vozdolska, R.R. and McComb, S.A. (2010) 'Team decision making in computer-supported cooperative work: how initial computer-mediated or face-to-face meetings set the stage for later outcomes', *Decision Sciences*, **41**(4): 933–54.

73 Shin, Y. and Song, K. (2011) 'Role of face-to-face and computer-mediated communication time in the cohesion and performance of mixed-mode groups', *Asian Journal of Social Psychology*, **14**(2): 126–39.

74 Burke, K., Aytes, K., Chidambaram, L. and Johnson, J.J. (1999) 'A study of partially distributed work groups: the impact of media, location, and time on perceptions and performance', *Small Group Research*, **30**(4): 453–90.

75 Markman, K.M. (2009) '"So what shall we talk about": openings and closings in chat-based virtual meetings', *Journal of Business Communication*, **46**(1): 150–70.

76 Giambatista, R.C. and Bhappu, A.D. (2010) 'Diversity's harvest: interactions of diversity sources and communication technology on creative group performance', *Organizational Behavior and Human Decision Processes*, **111**(2): 116–26.

77 Kerr, N.L. and Tindale, R.S. (2004) 'Group performance and decision making', *Annual Review of Psychology*, **55**: 623–55.

78 Rennecker, J. and Godwin, L. (2005) 'Delays and interruptions: a self-perpetuating paradox of communication technology use', *Information and Organization*, **15**(3): 247–66.

79 Sillince, J.A.A. and Saeedi, M.H. (1999) 'Computer-mediated communication: problems and potentials of argumentation support systems', *Decision Support Systems*, **26**(4): 287–306.

80 Montoya-Weiss, M.M., Massey, A.P. and Song, M. (2001) 'Getting it together: temporal coordination and conflict management in global virtual teams', *Academy of Management Journal*, **44**(6): 1251–62.

81 Johnson, S.K., Bettenhausen, K. and Gibbons, E. (2009) 'Realities of working in virtual teams: affective and attitudinal outcomes of using computer-mediated communication', *Small Group Research*, **40**(6): 623–49.

82 Hambley, L.A., O'Neill, T.A. and Kline, T.J.B. (2007) 'Virtual team leadership: the effects of leadership style and communication medium on team interaction styles and outcome', *Organizational Behavior and Human Decision Processes*, **103**(1): 1–20.

83 Nam, S.C., Lyons, J.B., Hwang, H.-S. and Kim, S. (2009) 'The process of team communication in multi-cultural contexts: an empirical study using Bales' interaction process analysis (IPA)', *International Journal of Industrial Ergonomics*, **39**(5): 771–82.

84 Carmel, E. (1999) *Global Software Teams: Collaborating across Borders and Time Zones*, Upper Saddle River, NJ: Prentice-Hall.

85 Sohrabi, B., Gholipour, A. and Amiri, B. (2013) 'The influence of information technology on organizational behavior: study of identity challenges', *International Journal of e-Collaboration*, **7**(2): 19–34.

86 Gibbs, J. (2009) 'Dialectics in a global software team: negotiating tensions across time, space, and culture', *Human Relations*, **62**(6): 905–35.

87 Ibid.

88 Kumar, K., van Fenema, P.C. and Von Glinow, M. (2005) 'Intense collaboration in globally distributed work teams: evolving patterns of dependencies and coordination', *Advances in International Management*, **18**: 127–53.

89 Daim, T.U., Ha, A., Reutiman, S., Hughes, B., Pathak, U., Bynum, W. and Bhatla, A. (2012) 'Exploring the communication breakdown in global virtual teams', *International Journal of Project Management*, **30**(2): 199–212.

90 Weisband, S. (2002) 'Maintaining awareness in distributed team collaboration: implications for leadership and performance', in P. Hinds and S. Kiesler (eds), *Distributed Work*, Cambridge, MA: MIT Press.

91 Sarker, S., Ahuja, M., Sarker, S. and Kirkeby, S. (2011) 'The role of communication and trust in global virtual teams: a social network perspective', *Journal of Management Information Systems*, **28**(1): 273–309.

92 Weisband, S. and Atwater, L. (1999) 'Evaluating self and others in electronic and face-to-face groups', *Journal of Applied Psychology*, **84**(4): 632–9.

93 Janssens, M. and Brett, J.M. (1997) 'Meaningful participation in transnational teams', *European Journal of Work and Organizational Psychology*, **6**(2): 153–68.

94 Krebs, S.A., Hobman, E.V. and Bordia, P. (2006) 'Virtual teams and group member dissimilarity: consequences for the development of trust', *Small Group Research*, **37**(6): 721–41.

95 Wegge, J., Bipp, T. and Kleinbeck, U. (2007) 'Goal setting via videoconferencing', *European Journal of Work and Organizational Psychology*, **16**(2): 169–94.

96 Roch, S.G. and Ayman, R. (2005) 'Group decision making and perceived decision success: the role of communication medium', *Group Dynamics*, **9**(1): 15–31.

97 Olson, G.M. and Olson, J.S. (2000) 'Distance matters', *Human-computer Interaction*,**15**(2): 139–78.

98 Hinds, P.J. and Mortensen, M. (2005) 'Understanding conflict in geographically distributed teams: the moderating effects of shared identity, shared context, and spontaneous communication', *Organization Science*, **16**(3): 290–307.

99 Gibson, C.B. and Gibbs, J.L. (2006) 'Unpacking the concept of virtuality: the effects of geographic dispersion, electronic dependence, dynamic structure and national diversity on team innovation', *Administrative Science Quarterly*, **51**: 451–95.

100 Walther, J.B. (1996) 'Group and interpersonal effects in international computer-mediated collaboration', *Human Communication Research*, **23**(3): 342–69.

101 Jarvenpaa, S.L., Knoll, K. and Leidner, D.E. (1998) '"Is anybody out there?":
antecedents of trust in global virtual teams', *Journal of Management
Information Systems*, **14**(4): 29–64.

102 Ibid.

103 Zolin, R., Hinds, P.J., Fruchter, R. and Levitt, R.E. (2004) 'Interpersonal trust in
cross-functional, geographically distributed work: a longitudinal study',
Information and Organization, **14**(1): 1–26.

104 Kuo, F.-Y. and Yu, C.-P. (2009) 'An exploratory study of trust dynamics in work-
oriented virtual teams', *Journal of Computer-Mediated Communication*, **14**:
823–54.

105 Walther, J.B. and Bunz, U. (2005) 'The rules of virtual groups: trust, liking, and
performance in computer-mediated communication', *Journal of
Communication*, **55**(4): 828–46; Altschuller, S. and Benbunan-Fich, R. (2010)
'Trust, performance, and the communication process in ad hoc decision
making virtual teams', *Journal of Computer-Mediated Communication*, **16**(1):
27–47.

106 Eckert, P. (2006) 'Communities of practice', in K. Brown (ed.), *Encyclopaedia of
Language and Linguistics*, Amsterdam, Elsevier. pp. 683–5.

107 Brown, J.S. and Duguid, P. (1991) 'Organizational learning and communities-of-
practice: toward a unified view of working, learning, and innovation',
Organization Science, **2**(1): 40–57.

108 Wenger, E.C. and Snyde, W.M. (2000) 'Communities of practice: the organizational frontier', *Harvard Business Review*, **78**(1): 139–46.

109 Shin, H.K. and Kim, K.K. (2010) 'Examining identity and organizational citizenship behaviour in computer-mediated communication', *Journal of Information
Science*, **36**(1): 114–26.

110 Vaast, E. (2004) '"O brother, where are thou?" From communities to networks
of practice through intranet use', *Management Communication Quarterly*,
18(1): 5–44.

111 Kirkman, B.L., Cordery, J.L., Mathieu, J., Rosen, B. and Kukenberger, M. (2013)
'Global organizational communities of practice: the effects of nationality diver-
sity, psychological safety, and media richness on community performance',
Human Relations, **66**(3): 333–62.

CHAPTER 11 MANAGEMENT AND LEADERSHIP

1 Wilson, H.J., Parise, S. and Weinberg, B.D. (2011) 'What's your social media
strategy?', *Harvard Business Review*, **89**(7/8): 23–5.

2 At www.mckinsey.com/insights/business_technology/bullish_on_digital_mckinsey_
global_survey_results (accessed 28 November 2013).

3 Kirkland, R. (2012) 'Making internal collaboration work: an interview with Don
Tapscott', *McKinsey Quarterly*, at www.mckinsey.com/insights/organization/
making_internal_collaboration_work_an_interview_with_don_tapscott
(accessed 24 June 2014).

4 At www.mckinsey.com/insights/business_technology/bullish_on_digital_mckinsey_
global_survey_results (accessed 28 November 2013).

5 Dieser, R. and Newton, S. (2013) 'Six social media skills every leader needs', *McKinsey Quarterly*, at www.mckinsey.com/insights/high_tech_telecoms_internet/six_social-media_skills_every_leader_needs.

6 Shaw, R.E. (2012) 'Kicking the habit: that email addiction', *TheHuffington Post*, 22 June (accessed 28 November 2013).

7 Dieser and Newton, op. cit.

8 King, W.R. (ed.) (2009) *Knowledge Management and Organizational Learning, Vol. 3: Annals of Information Systems 4*, at www.uky.edu/~gmswan3/575/KM_and_OL.pdf.

9 Chini, T.C. (2004) *Effective Knowledge Transfer in Multinational Corporations*, Basingstoke, UK: Palgrave Macmillan.

10 *McKinsey Quarterly* (7 February 2013), op. cit.

11 Srikanth, K. (2007) 'Co-ordination in distributed organizations', at http://ssrn.com/abstract=939786.

12 Hrastinski, S., Sjöström, S., Lundström, J.E., Larsson, A.O. and Ozan, H. (2011) 'Encouraging participation in an intra-organizational online idea community: a case study of a Swedish municipality', *First Monday*, **16**(10), at http://firstmonday.org/ojs/index.php/fm/article/view/3603 (accessed 25 June 2014).

13 Wenger, E.C. and Snyde, W.M. (2000) 'Communities of practice: the organizational frontier', *Harvard Business Review*, **78**(1): 139–46.

14 Chini, op. cit.

15 Curado, C. and Bontis, N. (2006) 'The knowledge-based view of the firm and its theoretical precursor', *International Journal of Learning and Intellectual Capital*, **3**(4): 367–81.

16 Hedlund, G. and Nonaka, I. (1993) 'Models of knowledge management in the West and Japan', in P. Lorange, B. Chakravarty, J. Roos and A. Van de Ven (eds), *Implementing Strategic Processes: Change, Learning and Cooperation*, London: Blackwell, pp. 117–44.

17 De Graaf , F.J. and Velthuijsen, H. (2011) 'Network governance for dealing with IT-enabled interorganizational co-operation networks: when should network IT – such as social media – be used and how to govern it', at http://papers.ssrn.com/sol3/papers.cfm?abstract_id=1749367 (accessed 23 November 2013).

18 Guirdham, M. (2011) *Communicating Across Cultures at Work*, 3rd edn, Basingstoke, UK: Palgrave Macmillan.

19 Vitak, J., Crouse, J. and LaRose, R. (2011) 'Personal internet use at work: understanding cyberslacking', *Computers in Human Behavior*, **27**(6): 1751–9.

20 Liberman, B., Seidman, G., McKenna, K.Y.A. and Buffardi, L.E. (2011) 'Employee job attitudes and organizational characteristics as predictors of cyberloafing', *Computers in Human Behavior*, **27**(6): 2192–9.

21 Weatherbee, T.G. (2010) 'Counterproductive use of technology at work: information and communications technologies and cyberdeviancy', *Human Resource Management Review*, **20**(1): 35–44.

22 Buckner, V., Christopher, J.E., Castille, M. and Sheets, T.L. (2012) 'The Five Factor Model of personality and employees' excessive use of technology', *Computers in Human Behavior*, **28**(5): 1947–53.

23 Ibrahim, M. and Ribbens, P.M. (2009) 'The impacts of competence-trust and

openness-trust on interorganizational systems', *European Journal of Information Systems*, **18**: 223–34.

24 Clarke, I., Kwon, W. and Wodak, R. (2012) 'A context-sensitive approach to analysing talk in strategy meetings', *British Journal of Management*, **23**: 455–73.

25 Nielsen, M.F. (2009) 'Interpretative management in business meetings: understanding managers' interactional strategies through conversation analysis', *Journal of Business Communication*, **46**(1): 23–56.

26 Benoit-Barné, C. and Cooren, F. (2009) 'The accomplishment of authority through presentification: how authority is distributed among and negotiated by organizational members', *Management Communication Quarterly*, **23**: 5–31.

27 Erickson, R.A. and Roloff, M.E. (2008) 'Reducing attrition after downsizing: analyzing the effects of organizational support, supervisor support, and gender on organizational commitment', *International Journal of Organizational Analysis*, **15**(1): 35–55.

28 Kacmar, K.M., Bachrach, D.G., Harris, K.J. and Noble, D. (2012) 'Exploring the role of supervisor trust in the association between multiple sources of relationship conflict and organizational citizenship behavior', *Leadership Quarterly*, **23**(1): 43–54.

29 Mackenzie, M.L. (2010) 'Manager communication and workplace trust: understanding manager and employee perceptions in the e-world', *International Journal of Information Management*, **30**(6): 529–41.

30 Thomas, G.F., Zolin, R. and Hartman, J.L. (2009) 'The central role of communication in developing trust and its effect on employee involvement', *Journal of Business Communication*, **46**: 287–310.

31 Khazanchi, S. and Masterson, S.S. (2011) 'Who and what is fair matters: a multi-foci social exchange model of creativity', *Journal of Organizational Behavior*, **32**(1): 86–106.

32 Harris, K.J., Harvey, P. and Kacmar, K.M. (2011) 'Abusive supervisory reactions to coworker relationship conflict', *Leadership Quarterly*, **22**(5): 1010–23.

33 Madlock, P.E. and Kennedy-Lightsey, C. (2010) 'The effects of supervisors' verbal aggressiveness and mentoring on their subordinates', *Journal of Business Communication*, **47**(1): 42–62.

34 Darioly, A. and Schmid Mast, M. (2011) 'Facing an incompetent leader: the effects of a nonexpert leader on subordinates' perception and behaviour', *European Journal of Work & Social Psychology*, **20**(2): 239–65.

35 At www.youtube.com/watch?v=TfswNRqSegg (accessed 28 November 2013).

36 Hui, M.K., Au, K. and Fock, H. (2004) 'Empowerment effects across cultures', *Journal of International Business Studies*, **35**(1): 46–60.

37 Robert, C., Probst, T.M., Martocchio, J.J., Drasgow, F. and Lawler, J.J. (2000) 'Empowerment and continuous improvement in the United States, Mexico, Poland, and India: predicting fit on the basis of dimensions of power distance and individualism', *Journal of Applied Psychology*, **85**(5): 643–58.

38 Pellegrini, E.K. and Scandura, T.A. (2006) 'Leader–member exchange (LMX), paternalism, and delegation in the Turkish business culture: an empirical investigation', *Journal of International Business Studies*, **37**(2): 264–79.

39 Jarvenpaa, S.L. and Leidner, D.E. (1999) 'Communication and trust in global virtual teams', *Organization Science*, **10**(6): 791–815.

40 Kirkman, B.L., Rosen, B., Tesluk, P.E., and Gibson, C.B. (2004) 'The impact of team empowerment on virtual team performance: the moderating role of face-to-face interaction', *Academy of Management Journal*, **47**(2): 175–92.

41 Zhang, S., Tremaine, M., Egan, R., Milewski, A., O'Sullivan, P. and Fjermestad, J. (2009) 'Occurrence and effects of leader delegation in virtual software teams', *International Journal of e-Collaboration*, **5**(1): 47–68.

42 Paré, G. and Dubé, L. (1999) 'Virtual teams: an exploratory study of key challenges and strategies', in *Proceedings of the 20th International Conference on Information Systems*, Association for Information Systems, pp. 479–83, at http://dl.acm.org/citation.cfm?id=352978.

43 Van Dijk, D. and Kluger, A.N. (2011) 'Task type as a moderator of positive/negative feedback effects on motivation and performance: a regulatory focus perspective', *Journal of Organizational Behaviour*, **32**: 1084–105

44 Sparr, J.L. and Sonnentag, S. (2008) 'Fairness perceptions of supervisor feedback, LMX and employee well-being at work', *European Journal of Work and Organizational Psychology*, **17**(2): 198–225.

45 Melwani, S. and Barsade, S.G. (2011) 'Held in contempt: the psychological, interpersonal, and performance consequences of contempt in a work context', *Journal of Personality and Social Psychology*, **101**(3): 503–20.

46 Lam, C.F., DeRue, D.S., Karam, E.P. and Hollenbeck, J.R. (2011) 'The impact of feedback frequency on learning and task performance: challenging the "more is better" assumption', *Organizational Behavior and Human Decision Processes*, **116**(2): 217–28.

47 Asmuß, B. (2008) 'Performance appraisal interviews: preference organization in assessment sequences', *Journal of Business Communication*, **45**(4): 408–29.

48 Clifton, J. (2012) 'Conversation analysis in dialogue with stocks of interactional knowledge: facework and appraisal interviews', *Journal of Business Communication*, **49**: 283–311.

49 Hebert, B.G. and Vorauer, J.D. (2003) 'Seeing through the screen: is evaluative feedback communicated more effectively in face-to-face or computer-mediated exchanges?', *Computers in Human Behavior*, **19**(1): 25–38.

50 Watts, S.A. (2007) 'Evaluative feedback: perspectives on media effects', *Journal of Computer-mediated Communication*, **12**(2): 384–411.

51 Mumm, J. and Mutlu, B. (2011) 'Designing motivational agents: the role of praise, social comparison and embodiment in computer feedback', *Computers in Human Behavior*, **27**(6): 1643–50.

52 Balvin, N. and Tyler, C. (2006) 'Emotions in cyberspace: the advantages and disadvantages of online communication', *Organizational Psychology*, (University of Melbourne legal studies research paper no. 277), at SSRN: http://ssrn.com/abstract=1027510.

53 Smidts, A., Pruyn, A.T.H. and Van Riel, C.B.M. (2001) 'The impact of employee communication and perceived external prestige on organizational identification', *Academy of Management Journal*, **44**(5): 1051–62.

54 Kim, T.-Y., Rosen, B. and Lee, D.-R. (2009) 'South Korean managerial reactions to voicing discontent: the effects of employee attitude and employee communication styles', *Journal of Organizational Behavior*, **30**(7): 1001–18.

55 Smidts et al., op. cit.

56 Shin, J., Taylor, S. and Gu, M. (2012) 'Resources for change: the relationships of

organizational inducements and psychological resilience to employees' attitudes and behaviors toward organizational change', *Academy of Management Journal*, **55**(3): 727–48.

57 Van de Ven, A.H., Rogers, R.W., Bechara, J.P. and Sun, K. (2008) 'Organizational diversity, integration and performance', *Journal of Organizational Behavior*, **29**(3): 335–54.

58 Allen, J., Jimmieson, N.L., Bordia, P. and Irmer, B.E. (2007) 'Uncertainty during organizational change: managing perceptions through communication', *Journal of Change Management*, **7**(2): 187–210.

59 Lawrence, S.A. and Callan, V.J. (2011) 'The role of social support in coping during the anticipatory stage of organizational change: a test of an integrative model', *British Journal of Management*, **22**(4): 567–85.

60 Leonardi, P.M., Neeley, T.B. and Gerber, E.M. (2012) 'How managers use multiple media: discrepant events, power, and timing in redundant communication', *Organization Science*, **23**(1): 98–117.

61 Bies, R.J., Shapiro, D.L. and Cummings, L.L. (1988) 'Causal accounts and managing organizational conflict: is it enough to say it's not my fault?', *Communication Research*, **15**: 381–99.

62 Timmerman, P.D. and Harrison, W. (2005) 'The discretionary use of electronic media: four considerations for bad news bearers', *Journal of Business Communication*, **42**(4): 379–89.

63 Hertel, G., Konradt, U. and Orlikowski, B. (2004) 'Managing distance by interdependence: goal setting, task interdependence, and team-based rewards in virtual teams', *European Journal of Work and Organizational Psychology*, **13**(1): 1–28.

64 Dzuranin, A.C. (2010) 'Mitigating escalation of commitment: an investigation of the effects of priming in team decision making settings', University of South Florida working paper, at http://dx.doi.org/10.2139/ssrn.1662539 (accessed 26 December 2013).

65 Berry, G.R. (2011) 'Enhancing effectiveness on virtual teams: understanding why traditional team skills are insufficient', *Journal of Business Communication*, **48**: 186–206.

66 Mackenzie, op. cit.

67 Van Dyne, L., Kossek, E. and Lobel, S. (2007) 'Less need to be there: cross-level effects of work practices that support work-life flexibility and enhance group processes and group-level OCB', *Human Relations*, **60**(8): 1123–54.

68 Bass, B. (1985) *Leadership and Performance Beyond Expectations*, New York: The Free Press.

69 Bass, B.M. (1999) 'Two decades of research and development in transformational leadership', *European Journal of Work and Organizational Psychology*, **8**(1): 9–32.

70 Walter, F. and Bruch, H. (2008) 'The positive group affect spiral: a dynamic model of the emergence of positive affective similarity in work groups', *Journal of Organizational Behavior*, Special Issue: Contexts of Positive Organizational Behavior, **29**(2): 239–61.

71 Spitzmuller, M. and Ilies, R. (2010) 'Do they [all] see my true self? Leader's relational authenticity and followers' assessments of transformational leadership', *European Journal of Work and Organizational Psychology*, **19**(3): 304–32.

72 Cunliffe, A.L. and Eriksen, M. (2011) 'Relational leadership', *Human Relations*, **64**(11): 1425–49.

73 Purvanova, R.K. and Bono, J.E. (2009) 'Transformational leadership in context: face-to-face and virtual teams', *The Leadership Quarterly*, **20**(3): 343–57.

74 Alimo-Metcalfe, B. and Alban-Metcalfe, J. (2005) 'Leadership: time for a new direction?', *Leadership*, **1**(1): 51–71.

75 Bolden, R. and Gosling, J. (2006) 'Leadership competencies: time to change the tune?', *Leadership*, **2**(2): 147–63.

76 Dickson, M.W., Den Hartog, D.N. and Mitchelson, J.K. (2003) 'Research on leadership in a cross-cultural context: making progress, and raising new questions', *The Leadership Quarterly*, **14**(6): 729–68.

77 Van Quaquebeke, Van Nippenberg, D. and Eckloff, T. (2011) 'Individual differences in the leader categorization to openness to influence relationship: the role of followers' self-perception and social comparison orientation', *Group Processes & Intergroup Relations*, **14**: 605–22.

78 Walvoord, A.A.G., Redden, E.R., Elliott, L.R. and Coovert, M.D. (2008) 'Empowering followers in virtual teams: guiding principles from theory and practice', *Computers in Human Behavior*, **24**(5): 1884–906.

79 Zhen, Z., Wang, M. and Shi, J. (2012) 'Leader-follower congruence in proactive personality and work outcomes: the mediating role of leader-member exchange', *Academy of Management Journal*, **55**(1): 111–30.

80 Mueller, B.H. and Lee, J. (2002) 'Leader-member exchange and organizational communication satisfaction in multiple contexts', *Journal of Business Communication*, **39**: 220–4

81 Jackson, E.M. and Johnson, R.E. (2012) 'When opposites do (and do not) attract: interplay of leader and follower self-identities and its consequences for leader-member exchange', *Leadership Quarterly*, **23**(3): 488–501.

82 Zhen et al., op. cit.

83 Jackson and Johnson, op. cit.

84 Van Quaquebeke, N. and Eckloff, T. (2013) 'Why follow? The interplay of leader categorization, identification, and feeling respected', *Group Processes Intergroup Relations*, **16**(1): 68–86.

85 Tröster, C. and van Knippenberg, D. (2012) 'Leader openness, nationality dissimilarity, and voice in multinational management teams', *Journal of International Business Studies*, **43**: 591–613.

86 Purvanova and Bono, op. cit.

87 Sosik, J.J., Kahai, S.S. and Avolio, B.J. (1998) 'Transformational leadership and dimensions of creativity: motivating idea generation in computer-mediated groups', *Creativity Research Journal*, **11**(2): 111–21.

88 Hambley, L.A., O'Neill, T.A. and Kline, T.J.B. (2007) 'Virtual team leadership: the effects of leadership style and communication medium on team interaction styles and outcome', *Organizational Behavior and Human Decision Processes*, **103**(1): 1–20.

89 Huang, R., Kahai, S. and Jestice, R. (2010) 'The contingent effects of leadership on team collaboration in virtual teams', *Computers in Human Behavior*, **26**(5): 1098–110.

90 Balthazard, P., Waldman, D.A. and Warren, J.E.(2009) 'Predictors of the emergence of transformational leadership in virtual decision teams', *The Leadership Quarterly*, **20**(5): 65163.

91 Whitford, T. and Moss, S.A. (2009) 'Transformational leadership in distributed work groups: the moderating role of follower regulatory focus and goal orientation', *Communication Research*, **36**: 810–37.

92 Sutanto, J., Tan, C.H., Battistini, B. and Phang, C.W.(2011) 'Emergent leadership in virtual collaboration settings: a social network analysis approach', *Long Range Planning*, **44**(5–6): 421–39.

CHAPTER 12 ORGANIZATIONAL STRUCTURES AND CULTURES

1 Bisel, R.S., Messersmith, A.S. and Kelley, K.M. (2012) 'Supervisor-subordinate communication: hierarchical mum effect meets organizational learning', *Journal of Business Communication*, **49**: 128–47.

2 Van Wijk, R., Jansen, J.J.P. and Lyles, M.A. (2008) 'Inter- and intra-organizational knowledge transfer: a meta-analytic review and assessment of its antecedents and consequences', *Journal of Management Studies*, **45**(4): 830–53.

3 Tsai, W. (2002) 'Social structure of "coopetition" within a multiunit organization: coordination, competition, and intraorganizational knowledge sharing', *Organization Science*,**13**(2): 179–90.

4 Courtright, J.A., Fairhurst, G.T. and Rogers, L.E. (1989) 'Interaction patterns in organic and mechanistic system', *Academy of Management Journal*, **32**(4): 773–802.

5 Cooren, F., Kuhn, T., Cornelissen, J.P. and Clark, T. (2011) 'Communication, organizing and organization: an overview and introduction to the special issue', *Organization Studies*, **32**(9): 1149–70.

6 Ibid.

7 Taylor, J.R., F. Cooren, N.G. and Robichaud, D. (1996) 'The communicational basis of organization: between the conversation and the text',*Communication Theory*, **6**(1): 1–39.

8 Uttal, B. (1983) 'The corporate culture vultures', *Fortune*, **17**: 66–72.

9 Schneider, B., Ehrhart, M.G. and Macey, W.H. (2013) 'Organizational climate and culture', *Annual Review of Psychology*, **64**: 361–88.

10 Quinn, R.E. and Spreitzer, G.M. (1991) 'The psychometrics of the competing values culture instrument and an analysis of the impact of organizational culture on quality of life', *Research in Organizational Change and Development*, **5**: 115–42.

11 Ibid.

12 Argyris, C. (1990) *Overcoming Organizational Defences*, New York: Prentice-Hall.

13 Schneider et al., op. cit.

14 Weber, W.G., Unterrainer,C. and Schmid, B.E.(2009) 'The influence of organizational democracy on employees' socio-moral climate and prosocial behavioral orientations', *Journal of Organizational Behavior*, **30**(8): 1127–49.

15 Smidts, A., Pruyn, A.T.H. and Van Riel, C.B.M. (2001) 'The impact of employee communication and perceived external prestige on organizational identification', *Academy of Management Journal*, **44**(5): 1051–62.

16 Brown A.D. and Starkey, K. (1994) 'The effect of organizational culture on

communication and information', *Journal of Management Studies*, **31**(60): 807–28.

17 Prasopoulou, E., Pouloudi, A. and Panteli, N. (2006) 'Enacting new temporal boundaries: the role of mobile phones', *European Journal of Information Systems*, **15**(3): 277–84.

18 O'Kane, P. and Hargie, O. (2007) 'Intentional and unintentional consequences of substituting face-to-face interaction with email: an employee-based perspective', *Interacting with Computers*, **19**(1): 20–31.

19 Kiesler, S. and Sproull, L. (1992) 'Group decision making and communication technology', *Organizational Behavior and Human Decision Processes*, **52**(1): 96–123.

20 Straus, S.G. (1996) 'Getting a clue: the effects of communication media and information distribution on participation and performance in computer-mediated and face-to-face groups', *Small Group Research*, **27**(1): 115–42.

21 Atai, M.R. and Chahkandi, F. (2012) 'Democracy in computer-mediated communication: gender, communicative style, and amount of participation in professional listservs', *Computers in Human Behavior*, **28**(3): 881–8.

22 Panteli, N. (2002) 'Richness, power cues and email text', *Information & Management*, **40**(2): 75–86.

23 Hastings, S.O. and Payne, H.J. (2013) 'Expressions of dissent in email: qualitative insights into uses and meanings of organizational dissent',*Journal of Business Communication*, **50**(3): 309–31.

24 Carlson, P.J., Kahn, B.K. and Rowe, F. (1999) 'Organizational impacts of new communication technology: a comparison of cellular phone adoption in France and the United States', *Journal of Global Information Management*, **7**(3): 19–29.

25 Markus, M.L. (1994) 'Finding a happy medium: explaining the negative effects of electronic communication on social life at work', *ACM Transactions on Information Systems*, **12**(2): 119–49. Markus, M.L. and Robey, D. (1988) op. cit.

26 Fukuyama, F. (1999) *The Great Disruption: Human Nature and the Reconstitution of Social Order*, New York: Free Press, pp. 194–211.

27 Stevenson, W.B. and Gilly, M.C. (1991) 'Information processing and problem solving: the migration of problems through formal positions and networks of ties', *Academy of Management Journal*, **34**(4): 918–28.

28 Albrecht, T.L. and Ropp, V.A. (1984) 'Communicating about innovation in networks of three US organizations', *Journal of Communication*, **34**(3): 78–91.

29 Monge, P.R. and Contractor, N.S. (2003) *Theories of Communication Networks*, New York: Oxford University Press, ch. 1.

30 Eveland, J.D. and Bikson, T.K. (1987) 'Evolving electronic communication networks: an empirical assessment', *Information Technology & People*, **3**(2): 103–28.

31 Bizot, E., Smith, N. and Hill, T. (1991) 'Use of electronic mail in a research and development organization', *Advances in the Implementation and Impact of computer systems*, **1**: 65–92.

32 Rice, R.E. (1994) 'Relating electronic mail use and network structure to R&D work networks and performance', *Journal of Management Information Systems*, **11**: 9–29.

33 Hinds, P. and Kiesler, S. (1995) 'Communication across boundaries: work,

structure, and use of communication technologies in a large organization', *Organization Science*, **6**(4): 373–93.

34 Ibid.

35 Gupta, A.K. and Govindarajan, V. (2000) 'Knowledge flows within multinational corporations', *Strategic Management Journal*, **21**(4): 473–96.

36 Peng, M.W. (2001) 'The resource-based view and international business', *Journal of Management*, **27**(6): 803–29.

37 Monge, P. and Fulk, J. (1999) 'Communication technology for global network organizations', in G. DeSanctis and J. Fulk (eds), *Shaping Organizational Form: Communication, Connection, and Community*, Newbury Park: Sage.

38 Tippmann, E., Scott, P.S. and Mangematin, V. (2012) 'Problem solving in MNCs: how local and global solutions are (and are not) created', *Journal of International Business Studies*, **43**: 746–71.

39 Andersen, T.J. and Foss, N.J. (2005) 'Strategic opportunity and economic performance in multinational enterprises: the role and effects of information and communication technology', *Journal of International Management*, **11**(2): 293–310.

40 Hansen, M.T. (1999) 'The search-transfer problem: the role of weak ties in sharing knowledge across organization subunits', *Administrative Science Quarterly*, **44**(1): 82–111.

41 Chang, Y.Y., Gong, Y. and Peng, M.W. (2012) 'Expatriate knowledge transfer, subsidiary absorptive capacity, and subsidiary performance', *Academy of Management Journal*, **55**(4): 927–48.

42 Johnson, K.L. and Duxbury, L. (2010) 'The view from the field: a case study of the expatriate boundary-spanning role', *Journal of World Business*, **45**(1): 29–40.

43 Mäkelä, K. (2007) 'Knowledge sharing through expatriate relationships: a social capital perspective', *International Studies of Management and Organization*, **37**(3): 108–25.

44 Beitler, M.A. and Frady, D.A. (2001) 'E-learning and e-support for expatriate managers', ERIC, Institute of Education Sciences of the US Department of Sciences, at http://files.eric.ed.gov/fulltext/ED452391.pdf

CHAPTER 13 INTER-ORGANIZATIONAL RELATIONS

1 Gittell, J.H. and Weiss, L. (2004) 'Coordination networks within and across organizations: a multi-level framework', *Journal of Management Studies*, **41**(1):127–53.

2 Dekker, H.C. (2004) 'Control of inter-organizational relationships: evidence on appropriation concerns and coordination requirements', *Accounting, Organizations and Society*, **29**(1): 27–49.

3 Farrell, J. and Klemperer, P. (2006) 'Coordination and lock-in: competition with switching costs and network effects', at http://ssrn.com/abstract=917785.

4 Tsui, S.S. and Ngo, H.-Y. (2012) 'Drivers and outcomes of long-term orientation in cooperative relationships', *British Journal of Management*, **23**: 80–95.

5 Fryxell, G.E., Dooley, R.S. and Vryza, M. (2002) 'After the ink dries: the interac-

tion of trust and control in US-based international joint ventures', *Journal of Management Studies*, **39**(6): 865–86.

6 Malhotra, D. and Murnighan, J.K. (2002) 'The effects of contracts on interpersonal trust', *Administrative Science Quarterly*, **47**(3): 534–59.

7 Dekker, op. cit.

8 Feng, J., Du, R., Ai, S., Zheng, Y. and Abbott, P. (2011) 'An empirical research of relation norms on IT outsourcing performance', *Procedia Engineering*, **24**: 214–18.

9 Arranz, N. and de Arroyabe, J.C.F. (2012) 'Effect of formal contracts, relational norms and trust on performance of joint research and development projects', *British Journal of Management*, **23**: 575–88.

10 Dickey M.H., McKnight D.H. and George, J.F. (2008) 'The role of trust in franchise organizations', *International Journal of Organizational Analysis*, **15**(3): 251–82.

11 Molm, L.D., Melamed, D. and Whitham, M.M. (2013) 'Behavioral consequences of embeddedness: effects of the underlying forms of exchange', *Social Psychology Quarterly*, **76**(1): 73–97.

12 Myers, P. (2007) 'Sexed up intelligence or irresponsible reporting? The interplay of virtual communication and emotion in dispute sensemaking', *Human Relations*, **60**(4): 609–36.

13 Williams, P. (2002) 'The competent boundary spanner', *Public Administration*, **80**: 103–24.

14 Yagi,N. and Kleinberg, J. (2011) 'Boundary work: an interpretive ethnographic perspective on negotiating and leveraging cross-cultural identity', *Journal of International Business Studies*,**42**: 629–53.

15 Beechler, S., Søndergaard, M., Miller, E.L. and Bird, A. (2004) 'Boundary spanning', in H.W. Lane, M. Maznevski, M.E. Mendenhall and J. McNett (eds), *The Blackwell Handbook of Global Management: A Guide to Managing Complexity*, Malden, MA: Blackwell, pp. 121–33.

16 Johnson, K.L. and Duxbury, L. (2010) 'The view from the field: a case study of the expatriate boundary-spanning role', *Journal of World Business*, **45**(1): 29–40.

17 Au, K.Y. and Fukuda, J. (2003) 'Boundary spanning behaviors of expatriates', *Journal of World Business*, **37**(4): 285–96.

18 Susskind, A.M., Odom-Reed, P.R. and Viccari, A.E. (2011) 'Team leaders and team members in interorganizational networks: an examination of structural holes and performance', *Communication Research*, **38**: 613–33.

19 Aldrich, H. and Herker, D. (1977) 'Boundary spanning roles and organization structure', *Academy of Management Review*, **2**(2): 217–30.

20 Manev, I.M. and Stevenson, W.B. (2001) 'Balancing ties: boundary spanning and influence in the organization's extended network of communication', *Journal of Business Communication*, **38**: 183–205.

21 Yagi and Kleinberg, op. cit.

22 Kumar, K., van Fenema, P.C. and Von Glinow, M. (2005) 'Intense collaboration in globally distributed work teams: evolving patterns of dependencies and coordination', *Advances in International Management*, **18**: 127–53.

23 Yagi and Kleinberg, op. cit.

24 Ramarajan, L., Bezrukova, K., Jehn, K.A. and Euwema, M. (2011) 'From the outside in: the negative spillover effects of boundary spanners' relations with members of other organizations', *Journal of Organizational Behaviour*, **32**: 886–905.

25 Mowery, D.C., Oxley, J.E. and Silverman, B.S. (1996) 'Strategic alliances and interfirm knowledge transfer', *Strategic Management Journal*, **17**: 77–91.

26 Bresman, H., Birkinshaw, J. and Nobel, R. (2010) 'Knowledge transfer in international acquisitions', *Journal of International Business Studies*, **41**: 5–20.

27 Ibid.

28 Zander, U. and Zander, L. (2010) 'Opening the grey box: social communities, knowledge and culture in acquisitions', *Journal of International Business Studies*, **41**: 27–37.

29 Lane, P.J. and Lubatki, M. (1998) 'Relative absorptive capacity and interorganizational learning', *Strategic Management Journal*, **19**(5): 461–77.

30 Hotho, J.J., Becker-Ritterspach, F. and Saka-Helmhout, A. (2012) 'Enriching absorptive capacity through social interaction', *British Journal of Management*, **23**: 383–401.

31 Moller, K. and Svahn, S. (2004) 'Crossing East-West boundaries: knowledge sharing in intercultural business networks', *Industrial Marketing Management*, **33**: 219–28.

32 Du, R., Ai, S., Abbott, P. and Zheng, Y. (2011) 'Contextual factors, knowledge processes and performance in global sourcing of IT services: an investigation in China', *Journal of Global Information Management*, **19**(2): 1–26.

33 Ruey-Jer, B.J., Sinkovics, R.R. and Cavusgil, S.T. (2010) 'Enhancing international customer–supplier relationships through IT resources: a study of Taiwanese electronics suppliers', *Journal of International Business Studies*, **41**: 1218–39.

34 Kraut, R., Steinfeld, C., Chan, A.P., Butler, B. and Hoag, A. (1999) 'Coordination and virtualization: the role of electronic networks and personal relationships', *Organization Science*, **10**(6): 722–40.

35 Lee, J.Y.-H. and Panteli, N. (2010) 'Conflict escalation in inter-organizational virtual communication', at http://dx.doi.org/10.2139/ssrn.1612545 (accessed 30 November 2013).

36 Ibid.

37 Kasper-Fuehrera, E.C. and Ashkanasy, N.M. (2001) 'Communicating trustworthiness and building trust in interorganizational virtual organizations', *Journal of Management*, **27**(3): 235–54.

38 Thomas, G.F. (2007) 'How can we make our research more relevant? Bridging the gap between workplace changes and business communication research', *Journal of Business Communication*, **44**: 283–96.

39 Ai, S., Du, R., Abbott, P. and Zheng, Y. (2012) 'Internal and contextual factors, knowledge processes and performance: from the Chinese provider's perspective', *Expert Systems with Applications*, **39**(4): 4464–72.

40 MacDuffie, J.P. (2011) 'Inter-organizational trust and the dynamics of distrust', *Journal of International Business Studies*, **42**: 35–47.

GLOSSARY OF TERMS

Accountability An actor's responsibility for his or her behaviour towards someone else; or, in the context of governance, the ability of an entity to satisfy stakeholders about its conduct.

Actor Person who takes action, including communicating.

Affective-cognitive consistency Level of evaluative agreement between the affective (feeling) and cognitive (thought/belief) elements of an attitude.

Affordance The design aspect of an object which suggests how the object should be used (see also **social affordances**).

Ageism Prejudice or discrimination on the grounds of age.

Agency The capacity of individuals and/or groups to act with intention.

Agreeableness Five-factor personality trait of general concern for social harmony, resulting in considerate, kind, generous, trusting and trustworthy, and helpful behaviour and an optimistic view of human nature.

Anxiety A state of diffuse fear, often without identifiable cause.

Approach Way of handling relationships by reaching out to the other.

Association rules An individual's tendency to link an identified state or quality with another: for example, associating identified anger with being cruel, high in social status, and so on.

Attachment A positive affective and attitudinal state towards another person or entity; it is probably a precondition of trust, but trust also requires the parties to accept vulnerability (risk) based on those positive attitudes.

Attribution The process by which people decide what mainly caused (or is causing) another person's action. Attribution theory asserts that people tend to attribute behaviour either to a person's disposition or to their situation and defines factors that influence this tendency.

Attribution style A tendency to over-attribute others' behaviour to the situation or to their disposition.

Authority Legitimated power.

Avatar Online representation of an actual person.

Avoidance Way of handling conflict by avoiding contact.

Boundary objects Physical objects, such as sketches, photographs, tables of data, graphs, research reports and computer-aided drafting models that enable people to understand a message.

Boundary spanning Interactions aimed at establishing or maintaining relationships with external individuals or organizations in support of organizational or team goals.

Broker Person who performs the function or act of liaising across gaps in a **network**.

Calculus-based trust Trust 'based on instrumental considerations and relying on credible information, such as reputations and information from network relationships, about another's goodwill and competencies. It also relies on opportunities for deterrence whenever malfeasance may occur, such as withdrawing future business opportunities and spreading of information about someone's behaviour among networked partners, affecting other current and future relationships the partner is and may get involved in'.[1]

Closure, need for A need individuals have for information that will allow them to feel certainty about an issue.

Cognitive consistency Psychological pressure to maintain consistency among strongly held attitudes or beliefs and between beliefs and behaviour.

Collaborative network organizations Computer-supported collaboration between a number of autonomous individuals or organizations.

Collectivism Cultural value that prioritizes the group to which a person belongs over the individual him- or herself.

Common ground Knowledge (often tacit and based on shared experience) that facilitates communication (see also **grounding**).

Communication Conveyance of meaning through its encoding in messages by a sender and their transmission, reception and interpretation by a receiver.

Communication accommodation Process of adapting communication to make it more similar to or more different from an interaction partner's (by **convergence** or **divergence**).

Communication apprehension Fear of communicating experienced beforehand.

Communication modes Ways of communicating including both face-to-face and all forms of mediated communication. Some other authors use the term 'communication modalities' to mean this.

Communication style An individual's 'natural' and learned preferred way of expression, which they may adapt to a specific interlocutor or environment; it affects how they are usually perceived. Communication styles differ by culture. (For examples of how culture affects communication style, visit the companion website ... Glossary.)

Competence-based trust Level of confidence a user has in another person's or organization's ability to perform.

Computer self-efficacy Belief in own ability to use computer technology to achieve a given outcome.

Conscientiousness Five-factor personality trait of a tendency to show self-discipline, act dutifully and aim for achievement against standards.

Context Aspects of the environment of an encounter that are present in the minds of participants and may influence them; a context may be physical, social (such as the participants' work roles), relate to its purpose or other aspects such as past encounters.

Convergence Process of adjusting communication style to be more like that of an interaction partner's.

Conversational maxims 'Rules' to which participants in conversations must conform in order to understand and be understood by their co-participants.

Cooperation Process of working or acting together for the common benefit.

Cooperation script A procedural sequence of collaborative, tightly interwoven events that participants are either requested or obliged to carry out.

Coordination Effectively combining the work of two or more individuals or groups.

Cultural distance Extent to which two cultures differ, based on an assumption that this can be measured. (To learn more about cultural distance, visit the companion website: Glossary.)

Culture Socially constructed set of actions, ideas and objects that people share as members of an enduring, communicatively interacting social group; in this book 'culture' is generally applied only to whole social systems. The term 'subculture' is used for parts of social systems such as an age group within a culture.

Demographic factors Elements of an individual's or group's description in terms of ethnicity, age, gender, (dis)ability level, sexual orientation, nationality, education and socio-economic status.

Divergence Process of adjusting a communication to be less like an interaction partner's.

Diversity Presence of, or stakeholding by, a range of groups of people differentiated, usually, by demography, but occasionally by occupation, profession or opinions.

Embodied agents Human-like representations of computer algorithms.

Enterprise resource planning systems (ERPs) Large-scale software packages used to support the varied business processes of organizations. ERPs catalogue a wide range of data, including financial accounting systems, financial management systems, product design, information warehousing, communication systems, human resources and project management in order to produce plans for businesses.

Entitativity Condition of possessing unity and coherence: as when a collection of individuals is perceived as a unified group.

Epistemic motivation Motivation (or need) to hold accurate perceptions about the world.

Ethics Moral systems.

Ethnicity Membership of a population whose members believe that in some sense they share common descent and a common cultural heritage or tradition, and who are so regarded by others.

Ethnic minority Ethnic group, which, for reasons of relative numbers or history, has subordinate status within a society.

Ethnocentrism Belief that one's own culture or ethnic group is superior to others'.

Expectation of accountability A person's belief that he or she will be held to account for his or her actions.

Expertise directories See **knowledge directories**.

Extraversion Five-factor personality trait of being energetic, positive, assertive, sociable and talkative.

Face Social value people assume for themselves, the image they try to project; positive face is based on the need for others' approval; negative face on the need to be independent of others and their approval.

Face-threatening acts Communications that threaten the positive or negative 'face' of either the speaker or the hearer of a communication.

Facework Communication strategies and actions aimed at meeting the communicator's 'face' needs.

First advocacy Being first to support a particular solution. There is evidence that both the first advocated solution and the person advocating it have increased influence.

Five-factor model Trait theory of personality that postulates that in most people's implicit personality theory five factors predominate: extraversion, openness to experience, agreeableness, conscientiousness and neuroticism.
- Extraversion means being sociable, fun-loving, affectionate, friendly, talkative.
- Openness to experience means being original, imaginative, having broad interests and daring. It is seen as quite different from intelligence.
- Agreeableness is most easily understood in terms of its obverse, antagonism, which means mistrustful, sceptical, callous, unsympathetic, uncooperative, stubborn and rude, but is not related to dominance.
- Conscientiousness means being hardworking, ambitious, energetic, persevering. Its other pole is undirectedness.
- Neuroticism is opposed to emotional stability.[2]

Framing Interpreting a sequence of activities as a particular kind of event.

Globalization Processes facilitated by modern technology and communications by which businesses and other organizations operate globally.

Governance Set of formal or informal processes and decision rights that together support accountability. See also **network governance**.

Grounding Process by which people establish and continuously update their shared understanding in conversations.

Groupthink The tendency of groups that have worked together over a period and been successful to take conformity to an extreme, especially in crises.

Hidden profile problem Problem in which information critical to its solution is dispersed among team members and which they must share to solve the problem.

High-context communication Culturally endorsed communication style that assumes high levels of shared knowledge and so uses elliptical speech.

Human-computer interaction Study of the region of intersection between psychology and the social sciences, on the one hand, and computer science and technology, on the other.[3]

Identification rules Rules people apply to make inferences from observed cues: for example, using the observed cue of a person shouting and frowning to identify that the person is angry. These rules are generally personal.

Individualism Cultural value that prioritizes the individual over the group(s) to which he or she belongs.

Information overload Difficulty in understanding an issue and making decisions that can be caused by the presence of too much information.

Intercultural communication Communication between members of two or more cultures, especially, but not only, when their cultural memberships are salient.

Interlocutor (Other) participant in a dialogue or conversation; interaction partner.

Interpersonal communication Two-way communication (or message exchange) between two or more people.

Interpersonal sensitivity Ability to assess other people accurately.

Intranets Technological networks for sharing information, operational systems or computing services within an organization.

Joint ventures Enterprises created by agreement between two or more organizations.

Kinesics Analyses of human movement.

Knowledge directories (aka expertise directories) Directories of who knows what; at an individual level, they are defined as 'individual mental maps of knowledge distribution'; when shared, they are referred to as 'compositional' or 'collective' knowledge directories; when held in digital format they are called 'digital knowledge repositories'.

Knowledge sharing Process through which organizational actors – individuals, teams, units or entire organizations – exchange, receive and are influenced by the experience and knowledge of others.

Knowledge stickiness Tendency of knowledge to flow between possessors and locations only with difficulty.

Locus of control Belief in one's capacity to impact on the environment and produce desired effects.

Long and short-term orientation Tendency to emphasize the long term or the short term when considering the future.

Low-context communication Culturally endorsed communication style that assumes low levels of shared knowledge and so uses verbally explicit speech.

Masculinity Cultural value that prioritizes assertiveness and competition over modesty, compromise and cooperation.

Mental model A representation of some domain or situation that supports understanding, reasoning and prediction. They are used to explain reasoning about physical systems and mechanisms such as spatial representation and **human–computer interaction**.

Mindfulness An active state of attending to, responding to and perceiving information correctly.

Minority influence Extent to which a group decision can be or is affected bythe opinion of a minority (which may be a numeric minority or a subgroup low in status).

Multinational enterprises (MNEs) and multinational companies (MNCs) Organizations that operate in several countries simultaneously; usually applied only when production as well as marketing are operated multinationally.

Network governance A select, persistent and structured set of autonomous entities (individuals or companies as well as non-profit agencies) engaged in creating products or services based on implicit and open-ended contracts to adapt to environmental contingencies and to coordinate and safeguard exchanges.

Network governance theory A theory of how to achieve results and safeguard information exchanges. Key concepts: **social embeddedness** (relationships are not just dyadic but embedded in a network), informal social contracts and reputation (or a social commodity that participants in a network seek to maximize).

Neuroticism Five-factor personality trait of tending to experience negative emotions, such as anger, anxiety, or depression.

Norms Unwritten rules for how to behave in a given role or situation.

Offshore outsourcing The practice of subcontracting work to low-cost countries.

Openness to experience Five-factor personality trait of a general appreciation for and willingness to adapt to a wide range of experiences.

Openness-based trust The level of confidence that a counterpart will handle information relevant to the relationship with transparency and equity.

Organization A multi-component entity within which there are defined-structural relationships and distinct roles among the constituent components or participating actors, as well as the means for coordinating their actions and interactions so as to produce coherent outcomes that link the entity to a supporting environment.

Organizational citizenship behaviour Willingness to contribute efforts to a community or organization, even though these efforts are not accounted for or rewarded under traditional definitions of performance.

Organizational culture A set of values and practices embedded in an organization.

Orientation A combination of attitudes towards and intentions regarding a phenomenon such as cooperation.

Paralinguistics Ways of speaking that include turn-taking, voice tone, speed of speech and length of time that one speaker speaks.

Perceptual distortion Inaccurate perception of events, objects and people as a result of inaccurate processing of information through omission, expectation or assumption.

Perspective taking The process of approaching an interaction from another's point of view.

Power distance Cultural value dimension which contrasts acceptance that power is distributed unequally with its opposite.

Proxemics Spatial positioning.

Psychological contract 'The mutual expectations held by employees and their employers regarding the terms and conditions of the exchange relationship.' It 'creates an enduring mental model of the employment relationship, which provides a stable understanding of what to expect from each other and guides efficient actions by both parties.'[4]

Reactance Motivational reaction when a person feels that a rule, regulation or person is taking away their freedom of action and which leads them to strengthen the attitude that is targeted.

Regulatory focus An individual's focus on desired end states, and the approach motivation used to go from the current state to the desired endstate. Regulatory focus theory differentiates a promotion focus on hopes and accomplishments from a prevention focus on safety and responsibilities. Promotion focus is more concerned with higher level gains such as advancement and accomplishment. Prevention focus emphasizes security and safety by following guidelines and rules.

Relational trust Trust which 'emerges from repeated interaction between trustor and trustee and is based on information available to the trustor from within the relationship itself'. Mechanisms to build relational trust include 'deliberate risk taking and increasing interaction, for instance by joint goal setting, problem solving, decision making and partner development activities'.[5]

Roles Expectations regarding how individuals who occupy positions or offices are to behave.

Self-disclosure A process of communicating one's identity by, for instance, sharing personal information, expressing opinions and telling stories about oneself.

Self-efficacy An individual's or group's belief in his or her ability to succeed in specific situations.

Self-esteem Individuals' or groups' appraisals of their own self-worth.

Signalling theory The theory that some 'signals' can be manipulated easily (words, for example), others less so, and that people know this and use it to help detect deceptions.

Situatedness A feeling of being physically present in a situation or **context**.

Social affordances Properties of an object that enable or constrain interaction, depending on the social norms in different situations.

Social capital Expected collective or economic benefits derived from cooperation between individuals and groups.

Social categorization Process of fitting other people and oneself into categories, based on social comparison.

Social comparison Process of comparing oneself with others on a variety of variables including abilities, personality, performance, reward, which strongly influences a range of work attitudes and behaviours.

Social contagion The largely unconscious adoption by one person of another interactor's communication style, emotions and attitudes.

Social embeddedness The size, density and quality of employees' networks of multiplex (many-sided) reciprocated exchange relationships with colleagues.

Social influence Theory that individuals' thoughts, actions and feelings are influenced by other people and social groups in various ways – by contagion (which is semi-automatic), by persuasion or normatively.

Social loafing Tendency to work less hard in a group than individually, partly because effort is less likely to bring personal reward.

Social psychology The study of the ways in which people affect, and are affected by, others.

Stereotypes Widely held but fixed and oversimplified images or ideas of a particular type of person or thing.

Stereotyping The construction of schemas to categorize people that allow us to cope cognitively with the variety of people and impressions. Stereotyping does not necessarily imply prejudice; however, prejudice can be found in over-reliance on stereotypes, which distorts our understanding of others.

Swift trust Suspension of doubts and disbelief that result from lack of trust-building prior to relationships in order to work cooperatively on a task. See also **calculus-based trust, relational trust, competence-based trust** and **openness-based trust**.

Transactive memory systems Group information-processing system made up of the memory systems possessed by individuals as well as the communication processes linking these individual memory systems together.

Trust Willingness of a party to be vulnerable to the actions of another party based on the expectation that the other will behave in a way that does not damage the trustor, irrespective of the ability to monitor or control that party. See also **calculus-based trust, relational trust, competence-based trust** and **openness-based trust**.

Turn-taking conventions Accepted ways of alternating (taking turns) to speak and listen in a face-to-face interaction.

Uncertainty avoidance Cultural value dimension which refers to the extent to which a culture prefers to avoid ambiguity and to the way in which it resolves uncertainty.

Values Favourable valences associated with abstract concepts such as freedom and equality.

Virtual groups and teams Groups and teams that communicate exclusively or predominantly by cmc; they are usually physically dispersed.[6]

Warranting principle The principle that people place more reliance on information that is 'guaranteed' free of self-interested manipulation by its supplier.

Warranting value The value that derives from information being 'guaranteed' free of self-interested manipulation.

Work roles An accepted set of expectations about how a job will be done and about related aspects of behaviour.

NOTES

1 Lau, R.S. and Cobb, A.T. (2010) 'Understanding the connections between relationship conflict and performance: the intervening roles of trust and exchange', *Journal of Organizational Behavior*, **31**(6): 898–917.

2 McCrae R.R. and Costa, P.T. Jr. (1987) 'Validation of the five factor model of personality across instruments and observers', *Journal of Personality and Social Psychology*, **52**: 81–90.

3 Carroll, J.M. (1997) 'Human–computerinteraction: psychology as a science of design', *Annual Review of Psychology*, **48**: 61–83.

4 Chen, Z.X., Tsui, A.S. and Zhong, L. (2008) 'Reactions to psychological contract breach: a dual perspective', *Journal of Organizational Behavior*, **29**(5): 527–48.

5 Lau and Cobb, op. cit.

6 Lowry, B.P., Zhang, D.Z.L. and Fu, X. (2007) 'The impact of national culture and social presence on trust and communication quality within collaborative groups', paper presented at the 40th Annual Hawaii International Conference on System Sciences, Hawaii, January 3–6, at http://ssrn.com/abstract= 958530.

INDEX

Abel, M.   98, 361
abilities   184, 185–6, 189
About This Book   25–6
accommodation, communicative   113, 122–4, 406
accountability   100, 283, 405
    expectation of   143, 145
accuracy, in goal detection   159
actor(s)   9–10, 14, 405
advocacy   215
affect   161–7
affective–cognitive consistency   177, 405
affordance(s)   14–15, 23, 28–37, 405
age   42–3
ageism   405
agency   191, 405
agreeableness   56, 118, 186, 187, 405, 408
Al-Badi, A.H.   45
Albrecht, T.L.   315, 401
Algahatani, M.A.   45
America(ns)   100, 116, 183, 187, 208, 214, 255, 314
Andersen, T.J.   317, 401
anger   162
'Anglo' cultures   214
anonymity   32
answering machine   3
anxiety   162–3, 213, 405
approach   158, 192, 405
apps   13
argument   201
argumentation support systems   19, 268
Ashforth, B.E.   165, 372
assimilation motivation   157
association rules   61, 405
assumptions   168–70
    negotiations and   169
    work-related   169–70
asynchronicity   33

asynchronous communication   269
Atos   279
attachment   309, 405
attention   57
    gaining   32
attitudes   177–82
attribution(s)   54, 60–1, 106, 123, 322, 405
    errors in   60
audibility   31
Australia/n   165, 183
authentic leaders/ship   300, 301
authority   69, 197, 286, 290, 294, 405
avatar(s)   20, 21, 87, 109, 203, 405
avoidance   207, 159, 207, 405

back-covering   228
Bandura, A.   170, 373
barriers   55, 83,184, 239,
    to communication   113–14, 115, 259
    to coordination   29
behavioural mimicry   143
beliefs   168–76
Benetton   326
Bergsieker, H.B.   100, 361
Berry, G.R.   112, 298, 362, 398
Berson, Y.   310
Bikson, T.K.   10, 11, 315, 401
Bizot, E.   315, 401
body language   109
Bond, R.   187, 377
boundary objects   235–6, 405
boundary spanners/ing   245, 320, 323–6, 405–6
Bourne, E.J.   138, 367
brainstorming   242–3, 252–3
Brett, J.M.   169
broker(s)   10–11, 406,
Brown, B.   86, 359
Bruch, H.   258
bullying at work   206

calculus-based trust   206, 274–5, 322, 406

Canada/Canadian   68, 183, 214

Carli, L.L.   199, 378

Carlo, J.L.   120, 362

Carone, Crista   146

Cassell, C.   185, 377

change, communication of   294–6

charismatic leaders/ship   300, 301

China/ese   208, 214, 215, 255, 327

clarity   118–19

   at work   119–20

   in writing   119

Clarke, I.   286

closure   214, 406

cmc

   abilities and   186

   adapting for differences   129–30

   affect and   166–7

   attribution and   60–1

   attention and   57

   communication accommodation and 123–4

   communication competence and 116–17

   communicative control and   113

   communicator style and   91–2

   conflict and   323

   conflict-handling and   209–11

   conversational rules and   86

   cooperation at work and   223–5

   culture and   140–1

   deceptions and   74, 87–8

   delegation and   290–1

   expectations and   173–4

   facework and   94–5

   feedback and   292–3

   group member satisfaction and 263–4

   group performance and   261–3

   groupwork and   261–7

   impression formation and   63–4

   impression management and   102, 104

   intentions and   84–5

   interaction and   109–10

   intercultural communication and 140–1

   inter-organizational relations and 327–9

   judgements and   70

   knowledge sharing and   237–9

   leadership and   303–4

   manager-subordinate relations and 299–300

   messages and   56, 81–3, 85

   motives and   160

   negotiation and   215–7

   norms and   175–6

   observing cues and   58–9

   organizations and   312–14

   persuasion and   202–4

   politeness and   96–9

     at work and   97–8

   power and   199–200

   prejudice and   181–2

   problematic use at work   228–9

   reciprocity and   86–7

   responding and   110–1

   self-efficacy and   171

   sex/gender and   134–6

   SIDE and   150–1

   SIPT and   152–3

   social comparison and   77

   social influence and   144–5

   stereotypes and   68–9

   the self and   192

   traits/personality and   188

   trust and   179–80, 181–2

   turn-taking and   111–13

   uncertainty management and   124–5

   values and   183

   virtual teamwork and   272–4

   work and affect   167

   work and status   167

   work relations and   227–9

Cobb, A.T.   206, 380

cognitions   167–76

cognitive consistency   177, 406

cognitive schemas   59–60

collaboration   271

collaborative network organizations   320, 406

collaborative tools   20, 242

collectivism   136, 141, 199, 406

co-location   12, 13, 15, 241

common ground 120, 121, 128, 240–1, 281–2, 406
communication 5, 6, 7, 12, 146
  accommodation 113, 122–4, 406
  apprehension 163, 406
  barriers 114
  breakdown 271
  climate 293–4
  competence 114–16, 159
    at work 116–17
    of interviewees 116
  contributions 80–9
  management 278–81
  mode(s) 2, 4, 27–50, 129–30, 145–53, 312, 327–9, 406; feedback and 292
  groupwork and 261–7
  knowledge sharing and 237–9
  management and 1
  perspective 307–8
  style(s) 43–4, 406
  technologies 3,8,268
  work relations and 227
communicative control 113
communicator style 90–2
communities of practice 275–6, 282
competence in communication 114–7
competence judgements 69
competence(-based) trust 285, 406
competencies 185
competition 222–3
compliance 194
computer apprehension 163
computer self-efficacy 171, 406
computer-generated feedback 293
computer-mediated communication see cmc
computer-supported collaborative software 20
conference calls 16, 17, 112, 268
conflict 323, 328
conflict handling 193, 205–11
conscientiousness 24, 187, 407
context 20–1, 407
contextual influences, on negotiations 213–15
control 320–2
convergence 122, 123, 126, 214, 407

conversational maxims 85–6, 407
cooperation 24, 221–5, 407
cooperation script 30, 407
coordination 24, 221, 239–43, 321, 407
copresence 31, 34–5
Côté, S. 185, 377
cotemporality 31
critical mass of users, media usage and 49
critique(s) 96, 137–8, 150
crowd sourcing internet marketplaces 21–2
cues 57–9
  cultural difference and 58–9
  unintentional 58–9
Culnan, M.J. 4, 347
cultural difference 58–9, 128–9
cultural distance 183, 407
cultural factors 42–5
cultural norms 215
cultural values 183
culture 14, 43–4, 136–8
  attribution and 138
  communication accommodation and 123
  communication and 136–41
  communication competence and 115–16
  conflict-handling and 208
  coordination and 240
  deception and 141
  delegation and 290
  emotions and 165
  group decision-making and 255
  groupwork and 250
  impressions and 63
  inter-organizational relations and 327
  knowledge management and 283
  knowledge sharing and 232
  leadership and 301
  negotiation and 214–15
  norms and 175
  personality and 187
  persuasion and 202
  power and 199
  stereotypes and 68
  traits and 187
Currall, S.C. 209, 380

customer complaints 173
cyberdeviancy 19
cyberloafing 19
cyberslacking 19

dc Jonge, S. 41
De Vries, R.E. 90, 360
decentralization 306-7
deception(s) 72-4, 87-8
    culture and 141
decision-making 251-5, 262-3
deindividuation 152
delegation 288-91
demographic factors 42-5
    communication and 132
'deviants', in groups and teams 260
Digman, J.M. 187, 377
dissonance theory 200-1
distributed problem-solving networks 21
distributive bargaining 211
divergence 407
diversity 8, 272, 276, 407
    cognitive 260
    in groups and teams 259-60, 267
Dubai 102
Dubé, L. 291, 396
Dunham, P.J. 122, 363
Dvir, T. 310

effective sales calls 205
e-lancers 316
electronic mail see email
electronic networks 10
    of practice 22
Ellis, D.G. 105, 106, 361
email 15-16, 88-9, 189, 229, 314, 323,
    328
    intercultural negotiation and 215
email monitoring 229
email(s), effective 88-9
embodied agents 20, 407
emergent perspective 314, 316
emotional intelligence 185-6
emotional labour 165
emotional transitions 165
emotions 161-7
    in negotiations 213
    work-related 161-7

employability skills 23- 24
employees 47-50, 222-9, 286-304
encoding/decoding models 80-3
enterprise resource planning systems
    171, 407
entititavity 66, 407
environments 75-6
epistemic motivation 157, 212, 247, 407
Epley, N. 68, 173, 356
equity theory 106
Erez, A. 190
ethical communication 117-18
ethical issues 195
ethics 23, 117-8, 408
ethnic minority 171, 408
ethnicity 43, 408
ethnocentrism 128, 408
evaluating 69-70
Eveland, J.D. 10, 11, 315, 401
events 71-5
expatriate relationships 318-9
expatriates 319, 324
expectation(s) 123, 171-3
    of accountability 143, 145
expertise directories 236, 408
explanatory objects 235-6
extraversion 46, 64, 186, 188, 408

'face' 92, 408
face-threatening acts 95-6, 408
Facebook 279
face-to-face communication 12-14, 22
face-to-face networks 10
facework 92-5, 408
Fairhurst, G.T. 103, 361
fairness 69, 75-6, 77, 287
fax 3
fear 162-4
Feaster, J.C. 95, 350
feedback 251, 291-
first advocacy 254, 408
five-factor model 187, 408
Flynn, F.J. 195, 378
formal control 321-2
Foss, N.J. 317, 318, 401
frames 71-2
framing 103, 408
France/French 139, 314

franchise operations   322
free riders   69–70
Friedman, R.A.   209, 380
Fryxell, G.E.   321, 402
Fukuyama, F.   315, 401
Fulk, J.   149, 317, 318, 369, 401
Furner, C.P.   141

Garicano, L.   230, 384
GE (General Electric Co.)   279
Geiger, I.   216, 382
Gelfand, M.J.   169
gender   *see sex/gender*
geographical dispersion   269
George, J.F.   141
German/s/y   139, 214
Gibbs, J.M.   269
Gibson, D.E.   167, 372
Gilly, M.C.   315, 401
global virtual teams   267, 269–72
globalization   7, 408
goal contagion   160
goals   158–60
   negotiations and   213
   power and   197
Goffman, E.   93, 357
governance   21, 278, 283–5, 321–2, 327,
      408
Govindarajan, V.   316, 401
Great Britain   214
Groce, J.   41
grounding   251–5
group decision-making   30, 31, 120–2,
      409
group decision support systems   19, 245
group development   245
group performance   244–76,
groups   244–78
   as information processors   247–8
   knowledge sharing and   252, 410
groupthink   252, 272–3, 409
groupware   19, 111–12
groupwork   244–50, 251–5
Guinote, A.   197
Gupta, A.K.   316, 401

Hancock, J.T.   122, 363
Harvard Business Review   275

Hedlund, G.   283, 395
Herring, S.C.   135
hidden profile problem   248, 409
hierarchical organizations   306
hierarchical mum effect   306
hierarchy bias   75
high-context communication   44, 137, 409
Hong Kong   68, 138, 215, 250
Hiltz, S.R.   82, 359
Hinds, P.   315, 401
Hui, M.K.   290, 396
human–computer interaction   409
Humphrey, R.H.   165, 372
hyperpersonal theory   151

Ibrahim   285, 395
identification rules   59–60, 409
identity   188–9
IM   17
implicit personality theories   187
impression formation   63–9
   at work   63, 65
   in distributed work   65
   of groups   65–9
impression management   99–104
   guidelines for   101–2
impressions   62–71
   culture and   63
   of groups   65–7,
India/ns   116, 130, 270, 290
individual factors in mode choice   45–6
individualism   136, 199, 409
influence, in groups   253–4
influencing   193, 194–205
informal networks   314–6
information control   35
information overload   186, 227–8, 246,
      409
information processing, in groups   247–8
information seeking, in negotiations   212
instant messaging   17, 28–9, 45, 166, 284
integrative negotiation   211, 212,
intelligence   185
intentions   84–5, 184
interaction(s)   105–30
   face-to-face   108–10
   patterns in teams   256
   social influence and   142–5

interaction skills   113–130
interactional goals   158–9
interactivity   20, 34, 36, 107
intercultural communication   105, 123,
    128–9, 130, 139–41, 409
  cmc and   140–1
intercultural knowledge sharing   234
interdependence   240, 321
interlocutor   406, 409
inter-organizational relations   285,
    320–30
inter-organizational nets   326–7
interpersonal communication   4, 5–11,
    409
    skills of   23–5, 113–30
interpersonal sensitivity   409
interpersonal theory   106
intranet(s)   40, 276, 409
Iran   68
issues, communication of   293–4

Jackson, S.   14
Japan/ese   118, 255, 283, 324–5
    culture   141, 175
job applicants   173, 174
joint venture(s)   208, 285, 322, 409
Judge, T.A.   190
justice   69, 75–6, 77, 287

Kalman, Y.M.   63, 175, 355, 374
Kashima, Y.   138, 367
Keller, W.   230, 384
Kerr. N.L.   247
Keyton, J.   14, 347
Kiesler, S.   315, 401
kinesics   12, 409
Kirkman, B.L.   291, 396
Klein, L.R.   34, 350
knowledge directories   236, 409
knowledge management   278, 281–3
knowledge sharing   22, 221, 229–30,
    232–9, 242, 281, 409
knowledge stickiness   230–2, 410
knowledge transfer   29–30
knowledge, characteristics of   230–2
Korczynski, M.   165, 372
Korea/n(s)   44–5, 87, 208, 294
Kraut, R.   327, 404

Kreuz, R.J.   83, 359
Kruger, J.   68, 82, 173, 356, 358
Ku, L.   167, 372

'Latin' cultures   214
Lau, R.S.   206, 380
Lawler, E.E. III   223, 383
leaders, in groups and teams   254, 260
leadership   277, 300–3
learning   266–7
Lee, C.S.   119, 347
Lee, J.Y.-H.   328, 362
Lin, C.-P.   239, 387
Lindebaum, D.   185, 377
linguistic style matching   122–3
LMX theory   302–3
locus of control   118, 409
lock-in   321
long-term orientation   136, 410
low-context communication   44, 137, 410

Mackenzie, M.L.   298, 396
managers/ment   173, 200, 277
management interactions   286
managerial values   183
manager–subordinate relations   286–300
market imperfections   318
Markus, M.L.   4, 50, 347, 352
masculinity   141, 410
Mayer, R.C.   178, 375
Mayhew, P.J.   45
McCroskey, J.C.   91, 360
McKinsey Quarterly   47–8, 282, 352
McLuhan, M.   81
media choice   see mode choice
media richness   36, 303
    at work   149
media richness theory   148–50
media usage patterns   37–42
mediated communication   4, 8, 14–23
Meglino, B.M.   8
Mejias, R.J.   182, 376
mental model(s)   214, 256, 257–8, 263,
    264, 391, 410
messages   55–6, 80–3, 214
    interpretive errors in   56
Mexico   214
Middle East   105

mindfulness 126, 410
Miners, C.T.H. 185, 377
minority influence 254–5, 410
Mintzberg, H. 3
mixed-mode groups 266
MNCs/MNEs 232–3, 240, 316–19, 410
mobile phones 311
mobility 29, 30, 37–50
mode choice 42–50, 108, 326
Moller, K. 317, 326, 401, 404
Monge, P.R. 317, 347
moods 161
moral agency 191
morality 69
Morand, D.A. 96, 358
motivation 157–8
    in negotiations 213
    work-related 157
motives 156, 160
multinational enterprise(s) *see*
    MNCs/MNEs

Nadler, J. 153, 217, 370
negotiating 193, 211–18
negotiators' assumptions 169
Neo, R.L. 188, 377
network advantages 10
network density 10–11
network economy 22
network governance 285, 410
network organizational forms 316
network(s) 6, 9–11, 245
    knowledge sharing in 233
neuroticism 64, 410
Nonaka, I. 283, 395
non-verbal behaviour 56, 58, 108–9
Norman, D.A. 14
norms 42, 174–6, 223, 410
Norway 221
Nowak, K.L. 46, 352

Ocker, R.J. 96, 358
Olekalns, M. 215, 382
Olson, G.M. 255, 273, 389
Olson, J.S. 255, 273, 389
openness to experience 25, 410–11
openness(-based) trust 285, 411
Oreg, S. 310

organization 411
organizational adoption, media choice and
    47–8
organizational citizenship behaviour 178,
    411
organizational climate(s) 308–11
organizational culture(s) 236, 305,
    308–11, 411
    knowledge sharing and 234
organizational imperative 314
organizational rules and norms 49
organizational structures 305–8
organizational support 48
organizations, conflict in 205–6, 207
    cooperation in 221–5
    decision-making in 251–5
    influencing in 194
    negotiation in 211
orientation(s) 127, 411
O'Sullivan, B. 94–95, 360
outsourcing 8, 239, 313, 322, 329, 410

Panteli, M. 199, 328, 378, 404
paralinguistics 3, 411
Paré, G. 291, 396
participation, mode effects on 251, 264
participative decision-making 251
Pazos, P. 50, 353
Pelaprat, E. 86, 359
Pellegrini, E.K. 290, 396
Peng, M.W. 316, 401
perceiving 53–61
perceiving groups 62
perceptual distortion 411
performance appraisal 291–3
Perkins, A.M. 163, 371
personality 187–8, 191
perspective taking 125–6, 411
persuading/persuasion 194, 200–204
Polanyi, M. 231, 384
policies, communication of 293–4
politeness 95–8
politeness theory 95–6
power 164, 194, 195–200, 204, 321
    mode effects on 265
    negotiation and 215
power distance 136, 411
prejudice 180–2

presenting change 158, 295–6
prevention focus 158, 228
privacy concerns 33
problematic internet use 246, 250, 264
process gains 246, 250, 264
process losses 246, 249, 250, 257, 264
production blocking 158, 250, 253
promotion focus 34, 37
propinquity 34
proxemics 12, 411
psychological capital 245
psychological contract 411
psychological factors 45–6, 232, 233–4
    knowledge sharing and 232, 233–4

Qatar/i(s) 214
Quest Software, Inc. 284
Quinn, R.E. 309, 400

Ravlin, E.C. 182, 376
reactance 194, 411
reciprocal exchange 322–3
reciprocity 86–7
reduced social cues theory 148, 150
regulatory focus 158–9, 192, 411
relational leaders/ship 300–1
relational trust 322, 411–12,
relationship values 183
resolving conflicts 208–9
respect 164
responding 110–1
Rettie, R. 8, 130, 365
reviewability 31
revisability 31
Ribbens, P.M. 285, 395
Rice, R.E. 315, 401
Rimbau-Gilabert, E. 203
Riordan, M.A. 83, 359
Robbins, S. 120. 362
Robert, C. 290
roles 8, 412
Ropp, V.A. 315, 401
rules 85–6
    that increase trust in groups 275
Russia 111, 363

Sacks, H. 237, 386
Saeedi, M.H. 111, 362

sales calls/communication 180, 205
Saudi Arabia 44, 45,
Scandura, T.A. 290, 396
Schmitz, J. 149, 369
Schroeder, S.J. 167, 372
scripted cooperation 30
selection interviews/ers 84, 100, 172,
        173, 182
    interviewee skills in 84, 90, 101, 116,
self, the 188–92
self-disclosure 81, 412
self-efficacy 168, 170–1, 412
self-esteem 106, 412
self-evaluations 189–91
self-fulfilling prophecy 172
self-presentation 90–9, 189
    culture and 139
    sex/gender and 133–4
self-regulation/control 191
sequentiality 31
service encounters 165
sex/gender, communication and 43, 132–6
    cmc and 134–6
    groupwork and 250
    persuasion and 202
    power and 199
shared mindfulness 126–7
shared reality 127–8
    theory 191
Sherif, M. 127, 364
short message service see texting
short-term orientation 136, 410
Shweder, R.A. 138, 367
SIDE 152–3, 225
Siegel, J. 82, 359
signalling theory 237, 386
Sillince, J.A.A. 74, 412
simultaneity 31
Singapore 43–4, 200
situatedness 20, 412
situation, influence on communication
        145–53
skills 6
Skoric, M.M. 188, 377
Smith, P.B. 187, 377
Smith, P.L. 215, 382
SMS 16–17, 85
social affordances 29–37, 405, 412

social capital   245, 412
social categorization   65–7, 412
social cognition   53–61
    bias(es)   57, 60, 63, 64–5, 66–8, 73, 75
    inputs   53–56
    processes   56–61
social comparison   76–7, 412
social contagion   143, 412
social control   174–5, 321–3
social embeddedness   226, 411, 412
social exchange theory   106
social factors, knowledge sharing and
    232
social identity   152
    model of deindividuation effects
    152–3, 225
social influence   39, 49–50, 412
social information processing theory
    150–1
social loafing   246–7, 412
social media/websites   18, 279–81
social perception, culture and   138–9
    sex/gender and   133
social presence   34–5
social presence model   147–8, 150
social psychology   412
social tuning   128
social websites/media   18, 279–81
socio-moral climate   310
Spain   139
Spears, R.   152, 370
Spitzberg, B.H.   8, 345
Spreitzer, G.M.   309
St. Amant, K.   130, 365
Stasser, G.   247, 388
status   167, 198, 291
    mode effects on   200, 265
    trust and   178–9
status quo bias   75
Steizel, S.   203, 379
stereotypes   43, 67–9
 at work   67–8
Stevenson, W.B.   315, 401
Stinson, D.A.   190
Straus, S.G.   264, 352
Sussman, N.M.   135, 365
Svahn, S.   326, 404
Swed/en/ish   47

swift trust   274, 413
synchronicity   33

Taiwan/ese   241, 327
Tacit coordination   182, 214
Tapscott, D.   16, 278, 281
task requirements   50
task, cmc and group performance and
    263
Taylor, J.R.   308, 400
team performance   256–9
team work, factors for improvement
    273–4
teams   244, 256–75
    knowledge sharing and   236–7
teamwork   182, 210, 239, 256–9, 270–1
technological imperative   314
teleconferencing   227–8
telework/ers/ing   166, 227–8, 298
telephone   3, 16
telepresence   34–5
temporal independence   112
text messages   85
texting   16–17
Thompson, L.   32, 33, 45, 61, 153, 217, 370
thoughts   168
'ties'   9–10, 318
time, interaction and   109–10
Tindale, R.S.   247
Titus, W.   247, 388
Tjosvold, D.   205, 206, 379
Toyota   326
training, media usage patterns and   48
trait impressions   62
trait perspective   91
traits   187–8
transactional leaders/ship   300, 301, 303
transactive memory   248–9, 268, 413
transformational leaders/ship   300, 301,
    303
Trevino, L.K.   38, 351
trust   178–80, 206, 274–5, 285, 287, 322,
    328, 413
    communication and   178
    virtual team effectiveness and   274–5
    work-related   178, 180
Tu, C.H.   81
Turk/ey/ish/(s)   214, 290

turn-taking   29, 111–13, 121–2, 413
   conventions   29, 43
Twitter   279
Tyson, D.H.   135, 365

ubiquity   32
UK   68, 185–6, 301, 323,
uncertainty avoidance   136, 413
uncertainty management   124–5
United States/US/USA   138, 200, 214, 301, 314
user identifiability   32, 36

values   177, 182–3, 413
van den Hooff, B.   39–40, 41, 351
Van der Schalk, J.   212, 381
Van Dyne, L.   298, 398
Varela   131
video-mediated communication   18
virtual groups/teams   8, 102, 267–76, 298, 413
   managing   298
virtual worlds   20, 242
visibility   31
Voice over internet provider service   13, 18

Walter, F.   258
Walther, J.B.   150, 151, 174, 274, 369,
warmth judgements   69
warranting principle   74–5, 413
warranting value   18, 413
Watson, W.   252, 389
ways of working   12–23
Weatherbee, T.G.   283, 395

Weisband, S.P.   261, 265, 390
Williams, E.   6
Williams, P.   323
Wilson, H.J.   278, 394
women, negotiation by   215
work communication   5–11, 23–5, 61, 63, 65, 67–8
   core processes   51, 53–218
   revolution in   1
work context   23–4, 55, 83,
work environments   75–6
work relations   221, 225–9
work roles   223, 413
work values   182–3
work, emotional intelligence and   185–6
work, self-evaluations and   190, 191
workflow   268
workforce diversity   8
   see also diversity
work-related conflict handling   205–6, 207, 210–11
work-related cooperation   221, 222–3
work-related influencing   194, 195
work-related personality   187
work-related traits   187
World Bank   275
writing apprehension   164
Wu, Y.   230, 384

Yates, J.F.   255, 389
Yoo, Y.   120, 362

Zander, L.   326, 403
Zander, U.   326, 403